INTRODUCTION TO ALGORITHMS IN PASCAL

INTRODUCTION TO ALGORITHMS IN PASCAL

THOMAS W. PARSONS

Hofstra University

John Wiley & Sons, Inc.
New York   Chichester   Brisbane   Toronto   Singapore

ACQUISITIONS EDITOR	Steve Elliot
DEVELOPMENTAL EDITOR	Sean M. Culhane
MARKETING MANAGER	Susan Elbe
ASSISTANT MARKETING MANAGER	Laura Eckley
SENIOR PRODUCTION EDITOR	Nancy Prinz
COVER DESIGNER	Michael Jung
MANUFACTURING MANAGER	Susan Stetzer

Composition and illustrations by the author in LaTeX. This book was printed
and bound by R. R. Donnelly & Sons Company. The cover was printed by The Lehigh Press, Inc.

Trademark Information

VAX is a trademark of Digital Equipment Corporation.
IBM, System/360, and IBM PC are trademarks of International Business Machines, Inc.
TeX is a trademark of the American Mathematical Society.
Turbo Pascal is a trademark of Borland International, Inc.
Unix is a trademark of AT&T Bell Laboratories.

Library of Congress Cataloging-in-Publication Data
Parsons, Thomas W.
    Introduction to algorithms in Pascal / Thomas W. Parsons.
        p.   cm.
    Includes bibliographical references.
    ISBN 0-471-30594-4
    1. Pascal (Computer program language).   2. Computer algorithms.
    I. Title
    QA76.73.P35P37   1994
    005.13'3—dc20   94-5246
                                                                              CIP
Printed in the United States of America

10 9 8 7 6 5 4 3 2 1

To Thomas B. Steel, Jr.

PREFACE

A computer-science curriculum normally begins with a course in programming. These days it is apt to be called something like fundamentals of computer science, but its main purpose is to make the student literate in some language for communicating with and controlling the computer. It is like a course in English grammar and spelling. We usually hope to make people good programmers at the same time—which is like teaching English composition—and sometimes we even succeed. The second term usually introduces students to the elementary data structures, now generally approached as abstract data types: arrays, character strings, stacks, queues, and linked lists, and to the use of recursion as a programming strategy. If we have time, we may provide an introduction to trees as well, and to a few basic algorithms for sorting and searching. These are, for example, the agenda in McCracken's admirable text, *A Second Course of Computer Science with Pascal.* (New York: John Wiley, 1987.)

What then? The course that followed used to be a course in data structures, but much of what went into the traditional data structures course has now been absorbed by that second course. The trend now seems to be a course in elementary algorithms. This has been for some years a component of most data structures courses; most data structures have a set of algorithms associated with them. Many of the data structures have moved back into CS 2, but the algorithms remain.

This seems the logical development. There is now a large body of standard techniques, standard solutions to frequently occurring problems, which the student should know relatively early on and before addressing more advanced aspects of program design. This book is written for such a course. Of the principal algorithms texts now available, many strike me as too difficult for second-year undergraduates. I have yet to find an algorithms book pitched at the sophomore level that provides the menu of topics that I feel should be included.

The prerequisites for my book are the things a sophomore can normally be expected to have seen: elementary programming and the use of arrays, dynamic allocation of memory, linked lists, stacks, queues, and recursion. Most students these days have had at least a term of discrete mathematics, and I assume a familiarity with sets, logic, some combinatorics, and the theory of graphs and trees. Since it sometimes helps to take a second look at recursion, the first chapter includes a brief review of recursion, although I hope that most students will be able to skim this material or to skip it altogether.

I have tried to provide all the essentials. There are chapters on searching, sorting, the growth and maintenance of binary trees, tree algorithms in general, and elementary graph algorithms. This seems to be the minimum, and the inclusion of searching and sorting provides enough overlap that the book will accommodate students with different amounts of previous preparation. Since instructors' preferences vary, I have tried to provide a reasonable choice of additional topics: external searching and sorting, dynamic programming, pattern matching in strings, text compression, random numbers, and random sampling.

In the same spirit, I have tried to provide a little more on each topic than might be considered strictly necessary. It is better to have to omit material than to find the coverage inadequate. This is particularly true in the case of the chapters on searching and sorting; here much of the elementary material may have been studied in a previous course and it is well to go a little beyond the usual extent in case the instructor wants to cover advanced topics. I have chosen to discuss searching before sorting, on the grounds that searching is conceptually simpler and usually results in simpler algorithms, with the possible exception of some of the hashing techniques.

The chapters on pattern matching and text compression and, to a lesser degree, the chapter on random numbers, also serve as case studies in which some of the algorithms the reader has seen earlier find application. I have found that classes enjoy learning about these topics; in particular, students who have used ARC or PKZIP like to find out how they work their magic. In the chapter on pattern matching in strings, I have somewhat reluctantly included the Knuth-Morris-Pratt (KMP) algorithm. It is a difficult algorithm to explain (and not that easy to program, in my experience), and it is now outperformed by the new, simpler, and more flexible algorithm of Baeza-Yates and Gonnet. Students will no doubt wonder why I bothered with KMP in the light of BYG, but there seemed no choice but to include it, because of its historical importance, because of its relation to finite-state automata, and because it is still widely used.

The generation and use of pseudorandom numbers is a topic that is frequently slighted in algorithms texts; but random sampling and similar applications are things our graduates will have to cope with in the profession. I have seen a surprising amount of confusion surrounding relatively simple applications, and of course the question of finding a better generator than is supplied in the language implementation is one that also rises occasionally. Hence I have thought it a good idea to include a chapter on random numbers.

My approach is casual and, I hope, intuitive. I have tried to provide clarity without spoon-feeding. Clarity, indeed, has been given top priority, and any topic in which my exposition is not at least as clear as any other book's is a topic in which I have failed. I have tried to explain *why* a particular technique has been developed and have tried as far as possible to introduce the unfamiliar in terms of the familiar. I have generally sacrificed rigor to clarity; rigor is for advanced courses. For example, I invoke heavy mathematics only where I have found it unavoidable or where I need it to derive a standard result; in most cases I am content to follow the shortcuts outlined in the first chapter for determining the time complexity of an algorithm in big-O terms.

You will notice also that I frequently give two definitions of a thing. The first is informal and usually not quite right; but it prepares the reader's mind and lays the groundwork for the formal definition by presenting the idea behind it. I think many teachers do this; Knuth's admirable *Mathematical Writing* goes so far as to say, "Lie, if it helps." I draw the line at lying, but I find the occasional half-truth very effective in the classroom. The fact is that, just as we program by iterative refinement, we *learn* by iterative refinement, and I find that telling our students too much too soon just interferes with this process.

My general procedure in introducing an algorithm is to describe its basic logic in narrative prose, to provide a step-by-step outline, and then to show an implementation in commented code, usually following the code with further explanation. (In some places I have departed from this sequence when it seemed desirable to do so, usually where the algorithm is so detailed that an outline would be as hard to read as the code.)

For the code, I have used Pascal in this version. At this writing, Pascal is still the language of choice in the majority of undergraduate programs, and for lucidity it is unparalleled. I have started work on a C version of the book, and it is amazing how the clarity disappears as one moves the code over to C. The principal drawbacks of standard Pascal are its miserable string handling and the lack of any bit-oriented primitives. I have met these problems by using Turbo Pascal, and I have covered the relevant features of Turbo by introducing them as examples in the process of discussing abstract data types in Chapter 1. In writing Pascal code I have followed what, in C, would be called the Whitesmith style of indentation. I find that no other style marks the boundaries of blocks as well as this does, and my experience is that it enhances the readability of Pascal as much as it does that of C.

I have always found dynamic programming a particularly difficult topic to get across, mostly because it isn't an algorithm but an approach to algorithm design. The only way to present it seems to be to show lots of examples and to show how each example illustrates the approach. I have introduced the topic by reviewing Dijkstra's algorithm, presenting it this time as a dynamic-programming algorithm instead of a greedy algorithm. This means that the reader's first exposure to dynamic programming is by way of an algorithm that is already familiar. I have included a simplified version of Donald Knuth's line-breaking algorithm among my examples, partly because it is one of the most ingenious applications of dynamic programming I have seen, partly because it addresses a problem whose importance is immediately apparent to the reader, and partly because my version reduces to yet another application of Dijkstra's algorithm.

I am deeply indebted to the many people who assisted and encouraged me in the writing of this book. First, to my wife, Pat, who has seen me through the rough places and provided unfailing support and confidence. Next, to Steven Elliot, Sean Culhane, and the many other people at John Wiley & Sons who have guided me through this project. Finally, to my reviewers: Maria Bleyberg, Heather Booth, Marek Chrobak, Teofilo Gonzalez, Owen Murphy, Stephan Olariu, Andrzej Proskurowski, Susan Rodger, and Diane Spresser. I owe more than I can say to their valuable criticism.

Brooklyn, New York
July, 1994

CONTENTS

CHAPTER 1

INTRODUCTION

This book is about algorithms and algorithm analysis. It is intended for use in a course that immediately follows a first programming course. In a programming course you get the fundamentals of a programming language, an introduction to good programming practices and the principles of software design, and an introduction to the most important data structures and their use. But there are many problems that come up repeatedly in computer applications, and these problems have received a lot of study. This book is about these problems and the solutions people have found for them.

I assume you are familiar with linked lists, stacks, and queues. (You may also have had an introduction to methods for sorting and searching, but we will take these up in greater detail here.) I assume you are familiar with recursion and with writing and using recursive programs. This is very important; recursive solutions frequently offer simple solutions to otherwise nasty problems, and we will be using recursion a lot in what follows. This chapter includes a brief review of recursion.

I assume you have had enough discrete math to know what sets are, the basics of logic, and some graph theory. Discrete math courses vary widely, but these topics are almost always included. Other material that may not have been covered will be discussed as it occurs or, in some cases, in the appendices.

1.1 WHAT IS AN ALGORITHM?

An algorithm is, roughly, a description of how to perform a certain task. How does an algorithm differ from a computer program? A program that carries out a particular algorithm can be thought of as an *implementation* of the algorithm. It may be difficult to keep this distinction in mind, because an algorithm must be *described*. The description must use a notation that is precise enough and familiar to the reader, and for practical purposes it is realistic to use a programming language to do this. For clarity and conciseness, I have never seen an algorithmic notation to compare with Pascal, and that is what we will use here. But the program is an implementation or an embodiment of the algorithm, not the algorithm itself.

An algorithm has certain distinguishing characteristics that set it apart from just any procedure for doing things. Knuth [1968] lists these:

1. An algorithm always terminates. A program that hangs up in an infinite loop may have been intended as the embodiment of an algorithm, but it didn't turn out that way. More realistically, a procedure for computing a transcendental number like π cannot be termed an algorithm unless it has some sort of escape clause, such as "Terminate when the last two estimates differ by less than 10^{-9}," because otherwise it would go on forever.

2. Every step is described precisely and unambiguously. This is what sets an algorithm apart from a recipe that says, "Add a pinch of salt." A recipe could conceivably be made into an algorithm by (among other things) saying something like "Add 2.5 milligrams of salt."

3. Every step is simple enough so that it can be performed in a reasonable amount of time.

4. An algorithm produces an output. It may or may not require an input, but it eventually disgorges one or more results, usually numbers like "42" but not always.

To this I would add, an algorithm solves an interesting or important problem. By the previous criteria, just about any working computer program could qualify as the implementation of an algorithm, but one does not normally call (say) a payroll program an algorithm. However, the method used for sorting the employees' records could be called an algorithm, because sorting is an important problem in computation that comes up frequently and has a number of clever solutions.

In this book, we will consider many different types of algorithms. We will study how they work and why they work, and when, as usually happens, there are several algorithms from which to choose, we will compare their performance in an attempt to get some idea of which one to choose for a particular application.

Digression on the word algorithm: This word has a curious history. In the ninth century an Arabic mathematician wrote a book about computing. The book's title was *Kitab al jabr w'al-muqabala*, "The book of reduction and restoration," and the author was called al-Khowârizmî because he was a native of Khowârizm. From the title of the book we get the term *algebra* and from the author's name we get the term *algorism*. Algorism originally meant computing with Arabic numbers (as opposed to computing with an abacus; nobody did arithmetic with Roman numerals). You were an algorist if you used Arabic numbers; you were also politically or religiously suspect, because they were (in the opinion of the Western Church) the work of infidels. (The Arabs got their numbers from the Indians, in fact, but that's another story.) The word apparently got confused with *arithmetic*, and so the final *-sm* turned into *-thm*. As computation with Arabic numbers became commonplace, the word was gradually applied to methods of computation in general and lost its original meaning.

1.2   COMPLEXITY AND BIG *O* NOTATION

We will be considering many different algorithms in this book. Some run fast, some run slowly, and naturally we take speed into consideration when choosing among alternative algorithms for the same task. We can come up with a formula for the run time of just about any algorithm. But the formulæ are generally long winded, and when you look closely, it turns out that most of the terms in the formula are negligible.

Here is an example. In a later chapter, we will show that the cost of sorting a list of data depends on how many comparisons we must make and on how often we have to move data around. One popular sorting method is the selection sort. Analysis of this sort shows that the number of comparisons needed to sort an array of n elements is, on the average, $\frac{1}{2}(n^2 - n)$. On the other hand, Mergesort, another popular sorting algorithm, requires, on the average, $n \log_2 n$ comparisons.

Now if we are sorting a list of 10 numbers, any old sort will do. But if we have to sort a massive amount of data, we don't want the job to tie up the computer for hours. So what matters in most cases is how the cost behaves for really large n. What is "massive"? Computer programs may have to sort millions of items, but we can regard 10,000 items as fairly massive, and in this case the cost of the selection sort comes to

$$\frac{1}{2}(100{,}000{,}000 - 10{,}000) = 49{,}995{,}000$$

comparisons, while the cost of Mergesort is

$$10{,}000 \log_2 10{,}000 \approx 132{,}877$$

comparisons. Without knowing how much computer time a comparison will cost, we can see at once that for a list of this size, Mergesort takes approximately 1/375 the time required by the selection sort. If the selection sort takes an hour, Mergesort will take less than 10 seconds. It is because of numbers like this that we are concerned with the execution time of an algorithm.

To make comparisons like these quickly and easily, we would like to have the differences in the execution times show up clearly, with a minimum of distracting terms in the formulæ. Let us take another look at that figure for the selection sort. We can write it as

$$\frac{1}{2}(100 \text{ million} - 10{,}000).$$

In a job this size, the 10,000 pales into insignificance beside that 100 million. So for all practical purposes, we can forget about the n in that formula and say that the cost is

$$\frac{1}{2}(n^2) + \text{other stuff}.$$

(We always use a plus sign; in this particular case "other stuff" happens to be negative.)

This always happens. There is always a *dominant term*, which accounts for nearly all the cost for large n, and we always want to focus our attention on that dominant term. "Other stuff" is imprecise and rather undignified, so the way we do this is to write,

$$\text{The cost is } O(n^2).$$

That is read as "the cost is Big O of n squared," and this is called Big O notation. Some people also say, "the cost is of the order of n squared," or better, "the cost is of the order of at most n squared."

> *Note:* There is a temptation to write "cost $= O(n^2)$," or worse yet, "$1/2(n^2 - n) = O(n^2)$." Avoid this; otherwise you may be tempted to reverse the equation and say, "$O(n^2) = 1/2(n^2 - n)$"; and this is nonsense. It is safest to avoid the equals sign and say, "*is* $O(n^2)$" (or whatever), and that is what we will do here.

Big O notation compares the growth rates of two functions of n: a cost function $f(n)$, which is unwieldy and which we want to simplify as much as possible, and $g(n)$, the simplification. The purpose of Big O notation is to throw the most expensive part of a function into relief while suppressing irrelevant details.

An informal definition of Big O is:

> $f(n)$ is $O\big(g(n)\big)$ if their ratio is bounded for really big n.

The formal definition is:

> $f(n)$ is $O\big(g(n)\big)$ iff[1] there is a $c > 0$ and an $N > 0$ such that $|f(n)| \leq c|g(n)|$ for all $n > N$.

When we measure costs, $f(n)$ and $g(n)$ are always nonnegative for $n \geq 0$. In that case, the condition simplifies to "if $f(n) \leq c \cdot g(n)$." The reason I said that their ratio is bounded is that if you divide through by $g(n)$, you get

$$\frac{f(n)}{g(n)} \leq c \text{ for all } n > N. \tag{1.1}$$

(We can't divide through if $g(n) = 0$ for some n of interest, but since no known algorithm has zero cost, we need not worry about that.) If the ratio never gets any bigger than the constant c, it is bounded. This form is usually easier to work with. The constants c and N are unspecified; all we need to know is that they exist. If in comparing two algorithms A and B, we find that A is $O(n)$ and B is $O(n^2)$, the constants c and N don't have to be the same for A and B for us to be able to say that A tends to be faster than B. On the other hand, if we want to *prove* that $f(n)$ is $O\big(g(n)\big)$, we have to show that c and N exist by giving sample values.

> *Example 1:* $f(n) = 1/2(n^2 + n)$ is $O(n^2)$, because
>
> $$\frac{1/2(n^2 + n)}{n^2} = \frac{1}{2} + \frac{1}{2n} \leq 1 \text{ for integer } n > 0.$$

---

[1] *Iff* is a standard abbreviation for *if and only if*.

Here $g(n)$ is n^2, $c = 1$, $N = 0$. When $n = 1$, the ratio is exactly 1; when $n > 1$, the ratio is less than 1. (We could have used $c = 5$, $N = 10$, and many other combinations as well; but it is enough to show one possible pair of values since we need only show that they exist.)

Example 2: $f(n) = 2^n + n^2$ is $O(2^n)$, because

$$\frac{2^n + n^2}{2^n} = 1 + \frac{n^2}{2^n}.$$

In this case, $g(n)$ is 2^n, and I will select $c = 2$, $N = 4$. It is instructive to see how this ratio behaves:

n:	0	1	2	3	4	5	6	7
ratio:	1	1.5	2	2.125	2	1.781	1.562	1.383

Briefly, at $n = 3$, the ratio is actually greater than 2; but as n keeps getting bigger, the ratio decreases as 2^n begins to grow faster than n^2 does. In the limit as $n \to \infty$, the ratio tends toward 1. This is the reason for the $n > N$ in the definition. The stipulation that $n > N$ protects us from these temporary irregularities and focuses our attention on what happens when n is really big.

Example 3: $f(n) = n^2$ is *not* $O(n)$, because

$$\frac{n^2}{n} = n, \text{ which grows without limit as } n \text{ increases.}$$

Notice that if $f(n) \leq g(n)$ for $n > N$, then we know automatically that $f(n)$ is $O\big(g(n)\big)$ since $c = 1$ is an obvious possibility in this case.

Big O notation is used in two ways:

1. To show in a general way how fast $f(n)$ grows;
2. To show how good an approximation is by showing in a general way how bad the error is.

We have seen examples of 1. An example of 2 is,

$$\tfrac{1}{2}(n^2 + n) = \tfrac{1}{2}n^2 + O(n). \tag{1.2}$$

This provides a little more information than $O(n^2)$ does; it provides the constant factor (which is usually unimportant), but it also tells us what was the most important thing that was left out. As another example,

$$\ln n! \text{ is } O(n \ln n), \tag{1.3}$$

but

$$\ln n! = n \ln n + O(n). \tag{1.4}$$

The latter form gives us an idea (a very good idea, as it happens) of just how close an approximation $n \ln n$ is. Most of the time, this extra information is unimportant to us, but occasionally we will want to know it.

Note on notation: Logarithms come up repeatedly in algorithm analysis. We will follow the custom of using $\ln x$ to represent the natural logarithm of x—that is, $\log_e x$—and of using $\lg x$ to represent the logarithm to the base 2 of x. (Logs to the base 2 are by far the most common.) If the base is immaterial, we will write $\log x$.

Big O has a lot of uses, but we will usually use it to describe the way the execution time of an algorithm changes with the amount of data it is given. In particular, the *time complexity* of an algorithm is the *longest* time the algorithm will take for any input of size n. We measure the time by counting the number of times some significant operation, like comparison or data movement, must be carried out. That term suggests that there's another kind of complexity, and there is: We can also estimate the memory requirements of the program; that's known as *space complexity*.

We will mostly be interested in time complexity, however; memory is getting to be more and more abundant (personal computers may have more memory than many mainframes had 25 years ago), and in the worst case we can always resort to external storage; but time is always in short supply. This does not mean we can forget about space complexity, only that for us time complexity will always be the primary issue. (I suppose we could consider a third kind of complexity: Is the algorithm devious and hard to understand, or is it simple and straightforward? Unfortunately, algorithm analysis never bothers with this kind of complexity.)

The only problem with Big O is that it's too loose. It gives us *an* upper bound on the time complexity, but not necessarily the *least* upper bound. All it has to be is less than something, after all; it could be less than something huge. For example, $f(n) = \frac{1}{2}(n^2 + n)$ is arguably $O(n^4)$, because you can surely find constants c, N such that the run time is $\leq cn^4$. (In fact, $c = 1$, $N = 1$ will do.) This is a red herring, however. In the analysis of algorithms, we typically find a cost function $f(n)$ that the algorithm can never exceed, and we say that the cost is $O(f(n))$.

Here is a set of rules that can enable us to compute the Big O form of any complexity function. In the following, "dominates" means "grows as fast or faster than"; $g(n)$ dominates $f(n)$ if $f(n)$ is $O(g(n))$. I use this term because $g(n)$ is usually taken from the dominant term in $f(n)$ and because it suggests vividly what we are driving at. For brevity, I will omit the arguments of the functions, since they are always n: I will write, "x is $O(y)$" instead of "$x(n)$ is $O(y(n))$."

1. Any function is big O of itself.

   Proof: Follows from the definition of Big O.

2. Constant factors like the $\frac{1}{2}$ in $\frac{1}{2}(n^2 - n)$ are ignored.

   Proof: This follows because we can lump any constant factors together with that constant c used in the definition of Big O.

3. Big O of a sum is equal to the fastest-growing term in the sum.

   Proof: Suppose $f(n) = a(n) + b(n)$, and suppose $a(n)$ grows faster than $b(n)$. Then by definition, b is $O(a)$; hence f is $O(2a)$, which is $O(a)$ by rule 2.

4. Big O is transitive. If $z(n)$ grows faster than $y(n)$ and $y(n)$ grows faster than $x(n)$, then clearly $z(n)$ grows faster than $x(n)$. Translated into Big O notation, this says, if x is $O(y)$ and if y is $O(z)$, then x is $O(z)$.

Proof: If x is $O(y)$, then $x(n)/y(n) \leq c$ for $n > N_1$. If y is $O(z)$, then $y(n)/z(n) \leq d$ for $n > N_2$. But then clearly

$$\frac{x(n)}{z(n)} = \frac{x(n)}{y(n)}\frac{y(n)}{z(n)} \leq c \cdot d \text{ for } n > N_3,$$

where N_3 is the greater of N_1 and N_2. $\big(N_3 = \max(N_1, N_2).\big)$

5. Big O is multiplicative. If a is $O(x)$ and b is $O(y)$, then $a \cdot b$ is $O(x \cdot y)$.

Proof: If a is $O(x)$, this means $a(n)/x(n) \leq c$ for $n > N_1$. If b is $O(y)$, then $b(n)/y(n) \leq d$ for $n > N_2$. But then, multiplying and substituting, we have

$$\frac{a(n)b(n)}{x(n)y(n)} \leq c \cdot d \text{ for } n > \max(N_1, N_2).$$

But that means that this ratio is also bounded; hence $a \cdot b$ is $O(x \cdot y)$.

6. Higher powers of n dominate lower powers of n.

Proof: This follows from the definition of Big O, and also from rule 5.

7. If $f(n)$ is a polynomial in n—that is, if $f(n)$ has the form,

$$f(n) = a_p n^p + a_{p-1} x^{p-1} + \cdots + a_2 n^2 + a_1 n + a_0$$

—then $f(n)$ is Big O of the highest power of n in the polynomial: $f(n)$ is $O(n^p)$.

Proof: This follows directly from rules 6, 3, and 2. We saw a case of this in our first example.

In proving the following rules, we will take advantage of the fact I mentioned before: if $a(n)$ and $b(n)$ are both positive and $a(n) \leq b(n)$ for $n > N$, then $a(n)$ is $O\big(b(n)\big)$.

8. Any exponential dominates any power: n^p is $O(y^n), y > 1$. (Anyone who has ever observed the way e^n flies off toward infinity as n gets big can easily believe this.)

Proof: We will start by showing that e^n dominates n^p; probably the easiest way to show it is to note that the power series for e^n is

$$e^n = \sum_{k=0}^{\infty} n^k / k!. \tag{1.5}$$

Now for any positive n, all the terms in this sum are positive; therefore they all add up. Hence if we truncate that sum at some finite power $p + 1$, our answer will be too small:

$$e^n > \sum_{k=0}^{p+1} n^k / k!.$$

But by rule 7, the second sum is $O(n^{p+1})$; and this clearly dominates n^p by rule 6. But if that smaller sum dominates n^p, then *certainly* e^n does. We can generalize this result to any exponential function by observing that $y^n = e^{an}$, where $e^a = y$. We can then use this same argument, substituting an for n.

9. Any positive power of n dominates $\ln n$.

Proof: If $p \geq 1$, then to show that n^p dominates $\ln n$ it is sufficient to show that n dominates $\ln n$, because of rule 6. But for $n > 0$, $\ln n < n$. For any positive power at all, we note that

$$\lim_{n \to \infty} \frac{\ln n}{n^p} = \lim_{n \to \infty} \frac{1/n}{pn^{p-1}}$$

by L'Hospital's rule. But this is

$$\lim_{n \to \infty} \frac{1}{pn^p},$$

which is clearly 0.

10. All logs grow at the same rate: that is, $\log_a n$ is $O\left(\log_b(n)\right)$ and $\log_b n$ is $O\left(\log_a(n)\right)$.

Proof: An elementary property of logs is that $\log_a n = \log_a b \cdot \log_b n$. Since $\log_a b$ is a constant, the result follows from rule 2.

11. $n \log n$ grows faster than n but more slowly than n^2. (The proof is left as an exercise.)

The first thing these rules give us is a table of functions in order of rates of growth. Every function in this table is Big O of the functions above it.

1. 2^n
2. $n^p, p > 1$
3. $n \log n$
4. n
5. $\log n$
6. 1

Putting these rules together gives us a more-or-less cookbook formula for finding the order of a complexity function. Most complexity formulæ can be written as sums of terms in n, with maybe a constant multiplier out in front. We begin by dropping that constant multiplier. Then we look for the fastest-growing term in the sum with the aid of the table above; $f(n)$ is Big O of that fastest-growing term.

In analyzing the time complexity of an algorithm from the code, we must count something. For example, in sorting and searching algorithms, we usually count comparisons. The starting point is normally to look for loops; very few algorithms are loopless. The limits on the loop tell us how many times it executes. For example, if the code says

```
for i := 1 to n do
    ...something...;
```

the loop will execute n times and the total cost is the sum of the costs of doing that something that forms the body of the loop. If the cost of the body depends on the particular value of i—specifically, if the cost is $g(i)$, then the cost of the loop is

$$\sum_{i=1}^{n} g(i).$$

If the cost is independent of i, as in this loop,

```
for i := 1 to n do
    sum := sum + a[i];
```

the cost reduces to n times what happens within the loop. In this case, for example, the body of the loop consists of an addition and the operations needed to access `a[i]`. We may take this to be a constant cost; hence the body of the loop is $O(1)$ and the cost of the loop as a whole is $nO(1)$, which, by the multiplicative property, is $O(n)$. Note that if the limits of the loop had been `i := 2 to n`, the cost would still have been $O(n)$: the cost is $n-1$ times whatever happens in the loop, but $n-1$ is $O(n)$.

If the loop is of uncertain length, as in a `while` loop, we reason similarly. For example, suppose we have

```
found := false;
while (p <> nil) and not found do
    if p^.key = k then
        found := true
    else
        p := p^.next;
```

This loop is clearly "walking down" a linked list looking for a key k. It will terminate when it finds k or when it reaches the end of the list. If the list contains n nodes, the cost of an unsuccessful search will be n. If we know where k is likely to be found, we can use that information to estimate the cost of a successful search. In most cases, however, k is apt to be almost anywhere: that is, each of the n nodes is equally likely to contain k. But recall that the time complexity of an algorithm is the longest time it can be expected to take for any given n; hence we assume that k will be in the worst possible place, at the end of the list. In either case, we get $O(n)$ as our answer.

If there are two nested loops, and if the limits on the inner loop do not change, then the costs of the two loops multiply. For example, in the following code,

```
for i := 1 to n do
    for j := 1 to n do
        x[i, j] := 0;
```

the cost of the outer loop is n times the cost of whatever happens inside it. But what happens inside it is another loop which also costs n; hence the overall cost is n^2. This principle can be generalized to any number of nested loops.

If the limits on the inner loop are variable, then the total cost of the nested loops is the sum, over the limits of the outer loop, of the costs of the various repetitions of the inner loop. Suppose our previous example were modified to read

```
for i := 1 to n do
    for j := 1 to i do
        x[i, j] := 0;
```

In this case the durations of the inner loop are $1, 2, 3, \ldots$, and the total cost is given by

$$\sum_{i=1}^{n} i = \tfrac{1}{2}n(n+1).$$

In finding the cost of recursive procedures, we must consider how many recursive calls are made at each level of recursion, how deep the recursions are likely to go, and what the cost of each recursion will be. If there is only one recursive call, the recursion can be thought of as a special case of a loop. For example, in this simple-minded recursion, found in many elementary texts,

```
function FACTORIAL (x: integer): integer;      { Computes n!   }
    begin                                      {   (Recursive) }
    if x <= 1 then
        factorial := x
    else
        factorial := x*factorial(x - 1)
    end;  { Factorial }
```

there is one recursive call each time around. The cost of the nonrecursive portions is one comparison and one multiplication; we may take these to be $O(1)$. Since the argument is diminished by 1 on every new recursion and since the recursions stop when $x = 1$, then if we are computing $n!$, the depth of the recursions is $n - 1$. Hence this behaves in the essentially same way as a loop from 2 to n and its cost is $O(n)$.

Here is an example with more than one recursive call:

```
function FIB (n: integer): integer;     { Fibonacci numbers     }
   begin                                {     (recursive)        }
   if n < 2 then
      fib := n
   else
      fib := fib(n - 1) + fib(n - 2)
   end;  { Fib }
```

This computes the Fibonacci numbers and it is based on their definition: for integer $n \geq 0$,

$$F_n = \begin{cases} n, & n < 2, \\ F_{n-1} + F_{n-2} & \text{otherwise.} \end{cases}$$

(This is a terrible way to compute Fibonacci numbers; it's suitable as a textbook example and for nothing else.) We have two recursive calls, and for really big n most of the recursions will also make two recursive calls. Hence as a first approximation we assume that the number of recursive calls will double each time. The argument is diminished by 1 in one call and by 2 in the other. If we ignore the difference, we can guess that the depth of the recursions is roughly n. When the cost doubles each time around, the overall cost will be exponential. You can see that from the fact that the recurrence relation

$$c_{i+1} = 2c_i$$

with initial condition

$$c_0 = 1$$

has the solution

$$c_i = 2^i. \tag{1.6}$$

Thus we guess that this algorithm is $O(2^n)$. This is not a bad first guess; detailed analysis will show that the actual cost of computing F_n recursively is in fact F_n. We also know that the nth Fibonacci number is approximately $\phi^n/\sqrt{5}$, where $\phi = (\sqrt{5} + 1)/2 \approx 1.61803$. This is $O(\phi^n)$. Since $\phi^n = 2^{n \lg \phi} = 2^{0.6942n}$, we see that $O(2^n)$ is not a bad starting guess (although note that 2^n is not $O(\phi^n)$).

There is one thing that I must add: In considering the complexity of an algorithm, we must not let ourselves be hypnotized by Big-O numbers. With rare exceptions, the more efficient algorithms entail considerable overhead, and when they are used on small amounts of data the overhead may wipe out the supposed benefits of the algorithm. A professional programmer will examine the problem at hand to determine the most appropriate algorithm to be used.

Our main concern will be efficiency, as measured by big O. But in considering efficiency there are two caveats. First, you must never forget the rule, *Make it work first before you make it work fast.*[2] The right answer in an hour is better than the

---

[2] Attributed to Bruce Whiteside. See Bentley [1988].

wrong answer in a minute. In many cases, the simplest, most direct approach is the best one to take.

Second, you must be aware that sometimes the greatest gains in efficiency will result from mundane considerations that are beneath the dignity of an algorithm theorist. For example, many programs can be sped up dramatically simply by managing input and output more efficiently; reductions of 80 to 90 percent are not uncommon. In FORTRAN as implemented on some computers, the statement

```
read (5, 901) (x(i), i = 1, 100)
```

requires 100 calls to the i/o handler to read the x array, while the statement

```
read (5, 901) x
```

requires only one. This is an implementation detail of the sort we never consider in algorithm analysis—in fact, it is a programming consideration rather than an algorithm consideration—but taking advantage of it once made a program run ten times as fast as it did previously. The theory we discuss in the ensuing chapters is important, but it is not the whole story. Everything we learn in life has a larger context in which we must place it and consider it.

1.3   ABSTRACT DATA TYPES

One of the most troublesome problems in implementing algorithms is the risk of being swamped by details. It's a hard problem to avoid, because programming is full of details, and if all the details are not exactly right, the program won't work. Since the mind can deal with only a limited number of things at one time (see, for example, Miller [1956]), it is essential to partition the program in ways that avoid overburdening our minds. There are a number of techniques for controlling complexity; the one we will discuss here is the use of abstract data types (ADTs).

They are called abstract because their implementation is hidden from the user. The name is actually misleading, since what is concealed is not only the implementation of the data type but also the implementation of the operations to be done on the type. Hiding these implementations means that we don't have to worry about the details of any operation on the data type; thus we can concentrate on what we want to do with a data object of that type and not on how to do it.

All the primitive data types in a language are abstract in this sense. If we have two **real** variables x and y and want to add them, we simply write x + y. We don't concern ourselves with how the addition is done; the implementation is hidden in the hardware and we trust the hardware to do it correctly. In a language, like Turbo Pascal, that includes character strings as a primitive data type, we find a similar abstraction. In Turbo Pascal we concatenate two character strings v and w by writing v + w. The details of how w is tacked onto the end of v, how the length of the resulting string is determined, and how the result is returned, are all concealed from us, and we don't worry about them.

Contrast that with a stack in a language like Pascal. We must decide whether to implement the stack as an array or as a linked list, and whenever we want to do anything with the stack, we must concern ourselves with the details of doing it. Thus we must spend time writing things like

```
const
   maxstack = 96;
type
   stacktype = record
                  top: integer;
                  node: array [1..maxstack] of integer;
                  end;
var
   my_stack: stacktype;
```

and

```
function POP (var newdata: integer): boolean;
                     { If stack is not empty, pops topmost  }
                     {   element from stack & returns it in  }
                     {   newdata.  Value of function indi-   }
                     {   cates success: if stack empty,      }
                     {   returns False; else returns true    }
   begin
   pop := false;          { Assume the worst       }
   with my_stack do
      if top > 0 then
         begin
         newdata := node[top];
         top := top - 1;
         pop := true    { Succeeded              }
         end
   end;  { Pop }
```

Writing and debugging all these things distracts our attention from the problem at hand; it's as if, every time we wanted to add two reals, we had to include code that would separate the exponents from the fractions, adjust the numbers so that the exponents agreed, add the fractions, and adjust the result so that it was normalized. The beauty of floating-point hardware is that it takes care of all these grubby details for us. Wouldn't it be nice if we could wrap the whole implementation of a stack—the declaration and the code for all the desired operations—into a package that would handle stack operations for us the way the hardware handles floating-point operations for us? ADTs let us do just that.

To pursue this comparison, recall that when we learn about doing arithmetic with reals, all we learn is how to declare them and how to write the operations. We are told, in effect,

A real variable is a data object that contains integer or noninteger numerical data.

The permissible operations are:

- Addition, written x + y;
- Multiplication, written x*y;
- ... etc.

The specification summarizes those aspects of real arithmetic that are visible to the user; it says nothing about how the real variables are implemented or how the operations are carried out. Ideally, if we move our programs to a new computer (say, from a PC to a Vax), any program that worked on the old system should work on the new one as well.

We wish to do the same thing with a stack: all the user will be told is,

A stack is a list of data objects of ⟨some data type⟩.

The permissible operations are:

- Making the stack empty, written clear_stack;
- Determining whether the stack is empty, written empty_stack;
- Pushing a new object onto the stack, written push (newdata);
- ... etc.

Again, the specification summarizes those aspects of the stack data type that are visible to the user. (In an ADT, this portion is frequently called the *interface*.) It says nothing about how the stack is implemented or how the operations are carried out. If we should choose later on to switch from an array implementation to a linked-list implementation, this change should be invisible to the user, and any program that worked before the change should work after it.

In creating an ADT, we must, of course, write and debug all the code that I have imagined: the declarations, and the procedures and functions that carry out all the operations we need. But then we simply save the resulting package in a file somewhere, and in any program that requires a stack, we just include the package. How the package is to be included depends on the version of Pascal we are using. Some versions provide a compiler directive for including a file. For example, Vax Pascal has the directive, #include ⟨*filename*⟩ and Turbo Pascal uses {$I ⟨*filename*⟩}. Turbo Pascal also provides a construct called a unit; this comes close to the ideal ADT, because it is compiled separately and included in compiled form and because it explicitly separates the interface (the part visible to the user) and the implementation (the part that is hidden). In versions of Pascal that do not provide a facility for automatically including files, we must simply copy the package into our program, but having done so, we forget that it is there and simply use the operations.

It helps to see an example of all this. Let us suppose that we wish to create an ADT for a stack. What the user sees, in effect, is the following definition:

A stack is a sequential arrangement of data items, with the following operations:

- `Clear_Stack` removes all data items from the stack;

- `Empty_Stack` determines whether the stack contains any data items;

- `Push` adds an item at the top of the stack, unless the stack is full;

- `Pop` removes an item from the top of the stack, unless the stack is empty.

The form in which the user sees this is apt to be as follows:

```
{ Interface: }
procedure CLEAR_STACK;              { Deletes all data from stack  }
function EMPTY_STACK: boolean;      { Tests for presence of data    }
function PUSH                       { Pushes x onto stack; returns  }
         (x: integer): boolean;  {    true if successful, false   }
                                 {    if stack already full.      }
function POP (var                   { Pops x from stack; returns     }
         x: integer): boolean;   {    true if successful, false   }
                                 {    if stack already empty.      }
```

(The word `interface` is added for clarity; but in a Turbo Pascal unit, **interface** (without the braces or the colon) is a keyword identifying those parts of the unit that will be visible to the user's program.)

What goes on behind the scenes might be this:

```
{ Implementation: }
const
   maxstack = 96;
type
   stacktype = record
               top: integer;
               node: array [1..maxstack] of integer;
               end;
var
   my_stack: stacktype;

procedure CLEAR_STACK;
   begin
   my_stack.top := 0    { Makes all previous data inaccessible  }
   end;  { Clear_Stack }

function EMPTY_STACK: boolean;
   begin
   empty_stack := my_stack.top = 0
   end;  { Empty_Stack }

function PUSH (x: integer): boolean;
```

```
begin
push := false;          { Assume the worst      }
with my_stack do
   if top < maxstack then
      begin
      top := top + 1;
      node[top] := x;
      push := true   { Succeeded             }
      end
end;  { Push }

function POP (var x: integer): boolean;
   begin
   pop := false;          { Assume the worst      }
   with my_stack do
      if top > 0 then
         begin
         x := node[top];
         top := top - 1;
         pop := true   { Succeeded             }
         end
   end;  { Pop }
```

The code shown here is written on the assumption that we are implementing the stack by means of an array. But note that if we were to change the implementation later on to a linked list, the user would not need to be told this; the interface would be unchanged and the procedures and functions listed there would still work as expected.

Besides the stack, two ADTs of particular importance for us are *queues* and *character strings*. We may define a queue as follows:

A queue is a sequential arrangement of data items, with the following operations:

- Clear_Queue removes all data items from the queue.

- Empty_Queue determines whether the queue currently contains any data items.

- En_Queue stores an item at one end of the queue (called the *tail* of the queue), if there is room for it in the queue.

- De_Queue removes an item from the other end of the queue (called the *head* of the queue), unless the queue is empty.

We will assume that these operations are invoked as follows:

```
procedure CLEAR_QUEUE;           { Removes all data from queue   }
function EMPTY_QUEUE: boolean;   { Tests for presence of data    }
function EN_QUEUE                { Puts x on tail of queue;      }
```

```
          (x: <type>): boolean;  {   returns true if successful, }
                                 {    false if queue already full }
function DE_QUEUE (var          { Removes x from head of queue; }
       x: <type>);             {   returns true if successful, }
                                 {    false if queue empty       }
```

The data type of the parameters (indicated here by **type** enclosed in angle brackets) depends on how the queue is to be used.

The string ADT is an enhancement of standard Pascal provided in Turbo Pascal. When we need to handle strings in our code, we will use the Turbo Pascal conventions, which are as follows:

function LENGTH (x: string); Returns current length of x.

function CONCAT (x, y: string): string; Returns the concatenation of strings x and y.

function COPY (x: string; m, n: integer): string; Returns a substring of x starting with the mth character of x and n characters long.

function POS (x, y: string): integer; Returns the location of the first instance of x in the string y and 0 if no instance is found.

procedure DELETE (var s: string; loc, n: integer); Deletes n characters from s starting at position loc.

procedure INSERT (x: string; var y: string; loc: integer); Inserts x into s at the locth position.

(Concat(x, y) can also be written as x + y. The plus operator is *overloaded*: it has a new meaning when applied to strings.) The string is stored inside the computer as an array of **char**, with the current length represented in various ways, but we do not need to know that: we invoke the operations, and they do what we want.

We will occasionally need to examine or manipulate the bits in an integer; for this purpose we will assume that the ADT **integer** has associated with it the following operations in addition to the normal arithmetic operations:

x **and** y returns the bitwise AND of the binary representations of the integers x and y;

x **or** y returns the bitwise OR of the binary representations of the integers x and y;

not x returns the bitwise complement of the binary representation of x;

x **shl** n shifts the bits of the binary representation of x to the left by n bits, putting 0's in the vacated bit positions;

x **shr** n shifts the bits of the binary representation of x to the right by n bits, putting 0's in the vacated bit positions.

Thus the Pascal **and**, **or**, and **not** operators are overloaded; when applied to Boolean variables they function in the usual way, but when applied to integers they operate as described here.

The main advantage of ADTs is that they hide the details of implementation from the user, as we have seen. This simplifies life for the programmer who uses the ADT and results in greater clarity in the end product; this clarity in turn makes maintenance and modification of the program (always a major cost item over the program's life) easier, safer, and cheaper to do. A second advantage is that an ADT is *reusable*. Once we have debugged our stack ADT, for example, we can use it in *any* program that requires a stack of integers. This spares us the work of coding and debugging a set of stack routines for every new program that requires them. (In object-oriented programming (for example, the type of programming supported by C++), we can go further and make the ADT support stacks of any desired data type. Object-oriented programming is not supported by standard Pascal, however.)

1.4   REVIEW OF RECURSION

You have probably been exposed to recursive procedures in your previous programming course(s), but it sometimes helps to come back for a second look, particularly since we will be seeing lots of recursive functions and procedures in the material to come.

1.4.1   Basics of Recursion

A recursive procedure or function deals with a problem by solving a simpler version of the problem and building on that solution. The trick is to find that simpler version. Sometimes it is implicit in the statement of the problem. For example, the Chebyshev polynomials are defined this way:

$$T(n,x) = \begin{cases} 1, & n = 0, \\ x, & n = 1, \\ 2xT(n-1,x) - T(n-2,x) & \text{otherwise.} \end{cases} \tag{1.7}$$

(I have deliberately chosen these unfamiliar polynomials to emphasize that we can reduce a definition like this to code without knowing anything about what the definition is defining.) In this example, the simpler form of the problem is given in the third line: You find $T(n,x)$ from two smaller Chebyshev polynomials. We can go from this definition right into code, in fact:

```
function CHEB (n: integer; x: real): real;      { Chebyshev     }
   begin                                         {    Polynomials }
   if n = 0 then cheb := 1                 { Line 1 }
   else if n = 1 then cheb := x            { Line 2 }
   else                                    { Line 3 }
      cheb := 2*x*cheb(n - 1, x) - cheb(n - 2, x)
   end;  { Cheb }
```

This isn't the world's greatest way to compute these polynomials, if you need a great many of them, but it does the job and can be obtained directly from the definition, as the comments in the code imply.

One of the classic examples, used in nearly every text, is the Towers of Hanoi puzzle. On the remote chance that you have never seen this, here is how it goes: You are presented with a board with three pegs. Stacked on one peg are a set of n discs of graduated sizes, as shown in Fig. 1.1 (a). Your problem is to move the discs from peg 1 to peg 3 subject to the following constraints:

1. You may move only one disc at a time;

2. You may not put a larger disc on top of a smaller one.

These constraints rule out the two obvious solutions: that of picking up the entire stack and moving it and that of putting the discs on peg 2 in reverse order and then putting them on peg 3 in their correct order.

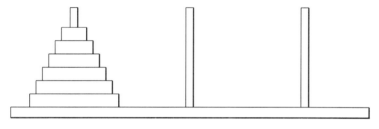

Figure 1.1 (a)

The reason this is such a popular example is that there is no intuitive idea of how you would program a solution without using recursion. But with recursion, we get the following solution:

1. Recursively move the top $n-1$ discs to the temporary peg, as shown in Fig. 1.1 (b);

2. Move the remaining disc to the destination peg as suggested by the dotted arrow;

3. Recursively move the $n-1$ discs from the temporary peg to the destination peg.

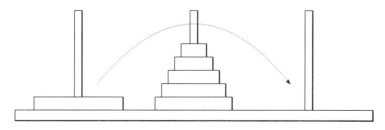

Figure 1.1 (b)

This solution will obey the rules because in each recursion only one disc is moved; furthermore, it is the largest remaining disc, so any other discs put on top of it in subsequent recursions will be smaller.

We can implement this algorithm as follows:

```
procedure HANOI (n, source, dest: integer);
                                    { Solves Towers of Hanoi }
      var                           {   with n discs          }
         temp: integer;             {   (recursive)           }
      begin
      if n = 1 then
*        writeln ('Move disc from peg ', source, ' to peg ', dest)
*     else
         begin
         temp := 6 - source - dest;
         hanoi (n - 1, source, temp);
         writeln ('Move disc from peg ', source, ' to peg ', dest);
         hanoi (n - 1, temp, dest)
         end
      end;  { Hanoi }
```

Since $1+2+3 = 6$, we can compute the number of the temporary peg by subtracting **source** and **dest** from 6, as shown. (This program can be made even shorter by changing the **if** to **if n > 0 then** and deleting the two starred lines. I've left it as shown in order to separate the recursive and nonrecursive parts.)

The main problem with using recursion is guaranteeing that the recursions won't go on forever. We protect ourselves by providing every recursive procedure with a "safety net" or escape clause. In **Cheb**, the escape clauses were the first two **ifs**. Since the recursive calls keep decreasing n, we will eventually trigger one or the other of these **ifs** and the recursions will stop. In the case of **Hanoi**, the safety net is also an **if**: If you are down to one disc, stop making recursions. We will find that every recursive procedure or function has such an escape clause.

There are probably three main problems in learning about recursion. One is trying to believe that recursion is good for anything. This is difficult because the elementary examples we must consider seem so foolish: children's puzzles like the Towers of Hanoi, or problems obviously solved the hard way, like recursive computation of factorials. That problem will disappear in the chapters ahead, because we will see many problems for which a nonrecursive solution is too awkward to consider.

The second problem is understanding how a recursive program works. The solution to this problem is to *assume the recursive call will, in fact, do what it is supposed to do.* In **Hanoi**, we can see that, if the recursive calls do indeed move the top $n - 1$ discs legally, then the procedure will work.

The third problem is convincing yourself that you can get away with it—convincing yourself, in fact, that it works. This can be particularly troublesome when the procedure has local variables, because it is hard to see which values of these variables apply at any particular time and hard to see how the language implementation can avoid getting mixed up. (Computers never get mixed up.)

I think this third problem is alleviated considerably if one knows how recursion is actually implemented. The implementation uses a stack. A call to a recursive subprogram is sometimes called an *activation* of the subprogram, and for every activation, the system pushes a number of data items onto the stack. These data items are called an *activation record*. It contains the return address (so the computer knows how to get back from the activation), the current parameters, and all local variables. There is one activation record for every recursive call, so as the recursions continue the stack gets bigger and bigger. Every time the program returns from a call, it pops the stack, uncovering the next record down. Beginning programmers sometimes worry about all that stack space, but there is no need to; if the program is designed intelligently, the stack usage is minimal and in any case memory is plentiful. Recursive procedures were first conceived and implemented when 256 kilobytes of memory was considered a generous amount; now many personal computers have more than that.

It may be helpful to watch the stack as a recursive procedure is executed. Imagine that we have a linked list, like that shown in Fig. 1.2, and that we need to list its contents starting with the last node and working back. (For example, if this were the implementation of a stack ADT and we wanted to list the contents of the stack from the bottom up, we would need such a procedure.) So, for the example in the figure, we would want the program to output 19, 37, 12.

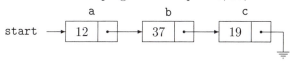

Figure 1.2

(We use the symbol ⇌ to represent a `nil` pointer.)

Here is a procedure for listing the contents as desired:

```
1   procedure SHOW_LIST_REVERSE (start: listptr);
                                    { Displays linked list }
2       begin                       {  backwards           }
3       if start <> nil then
4           begin
5           show_list_reverse (start^.next);
6           write (start^.data:4);
7           end;
8       end;  { Show_List_Reverse }
```

I said recursive procedures work by solving a simpler version of the problem; in this example, the simpler version consists of displaying all of the list except the first node. It works its way out to the end of the list by a series of recursive calls. Then, as the recursions unwind, it writes out the **data** field of each node. To analyze it as I recommended before, we take it on faith that the call in line 5 will write out the remainder of the list; then there is nothing more to do than to write out the first item of the list, which is done in line 6.

We will assume that the call to this procedure is in line 46 of the main program:

```
46      show_list_reverse (head);
```

We will further assume that the stack maintained by the language implementation initially contains only data for the main program. (In some language implementations, the main program's data are in a different place, but it is easier to follow the whole picture if we assume that they are on the stack.) Thus before the first call to `Show_List_Reverse`, the stack looks like Fig. 1.3 (*a*). When the main program makes the call, an activation record goes on the stack, as shown in Fig. 1.3 (*b*). It contains the parameter `start` and the return address. This address is actually a memory address; since we don't have any idea what that memory address actually is, I will call it simply line 46. Similarly, the parameter `start`, which currently points to the head of the list is a memory address (that's what pointers are), and since we don't know where the nodes are, I will simply identify that node's address as a.

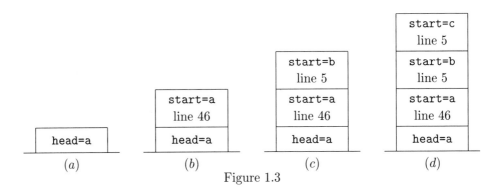

Figure 1.3

The first thing `Show_List_Reverse` does is test its parameter `start`. Since it isn't `nil`, it calls itself with the pointer value `start^.next` as a parameter. This puts a new activation record on the stack, as shown in Fig. 1.3 (*c*). This time the parameter is b (since that is `start^.next`) and the return address is line 5, since that is the point to which this recursive call must return.

We now have two activation records on the stack. But the language implementation has the rule that, in searching for local variables and parameters, it looks only at the *topmost* frame on the stack. This means that it will ignore the previous values of the parameter and return address and will look only at the current ones. But note that the previous values haven't been lost; they're one record down, awaiting the time when the program returns from this activation.

On the new activation, `Show_List_Reverse` examines `start`, finds it isn't `nil`, and calls itself again. Another activation record goes on the stack, as shown in Fig. 1.3 (*d*). This time `start` points to c, and once again the procedure examines `start` and calls itself again. The stack now looks like Fig. 1.3 (*e*).

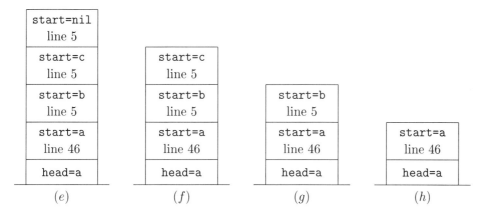

Figure 1.3 (continued)

Now when `Show_List_Reverse` tests `start`, it finds it is `nil`; therefore it does nothing and returns immediately. To return, it looks at the return address, which is line 5. When it returns, the activation record is popped from the stack, which now looks as shown in Fig. 1.3 (*f*). This activation of `Show_List_Reverse` has now finished with line 5 and goes on to line 6. In order to find `start^.data` so it can display it, it looks at the current value of `start`, sitting in the top stack frame. This value is `c`, hence it writes out `c^.data`, which is 12.

This activation now returns; the return address is line 5 and the system pops the stack, leaving it as shown in Fig. 1.3 (*g*). Again `Show_List_Reverse` looks at the parameter `start`, which is now `b`, so that when it writes the value of `start^.data`, we get 37 on the screen.

It then returns from this activation; the return address is line 5 again and the stack now looks as in Fig. 1.3 (*h*). It displays 19 and returns. But this time the return address is line 46; hence this return takes it back to the main program and we are done.

This example shows us several things. First, it shows how the subprogram finds its way back: the return address it is supposed to use is always in the topmost record on the stack. It also shows how the computer can find the correct parameters and local variables (if any): they are likewise in the topmost stack frame. Finally, it shows how the program avoids losing the previous return addresses, parameters, and local variables: they are all sitting in activations records further down the stack. The computer requires absolutely no intelligence to handle all this; it merely pushes when calling, pops when returning, and looks for all local information in the top frame of the stack. (How it accesses global and other non-local data is a topic that is beyond the scope of this discussion.)

1.4.2 Removing Recursions

There are two reasons why we might want to convert a recursive procedure to a nonrecursive form. First, we may be programming in some language that does not support recursions, in which case even if our first approach to a solution may have been recursive, we have no choice but to remove the recursions before we implement the procedure. Second, it may sometimes happen that a recursive form is unnecessarily complicated or too slow.

The recursive factorial function is an example of this second case; it is so simple to write

```
function FACT (n: integer): integer;
    var                              { Nonrecursive factorial}
        i, p: integer;
    begin
    p := 1;
    for i := 1 to n do
        p := p*i;
    fact := p
    end;  { Fact }
```

that it is hard to see why anyone should think the recursive form is better. An even worse case arises out of the Fibonacci numbers; we saw that the cost of computing F_n recursively was approximately exponential in n. But since each Fibonacci number is just the sum of the previous two Fibonacci numbers, the obvious course is to save those previous two numbers and use them to find the next:

```
function FIB (n: integer): integer;
    var                              { Nonrecursive Fibonacci}
        i,
        new, old, older: integer;
    begin
    older := 1;
    old := 0;
    new := 0;                { F(0) = 0      }
    for i := 1 to n do
        begin
        new := old + older;  { New number   }
        older := old;        { Save for     }
        old := new           {   next time   }
        end;
    fib := new
    end;  { Fib }
```

How much trouble it is to remove recursions depends on how many recursive calls there are and where they are in the code. The simplest case occurs when there is one recursive call that is the last executable statement in the procedure. If there is a single recursive call elsewhere in the procedure, it is more troublesome to remove it. The most complicated case involves two or more recursive calls at various points in the procedure. We now consider each of these cases.

Tail Recursion. When the subprogram ends with a recursive call, we refer to that call as *tail recursion*. A tail recursion can be replaced with an equivalent iterative structure, as follows:

> While there are recursive calls to be made:
>
> a. Do the nonrecursive part with the current parameters and local variables;
>
> b. Update the variables and parameters for the next recursion.

For example, consider this recursive procedure for writing out the contents of a linked list:

```
procedure SHOW_LIST (p: nodeptr);        { Displays linked list  }
   begin                                 {    (recursive)        }
   if p <> nil then
      begin
      write (p^.data:4);
      show_list (p^.next)
      end
   end;  { Show_List }
```

If the list is empty, we do nothing; otherwise we write the contents of the current node and then make a recursive call to write the remainder of the list. The only recursive call is the last executable statement in the function. We can replace it with a **while** loop as follows:

```
procedure SHOW_LIST (p: nodeptr);        { Displays linked list  }
   begin                                 {    (nonrecursive)     }
{  if p = nil then      }
      while p <> nil do
         begin
         write (p^.data:4);              { Nonrecursive part     }
         p := p^.next                    { Update                }
         end
   end;  { Show_List }
```

(The conversion is easier to follow if the **if** is left in, but it should be clear that it could be omitted, which is why I have made it into a comment.) The nonrecursive part is the writing of the current node's data, and the only thing that has to be updated here is **p**.

The reason we can get away with this is that there is nothing to be done after the recursive call has been made. The system puts the relevant data into an activation record when the recursive call is made, because normally when we come back from the call, we want to use those data again. But with tail recursion, we are never going to use them again, so we simply update them as we would for the call. This destroys the old values, but since we are never going to need the old values, it's safe to destroy them.

Single recursions. If the recursive part is not at the end, then we must use a stack to contain the saved values of the parameters and any local variables. We will use a version of our stack ADT as follows:

```
procedure CLEAR_STACK;                 { Makes stack empty    }
procedure PUSH (<parameters>);         { Pushes onto stack    }
procedure POP (<var parameters>);      { Pops from stack      }
function EMPTY_STACK: boolean;         { True if empty        }
```

This stack will take the place of the system stack the language implementation would use to store parameters and local data.

The rule for removing this kind of recursive call is:

1. Empty the stack.

2. While there are recursive calls to be made:

    a. Do the nonrecursive part that precedes the call;

    b. Push the current parameters and local variables onto the stack;

    c. Update the variables and parameters for the next recursion.

3. While stack not empty:

    a. Pop the stack;

    b. Do the nonrecursive part that follows the call.

As our example, let us take the following rather foolish procedure for displaying the nodes of a linked list from front to back and then from back to front. (My excuse for silly examples like this is that I want to keep the code simple so that the transformation will be as clear as possible.) We may write this procedure recursively as follows:

```
procedure LIST_FWD_BK (start: listptr); { Displays linked list }
                                         {   forward and back-  }
  begin                                  {   ward.  Recursive   }
  if start <> nil then
     begin
     write (start^.data:4);      { First node       }
     list_fwd_bk (start^.next);  { All the others   }
     write (start^.data:4)       { First node again }
     end
  end;   { List_Fwd_Bk }
```

Here the part that precedes the recursive call is just the first `write` and the part that follows the call is the second `write`. Following our rule, we get:

```
procedure LIST_FWD_BK (start: listptr); { Displays linked list }
                                         {   forward and back-  }
  begin                                  {   ward.  Nonrecursive }
  clear_stack;
  while start <> nil do
```

```
         begin
         write (start^.data:4);    { Before recursive call }
         push (start);
         start := start^.next      { Update                }
         end;
      while not empty_stack do
         begin
         pop (start);
         write (start^.data:4)      { After recursive call  }
         end
      end;  { List_Fwd_Bk }
```

Multiple Recursions. When the procedure has more than one recursive call, the process of removing them is much more difficult. I will consider only the case where there are two recursive calls. Sometimes the second call may be at the very end; in that case we may be able to remove it by tail recursion and then remove the remaining call with a stack, as shown previously.

Otherwise, we must handle both recursions with the aid of a stack. Doing this usually takes some ingenuity, and especially a thorough understanding of the specific algorithm we are modifying. The approach I am going to outline here is the nearest thing to a cookbook method. We have seen that a recursive call is replaced by a `push` and that a `pop` corresponds to a return from a recursive call. But when we pop the stack, we must know *which* recursive call we are returning from; hence when we do the `push`, we must also push some value that tells which call this corresponds to.

To see the basis for the conversion, consider a skeleton recursive procedure:

```
procedure R;
   begin
   if <condition> then
      begin
      A;
      R;          { First recursive call  }
      B;
      R;          { Second recursive call }
      C
      end
   end;  { R }
```

In this abstract model, A represents the statements preceding the first recursive call, B represents the statements in between the two calls, and C represents whatever happens after the last call. The condition that governs the escape clause for preventing infinite recursion is represented by ⟨condition⟩.

We can visualize what happens better if we look at a tree diagram illustrating how the recursions go. For simplicity, suppose that all the recursions terminate after the second call. Then we can represent the sequence of operations as shown in Fig. 1.4.

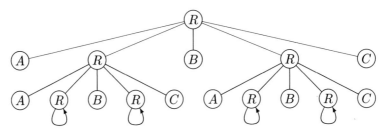

Figure 1.4

If we walk around the outside of this tree, going down the left side of each line to the circle and back up the right side, we see that the sequence of operations is $A, (A, B, C), B, (A, B, C), C$, and this is the sequence our nonrecursive version must yield. (The entries in parentheses are the ones resulting from the recursive calls.)

Each recursive call can be replaced by a **push** and a branch back to the beginning of the procedure, and each return can be replaced by a **pop** at the end of the procedure and a branch back to the point just after the call was made. Thus the nonrecursive version takes this form:

```
procedure R;
   label
       1, 2, 3, 10;
   begin
   clear_stack;
1: if <condition> then
       begin
       A;
       { adjust parameters and variables as needed }
       push (parameters and label 2);
       goto 1;
   2:    B;
       { adjust parameters and variables as needed }
       push (parameters and label 3);
       goto 1;
   3:    C
       if empty_stack then
           goto 10;
       pop (parameters and label);
       goto 2 (or 3) { depending on label popped }
       end
10:
   end;  { R }
```

When we pop the stack, we may branch either to 2 or 3, depending on where we were when we did the **push**. Thus, just as the language implementation stores a return address in the activation record, we must push a return address along with other data.

From this outline you can see that converting a subprogram to a nonrecursive version results initially in a morass of gotos. We normally refine the transformed version to get rid of those gotos in order to have an orderly, reasonably comprehensible program. We will apply this transformation to the Towers of Hanoi puzzle. The transformed version looks like this:

```
procedure NR_HANOI (n, source, dest: integer);  { Towers of    }
                                                 {   Hanoi      }
    label                                        { Nonrecursive }
      1, 2, 3, 10;        { Return addresses     }
    var
       ret_addr,
       temp: integer;
    begin
       clear_stack;
    1: if n > 0 then
          begin
          temp := 6 - source - dest;
          n := n - 1;
          push (2, n, source, dest);      { First recursive call  }
          dest := temp;
          goto 1;
    2:    temp := 6 - source - dest;
          writeln (source, ' --> ', dest);
          inc (count);
          push (3, n, source, dest);      { Second recursive call }
          source := temp;
          goto 1;
          end;
    3:    if empty_stack then
             goto 10;
          pop (ret_addr, n, source, dest);
          case ret_addr of               { How did I get here?   }
             2: goto 2;
             3: goto 3
             end;  { case }
    10:
    end;  { NR_Hanoi }
```

The resulting procedure is an example of particularly bad programming style, with all those gotos, but with some care the code can be cleaned up and the gotos eliminated. Kruse [1984] shows an elegant and compact version of the Towers of Hanoi, which he obtains by a series of transformations; Reingold and Hansen [1986] show an even tighter version. Either of these could be taken as a starting point for constructing nonrecursive versions of other algorithms.

1.5   PROGRAMMING STYLE AND STRATEGY

In a first programming course, we learn how to use a programming language to get the computer to do what we want. We are usually also told a great deal about program design and programming style.

Now, being taught a programming language is to computer science as being taught to read and write is to English literature. When we teach children to read and write, we do not try at the same time to teach them to write elegantly. But teaching about program design and programming style in an elementary programming course is like teaching those children to write beautiful English. Of course, we must start such training as soon as possible, in order to encourage good habits, but in my experience, good programming style and the knack of good program design comes only with time. Anyone who has developed a good style and has mastered the strategies needed to home in immediately on a clear and elegant solution to a programming problem in so short a time is to be congratulated.

Therefore, I am not going to spend much time preaching about programming style and strategy. But it may help to review a few pointers, which may guide your thinking as you become a more experienced programmer and develop those abilities you need to attain professional standing.

1. Top-down design.   There is a natural feeling that we must be able to walk before we can run, and we are usually taught early on that procrastination is a bad thing. In programming, these notions tempt us to write our programs from the bottom up. If we must process data read in from a file, we are apt to write the procedures for reading the data and for processing them right away.

I used to do this, too, and it was only through a lucky accident that I learned better. In programming, procrastination is a *virtue*. (Mark Twain: "Never put off to tomorrow what you can do the day after tomorrow.") Write the main program first, and every time you must do some real work, push the work off onto a procedure call. If you wish to compile the program, fool the compiler by writing each procedure along the following lines:

```
procedure FOO (x, y: parameters);
   begin
   end;  { Foo }
```

This is known as a *stub*; it makes the compiler think the procedure has been written and allows you to check out the logic of the main program.

You then apply this principle recursively: As you write each procedure, write its main logic first and every time something complicated comes up, push it onto yet another procedure call.

The reason this works is that when you get to writing the procedure itself, you know exactly what it is expected to do. If you write the procedure before the main program, you only *think* you know what it is supposed to do, and in my experience your estimate will usually be wrong. (Mine usually is.)

2. Simplicity. The best way to get from point a to point b is to stand at point a, look at point b, and follow your nose. The number of cases in which an indirect or roundabout approach pays off is remarkably small; in nearly all cases the simplest approach is the best.

For a truly horrible example, here is one adapted from Kernighan and Plauger [1978]:

```
for i := 1 to n do
    for j := 1 to n do
        a[i, j] := (i div j)*(j div i);
```

It is not at all obvious what this is supposed to do. The array a contains integers; after a little detective work you will realize that either i div j or j div i will be 0 except in the case when i = j. Hence this loop, which requires n^2 multiplications and $2n^2$ divisions—both expensive operations—merely sets all the elements of the a matrix to 0 except those on the main diagonal.

This isn't faster; it certainly is not clear. And yet programmers have been known to do things like this. But this is simpler and more clear:

```
for i := 1 to n do        { Make an identity matrix }
    for j := 1 to n do
        if i = j then
            a[i, j] := 1
        else
            a[i, j] := 0;
```

Evaluating n^2 ifs is faster than doing all those multiplications and divisions, and it should be immediately clear what is going on. In case it isn't, the comment will tell the reader.

3. Premature optimization. We have mentioned this previously, but it is worth mentioning again: We will spend a lot of time in this book looking at the costs of doing things. You must not be misled by this into thinking that speed is everything. It is certainly not everything the first time around: *Make it work first before you make it work fast.*

How important speed is depends on what we are trying to do. If we are writing a utility that will be used thousands of times on a big mainframe where we are billed for every millisecond of time used, speed is of the essence. But if we are using a personal computer to write a program that will be used only once, the only thing that counts is how long it takes to get the right answer. If it takes an hour to optimize and debug a program that would give us the right answer in five minutes if we didn't optimize it, and if we are going to use that program only once, why bother?

4. Variable names. You occasionally read fiction where the author has given the characters names that tell you something about them. In *David Copperfield,* you know from his name that Mr. Murdstone is not going to be a nice guy; the affinity to "murder" is not accidental.

It is a good idea to characterize your variables this way. It's probably acceptable to name loop counters `i` and `j` and pointers `p` and `q`, but when we have a total, it's best if we name it something like `total`. I also recommend adding a comment next to each variable where it is declared, saying what that variable is for.

I recommend using verbs for the names of procedures whenever it is practical to do so: call it `Read_Data` rather than `Data_Input`. Use nouns for variables and functions (but adjectives for Booleans).

5. Documentation and comments.   When we are writing a program, we are on top of everything. When we come back to it a week later—or even the next day, sometimes—we aren't. Comments are essential so that the programmer knows *why* the statement `left := left + 1` appears in the middle of that `else`. Thus we need to explain to ourselves what we are doing as we do it.

If the program is being written for others to use, it is a good idea to start by writing the documentation. Once we have written at least a draft of the user's manual, we have a much better idea of what the program is expected to do, and this will enable us to write the program more intelligently. Similarly, for each procedure it is a good idea to start with a comment explaining what the procedure does and, at least briefly, how it does it.

One way to learn good programming practice is to read good code. Hence I have tried to set a good example by following these rules in the examples in this book. The design is top-down when the complexity warrants it, and I frequently even explain the code top-down. The code is sometimes less concise than it might be, because in a textbook it's more important to be clear than to be terse. Once you know what is going on, you can streamline the code for yourself, as an exercise. You will find that the examples are provided with comments, although I usually omit the introduction, explaining how the procedure works, because that is covered in the surrounding text.

1.6   SUMMARY

We have seen an introduction to the concept of an algorithm and the basics of the rules for representing the time complexity of an algorithm; we have also had a brief look at the basics of recursive functions and procedures. We ended with a review of style and strategy.

Recursion is one of the fundamental tools of the programmer. It has the peculiarity that it starts out by being less important when we are beginners and becomes steadily more important as we learn more and penetrate more deeply into the mysteries of algorithm design. We will see, in the ensuing chapters, how often it provides the easiest way out of a tough problem. Beginners are apt to shy away from recursive solutions, but they are vital and frequently easier than iterative ones; an ease and familiarity with recursion is one of the marks of the professional.

Program design is an art; people do not learn it overnight. But we must work to develop it, and the ability to come up with a solution in short order is priceless. (You will sometimes be asked to write code in a job interview!)

1.7 PROBLEMS

1.1. Prove rule 11 (p. 8) from the definition of Big O.

1.2. Prove rule 11 from rules 9 and 5.

1.3. Show that $\log n$ is $O(\sqrt{n})$ by finding possible values of c and N.

1.4. Prove: If $f(n) > 0$ and increases monotonically for $n > N$, then $\lceil f(n) \rceil$ is $O(f(n))$.

1.5. For each of the following functions, find a $g(n)$ for which the given function is $O(g)$:

(a) $17n^3 + 1.7n^2 + n$
(b) $2n^2 + n \log n$
(c) $3n + n \log n$
(d) $2^n + n^9$
(e) $(n + \sqrt{n})(\log n + n + 3)$

1.6. Show that $n \log n$ is $O(n\sqrt{n})$.

1.7. We saw that $\log_a(n)$ was proportional to $\log_b(n)$. Does this hold for exponentials as well? That is, can we say that a^n is $O(b^n)$ and also b^n is $O(a^n)$? Justify your answer from the definition of Big O.

1.8. What is the cost of the following code?

```
for k := 1 to n do
   for i := 1 to n do
      for j := 1 to n do
         w[i, j] := w[i, j] or w[i, k] and w[k, j];
```

1.9. What is the cost of the following code?

```
for i := 1 to m do
   for j := 1 to p do
      begin
      sum := 0;
      for k := 1 to n do
         sum := sum + a[i, k] * b[k, j];
      c[i, j] := sum
      end;
```

1.10. What is the cost of the following code?

```
i := n;
while i > 1 do
    begin
    writeln (i);
    i := i div 2
    end;
```

1.11. Prove Eq. (1.6) by induction.

1.12. The text shows an implementation of the stack ADT using an array. Write an implementation that uses a linked list; be sure to make it compatible with the array version.

1.13. Suppose a queue is represented by a linked list and that its current contents are as shown:

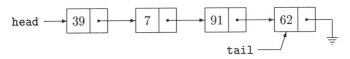

Problem 1.13

(a) Show how the queue looks after 21 and 49 have been added to the queue (in that order). (b) Show how the queue looks if one item is then removed from the queue.

1.14. Write a queue ADT using an array implementation. Include protection against trying to insert a data item when there is no room left in the queue.

1.15. Write a queue ADT using a linked-list implementation. Be sure to make it interchangeable with the array version.

1.16. (a) Suppose we have a string s containing the word `frangible`. What are the contents of the string after the two operations `Delete (s, 4, 1)` and `Delete (s, 6, 1)` (performed in that order)? (b) Suppose the string s contains the word `cuter`. What is the contents of the string after the operation `Insert ('omp', s, 2)`?

1.17. (a) If j is a 16-bit binary integer containing the value 1, what is the value of j after the statement `j := j shl 3`? (b) if `j = 341`, what is the value of j after the statement `j := j and 31`?

1.18. Trace the operation of the recursive `Hanoi` program assuming that the puzzle has four discs.

1.19. Trace the operation of the recursive version of `Show_List` assuming a list of the form shown in Fig. 1.2. Show how the system stack grows and shrinks as activation records are pushed onto and popped from the stack.

1.20. Euclid's algorithm for finding the greatest common divisor of two integers x and y can be outlined as follows:

$$gcd(x, y) = \begin{cases} y & \text{if } x \bmod y = 0 \\ gcd(y, x \bmod y) & \text{otherwise.} \end{cases}$$

Write a recursive function for Euclid's algorithm, based on this definition.

1.21. The answer to the preceding problem will use tail recursion. Write a nonrecursive version of the function.

1.22. Remove the recursion from the following function (note that this is an instance of tail recursion):

```
function SEARCH (p: pointer; key: keytype): pointer;
   begin
   if p = nil then
      search := p
   else if key = p^.data then
      search := p
   else if key < p^.data then
      search := search (p^.left, key)
   else
      search := search (p^.right, key)
   end;  { Search }
```

1.23. The following function for computing binomial coefficients makes use of the identity,

$$\binom{n}{k} = \frac{n}{k}\binom{n-1}{k-1}, \qquad 0 < k \le n:$$

```
function BCOEF (n, k: integer): integer;
   begin
   if (k > n) or (k < 0) then
      bcoef := 0
   else if (k = 0) or (k = n) then
      bcoef := 1
   else
      bcoef := (n*bcoef(n - 1, k - 1)) div k
   end;  { BCoef }
```

Notice that because of the sequence of computations in the last **else**, this is *not* tail recursion. (a) Remove the recursions with the aid of a stack. (b) Study the resultant function carefully and find a nonrecursive version that does not need a stack.

1.24. Remove the recursions from the following procedure. Do this in two stages: First, use tail recursion to remove the second call; then use a stack to remove the first call.

```
procedure INORDER (p: pointer);
   begin
   if p <> nil then
      begin
      inorder (p^.left);
      writeln (p^.data);
      inorder (p^.right)
      end
   end;  { InOrder }
```

1.25. The solution to the Towers of Hanoi problem given by Reingold and Hansen [1986] follows this general outline:

1. Clear the stack.

2. Push the problem onto the stack.

3. While the stack is not empty:

   a. Pop the stack

   b. If the item popped is the special case (here $n = 1$), then

       do the special case (move the disc)

   c. Else:

       i. Push the *second* subproblem;

       ii. Push the special case (here $n = 1$);

       iii. Push the *first* subproblem

Use this skeleton to write a nonrecursive Towers of Hanoi procedure.

CHAPTER 2

SEARCHING

Two of the most common problems in data processing are sorting and searching. Many kinds of data have to be arranged in alphabetical or numerical order, and locating particular data items must be done again and again. Both of these operations can be time-consuming, and a lot of study has been given to discovering efficient ways to do the job. In this chapter and the next two, we consider ways of doing these operations. Since searching is conceptually simpler and generally easier to implement than sorting, we will start with searching.

Throughout this chapter, we will assume that the list we are searching contains no duplicates. In practical applications, this is almost always the case; a bank may have two or more accounts for some customer, but they will be distinguished by different account numbers, and that difference will be enough to ensure that the records are not duplicates. If the list should contain duplicates, there is generally no way of knowing which duplicate will be found by the search.

Searching can be internal or external. With internal searching, all the data are in memory and we need only find where our target is. With external searching, the data are on some external storage device, like a disc or a tape. In that case, we must reduce the problem to one of internal searching by reading some or all the data into memory and doing an internal search. There are special ways of organizing external data that minimize the time needed to do an external search; we will consider these in Chapter 7; in this chapter, we consider only internal searching.

2.1 SEQUENTIAL SEARCHING

The simplest (and slowest) way to search a list for a data item is to start at the beginning of the list and examine every item until we have either found it or reached the end of the list. Since we look at all the items in sequence, this is called a *sequential* search.

If the list is an array, we can implement this search as follows. We assume that `searcharray` is a data type defined as

```
type searcharray = array[1..n] of {some appropriate type};
```

37

In many cases, the array will be an array of records. We will assume in such cases that the record contains some special identifying field which is commonly called its *key*. Thus the record might take this form:

```
type keytype = {as required};
     rectype = record
                  key: keytype;
                  {other things}
               end;
```

Now we can show the code for a sequential search of an array:

```
function ARRAY_SEARCH (a: searcharray; n: integer;
                  target: keytype): integer;
       var                        { Sequential search of array      }
          i: integer;
          found: boolean;
       begin
       i := 1;
       found = false;
       while (i <= n) and not found do
          if a[i].key = target then
             found = true
          else
             i := i + 1;
       if found then
          search := i
       else
          search := 0
       end;   { Array_Search }
```

In this procedure, n is the length of the array. `Array_Search` returns the subscript of the desired item; this gives the calling program direct access to it.

If the item is not found, `Array_Search` returns 0. This gives the caller a way to determine whether the record was found or not:

```
k := array_search (y, n, 42);
if k <> 0 then
   { do something with y[k] }
```

If the data are contained in a linked list, we do essentially the same thing, except that we walk through the list by following the pointer fields of the records. In such cases, let us assume that the list nodes have this structure:

```
type
   keytype = {as required};
   nodeptr = ^node;
   node = record
```

```
            key: keytype;
            { other fields }
            next: nodeptr;
         end;
```

In that case, the code takes almost the same form; the main difference is that we advance a pointer p with p := p^.next instead of a subscript i with i := i + 1:

```
   function LIST_SEARCH (start: nodeptr; target: keytype): nodeptr;
      var                     { Sequential search of linked list      }
         p: nodeptr;
         found: boolean;
      begin
      p := start;
      found = false;
      while (p <> nil) and not found do
         if p^.key = target then
            found := true
         else
            p := p^.next;   { Walk down list }
      search := p;
      end;   { List_Search }
```

Here start is a pointer to the beginning of the list. The pointer p walks down the list until it either finds the item or reaches the end of the list. A linear linked list is normally terminated by making the last item's pointer nil, and the test on p <> nil enables List_Search to recognize the end of the list. After the while loop has terminated, we don't need to test found because p will point to the desired record if it was found; otherwise it will be nil. In either case we return p to the caller. Again this gives the caller direct access to the desired record, and if p = nil, that fact will inform the caller that the record was not found. The calling code may look like this:

```
   p := list_search (list, 42);
   if p <> nil then
      { do something with p^ }
```

The strength of the sequential search is that it always works; you can search any list this way. When we look at faster methods, we will see that they always assume that the list is organized in some appropriate way. The sequential search requires no special organization. The weakness of this method is that it is slow. If we assume that the all locations in the list are equally likely to contain the target (if it is there), then the average number of comparisons needed to carry out a successful search of a list of n items is $(n + 1)/2$, which is $O(n)$. The worst case will occur if the target is at the very end of the list, so that the algorithm has to go over the entire list. This means examining every item, so the worst-case cost is n, which is also $O(n)$. If the target is not in the list, the search will have to go clear out to the end of the list to see this; hence the cost of an unsuccessful search will be n; this is also $O(n)$.

There is only one way to speed up such a search. If we find the item, we can move it up to the head of the list. If the list is an array, moving the item may entail very many shifts as we move things about in the array to make room for the new entry at a[1], but the speedup may be worth the cost. If the list is a linked list, we can move the selected item by a simple pointer manipulation. For example:

```
function SO_SEARCH(var start: nodeptr; target: keytype): nodeptr;
                          { Sequential search with self-  }
         var              {   organizing storage          }
            p, q: nodeptr;
            found: boolean;
         begin
         p := start;
         q := nil;
         done := false;
         while (p <> nil) and not found do    { Search loop  }
            if p^.key = target then           {   as before  }
               found := true
            else
               begin
               q := p;          { q lags p      }
               p := p^.next
               end;
         if found then                    { Found:                }
            if q <> nil then
               begin
               q^.next := p^.next;     { Patch around p^       }
               p^.next := start;       { Move p^ up            }
               start := p              {    to front           }
               end;
         search := p
         end;   { SO_Search}
```

If the target happens to be at the start of the list already, we do not need to shift it. But if the target is at the start of the list, q will still be nil; hence the if q <> nil tests for this condition and skips the relocation if it is unnecessary.

This is called *self-organizing storage*. Its advantage is this: In many applications, some data are accessed frequently and some are hardly ever accessed. This is true of accounts in a store or at a bank; some customers will do a lot of business with the organization while others will have occasion to do so only rarely. With self-organizing storage, the rarely accessed records will gradually drift out toward the end, while the frequently accessed ones will tend to cluster at the beginning of the list, where a sequential search will find them quickly. But if the most frequently accessed records can be found quickly, then the average search time will be less than $n/2$ if the search is successful. (The worst-case time will still be n, however, as will the time for an unsuccessful search.) Notice that we have already started thinking in terms of imposing an organization on the data.

2.2 BINARY SEARCH

If the data are contained in an array, and if the data items are sorted by the keys on which we are going to search, then we can do significantly better. If the target is there, it will obviously be either in the first half of the array or in the second half. If the array is sorted, we can find which half contains the target just by looking at the middle record (or the record nearest the middle). If the key we are looking for is less than the middle record's key, then the target will be in the first half, if it is there at all, and we can forget all about the second half.

But we can now search the first half in exactly the same way: If we look at *its* middle item, we can determine whether to look for the target in the first quarter or the second quarter. And we can apply the same technique to the indicated quarter, and then the eighth, and then the sixteenth.... When we get down to a single item, that will be the target if it is in the list at all.

This technique is called a *binary search*; we can outline the algorithm as follows:

1. Assume the array is dimensioned from 1 to n. Set *first* to 1 and *last* to n.

2. While *last* > *first*:

   a. Set *middle* to $\lfloor (first + last)/2 \rfloor$.

   b. Compare the target to the key of the element in position *middle*. (Call this the test element.)

   c. If the target is less than the test element's key, make *last* point to the test element. (This disposes of the upper half of the current subarray.)

   d. Otherwise, make *first* point to the element just past the test element. (This disposes of the lower half.)

3. If *last* points to a record whose key is equal to the target then the search is successful; otherwise the search fails.

The following code shows an implementation of this algorithm:

```
function BIN_SEARCH (a: searcharray; n: integer;
                key: keytype): integer;
    var                      { Binary search of sorted array }
       first, last,
       middle: integer;
    begin
    first := 1;
    last := n;
    while last > first do        { Invariant: desired    }
                                 {    item is in         }
```

```
                                         {   a[first]..a[last]    }
                                         {   or it is missing     }
         begin
         middle := (first + last) div 2;
         if key <= a[middle] then
             last := middle                { Throw away upper half }
         else
             first := middle + 1           { Throw away lower half }
         end;
     if a[last] = key then                 { Was it there?          }
         bin_search := last                {   --yes: return last  }
     else
         bin_search := 0                   {   --no: return 0       }
     end;  { Bin_Search }
```

The variables first and last bracket the range currently under consideration. At
the beginning, they are 1 and n, respectively, since initially we are considering the
entire array. The midpoint of this range is addressed by middle. The comparison
between key and a[middle] determines which half to discard. As the search continues, first and last gradually move in from the ends of the array and close in on
the target. Eventually they will meet, and at that point the while loop terminates.
If the target is in the list, then last will be pointing to it; otherwise last will point
to some number that is close to key. So the final test determines whether the limits
actually closed in on the target or on something nearby.

The execution time of this procedure is dominated by the while loop. Every
time we go around this loop, we decrease the range to be considered by half. Let
r_i be the length of the range on the ith pass through the loop; then we have

$$r_{i+1} = r_i/2. \tag{2.1}$$

(Actually, since r_i may be an odd number, we should say that $r_{i+1} = \lceil r_i/2 \rceil$, but
the math is simpler if we ignore this fine point.) The loop terminates when $r_i = 1$.
This gives us a recursion with the initial condition $r_0 = n$. It should not be difficult
to see that the solution to this recursion is

$$r_i = n/2^i, \tag{2.2}$$

and the number of passes through the loop, if it terminates when $r_i = 1$, must
be $\lceil \lg n \rceil$. There is one more comparison after the loop, so the total number of
comparisons is approximately $\lg n + 1$. Thus the cost of the binary search is $O(\lg n)$.
We will find that faster methods frequently reduce the cost of solving a problem in
the ratio of $\lg n : n$; as a rule of thumb, for the simple algorithms we are considering,
we can say that as soon as you discover this kind of speedup, you are at or near
the best you can do.

Is the binary search the best we can do? Yes, if we search by comparing keys.
Because every time we pass through the while loop we make a comparison. This
comparison can have only two outcomes: the target is or is not less than the middle

element. The algorithm now has two possible courses of action open to it, depending on the outcome. These two courses also involve choices, and each of *those* choices also has two possible outcomes.

We can diagram this situation with a tree, as shown in Fig. 2.1:

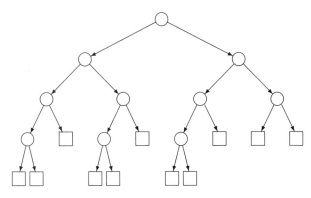

Figure 2.1

The interior vertices of this tree correspond to the comparisons. The edges from each interior vertex correspond to the outcomes. As the search proceeds, we work our way down the tree. The leaves of the tree correspond to the different possible locations of the target. If the list has a length of n, then there are n possible locations and so n leaves. This is a binary tree, and from the study of trees in discrete math we know that the height of a binary tree with n leaves is $\lceil \lg n \rceil$. But the height of this tree is the number of comparisons needed to find the target.

But this tree is completely general; it does not specify the structure of the algorithm. Hence this tree describes the best any algorithm can do. (An algorithm like the sequential search may do *worse* than this, but no algorithm based on key comparisons can do better.) We conclude that the best we can do, if we search by comparing keys, is $\lg n$.

> *Comment:* At first glance, there seems to be something missing in this argument. What if we make a couple of comparisons and find the target right away, without going all the way down to a leaf? It would appear that, in that case, we *could* do better than $\lg n$, at least sometimes. But consider that at each stage in the program we must then make *two* comparisons, not just one: one comparison to see whether we are now at the target and a second comparison to decide which way to go if we aren't. Furthermore, roughly half the vertices in the tree are leaves, and these tend to dominate the cost. So we are doubling the number of comparisons for a payoff that is significant only about half the time. The result comes out to be $O(\lg n)$ just the same, and furthermore there is a larger constant multiplier out in front, reflecting the fact that we made two comparisons most of the time. In fact, a binary search programmed this way takes roughly twice as long as the way we developed previously.

2.3 HASHING

There is a way to search without doing key comparisons, and in that case we can do better than $\lg n$. In this method, we let the key itself tell us where to store the record, and when we do a search later on, the key itself tells us where to look.

For a simple example, suppose we have only 100 records and suppose the keys are integers ranging from 0 to 99. Then we could use an array dimensioned [0..99] and place the record with key i in the element x[i]. Then when we search, we examine the key, see that it is some number i, and we know immediately that the target is in x[i]. It costs one array access to locate the record, so that in this case the cost of this method is $O(1)$.

The problem becomes more interesting when the keys aren't numbers. In many cases, they will be character strings, so that now we need some way of getting subscripts out of strings. We need a function h: {strings} → {legal subscripts}. For the time being, assume that we have such a function, and assume further that no two different strings will ever yield the same subscript. Then we could proceed as follows: Suppose the record we are dealing with is x. For storing the record in the first place, we would say

```
ix := h(x.key);
a[ix] := x;
```

and for retrieval later on we would say

```
ix := h(x.key);
x := a[ix];
```

It takes only one array access to find x; hence this method is still $O(1)$. If the function h is cheap to evaluate, then we have virtually instantaneous access to any record we want.

Hash Functions.   The key to this is the function h. We have to do something with the contents of the key to obtain a legal subscript. Historically, this method was developed for use with keys that were character strings, and we will focus on that case. The function h normally does some kind of simple arithmetic on the ASCII codes of the characters in the key. This operation chews up the key, of course; in fact, it makes *hash* of it. Because of this, the function has come to be called a *hash function* and this entire system of storage and retrieval is known as *hashing*.

We will consider two hash functions, both of which are widely used. In each case, we will assume that the array a has subscripts running from 0 instead of 1; that is, that we have declared

```
type
    hasharray = array [0..n] of {some record type or other};
var
    a: hasharray;
```

Then our first hash function takes this form:

```
function HASH (key: string; n: integer): integer;
   var                           { Modular hashing        }
      i, sum: integer;
   begin
   sum := 0;
   for i := 1 to length(key) do
      sum := sum + ord(key[i]); { Add ASCII codes        }
   hash := sum mod (n + 1)
   end;   { Hash }
```

Recall that the `mod` operation gives us the remainder when `sum` is divided by `n +`
1; this remainder will lie in the range $[0 \ldots n]$ and thus is guaranteed to be a legal
subscript. (This use of the `mod` operation is the reason for calling it modular hashing.) The beauty of this method, besides the fact that it executes very quickly, is
that the subscripts tend to end up distributed over the legal range in an apparently
random way, so that the records will be scattered more-or-less uniformly throughout the array instead of appearing in clusters. Whether they are *actually* randomly
distributed depends critically on n, however. Knuth [1973] shows that if $n + 1$, the
number of locations in the array, is a prime number, then the distribution of hash
values is most likely to be random. (Some people also shift the ith character $i - 1$
bits to the left, to make sure that a string like AB doesn't yield the same result as
BA.)

The second hash function is based on multiplication instead of division. Instead
of summing and using a `mod` operator (which is implemented by division), we multiply the sum by a positive real constant less than 1. We then multiply the fractional
part of this product by the table size and use the ceiling of the result as the hash
function:

```
function HASH (key: string; n: integer): integer;
   const                        { Multiplicative hashing}
      c = {some positive real number < 1};
   var
      i, sum: integer;
   begin
   sum := 0;
   for i := 1 to length(key) do
      sum := sum + ord(key[i]); { Add ASCII codes        }
   hash := trunc((n + 1)*frac(c*sum));
   end;   { Hash }
```

This method is particularly useful when implementing symbol tables in assem-
blers and compilers. The symbol table is a central repository of all information
about the programmer's identifiers (variable names, type names, procedure names,
and so on). Programmers frequently use identifiers like sum1, sum2, sum3, where the
names differ in only one character. The hash values for such identifiers will be close

together if we use the mod method, while the multiplicative method tends to scatter them more or less uniformly over the range of the subscripts. Figure 2.2 shows how a uniformly spaced sequence of keys is distributed over the range of subscripts when the constant $c = \phi = (\sqrt{5} - 1)/2 \approx 0.618034$, a popular value. Each of the thick horizontal lines represents an individual call to the multiplicative hash function, with the dot at the end indicating the value returned; the vertical lines along the bottom show how these values are distributed over the range of subscripts. You will notice that the distribution is approximately uniform; this explains the popularity of this constant, although ϕ is not unique in this respect.

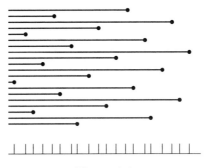

Figure 2.2

This method has the additional advantage that the table size can be any convenient number; it does not have to be prime, as it must be with modular hashing. There are other hash functions, but the two we have considered here are among the simplest and best.

2.3.1 Collisions

Here are some examples; we will use modular hashing and will take $n + 1$ to be 127. We need a source of words to use as examples; I will take the names of the books of the Bible. Suppose the key is Genesis. Then we have

G	71
e	101
n	110
e	101
s	115
i	105
s	115
	718

The numbers in the second column are the ASCII codes (in decimal) of the characters in the first column. Since 718 mod 127 = 83, the subscript for Genesis is 83 (we say that Genesis "hashes to 83"), and we would store the entry for Genesis in position 83 of the array. If the key is Exodus, we have

$$
\begin{array}{ll}
\text{E} & 69 \\
\text{x} & 120 \\
\text{o} & 111 \\
\text{d} & 100 \\
\text{u} & 117 \\
\text{s} & \underline{115} \\
& 632
\end{array}
$$

Since 632 mod 127 = 124, `Exodus` hashes to 124. Finally, suppose the key is `Isaiah`. This time we have

$$
\begin{array}{ll}
\text{I} & 73 \\
\text{s} & 115 \\
\text{a} & 97 \\
\text{i} & 105 \\
\text{a} & 97 \\
\text{h} & \underline{104} \\
& 591
\end{array}
$$

Since 591 mod 127 = 83, `Isaiah` hashes to 83. But that's the same subscript we had for `Genesis`!

When two keys hash to the same subscript, it is appropriately called a *collision*. I wish that I could now describe some ideal hash function that would never result in collisions. If there were such a function, how sweet life would be for programmers. But collisions are virtually inevitable, no matter what hashing function we use. A few collisions are avoidable; making `n + 1` a prime is one way of avoiding those. But our focus should be on what to do about collisions rather than how to avoid the inevitable.

(A situation occasionally arises where there are a definite number of keys, which are all known in advance. In this special case, we can sometimes custom-tailor a special hash function, which, for these keys only, will result in no collisions. This is known as *perfect hashing*. These applications are rare, however, and in the general case, we must consider how to cope with collisions.)

2.3.2 Collision Resolution

The ways of handling, or *resolving*, collisions fall into two broad categories: We can avoid the collision by finding an unoccupied slot in the hash table, or we can let the collision happen and deal with it more cleverly. Collision resolution that involves searching the array for a vacancy is known as *open addressing*; the alternative is called *chaining*. We will see that chaining is usually the method of choice, but open addressing is often used, and we will start with that.

Linear Probing. All these methods involve interrogating memory locations. Examining a memory location is known as *probing*. Our first alternative, *linear* probing, consists of going down the array, starting at the point at which the collision occurred, and looking for an unoccupied location. When we find one, that's where we put the item. It is called linear probing because we move through the array uniformly in our search for a vacant place.

This means that the array contents have to be marked somehow as empty before the process begins, so the program can recognize an empty slot when it sees one. The easiest way to do this is to set the **key** fields of all the table entries to the null string. If the array subscript runs off the end of the array in the process of probing, it must wrap around to the beginning again. We must also allow for the possibility that the table is already full and cannot accommodate another entry; we will use a Boolean parameter **full** to show this. Hence for insertion we have code like the following:

```
procedure HASHINSERT (var a: hasharray; data: datarec;
                          var dup, full: boolean);
     var                            { Insertion with linear probing }
        ix,                  { Array        }
        oldix: integer;    {    indices     }
     begin
     full := false;                 { Always the optimist   }
     dup := false;
     ix := hash(data.key, n);
     oldix := ix;                   { Note starting place   }
     repeat                         { Search for empty slot }
        if a[ix].key = data.key then
           dup := true
        else if a[ix] <> '' then
           ix := (ix + 1) mod n
     until dup or (a[ix].key = '') or (ix = oldix);
     if not dup then                { No duplicate:         }
        if a[ix].key = '' then
           a[ix] := data           {    Found slot          }
        else
           full := true            {    Didn't find slot    }
     end;  { HashInsert }
```

The bounds of a are 0 to n; hence the **mod (n + 1)** operation provides the wrap-around we require. If the table is full, the search for a vacancy will continue forever, if we don't provide some protection; that is the reason we saved the original hash value in **oldix** and bounced out of the loop when we met **oldix** again. If in the course of the search it encounters the key itself, then this is a duplicate entry, and **Insert** sets **dup** to TRUE and refuses to enter the record.

Notice that when we retrieve an item, we must examine the array location to which the key has hashed and verify that that is what is actually in the location. If it isn't, then we must do the same kind of linear probing until we find the matching entry. If we encounter an empty location along the way, that fact tells us that the data item we are after isn't in the list. Hence the code for retrieval is as follows:

```
function HASHSEARCH (var a: hasharray; k: str): integer;
                                { Search of hash table  }
   var                          {   with linear probing }
      ix,                  { Array          }
      oldix: integer;      {   indices      }
      found: boolean;
   begin
   ix := hash (k, n);
   oldix := ix;
   found := false;
   repeat               { Sequential probing     }
      if a[ix] = k then
         found := true
      else
         ix := (ix + 1) mod n;
   until found or (a[ix] = '') or (ix = oldix);
   if found then
      hashsearch := ix
   else
      hashsearch := -1
   end;   { HashSearch }
```

The result returned to the user is the subscript where the item was found or -1 if the item wasn't found.

This approach leads to two difficulties. The first is *clustering*. The array does not fill up uniformly; entries tend to bunch up. As long as the table is relatively empty, this is no great problem. But as the table fills up, the clusters begin to dominate the table and empty slots become scarce. But if a name hashes to a point within the cluster, the probing process must now search sequentially through the cluster until it finds a free location, or the desired record, and this adds to the storage and retrieval times.

It helps to look at an example. We will use an array with $n = 127$ locations, so our subscripts range from 0 to 126. We will use the modulo-n hashing function given above. For our data, we will take the names of the 80 books of the Bible—Old Testament, Apocrypha, and New Testament—and store them using this hashing scheme. When we have read in the Old Testament books (the first 39 names), the table looks like Fig. 2.3 (a):

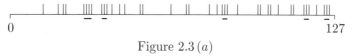

Figure 2.3 (a)

The hash-table addresses run from left to right in this figure, and each vertical line represents an occupied table location. You can see that clusters are already beginning to form; these are marked by lines drawn under the baseline. These clusters are small, so far; too small to give us any serious trouble. If a new name hashes to *any* place within one of these clusters, however, that cluster will grow.

When we have read in the entire list, the table looks like Fig. 2.3 (*b*):

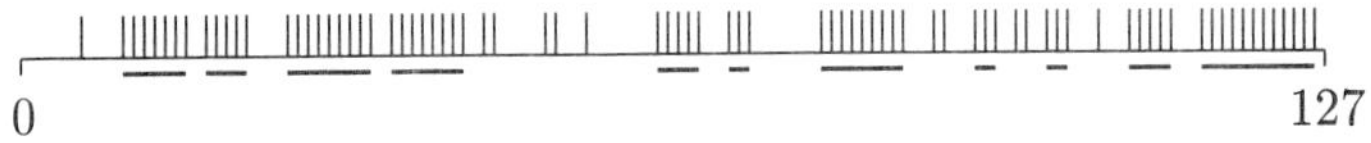

Figure 2.3 (*b*)

You can see that there are clumps of books interspersed with gaps in the array. The most significant cluster is that running from 115 to 126. We can see most clearly how clusters grow if we see how this one grew. Hosea went into location 115 initially; then Psalms hashed to 115 and was bumped to 116. Subsequently, Jonah hashed to 116 and was bumped to 117. So at this point we had a clump of three contiguous table entries resulting from two collisions; these are already visible in Fig. 2.3 (*a*). Later on, Romans occupied 118, Wisdom occupied 119, and Lamentations occupied 120. This cluster resulted from chance; but then when I Corinthians was entered, it hashed to 116; it was bumped successively to 117, 118, ... and did not find a vacancy until 121.

The experience with Jonah and I Corinthians shows an important point: When a collision lands in the middle of a cluster, it makes the cluster bigger. It is this phenomenon that makes clustering a problem. In fact, putting I Corinthians in location 121 plugged the only gap between 115–120 and another cluster at 122–126; these two clusters then became one big one. The presence of these large clusters means that there is an excessive time lost in storing and retrieving items. If there had been an 81st book, the probability that it would also land somewhere in that cluster stands at 0.15. The clusters marked in the figure comprise 69 entries, 54 percent of the table size, so there is a better than even chance that a new key will hash to a location inside a cluster, making the cluster bigger and making the item harder to retrieve.

The solution to this problem is to make the table size larger than the number of items you expect to store in it. Making the table two to three times as big is a good guess. This wastes space, to be sure; but we are trading wasted space for wasted time.

The second problem with linear probing is that of removing an entry. Suppose we saw fit to remove Psalms from the list. Psalms had ended up in location 116; when we remove it, we naturally mark a[116] empty. But what happens then if we look for I Corinthians? Its name hashes to 116. If 116 had still been occupied, linear probing would have led the program to 121 and it would have found it there. But now 116 is empty; the program will not look elsewhere; it will see the vacant entry and conclude that I Corinthians is missing from the list. One possible solution to ·this problem is to mark a deleted item with some special code so that it won't look empty and thus won't fool a subsequent search. Knuth [1973] describes another, more complicated way to work around this difficulty; it is addressed in a problem at the end of this chapter.

Quadratic Probing.   In that case, what are we to do? One possibility is to jump around a bit. We could take a step of 2 every time we found a vacancy. But it is better still to take a series of gradually increasing steps. We will hope that

as the jumps get bigger they will take us out of any nascent cluster. We can try
a[ix], a[ix + 1], a[ix + 4], a[ix + 9], a[ix + 16], ... Because these offsets
are perfect squares, we call this *quadratic probing*. Since consecutive squares are
separated by consecutive odd numbers, we can write

```
ix := hash(k, n);
step := 1;
inc := 3;    { Step-size increment  }
while a[ix] <> '' do                   { Search for vacancy    }
      begin
      ix := (ix + step) mod (n + 1); { Wrap around           }
      step := step + inc;
      inc := inc + 2                   { Bigger step next time }
      end;
a[ix] := data;
```

This method has its problems, too; sometimes the way in which ix jumps around
interacts with the size of the array in a manner that makes it miss certain array
entries altogether. With the [0..127] array we used in these examples, quadratic
probing reached the entries marked in Fig. 2.4:

0   127

Figure 2.4

There are 85 lines in this figure; there were 42 entries that were unreachable by
quadratic probing.

Chaining.   The best way to manage hashing is almost always to use a hash array
consisting of pointers to linked lists. Since we end up with chains of nodes dangling
from these entries, this method is called chaining. Insertion is just a mite more
troublesome, but chaining solves so many problems for us, and solves them so
neatly, that it is usually the method of choice.

We will declare linked-list nodes and the hash array as follows:

```
type
   chainptr = ^chainnode;
   chainnode = record
                  data: {some appropriate type};
                  next: chainptr;
               end;
   hasharray = array [0..n] of nodeptr;
var
   a: hasharray;
   p: chainptr;
```

At the beginning of the program, we set all entries in a to nil. Then for insertion,
we need do only the following:

```
read (inf, data);
ix := hash(data^.key, n);
new (p);
p^.data := data;
p^.next := a[ix];
a[ix] := p;
```

Every new node is added at the beginning of the chain. It doesn't matter where we enter it and adding it at the beginning requires no special cases: the code works whether there is already a chain there or not. If there is a collision, the new record is just added to the chain; since colliding records don't take up any extra address space, there is no problem with clustering. Of course, the collision will make the chain longer, but chains tend to be short in general, and it is quicker to search a short chain than a long cluster.

For retrieval, we do this:

```
ix := hash(key, n);
p := a[ix];
found := false;
while (p <> nil) and not found do
   if p^.data^.key = key then
      found := true
   else
      p := p^.next;
```

This is a simple sequential search of the chain; when the algorithm leaves the while loop, p will point to the desired item if it was there; otherwise p will be nil.

In addition, deletion from a chained table is easy. We find the table entry, run down the chain until we have found the key, and delete it in the usual way:

```
ix := hash(key, n);
p := a[ix];
q := nil;
found := false;
                              { Search for item            }
while (p <> nil) and not found do
   if p^.data^.key = key then
      found := true
   else
      begin
      q := p;                 { q lags p                   }
      p := p^.next
      end;
if found then
   begin
   if q = nil then
      a[ix] := p^.next    { Was first in list              }
```

```
else
    q^.next := p^.next; { Was later in list            }
dispose (p)
end;
```

This is a perfectly conventional deletion from a linked list, and there is no possibility of losing a wanted item as a result of deletion.

Chaining gives us an added bonus. Clearly, once the table is full, probing with open addressing will seek forever unless we put in some kind of test to make it stop when it has gone all around the array and ended up at the starting address. But with chaining, we can store *more data items than there are array addresses*. To see why this is possible, look at Fig. 2.5, in which I have stored 16 records using an array of only five entries:

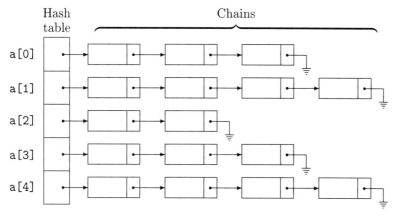

Figure 2.5

This is a pathological case, of course, intended only to prove a point, but the point is an important one: We do not have to worry about running out of array space.

The main drawback to chaining is the need for extra memory to hold the pointers. But you should bear in mind that linear probing also needs extra memory in order that the array will be big enough to avoid clustering. Moreover, if the chained records are large, the pointer cost is insignificant.

In all these cases, the number of probes depends on how full the table is. We can express this as the *load factor*,

$$\lambda = \frac{\text{Number of items stored}}{\text{Length of table}}. \tag{2.3}$$

Note that with chaining, λ can be greater than 1, as Fig. 2.5 shows.

For open addressing with linear probing, if we ignore clustering, it can be shown that the expected number of probes is

$$
\begin{aligned}
S(\lambda) &= \tfrac{1}{2}\left(1 + \frac{1}{1-\lambda}\right) &&\text{for successful search} \\
U(\lambda) &= \tfrac{1}{2}\left(1 + \frac{1}{(1-\lambda)^2}\right) &&\text{for unsuccessful search.}
\end{aligned}
\tag{2.4}
$$

Both of these approach infinity as $\lambda \to 1$, a fact that is consistent with our observation that you can search a full table for vacancies forever. Hence it is important to make the table big enough to guarantee that it will never fill up; indeed, to avoid excessive clustering, it is a good idea to make the table bigger by a factor of 2 or 3, as mentioned previously.

For chaining, the expected number of probes is dramatically smaller:

$$\begin{aligned} S(\lambda) &= 1 + \tfrac{1}{2}\lambda \quad \text{for successful search} \\ U(\lambda) &= \lambda \qquad\qquad \text{for unsuccessful search.} \end{aligned} \qquad (2.5)$$

Both these equations are a consequence of the fact that the average chain length is just λ. This is very fast retrieval: $O(\lambda)$, in fact. In almost all normal cases, λ will be less than 1. Even if the table is overloaded, λ is not likely to be any more than 2, so we will still get our result with an average of two probes.

Hashed storage is sometimes used to implement sets. Small sets are normally represented by bit vectors, but for large sets this is impractical. (We will discuss this at greater length in Chapter 6, Section 6.3.) But if we insert each element of the set in a hash array, then we can test for membership just by searching for the element. Other set operations like union, intersection, and complementation are more troublesome, however. In Chapter 7, we will also meet with a method that uses hashing very deftly to manage external storage.

2.4   SUMMARY

We have not seen the last of searching. We have seen an efficient method of searching in arrays, but none for linked lists, and nothing has been said about external searching. We will meet a linked data structure that is ideal for searching in Chapter 5 and will discuss external searching in Chapter 7.

The binary search is probably the most generally useful of all searching methods. Data are probably kept in sorted order more often than not, and in such cases, the binary search is the natural way to proceed. In Chapter 6, we will discover that the binary search can even indicate where a record would have been had it been present. On the other hand, if we are at liberty to store records where we wish with no need to keep them in sorted order, hashing, with its $O(\lambda)$ speed, is clearly the method of choice.

2.5   PROBLEMS

2.1. Verify that the sequential search correctly searches an empty list and a list with only one element.

2.2. It might appear that the use of the Boolean `found` in `Array_Search` is an unnecessary complication. We might be tempted to write simply

```
while (i <= n) and (x[i] <> target) do
   i := i + 1;
```

Why is this dangerous?

2.3. Trace the operation of the binary search when searching the array (2, 5, 7, 13, 18, 22, 25, 36, 39, 46, 59, 62, 77, 78, 94) for the keys 18 and 60.

2.4. (a) If the binary search is represented by a tree like that of Fig. 2.1, show that the leaves will all be on one level or on two adjacent levels. (b) Use this fact to show that the average cost of a binary search is $\lg n + 1$.

2.5. A successful sequential search costs $(n+1)/2$ comparisons on the average, while a binary search costs $\lg n + 1$ comparisons on the average. For very short lists, it should be clear that the sequential search is more economical, particularly because these estimates do not take into account the other operations inside the main loop of `Bin_Search`. But assuming that they can be taken at face value, find the first value of n for which the binary search is faster.

2.6. (a) If we are searching a linked list whose keys are in sorted order, why isn't it practical to use the binary search? (b) How can we speed the execution of an unsuccessful sequential search when traversing a list (linked or contiguous) whose keys are sorted? (c) What is the average cost of an unsuccessful search under these circumstances?

2.7. Verify that `Bin_Search` correctly searches a list with only one element. What difficulty will arise if the list is empty (*i.e.*, if `last = 0`)? Modify the procedure to avoid this problem.

2.8. The *interpolation search* is a variant of the binary search in which the next point to be examined is based on the *values* found at `first` and `last`. For example, if `key` turns out to be $3/4$ of the way between `a[first]` and `a[last]`, then we set `middle` to be $3/4$ of the way between `first` and `last`. Specifically, we write

```
middle := first + round((last - first - 1)
                *(x - a[first])/(a[last] - a[first]));
```

(This method assumes that the keys are distributed roughly uniformly and works best when they are.) Otherwise, the procedure is essentially the same as the binary search, except for some protections required to make sure the procedure terminates in all cases. Program an interpolation search.

2.9. For an illuminating example of the likelihood of collisions, consider a scheme where people are hashed by their birthdays. If nobody in a group of people has a birthday on February 29, how large must a group be for the odds to be even that two people in the group have the same birthday?

2.10. Double hashing is yet another way of combating clustering when using open addressing. Here we have two hash functions h_1 and h_2. The values from h_1 cover the range from 0 to n as usual (where n is the last subscript in hash table), but h_2 yields values from 1 to n that are relatively prime to $n+1$. (If $n+1$ is prime already, this will happen automatically.) We find an address with h_1 as usual, but if we must begin probing, we use h_2 to select a step size. (a) How does this avoid clustering? (b) Program this.

2.11. Knuth's method for deleting a record from hashed storage using open addressing and linear probing is to simulate the sequence of probes that would be made in the event of a collision. Search for the record in the usual way; when it is found, mark it as empty, note its location j, and continue probing until you find an empty location or a key whose hash address is before j. If you find such a key at location i, then copy the key to location j, mark location i as empty, update j to i, and continue searching; once you find an empty location, the algorithm terminates. The only tricky part of this procedure is accounting for wraparound when testing whether the hash address is less than j. Implement this deletion method.

2.12. Suppose we expect to store n entries in a hash table. Depending on the record size, it may take more storage to use chaining than to use open addressing with an oversized table. Assuming each record occupies b bytes, find the break-even point—that is, the value of b for which chaining begins to require less memory than open addressing. Assume that the hash table will be expanded to length $3n$ with open addressing, that it will be of length n with chaining, and that a pointer requires 4 bytes.

2.13. The code we showed for insertion into a hash table with chaining did not check for a duplicate key. Write a procedure `Insert` that does so, refuses to enter a duplicate, and returns a Boolean indicating whether a duplicate was found.

2.14. A *perfect* hash function is one that never results in any collisions. If we know the set of all possible keys in advance, we can frequently devise a perfect hash function. Given the keys

`Jan Feb Mar Apr May Jun Jul Aug Sep Oct Nov Dec,`

one obvious perfect hash function is `Jan` $\rightarrow 0$, `Feb` $\rightarrow 1$, and so on, which fits in an array `[0..11]`; but this means setting up a table of correspondences. Try to devise a perfect hash function based on the ASCII codes of the keys that fits in an array `[0..14]`. Better yet, try to write a program that will find the function for you.

CHAPTER 3

STRING SEARCHING

A special searching problem arises when we want to locate a particular sequence of characters in a file of ASCII text. This is known as *string searching* or *pattern matching*. Here a sequential search is inevitable, with an associated cost that we expect to be $O(n)$, and the trick is to make sure it isn't any worse than that. As usual, there are several methods for searching, and each has its advantages and drawbacks.

String searches are normally given the string to be searched and the string to be found as parameters. We will call the string we are seeking the *pattern* and the body of text we are examining the *text string*. We will assume that the text string is in memory. (When searching a file, we normally read the file, or a large chunk of it, into memory.) We will also assume that the length of the pattern is m characters and that of the text string n characters. When we need to distinguish between the pattern itself and an actual instance of the pattern in the text string, we will call the latter the *target*, and we will assume that the search function will return the location of the target, returning 0 if the target isn't found. If the pattern appears more than once in the text string, then the search normally returns the location of the first instance.

In describing and analyzing string searches, it is helpful to imagine the pattern placed over the portion of the text string with which it is to be compared:

Pattern: `problems`
Text string: `One of the commonest programming problems in text pro...`
          ⇑ $k = 0$ ⇑ target

where k is the number of characters from the start of the text string to the point over which we imagine the pattern being placed. Most searches proceed by sliding the pattern along the text string until a match is found. To program this, we use an offset into the text string. If this offset is in the variable k, if the length of the pattern is m, and if we temporarily ignore bounds checking, then we can test for a match by looping through the pattern and the string this way:

```
i := 1;
while (i <= m) and (pattern[i] = textstr[i + k]) do
```

```
i := i + 1;
```

It should be clear from this that to slide the pattern one character to the right we need only increment k. We will address the problem of bounds checking when we come to implement the various algorithms in code.

3.1   BRUTE-FORCE SEARCHING

The simplest way to search is to scan the text string and look for an instance of the first character of the pattern. If we find it, we see whether it is followed by the second character of the pattern. If it isn't, we go back to looking for another instance of the first character. If it is, we see whether the third character is there, and so on.

In terms of the sliding-pattern model, we can describe the brute-force method as follows:

1. Place the pattern at the start of the text string and see whether all the characters match.

2. If they do, the target is found. If not, then stop comparing after the first mismatch, shift the pattern one character to the right, and try again.

3. Keep trying until the search succeeds or the end of the pattern extends past the end of the text string.

Since we have tried all possible locations, we are guaranteed to find the target if it is there.

For example, if k is defined as above, then our search begins at $k = 0$. In the example given, there is a mismatch immediately: $p \neq 0$. So we try $k = 1$:

Pattern: `problems`
Text string: `One of the commonest programming problems in text pro...`
                    ⇑ $k = 1$ ⇑ target

If we continue this way, you will see that the pattern moves right along. In the absence of false alarms, we require only one comparison before we shift the string. When we find the target, it takes $m - 1$ additional comparisons to verify that we have indeed found it. In this example, we hit one false alarm. We have

Pattern: `problems`
Text string: `One of the commonest programming problems in text pro...`
                              ⇑ $k = 21$

Here the two p's match, as do the two r's and the two o's, but $b \neq g$ and we give up after two extra comparisons. We must advance the pattern one position, so that $k = 22$, and continue searching. When we finally succeed, we have this:

Pattern: `problems`
Text string: `One of the commonest programming problems in text pro...`
                                      ⇑ $k = 33$

We know we succeeded because all eight characters match. It cost us 33 shifts and 43 comparisons to locate the target.

We can now refine our algorithm as follows:

1. Let the pattern be P, with length m, and let the text string be T, with length n. Set $k = 0$; set $i = 1$;

2. While $i \leq m$ and $i + k \leq n$:

    a. If $P_i = T_{i+k}$ then increment i. Otherwise increment k and set i to 1.

3. If $i > m$, the search was successful and the target starts at position $k+1$; otherwise the search failed.

This leads directly to the following implementation; virtually the only change is the use of more expressive variable names than i, k, P, and T:

```
function BRUTE (var textstr: tstring; var pattern: pstring;
               n, m: integer): integer;
                                { Brute-force string searching  }
    var
        off,            { Offset (was i)              }
        pat: integer;   { Pattern subscript (was k) }
    begin
    pat := 1;
    off := 0;
    while (pat <= m) and (pat + off <= n) do
       if pattern[pat] = textstr[pat + off] then
          pat := pat + 1
       else
          begin
          off := off + 1;
          pat := 1
          end;
    if pat > m then
       brute := off + 1
    else
       brute := 0
    end;   { Brute }
```

How much time this search takes depends on the data. Since the pattern length is m and the length of the text string is n, the cost of a search (that is, the number of character comparisons required) is at best $O(n)$. This case arises if there are no false alarms. For example, suppose our pattern is **zz** and the text string is

```
This is a fairly long character string ending in zz.
```

There are no false alarms in this string and it takes n comparisons to locate the pattern. At worst, the cost will be $m(n+1-m)$, which we may take to be $O(mn)$ because typically $n \gg m$. For example, suppose the pattern is **aaaaaaab** and the text string is

```
aaaaaaaaaaaaaaaaaaaaaaaaaaaaaaaaaaaaaaaaaaaaaaaaaab
```

Here the search requires eight comparisons for every value of k as k runs from 1 to 50; the total is 400 comparisons. This case is not as pathological as it might appear; imagine that instead of a we had blanks. The blank is the most frequent character in text, and long strings of blanks are not uncommon.

3.2   THE KNUTH-MORRIS-PRATT ALGORITHM

D. E. Knuth [1977], together with J. H. Morris and V. R. Pratt, may have been the first investigators to realize that we are acquiring information as we do the character-by-character comparisons and that in simply shifting the pattern over by 1 after a false alarm we are throwing away that information. If we used that information intelligently, we might occasionally be able to shift the pattern by a longer distance and thus reduce the length of the search. In any case, we should never have to go back and reëxamine earlier characters in the text string, the way we did in the brute-force method, because we know what those characters are.

This not only speeds the process but solves another problem we hadn't addressed before: In searching very long text files, we may have to copy them piecemeal into a buffer area in memory, and if we need to back up past the beginning of the buffer, this can lead to awkward problems unless we use some sort of double-buffering scheme. For example, suppose the text string contains the sequence murmuring and we are searching for the pattern murder. It could just happen that murmuring runs off the end of the buffer:

```
adsworth Longfell    _ _ _    primeval the mur
```

When the algorithm reaches the word murmuring, it runs off the end of the buffer, too, and new text is read in from the file.

```
muring pines and    _ _ _    of exquisite musi
```

The brute-force algorithm sees the mismatch on that initial m. It must now back up to the second character of murmuring; but in doing this it runs off the beginning of the buffer. If it backs up in the file and replaces the old buffer contents, the algorithm can function, but only at the cost of a lot of disc accesses. A situation like this is admittedly unlikely, but it is not impossible, and when writing a utility, we have to assume that Murphy's Law will hold. With the KMP (Knuth-Morris-Pratt) algorithm, we never need to back up.

As an example of the KMP search, suppose we are searching for the substring problem in a string beginning, programming. When we make the comparisons, we have

Pattern: problem
Text string: programming
            ⇑ $k = 0$

When we hit the mismatch between b and g, we know immediately from the characters that have been matched so far and from the form of the pattern that 1 or 2 shifts will not work. But a shift of 3 might work, because that aligns the beginning of the pattern with the non-matching character in the text string:

Pattern: `problem`
Text string: `programming`
                 ⇑ $k = 3$

At this point, we can resume our scan of the pattern at position 4. The value of this shift depends only on the point in the pattern where the mismatch occurs. Before the search begins, therefore, the KMP algorithm constructs a table of optimum shifts. The actual search then makes use of this table.

In fact, all the high-speed string-searching algorithms we will consider use tables of this sort. This means that we must account for the cost of constructing the table in deciding whether the high-speed search is worth the trouble. For $n < 100$ and $m < 20$, it is probably better to save ourselves the trouble and use the brute-force algorithm unless we are searching a file and need to worry about the backup problem. In particular, functions like Turbo Pascal's `pos` are best implemented as brute-force searches, especially when the maximum permitted string length is 255 characters.

It is probably easiest to see how to program the KMP algorithm if we view it as a finite-state automaton (FSA) that runs over the text string, changing state as it goes. (FSA's are reviewed in Appendix C.) As is explained in the appendix, a FSA accepts a string if there is a path through its states whose edges spell out the string. Hence, as a point of departure, it should be a simple enough matter, given a pattern of length m, to create a FSA with $m + 1$ states with successive transitions depending on the successive characters in the pattern. For example, for the word `problem`, we would have a FSA like the one shown in Fig. 3.1.

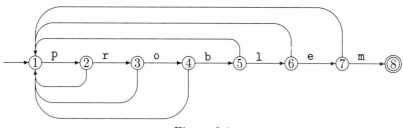

Figure 3.1

The starting state is state 1, marked by the arrow coming in out of the left; the accepting state (state 8) is identified by a double circle. The matching transitions are the ones from left to right, marked by the characters p, r, o, and so on, that enable each transition.

Normally such an automaton would have as its input alphabet all the characters that could conceivably appear in the file; but in fact for the purposes of the KMP algorithm, we can divide the inputs into two categories: matching characters and mismatches. If the automaton, in a particular state, expects to see some character

x that is a part of the pattern, then x is a match and any other character is a mismatch. In Fig. 3.1, the mismatching transitions are the unmarked arrows, taking the automaton back to an earlier (lower-numbered) state. The states play a dual rôle in this machine: They record how many consecutive matching characters have been encountered so far, but they also serve to index the pattern.

The KMP machine is not quite this simple. There is a special error state, and while the algorithm is looking for a match to the first character in the pattern, it alternates between this state and state 1. So the actual FSA for the word **problem** is as shown in Fig. 3.2.

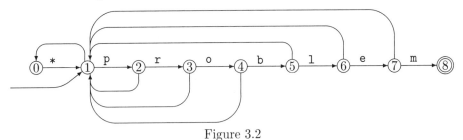

Figure 3.2

The starting state is still state 1; state 0 is the special error state. Normally, a FSA will advance to the next input character after every transition, but when we get to the implementation, you will see that on these mismatch transitions the machine does *not* advance to the next character. Otherwise, the logic of the transitions should be clear: If we get part of the way through what looks like the target, only to encounter a mismatch, then we must go clear back to the beginning again and start over; that's why the transitions on mismatches are to state 1. The * on the transition from state 0 to state 1 means that it always takes place; as it scans the text string looking for the beginning of the pattern, the automaton alternates between these two states until it finds a **p**.

The state table for this machine is as follows:

State	Match	Mismatch
1	2	0
2	3	1
3	4	1
4	5	1
5	6	1
6	7	1
7	8	1
8	–	–
0	1	1

(Since it is customary to put the starting state on the first line of a state table, I have moved state 0 down to the end. State 8 is underlined to mark it as the accepting state.) Because of the simple structure of this machine, the state numbers also correspond to the characters in the pattern; thus when the machine is in state 3 it is expecting to see **o**, the third character in the pattern.

We can implement this machine as follows. We do not need a full state table like the one shown above. We know that if a match is found for the jth pattern character, then the next state will be simply $j+1$, except at the end of the pattern. Therefore, we need only specify where to go in the event of a mismatch. (The next state in that case will not always be 1.) We will place the second column of the state table in an array next. Since the state transition for state 0 is always to state 1, we do not need an entry for next[0]. We take the length of the text string to be n and the length of the pattern to be m, as usual. Then the code will be

```
function KMP_SEARCH (var textstr: tstring; var pattern: pstring;
              n, m: integer): integer;
                          { Knuth-Morris-Pratt pattern matching   }
    var
        j,                    { Pattern subscript (& state)    }
        i: integer;           { Text string subscript          }
        next: array[1..maxpat] of integer;

    { ===>  Make_Table goes here  <=== }

    begin
    make_table;
    i := 1;
    j := 1;
                          { Main loop: on pattern and
    while (j <= m) and (i <= n) do
        begin
        if j = 0 then                              { O
            begin
            i := i + 1;            { Move forward in text string   }
            j := j + 1             {   & go to next state          }
            end
        else if textstr[i] = pattern[j] then      { Match:          }
            begin
            i := i + 1;            { Move forward in text string   }
            j := j + 1             {   & go to next state          }
            end
        else
            j := next[j];          { Mismatch: go to next state    }
        end;  { while }
    if j > m then                  { Out of loop: determine        }
        kmp_search := i - m        {   success                     }
    else
        kmp_search := 0            {   or failure                  }
    end;  { KMP_Search }
```

Add buffering.

(Maxpat is a constant specifying the longest allowable pattern.) Note that since j does double duty as the automaton state and the pattern subscript, the assignment `j := next[j]` has the effect of shifting the pattern the desired number of positions to the right. We may leave the `while` loop either because we found the pattern or because we ran off the end of the text string. The `if` following the loop determines what the reason was and announces success or failure accordingly.

There is some lost motion in this code, and the procedure can be tightened up to avoid this. The main loss of efficiency stems from the way the state switches between `j = 1` and `j = 0` while searching for the first matching character. Knuth *et al.* show a variant that deals with this and a couple of other inefficiencies, but it is spaghetti code and relies on sentinel characters at the ends of the pattern and the text string. The spaghetti code may not necessarily be bad, since high-speed searches are frequently implemented in assembly language, where `gotos` or their equivalent are common, but for some searches it may not be practical to use sentinels.

In illustrating the finite-state automaton, I chose a simple pattern. But if the pattern contains repeated substrings, we can take advantage of that fact. Suppose the pattern is `perpetrate`. This has a repeated `pe-`, and when a subpattern within the string matches a prefix of the pattern,[1] the rules change. If we find a mismatch to the first `t`, we are not going to want to go back to the start of the pattern. To see why that is, return to our shifting model of the algorithm and suppose that the text string is `perperpetrate` (presumably a typo). We are currently here:

$$\Downarrow \; j = 1$$

Pattern: `perpetrate`
Text string: `perperpetrate`

$$\Uparrow \; i = 1$$

If the automaton makes a transition to state 1, it will align the first character of the pattern with the non-matching text character. We will have this configuration—

$$\Downarrow \; j = 1$$

Pattern: `perpetrate`
Text string: `perperpetrate`

$$\Uparrow \; i = 6$$

—and we will miss the target. We must make a transition to state 3 instead; this will have the effect of lining the pattern up with the second `per-`:

$$\Downarrow \; j = 3$$

Pattern: `perpetrate`
Text string: `perperpetrate`

$$\Uparrow \; i = 6$$

Now the pattern is in the right position, and we can pick up where we left off in the text string and keep comparing. So in designing the FSA we must make sure that on such a mismatch the `next` table takes the machine back to the end of the prefix. The FSA for this pattern must therefore look as shown in Fig. 3.3.

---

[1] A *prefix* of a string is a substring that begins at the start of the string.

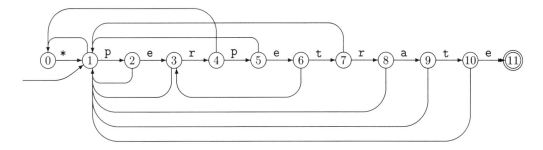

Figure 3.3

The main difference is the transition from state 6, which goes to state 3 instead of state 1. In state 6, the scanner has seen `perpe` followed by a mismatch, as in our previous example, and it returns to state 3 in case the second -pe- is the beginning of a target. Notice that if there are repeated substrings within the pattern that do not match a prefix of the pattern, they are ignored: the `next` array for the word `repetition` is just (0, 1, 1, 1, 1, 1, 1, 1, 1, 1).

The best way to recognize repeated subpatterns is to slide the pattern past itself, almost the way `KMP_Search` slides the pattern past the text string; in fact, `Make_Table` bears a close resemblance to the searching procedure:

```
procedure MAKE_TABLE;                { Builds state table }
   var                               {    for KMP search   }
      i,                   { Subscripts    }
      j: integer;          {  into pattern }
   begin
   i := 1;                 { Main pattern pointer      }
   j := 0;                 { Offset pattern pointer    }
   next[1] := 0;
   while i < m do
      if (j = 0) or (pattern[i] = pattern[j]) then
         begin
         inc (i);                 { Track matching }
         inc (j);                 {   characters   }
         if pattern[i] <> pattern[j] then
            next[i] := j
         else
            next[i] := next[j];
         end
      else
         j := next[j]
   end;   { Make_Table }
```

The sliding of the pattern is handled by the subscripts `i` and `j`. The initial values apply an initial one-character shift to the pattern. If $j = 0$, this starts the process moving through the pattern. If there are no matches, `j` alternates between 1 and 0 just as it does in `KMP_Search` when waiting for the first character of the pattern. On every alternation, next[i] is set to 1. When the beginning of a repetition is found, next[i] is set to 0; then the array is filled with 1's until the repetition ends. When that happens, j points just past the end of the prefix and i points just past the end of its repetition. Thus j contains exactly what next[i] should be. You can see this in Fig. 3.3: when i is 6, j is 3, and this is what produces the transition from state 6 to state 3.

Since KMP_Search examines every character in the text string until the pattern is found, its cost, measured by the number of comparisons made, cannot be less than $O(n)$. Since it must run through the entire pattern in the event of a match, the overall cost is at most $m + n$. Make_Table constructs the next table in essentially the same way that the search is carried out; therefore we conclude that its cost is $O(m)$. Since $m < n$, the entire search, including building the table, is $O(m + n)$.

3.3   THE BAEZA-YATES–GONNET (BYG) ALGORITHM

Another search algorithm, which runs 40 to 50 percent faster than KMP, was published in 1992 by R. Baeza-Yates and G. H. Gonnet. In this method, the table consists of an array of bit vectors, one for each character in the input alphabet, which act as *masks*. Each bit position in the vector corresponds to a character position in the pattern, and so the vectors must be as long as the pattern. These bit vectors are normally all 1's, but if the corresponding character appears in the kth position in the pattern, then the kth bit is a 0.

Bits are sometimes numbered from the left and sometimes from the right; some people start counting from 0 and others from 1. In this case, it is most convenient if we number the bits *from the right*, starting with 1. Then suppose the pattern for which we are searching is states. The table of bit vectors will then look like this:

```
      654321
a     111011
b     111111
c     111111
d     111111
e     101111
f     111111
...   ...
r     111111
s     011110
t     110101
u     111111
...   ...
```

For example, the letter a appears in the third position in the pattern states, so bit 3 is set to 0. The letter t appears in the second and fourth positions, so bits 2 and 4 are set to 0.

Now think of these bit vectors as masks, where the 0's are transparent and the 1's opaque, and imagine them lined up with the characters in the text string. Suppose the text string is `misstates`. Then if we line up the corresponding masks with each of these characters, we get a picture like Fig. 3.4 (*a*).

Masks

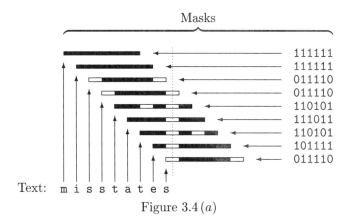

Text: m i s s t a t e s

Figure 3.4 (*a*)

Here the mask for `m` is lined up with the `m`, the mask for `i` with `i`, and so on. There is a match to the pattern in this string, and six of the transparent sections line up. If you could direct a beam of light at these bit patterns, as suggested by the dotted line, it would shine through the transparent parts; this is what tells us that we have found a match.

Contrast that with what happens if the text string contains the word `mistakes`, as in Fig. 3.4 (*b*). Now if you line up the masks the same way, the mask for `k` would block the light, indicating that there is no match. Notice that there is no explicit comparison against pattern characters in the BYG algorithm; the pattern is, in a sense, built into the masks.

Masks

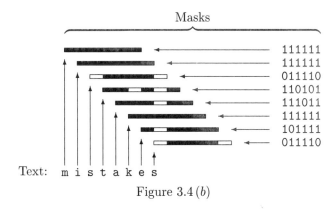

Text: m i s t a k e s

Figure 3.4 (*b*)

The BYG algorithm does digitally what we imagined being done with a beam of light. The masks are accumulated in a working variable `work`. The initial value of `work` is −1, which is all 1's in 2's-complement binary. As we look at each new text character, the contents of `work` are shifted one bit to the left (which corresponds to the offsets we saw in the masks in the figure) and the mask for the current character is ORed into work. The OR operations correspond to our attempt to shine a light through the masks; if all the characters match the pattern, one 0 will survive these shifts and ORs; if any of the characters doesn't match, that 0 will be wiped out by that character's mask. In each pass through the loop that implements all this, we test the relevant bit of the mask; if it is a 0, and if it appears in the right place, we have found the pattern.

We can write the code for the BYG search as follows:

```
function BYG_SEARCH (var textstr: tstring; var pattern: patstr;
              n, m: integer): integer;
                                  { Baeza-Yates-Gonnet pattern    }
                                  {    searching                  }
      const
         firstc = #0;        { First ASCII character }
         lastc = #255;       { Last ASCII character  }
      var
         table: array [firstc..lastc] of integer;
         i,
         test_bit,
         work: integer;      { Holds bit pattern      }
         cc: char;           { 1st char of pattern    }
         found: boolean;

      { ===>  Make_Table goes here   <=== }

      begin  { BYG_Search }
      make_table;             { Construct masks        }
      i := 1;
      found := false;
      cc := pattern[1];
      repeat
         while (i < n) and (textstr[i] <> cc) do
            i := i + 1;               { Look for start of pattern    }

                    { i now points to possible start of pattern    }
         work := -1;
         repeat
            work := work shl 1            { Shift-or operation    }
                    or table[textstr[i]];
            if work and test_bit = 0 then  { Test for match       }
               found := true
            else
               i := i + 1
         until (work = -1) or found;
      until found or (i >= n);
```

```
if found then
   byg_search := i + 1 - lgth
else
   byg_search := 0
end;   { BYG_Search }
```

This algorithm requires the ability to shift the contents of a variable one position to the left (which could be done as easily by addition, of course: `work := work + work`) and to do bitwise OR and AND operations. We have implemented these here using the extended ADT **integer** described in Section 1.3. The shift-OR loop is preceded by another loop that scans the incoming text string for a match to the first character of the pattern; only when that has been found does the procedure enter the shift-OR loop.

Suppose our pattern is `state` and our text string `misstates`, as before. The procedure scans down the text string until it sees the first `s`. At that point, it sets the working variable to -1; since this is a binary integer, that means `work` contains `1111111111111111`. In the loop, it shifts this one bit left and ORs it with the mask for `s`. When a binary integer is shifted left, the rightmost bit is set to a 0, and since the mask for `s` also has a 0 in its rightmost bit, `work` is now `1111111111111110`. It then advances to the next character, which is another `s`, and shifts and ORs again, with the same result as before.

To see what happens after that, it is best to use a table. The shifted value of `work` is in the first line, the mask is in the second line, and the result of the OR is in the third line. In the result, the position of the test bit is indicated by an underline.

Input	Bits	
	1111111111111110	Shift
s	1111111111011110	Mask
	11111111111<u>1</u>1110	Result
	1111111111111100	Shift
s	1111111111011110	Mask
	1111111111<u>1</u>1110	Result
	1111111111111100	Shift
t	1111111111110101	Mask
	1111111111<u>1</u>1101	Result
	1111111111101010	Shift
a	1111111111111011	Mask
	111111111<u>1</u>11011	Result
	1111111111110111	Shift
t	1111111111110101	Mask
	11111111111<u>0</u>0111	Result
	1111111111101111	Shift
e	1111111111101111	Mask
	1111111111<u>0</u>1111	Result

At this point, the test bit is a 0 and the pattern is recognized. This is the only 0 that survived that sequence of shifts and ORs.

It may also be useful to see what happens when the text string turns out not to contain the pattern. Suppose the text string is `mistakes`. Then after we arrive at the first `s` we have this:

Input	Bits	
	1111111111111100	Shift
s	1111111111011110	Mask
	1111111111111110	Result
	1111111111111100	Shift
t	1111111111110101	Mask
	1111111111111101	Result
	1111111111101010	Shift
a	1111111111111011	Mask
	1111111111111011	Result
	1111111111110111	Shift
k	1111111111111111	Mask
	1111111111111111	Result

At this point, `work` is -1 and the procedure leaves the `repeat` loop.

The code for forming the table of masks is as follows:

```
procedure MAKE_TABLE;              { Constructs masks       }
   var                             {    for BYG search      }
      i, j: integer;
      cc: char;
   begin
   for cc := firstc to lastc do { Default values           }
      table[cc] := -1;
   j := 1;
   for i := 1 to m do               { Punch holes           }
      begin                         {    in selected masks  }
      cc := pattern[i];
      table[cc] := table[cc] and not j;
      j := j + j;                   { Shift left            }
      end;
   test_bit := j div 2;             { Define test bit       }
   end;   { Make_Table }
```

The variable `j` is used to set selected bits in the masks to 0. It starts out as 1, and every time through the loop it is shifted one bit to the left by doubling it. We punch a hole in a mask by ANDing it with the bitwise complement of `j`. For example, if `j = 8`, then its binary value is 0000000000001000, its complement is 1111111111110111, and ANDing this with the mask puts a 0 in bit 4.

The cost of BYG is simply $O(n)$, in which n is the length of the text string. The constant multiplier is the cost of each pass through the shift-OR loop; this is only the shift, the OR and the test against `test_bit`. The space complexity can be considerable, however; if the input alphabet is Σ, then the storage required for the masks is clearly $m|\Sigma|$ bits.

The main drawback of BYG is that it requires the ability to do bitwise operations on integer variables. This is less crippling than it may seem; most high-speed pattern searches are implemented in assembly language in order to get a program that will run as fast as possible. A secondary drawback is the fact that the length of the masks limits the length of the pattern. Most computers provide 32-bit arithmetic, however, and many compilers support arrays of 32-bit integers, and few search patterns are longer than 32 characters.

These drawbacks are offset by the simplicity of the algorithm and also by its flexibility. For example, it is troublesome to write a search algorithm that is case-insensitive so that `The`, `THE`, and `tHe` will all be recognized as matching the pattern `the`. But all that is necessary in BYG is to make the masks for uppercase and lowercase letters match, and to provide a slight modification in the initial scanning loop. Indeed, Baeza-Yates and Gonnet show versions of the algorithm that can search for patterns made up of families of characters and that can recognize patterns containing errors.

3.4   QUICKSEARCH

While Knuth and his colleagues were writing the paper describing the KMP search, two other investigators, R. S. Boyer and J. S. Moore [1977], found a faster method. They obtain their speedup by working backward from the end of the pattern to the beginning. Their approach requires *two* tables, one of which is fairly complicated to construct, but their algorithm is less than $O(n)$ because we can frequently shift the pattern by its own length after a mismatch, and the back-to-front comparison means that we frequently skip portions of the text string. Hence this method has the potential of being almost $O(n/m)$. On the other hand, you will recall that moving backward poses problems when we are searching a text file buffered in memory.

KMP, BYG, and Boyer-Moore are all outperformed by an even faster search by D. M. Sunday [1990], called Quicksearch. It is not only faster than either of these, it is also simpler. (This is a rarity in computer science; so often faster algorithms are more complicated. It is noteworthy that both Sunday and BYG are not only faster but simpler than their predecessors.) As with the Boyer-Moore search, we can skip over characters in the text string, and the skip is frequently $m + 1$ characters. This means that the average cost of a Quicksearch is less than $O(n)$ and can approach $O[n/(m+1)]$. It thus completely eclipses the algorithms we have seen so far, except for very short patterns where division by $m+1$ has little effect. Furthermore, unlike the brute-force and Boyer-Moore methods, Quicksearch never moves backward in the text string.

The KMP and BYG searches remain useful in those applications where you must look at every character in the string exactly once. For example, suppose a program using a pattern-matching algorithm must identify the line number in which the target was found. Presumably, every time the search encounters a new-line indicator, it can increment a line counter. But if the searching algorithm regularly skips over characters in the text string, it may miss a new-line indicator and get the line count wrong. (Guess how I found this out.) For another example, character strings in C have their length indicated by a delimiter marking the end of the string. With Quicksearch (and with the Boyer-Moore algorithm), we must scan the string first to find its length, because the search itself may skip past the end-of-string marker and go on forever. If we are going to scan the string, we may as well do it in the course of a BYG search. But whenever it is safe to skip over characters during the search, it makes sense to do so and Quicksearch is the best choice.

Sunday's rule is simplicity itself: We do the character-by-character comparisons, as in the brute-force search, until we hit a mismatch. But at that point we look at the text character *just beyond the end of the pattern*. (I will call this the *test character*.) If the test character doesn't appear in the pattern, then no shift that puts any of the pattern over that character will work; hence we can shift the entire pattern *past* the test character. This is a shift by $m + 1$ characters, clearly much better than what we had in the brute-force method and better than the Boyer-Moore search. In this case, we also skip everything in the text string up to the new position of the pattern.

If the test character does appear in the pattern, then we shift the pattern by the smallest distance that will match the test character. This distance will normally be more than one character; it could put us right on the target, but if it doesn't, we know we will never overshoot the target and normally it will cost only one comparison before we shift again.

Returning to our original example, suppose we have

Pattern: `problems`
Text string: `One of the commonest programming problems in text pro...`
⇑ $k = 0$

The test character is the `h` in `the`. This does not appear in the pattern, so we shift the pattern by its own length plus 1 (*i.e.*, 9 characters); this puts it past the `h`:

Pattern: `problems`
Text string: `One of the commonest programming problems in text pro...`
⇑ $k = 9$

This time the test character is `e`, which occurs in the pattern. We now shift the pattern so those two `e`s line up. How big should this shift be? It must be one more than the distance from that `e` to the end of the pattern. The pattern is 8 characters long, and `e` is the sixth character. So we shift it by $8 - 6 + 1 = 3$ characters:

Pattern: `problems`
Text string: `One of the commonest programming problems in text pro...`
⇑ $k = 12$

Again we find a mismatch ($p \neq o$); this time the test character is a blank, which isn't in the pattern; and again we shift it by a full 9 characters:

Pattern: problems
Text string: One of the commonest programming problems in text pro...
⇑ $k = 21$

Here, as in the brute-force case, it takes three tests to find the mismatch. When we do, the test character (i) isn't in the pattern, hence it takes us another 9 characters down:

Pattern: problems
Text string: One of the commonest programming problems in text pro...
⇑ $k = 30$

Now we are approaching our target. The next test character is e again, so again we shift the pattern by $8 - 6 + 1 = 3$ characters:

Pattern: problems
Text string: One of the commonest programming problems in text pro...
⇑ $k = 33$

...and we have found our target. Finding it required five shifts and 15 comparisons. Quicksearch can be coded as follows:

```
function QUICKSEARCH (var textstr: tstring; var pattern: patstr;
              n, m: integer): integer;
                          { D. M. Sunday's string-          }
                          {   searching algorithm.          }
      const
         firstc = #0;        { First ASCII character }
         lastc = #255;       { Last ASCII character  }
      var
         shifts: array [firstc..lastc] of byte;
         off,                { Offset                    }
         lgth1,              { This is m + 1             }
         pat: integer;       { Pattern subscript         }

      procedure MAKE_TABLE;          { Construct shift table          }
         var
            i: integer;
            c: char;
         begin
         for c := firstc to lastc do       { Default = m + 1        }
            shifts[c] := lgth1;
         for i := 1 to lgth do
            begin
            c := pattern[i];
            shifts[c] := lgth1 - i;        {   else m - i + 1       }
            end;
         end; { Make_Table }
```

```
begin   { QuickSearch }
lgth1 := m + 1;
make_table;
pat := 1;
off := 0;
while (pat <= m) and (pat + off <= n) do
   begin
   if pattern[pat] = textstr[pat + off] then
      pat := pat + 1
   else
      begin
      off := off + shifts[textstr[off + lgth1]];
      pat := 1;
      end
   end;
if pat > m then
   quicksearch := off + 1
else
   quicksearch := 0
end;   { QuickSearch }
```

Notice that the code is nearly identical to that of **Brute**, except for looking up the shift value in the table.

The shift table is the array **shifts**. It is indexed by characters in order to avoid having to do a lot of bothersome **ord(c)** operations. The construction of this table simply embodies what we have already said about shifting. If the test character does not appear in the pattern, the default shift is the $m + 1$; this is what the first loop in **Make_Table** does. For characters that do appear in the pattern, we want the shift to be $m + 1$ minus the position of the character in the pattern. The second loop in **Make_Table** takes care of this.

In the best case, we will detect a mismatch on the very first character examined and the shift will always be $m + 1$ characters. Hence Quicksearch has the potential to be $O(n/(m + 1))$. A complete analysis of this algorithm is not yet available; Sunday conjectures that it is at worst $O(n)$. Experimental results on about 200,000 characters of text show (a) that the performance is better for longer patterns than for shorter ones and (b) that for the most common pattern lengths (six to eight characters), Quicksearch tests roughly $1/6$ of the characters in the text string.

My own experiments suggest that for these pattern lengths the average shift is just about the same as the length of the pattern and there are an average of 1.1 comparisons per shift. This suggests that the cost of a successful search is thus roughly $1.1/m$ times the distance from the start of the text string to the point where the target is found; for an unsuccessful search it must be roughly $1.1n/m$. These estimates are of necessity approximate, since the cost depends so much on the nature of the pattern. If the pattern is made up of infrequently appearing characters, the likelihood of a match against the test character is small, and the likelihood of a *mis*match between the first pattern character and the corresponding text character is high. This means that most of the shifts will be by $m+1$ characters and that there will be typically one comparison per shift. Thus a search for *cqjzx* will go faster than a search for *etaoi*, which is made up of the five most common letters in English text. (Searching for those two strings in a draft of this chapter gave the following results: Finding *cqjzx* took 2,720 comparisons, 20% below the predicted value of 3,323; finding *etaoi* took 3,338 comparisons against a predicted value of 3,332.)

Two further speedups are possible. First, the Boyer-Moore rule may occasionally indicate that the pattern can be shifted farther down the string than the distance given by the table `shifts`. Hence Sunday also considers computing the shift twice, once from the `shifts` table and once using the Boyer-Moore rule. In this case, we look up both shifts and choose the larger one. Sunday provides an implementation of this approach, which he calls the *maximal shift* algorithm.

Second, we have consistently done the character-by-character comparison from left to right. There is no need to do it this way, however. We could speed up the search further by a strategy that avoids false alarms. (In this connection, note that the `aaaaaaab` pattern we considered before is not handled much more intelligently by the Sunday search than by the brute-force method.) If we could predict which character is most likely to result in a mismatch, we could examine that one first. One possibility is to avoid repeated letters like `a` in this example and try the `b` first. Another method, preferable in practical cases, is to try infrequently occurring letters like `q`, `j`, `z` first and common letters like `e`, `t`, `a` last. Sunday calls this the *optimal shift* algorithm; in the experimental results included in his paper, this method showed the best performance. In view of our consideration of *cqjzx* and *etaoi*, this should come as no surprise.

Sunday found that the optimal shift algorithm averaged only about 5 percent better than the basic Quicksearch, however. Both of these speedups require extra preparation before the actual search begins, and this extra preparation increases the overhead of the algorithm. Hence they can probably be dispensed with unless you are searching text strings that are hundreds of thousands of characters long.

3.5   CASE

String searches may be case-sensitive or case-insensitive. If the search is case-insensitive, then lowercase letters are equivalent to uppercase letters. For example, a case-insensitive search will consider `The`, `the`, and `THE` to be all the same word. This can occasionally be an important feature to have. We observed that BYG can be made case-insensitive relatively easily; but case-insensitive searches are clumsy to implement in the other algorithms, because all alphabetics must be converted to a common case before comparing them.

In the ASCII code, uppercase alphabetics are assigned bit patterns from 41_{16} to $5A_{16}$ and lowercase alphabetics range from 61_{16} to $7A_{16}$. It would seem then that all one would have to do to convert to a common case is to add 20_{16} to the ASCII codes. Unfortunately, it isn't that simple, because this plays havoc with some of the nonalphabetics. For example, the character `[` ($5B_{16}$) is converted to `{` ($7B_{16}$).

Hence we must do something like

```
if (cc >= 'A') and (cc <= 'Z') then
    cc := chr(ord(cc) + $20);
```

where the dollar sign indicates that the following constant is in hex.

3.6 SUMMARY

There are many reasons to do pattern searching in character strings. Any search or search-and-replace operation in a text editor or word processor needs to do this. Certain utilities, like Norton's TextSearch, will search a file for all instances of a specified string.

For short string searches, the brute-force method is best, since the cost of constructing a table may outweigh the saving of a more powerful algorithm.

We can divide the fast searching algorithms into two categories: those that look at every character of the text string and thost that skip over characters. If it is important to count things like end-of-line markers, KMP or BYG is clearly indicated. In all cases where you are searching a very long string and you can safely skip over characters, Quicksearch is the method of choice.

3.7 PROBLEMS

3.1. If the text string is `One of the commonest programming problems in text processing is...`, how many shifts and comparisons are necessary to find the substring `process` by the brute-force method?

3.2. If the pattern appears more than once in the text string, the KMP algorithm always returns the location of the first instance. Modify the procedure so that each new call will find another instance if there is one. (*Hint:* you will need to make the location of the most recently found instance a parameter.)

3.3. In the KMP algorithm, state 0 seems superfluous, since there is always a transition to state 1. Experiment with changing all 0's in the **next** array and explain what happens.

3.4. Compute the KMP **next** array for the string `stepsister`.

3.5. Assuming a character set consisting of only the lowercase letters, construct a BYG mask table for the pattern `positive` and trace the operation of searching the text, `postpositive`.

3.6. Modify `BYG_Search` and its table-building procedure to do case-insensitive searches.

3.7. Modify `BYG_Search` so that it can search either forward or backward from the current position in the file. Notice that the test bit for a backward search will always be 1.

3.8. Modify `BYG_Search` so that each new call will find another instance of the pattern, if there is one. Test it with the text string `murmurmuring` and the pattern `murmur` and make sure it finds both <u>murmur</u>muring and mur<u>murmur</u>ing.

3.9. If the text string is the one given in Problem 3.1, how many shifts and comparisons are necessary to find the substring `process` by Sunday's method?

3.10. In shifting the pattern in Quicksearch, repeated letters in the pattern must be handled so that the *last* occurrence of a repeated letter is the one lined up with the test character. Show why the second loop in `Make_Table` takes care of this automatically.

3.11. Modify Quicksearch so that each new call will find another instance of the pattern if there is one.

3.12. Write a Quicksearch function that will find the *last* instance of a pattern by searching backwards through the text string.

3.13. Suggest a way in which Quicksearch could be applied to strings terminated with a null character without the risk of skipping over the null.

3.14. If very many searches are to be made in the same file, we might consider providing an array giving the location of every new-line indicator in the file. Then we could use Sunday's search and determine the line number by a binary search of the new-line table. Discuss the advantages and disadvantages of this method.

3.15. Sunday's optimal shift algorithm can be implemented by means of a permutation array that sets the order in which the pattern characters are matched against the text string. Write a procedure that takes the pattern and a table of letter frequencies as parameters and returns the permutation array. Modify Quicksearch to use this permutation array.

3.16. Sunday's optimal-shift idea can be applied to a brute-force search as well. Modify `Brute` to incorporate this feature.

CHAPTER 4

SORTING

The term *sorting* means rearranging the elements of a set of data objects into ascending or descending order, as, for example, we might alphabetize a list of words or names. Sorting may well be the most frequent task in general computer applications; it seems we are always arranging words or numbers this way, either to facilitate other operations, like the binary search, or to make the output easier to read. The sorting algorithms we examine here will without exception sort the data into ascending order, but it is a trivial task to modify any of them to sort into descending order.

Like searching, sorting can be either internal or external. In an internal sort, all the data to be sorted are in computer memory; in an external sort, they are on some mass storage device like a disc or, occasionally, a magnetic tape. External sorting is a big topic in itself, and we will defer treatment of external sorting to Chapter 8.

Usually we need to sort *records*; these records normally contain many fields— for example, if we are sorting a bibliography, the records will contain author, title, date, publication, publisher; or if it is an address book, then a record will contain name, address, phone number. We can sort on only one field at a time; we call the field on which we sort the *key*, as we did when searching.

A sort is *stable* if any two records with identical keys are left in the same order after sorting. This may or may not be important. Sometimes we want to sort a list by two categories. For example, suppose we want a list of books that is alphabetical by author and alphabetical by title within author. If we are using a stable sort, we can sort by title first and then by author afterward, and we will get the desired result. If we try this with an unstable sort, the entries under a particular author may be all jumbled up.

There is no "best" method to sort. Most of the simplest methods are good for small amounts of data but are prohibitively slow for large amounts; some of the faster methods are great for large amounts of data but involve so much overhead that they're wasteful for small amounts of data. One of the particularly fast sorts is better adapted to arrays than to linked lists, and so on.

If we rank the sorts we will consider by speed, we get this table:

$O(n^2)$:   selection sort, insertion sort, Quicksort
$O(n^{1.25})$:   Shell sort
$O(n \lg n)$:   Mergesort
$O(n)$:   bucket sort

In each case, n is the number of data items (records) that must be sorted. Quicksort is normally considered an $O(n \lg n)$ algorithm, but that is the average cost; the table above gives worst-case costs. (We will verify these table entries as we consider these different methods.) You must not be misled by this table, however: the faster sorting algorithms also tend to be more complicated. The overhead arising from these complications means that they really come into their own only when sorting large amounts of data. As a rule of thumb, it is probably best to use the simplest sorting method that can handle your data in a reasonable time. Computers are *fast*.

A word about the "bubble sort": this is also $O(n^2)$, but as $O(n^2)$ sorts go, it is by far the slowest. A lot of books describe this sort, but there's no reason to; selection and insertion sorts are both faster and easier to program; the only thing to be said for the bubble sort is that it has a cute name. To be useful, an algorithm needs more than just a cute name.

The things we sort will be arrays or linked lists. We will assume that the elements are records, each record containing a key, and that the sort is to permute the elements so their keys are in ascending order.

4.1 SELECTION SORT

The basic idea of the selection sort is this: find the greatest item in the array. Remove it and place it at the end of the sorted table. Then find the greatest remaining item; since the greatest is gone, that will be the second greatest. Remove that and place it in the second-last position in the sorted table. Continue this way until the unsorted table is empty and the sorted table is full.

Now, if we have n items to sort, sitting in an array of length n, then after we have sorted k of those items, we have $n - k$ left in the unsorted table and k in the sorted table. That adds up to n. So we should be able to do the whole process in place, using a single array instead of two arrays and moving the items into place by swapping. (Such a sort is called an *in-place* sort; the sorting algorithms we consider in this chapter are all in-place sorts.) In that case, after we've sorted k of the items, our array will look like Fig. 4.1.

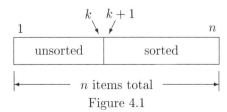

Figure 4.1

Note that because of our policy of selecting the largest unsorted key, the keys in the sorted part will all be greater than or equal to the keys in the unsorted part.

We can thus base the selection sort on a find-and-swap routine as follows:

1. Set i to n.

2. While $i > 1$:

  a. Find the record in the range from 1 to i with the greatest key.

  b. Exchange that record with the one in position i.

  c. Decrement i.

We stop when $i = 1$ because at that point there is only one element left. Since this record has a key no greater than all the keys previously considered, it is already in place.

At the start, the entire array is unsorted. Find-and-swap locates the greatest element in the array and swaps it with a[n]:

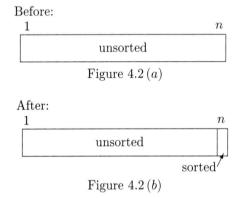

Figure 4.2 (*a*)

Figure 4.2 (*b*)

The next time around, it finds the greatest key between a[1] and a[n - 1] and swaps that into location a[n - 1]. As the main loop continues, the sorted part grows and the unsorted part shrinks.

We will declare our array as follows:

```
type
   keytype = integer;    { or whatever }
   datarec = record
                key: keytype;
                { other fields as needed }
             end;
   xarray = array [1..n] of datarec;
```

Then we can implement the algorithm this way:

```
procedure SELECT (var a: xarray; n: integer);
   var                              { Selection sort       }
      i, j,            { Array         }
```

```
    jmax: integer;    {    subscripts  }
begin
for i := n downto 2 do
            { Invariant: (a) a[i + 1] through a[n]  }
            {   are sorted; (b) these elements      }
            {   are all greater than than or equal  }
            {   to a[1] through a[i].                }
    begin
    jmax := 1;
    for j := 2 to i do          { Find greatest key     }
        if a[j].key > a[jmax].key then
            jmax := j;
    swap (a[i], a[jmax]);
    end;
end;  { Select}
```

I have added a shortcut here. We have to give `jmax` an initial value, and it is simplest to make it the start of the unsorted list: `jmax := 1`. But in that case we don't need to compare `a[jmax]` with itself. Hence the inner loop starts with 2 instead of 1.

The procedure for swapping is simple enough; it could have been embedded in `Select`, in fact, except that the sorting logic is clearer if the swap is kept separate.

```
procedure SWAP (var a, b: datarec);
    var
        temp: datarec;
    begin
    temp := a;
    a := b;
    b := temp
    end;  { Swap }
```

The implementation described here is for arrays, but we can do selection sorting with linked lists as well. In that case it is easier to select the smallest key and insert the sorted records at the head of the list; this implementation is left as an exercise.

How long does the selection sort take? We can count two things in sorting: the number of comparisons we must make, and the number of data items we must move. The inner loop makes $i-1$ comparisons every time; the outer loop goes from 2 to n. So the total number of comparisons is

$$
\begin{aligned}
C &= \sum_{i=2}^{n}(i-1) \\
&= \sum_{i=1}^{n-1} i \\
&= n(n-1)/2.
\end{aligned}
\tag{4.1}
$$

On each pass through the outer loop, we do one swap, so there are $n - 1$ swaps altogether. If you look at the code for swapping, you see that each swap requires 3 movements of data items. Therefore, the total number of data movements is

$$M = 3(n - 1). \tag{4.2}$$

So we have the result:

$$\begin{aligned} C &\quad \text{is} \quad O(n^2) \\ M &\quad \text{is} \quad O(n). \end{aligned} \tag{4.3}$$

4.2   INSERTION SORT

Insertion sort is another $O(n^2)$ sort. Here we again have an array that is partly sorted and partly unsorted:

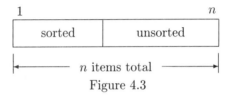

Figure 4.3

This time we pick an unsorted item and *insert* it in the proper place in the sorted part. The algorithm thus takes this form:

While there are unsorted records in the list:

- a. Select an unsorted record. (For simplicity, we normally select the *first* unsorted record.)
- b. Find j in the sorted part such that the jth key is greater than or equal to the unsorted record's key.
- c. Insert the unsorted record just before record j.

The insertion can be done in two ways, depending on the data structure being used to represent the list. Insertion in a linked list is somewhat easier, but the array case is probably the more common, and we will consider that case first.

4.2.1   Insertion Sort with Arrays

If we are going to insert the new item in the sorted part, we will have to shift the other sorted items over to make room for it. The rightmost shifted item will collide with first element in the unsorted part. The easiest way to handle that problem is to copy that first unsorted item into some temporary variable, so that when the shift overwrites the original, we haven't lost it.

First, how do we find a home for the new item? We will simply go through the sorted part until we find two items a[j - 1] and a[j] such that a[j - 1].key < temp.key and a[j].key ≥ temp.key. Then we can place temp in between these.

Second, how do we shift? We must shift everything to the right by one position. To do this without losing any data, we must start at the right end and work backward.

Now, if we must search the sorted part and shift the sorted part, it makes sense to do both simultaneously. So in the implementation we will have a search-and-shift loop that looks like this:

```
temp := a[i];
j := i;
found := false;
while (j > 1) and not found do  { Search and shift      }
    if a[j - 1].key <= temp.key then
        found := true
    else
        begin
        a[j] := a[j - 1];
        j := j - 1;
        end;
```

This loop will terminate when we've found those two items that bracket `temp.key`. At that point, everything from `a[j]` on has been shifted and we can just drop `temp` into `a[j]`:

```
a[j] := temp;
```

As far as we have gone, our overall procedure looks like this:

```
procedure ISORT (var A: xarray; n: integer);
    var                             { Insertion sort for arrays    }
        i, j: integer;
        temp: datarec;
    begin
    for i := 2 to n do              { Invariant: items 1 through    }
                                    {   i are in sorted order.      }
        if a[i].key < a[i - 1].key then
            begin                   { If invariant violated,        }
            { search-and-shift }    {   fix it.                     }
            a[j] := temp;
            end;
    end;  { Isort }
```

The loop on `i` begins with `i := 2` because an array containing one item is already sorted and thus satisfies the loop invariant. Notice the `if` inside that `for` loop: If it should happen that `a[i]` is already greater than or equal to `a[i - 1]`, then it is already in its proper position and we can skip the entire body of the outer loop in that case. Filling in the search-and-shift code we have this:

```
procedure ISORT (var A: xarray; n: integer);
    var                            { Insertion sort for arrays      }
        i, j: integer;
        temp: datarec;
        found: boolean;
    begin
    for i := 2 to n do             { Invariant: items 1 through     }
                                   {   i are in sorted order.       }
        if a[i].key < a[i - 1].key then
            begin                  { If invariant violated,         }
            temp := a[i];          {   fix it.                      }
            j := i;
            found := false;
            while (j > 1)          { Search and shift        }
                    and not found do
                if a[j - 1].key <= temp.key then
                    found := true
                else
                    begin
                    a[j] := a[j - 1];
                    j := j - 1;
                    end;
            a[j] := temp;          { Put a[i] in new home  }
            end;
    end;  { Isort }
```

4.2.2 Insertion Sort with Linked Lists

When we implement the insertion sort for a linked list, we do not have the problem of moving things around to make room for the new item, because by suitable pointer manipulations we can insert anything anywhere. We also do not need to search backwards to find a home for the new item; in fact, we *can't* search backwards unless the list is doubly linked. So the whole operation proceeds in a much more straightforward way.

We will assume that we have the following declarations in the main program:

```
type
    keytype = integer;
    nodeptr = ^node;
    node = record
                key: keytype;
                { other fields as needed }
                next: nodeptr
           end;
```

Where i marked the beginning of the unsorted part in the array version, we will use a pointer last to point to the *end* of the sorted part here. Where we used temp to hold the first unsorted element before, we will now use temp to *point* to the first unsorted element. Since we are going to do insertion by pointer manipulation, this makes more sense.

We search for the proper place to insert temp^ with a pair of pointers p and q. We will advance these pointers until the keys they point to bracket temp's key; then we will insert temp^ in between them.

```
procedure ILISTSORT (var list: nodeptr);
                         { Insertion sort for linked lists      }
   var
      last,      { Last sorted node       }
      temp,      { Node to be inserted    }
      p, q: nodeptr;
   begin
   last := list;         { Single node is already sorted }
   if last <> nil then   { Don't sort an empty list       }
      while last^.next <> nil do
                         { Invariant: everything from   }
                         {   list^ through last^ is     }
                         {   sorted.                    }
         begin
         temp := last^.next;    { Element to be inserted}
         if temp^.key >= last^.key then
            last := last^.next  { Already in place      }
         else
            begin              { Find a home for temp^ }
            p := list;
            q := nil;          { q lags p              }
            while p^.key < temp^.key do
               begin
               q := p;
               p := p^.next
               end;            { Keys of p^ and q^     }
                              {   bracket temp^.key   }
            last^.next := temp^.next;  { Insert temp^ }
            temp^.next := p;
            if q = nil then list := temp
                     else q^.next := temp
            end  { else }
         end  { if, while }
   end;  { IListSort }
```

If temp^.key $\geq$ last^.key, then temp^ is already in place and we need only advance last to the next node. Otherwise we enter a search-and-shift loop similar to the one we had when sorting an array. Notice that if we have had to move temp^, we do not advance last. The reason for this should be clear if you give it a little thought; giving it a little thought is the subject of Problem 4.5.

Figure 4.4 shows the process of inserting the key 6 in the correct position in the sorted portion of the list. The sorted portion ends with the key 11, pointed to by `last`. The pointer `temp` has been made to point to the node to be moved. In Fig. 4.4 (b), `p` and `q` are on either side of the place where 11 is to go, and the pointers have been set so the node is now in the proper place.

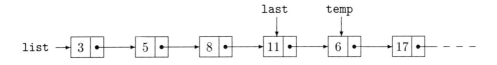

Figure 4.4 (a)

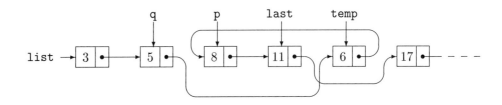

Figure 4.4 (b)

The analysis of the insertion sort runs roughly along the same lines as the analysis of the selection sort. The procedure makes $n - 1$ passes through the outer loop. In the worst case the inner loop is executed every time and its length is $i - 1$; each pass through the inner loop involves one comparison and one data movement. Hence the cost of the insertion sort is

$$C = M = \sum_{i=2}^{n}(i - 1) = n(n - 1)/2. \tag{4.4}$$

This is $O(n^2)$. In the linked-list version it is not necessary to shift records over to make room for the new one, and the number of data movements is thus only $O(n)$.

The insertion sort appears to be a more clumsy program than the selection sort, and the array version requires more data movement (which may be more costly than mere comparisons). On the other hand, the selection sort isn't stable, while this one is. In addition, if the list is already almost sorted—that is, if there are only a few misplaced records—the insertion sort will run faster, because whenever `x[i].key > x[i - 1].key` we skip the entire search-and-shift loop. If the procedure happens to try to sort a list that is already sorted, it should be clear that $C = n - 1$ and $M = 0$. In the selection sort, the inner loop runs to completion every time whether the list is sorted or not. Finally, the insertion sort is basic to the next sorting algorithm we will consider.

4.3   THE SHELL SORT

A significantly faster sort was invented by Donald Shell in 1959. The basic idea is this: An insertion sort takes longer than it should, because when it shifts data items it is moving them only one position at a time. If we could devise a sort that would move the items longer distances, we could cover long distances in fewer steps. After all, it costs no more to do

```
x[700] := x[3];
```

than it does to do

```
x[700] := x[699];
```

So instead of sorting all the elements in the list, suppose we sort every fifth element. Then the shifts will move things 5 places each time.

Of course, we may shift something too far. In order to take care of these errors, we'll do another sort, this time sorting every third element. Finally, we will take care of any remaining discrepancies by sorting every element.

It's not clear why three sorts should go faster than one sort, but before we address that question, let's look at an example: Suppose we have

12 2 9 16 3 25 1 7 16 4 3 24 6 19 32 16 9 31 18 7

First we sort every fifth element:

The first row under the array shows the elements in locations 1, 6, 11, and 16 in sorted order; the second shows the elements in locations 2, 7, 12, and 17, and similarly for the other rows. This gives us

3 1 6 16 3 12 2 7 16 4 16 9 9 18 7 25 24 31 19 32

Now we sort every third element:

This gives us

2 1 6 3 3 7 4 7 9 9 16 12 16 18 16 19 24 31 25 32

Now we sort all the elements:

2 1 6 3 3 7 4 7 9 9 16 12 16 18 16 19 24 31 25 32

1 2 3 3 4 6 7 7 9 9 12 16 16 16 18 19 24 25 31 32

Why is this faster? We know that an insertion sort is $O(n^2)$. In the first pass, instead of sorting 20 elements, we're sorting five subsets of 4 elements. Sorting 4 elements takes roughly 1/25 as long as sorting 20 elements; on the other hand, we must do it 5 times, as shown. We are still ahead: all five passes take a total of about 1/5 the time.

On the second time, we are sorting arrays of about 1/3 the size 3 times; this takes us a total of 1/3 the time. But there's an additional, more important speedup, because the array is already roughly sorted: the small elements have begun to cluster at the left end and the large ones at the right, as you can see in the output of that first pass. But we have seen that the insertion sort will run faster on an array that is almost sorted than on one that's completely random. In the example shown here, we skip the search-and-shift loop more than half the time. So in fact we'll take *less* than 1/3 the time for this pass.

In the final pass, the array is essentially sorted and only a few corrections need to be made. Most of our search-and-shift loops will be unnecessary, and the ones that remain will be short. That is why these three sorting passes are actually less expensive than one.

We can summarize Shell's algorithm as follows:

1. Let $step = n$. (n is the length of the array)
2. While $step > 1$:
   a. Set $step$ to $\lfloor step/3 \rfloor + 1$.
   b. For $i = 1$ to $step$:
      Sort every $step$th record beginning with record i.

The simplest approach to coding this is to modify our procedure ISort so that we can specify the starting point in the array and the step size:

```
procedure ISSORT (var x: sortarray; n, start, step: integer);
                              { Insertion sort modified      }
     var                      {    for use with Shell sort   }
        i,
        j: integer;        { Searching subscript   }
        temp: datarec;
        found: boolean;
     begin
     i := start + step;
     while i <= n do
        begin
        if x[i].key <= x[i - step].key then
           begin
```

```
            temp := x[i];
            j := i - step;
            found := false;
            while (j > 0) and not found do
                if x[j].key > temp.key then
                    begin
                    x[j + step] := x[j];
                    j := j - step
                    end
                else
                    found := true;
                x[j + step] := temp
                end;
        i := i + step
        end
    end;  { ISSort }
```

Here `step` indicates the spacing between elements, and where the plain insertion sort used to have j + 1, j - 1, and the like, we now have j + `step`, j - `step`, and so on. The location of the first element to be sorted is given by `start`. Thus this version will sort every `step`th element, starting from subscript `start`.

Then the body of the Shell sort looks like this:

```
procedure SHSORT (var x: sortarray; n: integer);
    var
        start,
        step: integer;
    begin
    step := n;
    while step > 1 do
        begin
        step := step div 3 + 1;
        for start := 1 to step do
            issort (x, n, start, step)
        end;
    end;  { ShSort }
```

In practice, the insertion sort is normally made a part of the Shell sort instead of being called as a separate procedure. I have shown it this way to emphasize the logic of the process. Where did I get that sequence of step sizes defined by `step := step div 3 + 1`? There is no known rule for finding the optimum sequence of step sizes (although we know that powers of 2 are a *bad* choice); the sequence resulting from the code shown here works well and is simple to compute.

Nobody has ever been able to analyze the Shell sort the way we have done with the other sorts, except with so many approximations as to make the results nearly worthless. Some estimates have been obtained and verified experimentally on the computer. The best we can say is that with a suitable sequence of step sizes, the cost is roughly $O(n^{1.25})$. This may not seem like much of an improvement, but on my PC a Shell sort of 2,000 elements takes about a second where an insertion sort takes 24 seconds.

4.4 QUESTIONS OF SPEED

We have now seen a sort that runs faster than the selection or insertion sorts. This leads to two questions we must consider: How fast can we sort? and How fast do we *need* to sort?

In answering the first question, we will assume that the sort must compare keys, and we will assume that we can measure the cost realistically by counting the number of comparisons needed. Every time the algorithm makes a comparison, there are two possible results: Either the keys are in the correct order or they aren't. This means that the program will follow at most two different courses of action after each comparison. If the data are sorted after a comparison, we are done; otherwise the next step will involve another comparison. Because of this, we can draw the possible sequences of comparisons as a tree, as in Fig. 4.5:

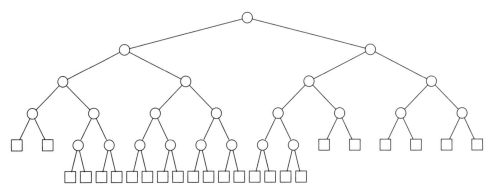

Figure 4.5

Every interior vertex on this tree represents a comparison; it has two children because each comparison has two outcomes. The top level (the root) of this tree represents the first comparison made. Every new level represents a subsequent step in the algorithm. This follows the structure of the tree we used to analyze searching; but there is a crucial difference, because in this case the leaves represent how the data have to be rearranged in order to get them sorted. If the sorting algorithm is ideal, then every leaf corresponds to a different permutation needed to sort the data. For any given set of input data, the algorithm starts at the root of the tree and works down, level by level, making comparisons as it goes, until it reaches the leaf corresponding to the permutation needed to sort that particular set of data. (We can relate this process to our analysis of searching by noting that we are, in effect, searching for the right permutation.[1]) The height of the tree is thus equal

---

[1] I am indebted to Murphy [1994] for this insight.

to the number of comparisons that must be made in sorting the data.

Now in constructing this tree, we have said nothing about what the algorithm is like: it is completely general. The final question is, how many leaves will there be and how does this relate to the height of the tree? From discrete mathematics we know that if we have n data items, there are $n!$ permutations; hence the tree has $n!$ leaves. We also know, from the study of graphs, that the height of a binary tree with k leaves is at least $\lceil \lg k \rceil$. Hence we conclude that the height of this tree will be, at best, $\lceil \lg n! \rceil$, and that is our result.

We can get this number in more familiar form by means of Stirling's approximation for factorials, given in Appendix A:

$$n! \approx \sqrt{2\pi n} \left(\frac{n}{e}\right)^n.$$

(4.5)

Taking the log (to the base 2) of this gives us

$$\lg n! \approx {}^1\!/{}_2 \lg n + n(\lg n - \lg e) + \lg \sqrt{2\pi}.$$

(4.6)

But this is $O(n \lg n)$, and that is the result we are after: The best we can do when sorting a list of n data items by comparing their keys is $O(n \lg n)$. This is of particular interest for us because we will shortly encounter two sorting methods whose cost, measured by the number of comparisons they must make, is in fact $O(n \lg n)$.

The second question, How fast do we *need* to sort, is a judgment call. I have promised you $O(n \lg n)$ sorts, but when we see them we will find that they all require a fair amount of overhead: the programs are not as simple as the ones for the insertion and selection sorts. This means that there is a trade-off to be considered: Will the saving in time be enough to justify the cost of the program? In many cases it will not be. As a quick rule of thumb, I would say that if you know your application will *never* need to sort more than 100 items, virtually any sort will do. Beyond that figure, it is probably a good idea to consider an $n \lg n$ sort instead.

This is an important point, because inexperienced programmers who know about the faster sorts tend to think that they are the only ones to use; but in many applications the amount of data involved is too small to justify using them. You don't drive a thumbtack with a sledge hammer.

4.5   DIVIDE AND CONQUER

Suppose a procedure costs $O(n^2)$. In fact, to to keep things simple, suppose it costs exactly n^2. Now, if we could split the job into two halves, would this buy us anything? The first part is now of size $n/2$, hence it costs $n^2/4$. The same is true of the second part; thus the cost is

$$n^2/4 + n^2/4 = n^2/2 + \text{cost of combining the results.}$$

So if the cost of combining the results isn't excessive, we've cut our work in half. (This is similar to the reasoning we saw in our discussion of the Shell sort.)

That looks so attractive that we might as well do it again. Suppose we split each half again. Now we have four parts, each of size n/4. The total cost is now

$$4(n^2/16) + \text{cost of combining the results}$$
$$= \quad n^2/4 + \text{cost of combining the results.}$$

The next question is, Do we ever need to stop doing this? Suppose the operation is sorting, and to make the example concrete suppose $n = 64$. Then we do

Split in half: $n = 32$ for each part.
Split in half again: $n = 16$ for each part.
Split in half again: $n = 8$ for each part.
Split in half again: $n = 4$ for each part.
Split in half again: $n = 2$ for each part.
Split in half again: $n = 1$ for each part.

But now our problem has vanished! Because a list containing only one element is already sorted. We have decomposed the problem into six levels, one level per split, and our cost is (6 levels)·(cost of combining per level).

Now, if n is a power of 2, then it requires exactly $\lg n$ splits to get down to 1 item per part. So then the total cost is

$$\lg n \cdot (\text{cost of combining operation}).$$

And if n isn't a power of 2, then it costs $\lceil \lg n \rceil$ splits, which is still $O(\lg n)$.

In the case of sorting, we know two methods in which the cost of combining (or of an equivalent operation) at each level is $O(n)$. One of these is Mergesort; the other is called Quicksort. Quicksort is best adapted to sorting arrays; Mergesort is best for sorting linked lists. In both these cases, the *average* cost of sorting is $O(n \lg n)$, which we just showed was optimal for sorts based on comparisons of keys.

This technique, of splitting a hard problem up into easy ones and then combining the results, has come to be known as "divide and conquer." There are a number of special programming techniques that are particularly powerful for certain kinds of problems, and divide-and-conquer is one of them.

4.6 MERGESORT

Our first divide-and-conquer sort is Mergesort. The Mergesort algorithm is as follows:

1. Split the list down the middle

2. Sort each half

3. Merge the halves

Here is an example. Our list consists of the numbers,

1   10   12   9   4   5   15   19   3   17

First, we split the list in two:

```
1   10   12   9    4
5   15   19   3   17
```

Next, we sort the two halves:

```
1   4    9   10   12
3   5   15   17   19
```

(How do we sort these two halves? By a recursive call to Mergesort.)

To merge the two sorted halves, we compare the leading numbers and remove the smaller, placing it in the output list. At the start, $1 < 3$, so we remove 1:

```
4    9   10   12
3    5   15   17   19
Output list:    1
```

Now $3 < 4$, so we remove 3:

```
4    9   10   12
5   15   17   19
Output list:    1    3
```

Now $4 < 5$, so we remove 4:

```
9   10   12
5   15   17   19
Output list:    1    3    4
```

Now $5 < 9$, so we remove 5:

```
9   10   12
15   17   19
Output list:    1    3    4    5
```

In the next three steps, 9, 10, and 12 are all less than 15:

```
[empty]
15   17   19
Output list:    1    3    4    5    9   10   12
```

At this point, the first list is empty; we can just tack the other list onto the end:

```
[empty]
[empty]
Output list:    1    3    4    5    9   10   12   15   17   19
```

and we are done.

We are now ready to look at an implementation. Our types, declared in the main program, are

```
type
   keytype = {Some type or other};
   nodeptr = ^node;
   node = record
              key: keytype;
```

```
                     { other fields as needed }
                     next: nodeptr;
                 end;
         var
            start: nodeptr;
```

and our procedure looks like this:

```
    procedure MSORT (var L: nodeptr);
        var                           { Mergesort for linked lists    }
           middle: nodeptr;
        begin
        if L <> nil then          { Else list empty         }
           if L^.next <> nil then { Else only one node      }
              begin
              split (L, middle);  { Make two halves         }
              msort (L);          { Sort                    }
              msort (middle);     {    each half            }
              merge (L, middle);  { Merge them              }
              end
        end;   { MergeSort }
```

Notice how closely this code matches our outline of the algorithm. There are two safety nets in this recursive procedure, because we will sort a list only if it has two or more nodes. To test this, we must examine both L and L^.next, and that explains the two nested ifs.

We split the list this way: We will advance a pointer, p, until it hits the end of the list. We will advance a second pointer, middle, *half as fast*. Then when p reaches the end of the list, middle will be half-way through the list. This gives us

```
    procedure SPLIT (var start, middle: nodeptr);
                        { Splits list for Mergesort          }
                        { start: head of input list          }
        var             { middle: head of second output list }
           p: nodeptr;
        begin
        p := start;
        middle := p;
        while p <> nil do                 { P traverses list      }
           begin
           if p <> start then             { Delay middle          }
              middle := middle^.next;     {    by one node         }
           p := p^.next;
           if p <> nil then               { P moves twice as fast }
              p := p^.next;               {    as middle          }
           end;
        p := middle;                      { Middle now at end     }
```

```
                                 {    of 1st half      }
    if middle <> nil then        {   ... now at start  }
       middle := middle^.next;   {     of 2nd half     }
    p^.next := nil               { Detach first half   }
    end;  { Split }
```

We delayed `middle` so that, at the end of the loop, it will be at the *end of the first half*:

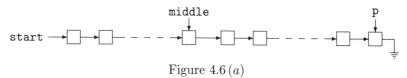

Figure 4.6 (*a*)

That's because we must detach the first half from the second half. We pick up that node with `p` and advance `middle` to where we want the second half to begin:

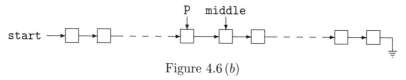

Figure 4.6 (*b*)

Then we detach the first half with the final statement:

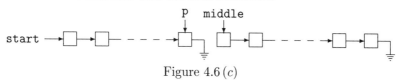

Figure 4.6 (*c*)

To merge the two sorted lists, we just duplicate the steps we took when we did it by hand. We will maintain two pointers, `head1` and `head2`, which we will use to go through the two lists. As long as neither list is empty, we will select the node with the bigger key, remove it, and attach it to the output list. When one of the lists is empty, we will simply append what remains in the other list to the output list. This gives us

```
procedure MERGE (var first: nodeptr; second: nodeptr);
                    { Merges two sublists for Mergesort     }
        { first: head of 1st list and also of output list  }
        { second: head of second list                      }
    var
       head1, head2,  { Heads of sublists      }
       p,             { Node to be removed     }
       q: nodeptr;    { End of output list     }
    begin
    head1 := first;
    head2 := second;
```

```
first := nil;                  { Output list initially empty  }
while (head1 <> nil) and (head2 <> nil) do
   begin
   if head1^.key < head2^.key then{ Select node              }
      begin                       {   with smaller key        }
      p := head1;
      head1 := head1^.next;       { Advance selected ptr  }
      end
   else
      begin
      p := head2;
      head2 := head2^.next;
      end;
   if first = nil then
      first := p                  { Link it to output list}
   else
      q^.next := p;
   q := p;
   end;
if head1 <> nil then             { Attach remaining list }
   q^.next := head1              {   to end of output     }
else                            {   list                 }
   q^.next := head2;
end;  { Merge }
```

Figures 4.7 (a)–(e) illustrate the operation of Merge. In Fig. 4.7 (a) the procedure has identified the smaller key, 12, at the head of the list pointed to by head1; accordingly it has set p to point to head1:

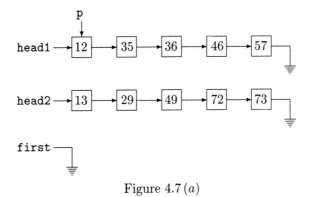

Figure 4.7 (a)

Figure 4.7 (b) shows the state after the last line of the while loop has been executed; the node containing 12 has been moved to the output list by attaching it to first. The pointer q now points to the end of the output list.

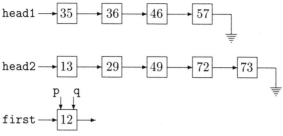

Figure 4.7 (b)

In Fig. 4.7 (c), the procedure has identified the new lowest key and set p to point to it.

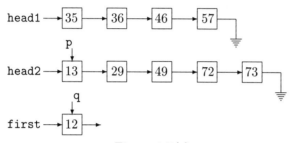

Figure 4.7 (c)

Here is the last line of the **while** loop again; the node containing 13 has been put at the end of the output list:

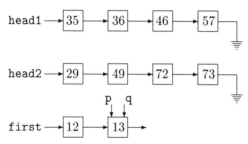

Figure 4.7 (d)

At the termination of the **while** loop, **head1**'s list is empty and the procedure is about to append the rest of **head2**'s list to the end of the output list.

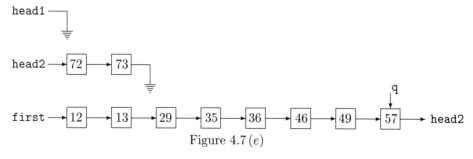

Figure 4.7 (e)

These three procedures—MSort, Split, and Merge—give you Mergesort. The analysis is straightforward: Every call to Split splits the list as nearly down the middle as possible. Hence it always takes $\lceil \lg n \rceil$ splits to get a list of n nodes down to lists that are either empty or consist of a single node. This means that there are $\lceil \lg n \rceil$ levels of recursions. The cost of merging is $O(n)$ per level of recursion; hence the total cost is $O(n \lg n)$.

The logic of Mergesort can be applied to arrays as well as linked lists, but there is a snag: merging an array onto itself is difficult, and the usual solution is to use an auxiliary array of a size comparable to that of the array being sorted. There does not seem to be much point in struggling with the merging problem since Quicksort works so well with arrays; writing a Mergesort for arrays is therefore left as an exercise.

4.7   QUICKSORT

Quicksort was published in 1961 by C. A. R. Hoare. The idea is this: Suppose we look for something much less ambitious than a full sort. Suppose we will settle for the following: Partition the array into three parts—a left part, a *pivot element P*, and a right part, as suggested in Fig. 4.8 (*a*):

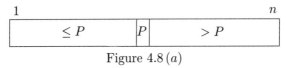

1   n

| $\leq P$ | P | $> P$ |

Figure 4.8 (*a*)

—in such a way that everything in the left part is less than or equal to the pivot and everything in the right part is greater than the pivot, as shown.

It turns out that this less ambitious project costs us only $O(n)$ comparisons. But look what it gets us: If we do the same operations on the two halves, we get the condition shown in Fig. 4.8 (*b*):

1   n

| $\leq Q$ | Q | $> Q, \leq P$ | P | $> P, \leq R$ | R | $> R$ |

Figure 4.8 (*b*)

Notice that this is approaching a sorted condition. If we go on and keep partitioning until all our partition sizes are down to 1, then we have a completely sorted array.

That's the essence of Quicksort. We may describe the algorithm as follows:

1. If the number of records to be sorted is > 1 then do steps 2–4.

2. Select a pivot record.

3. Partition the records so that all records with keys less than or equal to the pivot's key are to the left of the pivot and all records with greater keys are to the right of the pivot.

4. Do step 1 on each of the partitions.

We can outline an implementation of this algorithm immediately:

```
procedure QUICKSORT (var a: xarray; lb, ub: integer);
   begin
   if ub > lb then
      begin
      { Partition the array; let pivot be in location j      }
      quicksort (a, lb, j - 1);   { Sort left-hand partition }
      quicksort (a, j + 1, ub);   { Sort right-hand partition }
      end
   end;  { QuickSort }
```

Here lb and ub are the lower and upper bounds of the partition we're working on; the main program call is

```
quicksort (x, 1, n);          { n = length of x       }
```

As the code shown indicates, we handle the repeated partitionings by recursive calls: it's the easiest way. Let us demonstrate the overall process with a small array:

2	6	1	9	4	8	3	7	5	Unsorted (5 is pivot element)

2 6 1 9 4 8 3 7 5   Unsorted (5 is pivot element)
2 1 4 3 [5] 6 9 8 7   First partition
2 1 [3] 4 5 6 [7] 9 8   2nd and 3rd partitions (1..4 and 6..9)
1 [2] 3 4 5 6 7 8 [9]   (1..2, 4, 6, 8..9)

The portions to be partitioned are enclosed in rectangular boxes. After each partitioning, pivot elements are the ones in square brackets. (If the partition is of length 1, there is nothing to sort and hence no pivot element.) After the last step, the partition sizes are 0 or 1 and there's nothing more to do; the array is sorted.

If each partitioning step divides its piece of the array into two roughly equal parts, then it will take roughly $\lg n$ levels of partitioning to get down to sizes of 0 or 1. If each level costs $O(n)$, then the total cost will be $O(n \lg n)$.

We're left with the question, how to do the partitioning in $O(n)$ operations. There is more than one way to do this; I will start with a quick summary of the way Hoare himself used. Then I will cover in detail an alternative way which I recommend.

Hoare's method starts with two subscripts at opposite ends of the segment to be partitioned. First, we hold the left-hand pointer stationary. We compare the key it's pointing to with the key the right pointer is pointing to. As long as the right key is greater than the left key, we keep moving the right pointer to the left. If the left pointer is i and the right pointer is j, then we have

```
while A[i].key < A[j].key do
   j := j - 1;
```

When we find two elements out of order, we swap them; then we hold the right pointer steady and move the left pointer instead:

```
while A[i].key < A[j].key do
   i := i + 1;
```

Again, when we find two elements out of order, we swap them; then we go back to the first loop. We continue until the two subscripts meet.

So there is Hoare's partitioning. It's an appealing technique; it's very pretty to see those two subscripts marching through the array toward each other. The problem with this is that there are a number of ways in which i and j can meet, and making sure that we exit the partitioning loops in the right way, with j always pointing to the pivot element, is tricky and frequently a source of bugs.[2]

The following method is due to Lomuto (see Sedgewick [1978] and Bentley [1986]). We pick the right-hand element as our pivot value. There are still two subscripts, but only one moves continually through the array; it starts at the left end and works its way toward the pivot value. The other subscript moves only when there is a swap to be done. The code looks like this. Again I'm using the subscript lb ("lower bound") to mark the beginning of the portion to be partitioned and ub ("upper bound") to mark the end.

```
j := lb - 1;
pivot := x[ub].key;
for i := lb to ub do       { Invariant:  keys in         }
                           {   x[lb..j] <= pivot; keys    }
    begin                  {   in x[j+1..i-1] > pivot     }
    if x[i].key <= pivot then
        begin              { If invariant violated,       }
        j := j + 1;        {   correct it                 }
        swap (x[i], x[j]);
        end;
    end;
```

We can try this on a sample array. The array subscripts run from lb to ub; i is at lb and j is off the end of the array, at lb − 1; the pivot is 5, the last number in the array:

```
lb                      ub
 6  8  1  9  2  5  7  3  5      Pivot = 5
 j  i
```

As we go through the for loop, i moves from 6 to 8 to 1. Now 1 is less than the pivot value, so we advance j and swap the 6 and the 1:

```
 1  8  6  9  2  5  7  3  5
 j     i
```

Now i continues from 6 to 9 to 2. Here we have another element less than pivot, so we advance j and swap again:

```
 1  2  6  9  8  5  7  3  5
    j     i
```

Notice that the elements from lb through j are less than the pivot value, whereas those between j and i are greater, as predicted by our invariant. We go on: i

---

[2]See Bentley [1986], Chapter 10.

moves from 8 to 5; $5 \leq 5$, hence we advance and swap again:

```
1   2   5   9   8   6   7   3   5
        j           i
```

Now i advances from 6 to 7 to 3. Again, $3 \leq 5$, hence we bump j and swap:

```
1   2   5   3   8   6   7   9   5
        j               i
```

Now i finally reaches 5. But $5 \leq 5$, hence we advance and swap one more time:

```
1   2   5   3   5   6   7   9   8
            j               i
```

And there we are. Because we used $\leq$ in the test, the last pass through the loop swaps the pivot element itself, which is what puts the pivot itself on the boundary between the two partitions. In this method, the loop always terminates in the same orderly way, and at the end, j points to the pivot. The recursive calls then sort items (1, 2, 5, 3) and items (6, 7, 9, 8).

There is one shortcut it probably pays to add. Occasionally when we reach the swap instruction, i = j. In that case, there's clearly no need to swap. So we can save the program a little work by guarding the swap with an if i <> j.

We are going to write a recursive procedure, of course. For our safety net, we will require that there be something there to sort: that is, that ub > lb. (Remember that an empty array, or an array of only one element, is already sorted.) So here is the implementation:

```
procedure QUICKSORT (var a: sortarray; n: integer);

    procedure Q (lb, ub: integer);
        var                         { The Hoare-Lomuto partitioning }
            i, j: integer;
            pivot: keytype;
        begin
        if ub > lb then             { Safety net                    }
            begin
            j := lb - 1;            { Make the partitions:  }
            pivot := a[ub].key;
            for i := lb to ub do    { Main loop.   Invariant: keys  }
                                    {   in x[lb..j] <= pivot; keys  }
                                    {   in x[j+1..i-1] > pivot      }
                if a[i].key <= pivot then
                    begin                   { If invariant violated,}
                    j := j + 1;             {   fix it              }
                    if i <> j then          {   by swapping records }
                        swap (i, j);
                    end; { for; if }
            q (lb, j - 1);          { Recursive calls for   }
            q (j + 1, ub);          {   each partition       }
            end; { if }
```

```
        end;  { Q }

  begin  { QuickSort }
  q (1, n)
  end;  { QuickSort }
```

Cost. I said the partitioning operation was $O(n)$. Actually, its cost, measured by the number of comparisons needed, is $O(\mathtt{ub} + 1 - \mathtt{lb})$, plus one for the safety net, as you can see from the fact that the partitioning loop runs from lb to ub. That means that at any level of recursion—for example, going from Fig. 4.8 (*a*) to Fig. 4.8 (*b*)—several partitionings will have to be done; but at any level, the total number of elements to be partitioned is $\leq n$. In the ideal case, each partitioning will split its partition exactly down the middle, which means that there will be $\lg n$ levels. Hence we conclude that the best-case cost is at most $n \lg n$.

Finding the average cost is difficult, because the number of partitioning operations, and the length of each, depends on where the pivot element happens to lie. The math enmeshes us in probability theory; it is daunting and not particularly enlightening. I will simply state, without proof, that the average cost of Quicksort, over all permutations of the input data, is approximately $2n \ln n$ or $1.38n \lg n$. We already saw that the best case (splitting down the middle every time) was $n \lg n$; thus the average cost is not much greater than the optimum.

The worst case is another story. It is possible that the data may arrive in such an order that the splits are nowhere near the middle. In particular, suppose one partition were always empty:

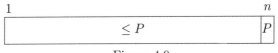

Figure 4.9

If this happened on every recursion, then it would take $O(n)$ recursions to get the left-hand partition down to a size of 1, and in that case the run time would be back up to $O(n^2)$. We would lose all the advantage of the Quicksort strategy. Can this happen? You bet it can! If the data arrive in sorted order, then the pivot is always the largest value in the partition, and the partitions go exactly as in this figure. Furthermore, if almost all of the data are sorted, with only a couple of elements out of order, the same problem arises.

Yes, but who would be dumb enough to sort an array that is already sorted? A computer would, that's who. Data files are frequently maintained in sorted order, and a program might well have code that changes certain elements in the array and then sorts it to get it in order again. Suppose nothing is changed, or suppose only one or two elements are changed: It is generally not easy to test an array to find out whether it is "almost" sorted. It is because of this worst-case behavior that we listed Quicksort as $O(n^2)$ in our table at the beginning of this chapter.

There are a number of ways out of this problem, and Quicksort is such a powerful method that it is worth taking the extra trouble. One possibility is to select the middle element of the partition as the pivot, swapping it into a[ub] before entering the partitioning loop. There are sequences of keys for which this will also result in $O(n^2)$ behavior, but such sequences are unlikely, while sorted and almost-sorted sequences are common. A better possibility is to pick the median of the first, middle, and last element of the partition and use that as the pivot. (The median element is the one whose value is in between the values of the other two.) Knuth [1973] suggests choosing an element from the subarray at random and using that as the pivot.

Bentley [1986] recommends sorting recursively until the partition size is less than some minimum size—say, 10 to 20 elements. At that point Quicksort quits, and we use a simple insertion sort to clean up the rest. (This is a little like the final pass of the Shell sort: it goes quickly because nearly everything is in place.) On the face of it, this doesn't look like a very smart approach, but Sedgewick [1978] studied this possibility and found that it was one of the best. We can enforce the minimum-size requirement by changing our safety net to read,

```
if ub - lb > minimumsize then ...
```

where `minimumsize` is some number between 10 and 20. (The speedup is not greatly sensitive to the value chosen.)

We have now seen one $O(n \lg n)$ sort—two, if we include the protected versions of Quicksort. There are more to come, most notably Treesort and Heapsort. These both make use of tree structures, however, and they will have to await the treatment of trees in Chapters 5 and 6, respectively.

4.8 RADIX-EXCHANGE SORTING

A completely different approach to sorting looks at pieces of the key rather than at the whole key. To see how such an approach works, we will start by taking integers as our keys and using the individual bits as the pieces. Suppose we have the array,

1, 4, 8, 6, 7, 9, 3

If we write these numbers as 4-bit binary numbers, we have

0001 0100 1000 0110 0111 1001 0011

We will now partition these keys almost as if we were doing a Quicksort, except that we will arrange them so that all the numbers whose high-order bit (which we will call bit 3) is 0 come before those whose high-order bit is 1:

0001 0100 0110 0111 0011 | 1001 1000

Next, within each partition, we order the keys so that the numbers with a 0 in the second-highest bit (bit 2) come before those with a 1 in bit 2:

0001 0011 | 0110 0111 0100 | 1001 1000

In the next pass, we order the contents of each new partition on bit 1:

0001 | 0011 | 0100 | 0111 0110 | 1001 1000

Finally, we order the contents of each new partition by bit 0:

| 0001 | | 0011 | | 0100 | | 0110 | 0111 | | 1000 | 1001 |

...and the numbers are sorted.

We can do the partitioning by swapping the numbers, using a variant of Lomuto's method. Because we are using the radix-2 digits of the keys as if they were keys themselves, this method is known as *radix-exchange* sorting. To sort by this method, we must have a way of testing individual bits of a key. This is awkward in standard Pascal; the function Odd will test bit 0 for us, and in computers that use two's-complement integers (nearly all of them these days), we can test the high-order bit. We can of course shift the numbers right by repeated division, so as to move the bit of interest into bit 0, but this is an expensive operation.

Turbo Pascal offers two extensions to standard Pascal that solve this problem. First, it has the **shr** and **shl** operators, which will shift an integer a specified number of bits to the right or left, respectively; second, it has extended the AND and OR operations so that they can do bitwise operations on integers. (We discussed this in Section 1.3 in Chapter 1.) Hence we can write a function bit that selects and tests a specified bit:

```
function BIT (a: integer; b: integer): boolean;
  begin                          { Returns true if bit  }
  bit := a and (1 shl b) = 0     {   b of a is 0  (Bit 0 }
  end;  { Bit }                  {   is rightmost bit.)  }
```

With this function, we can now write a modified Lomuto partitioning procedure. We nest it inside the main sorting procedure as follows:

```
procedure RSORT (var x: sortarray; n: integer);
                           { Radix-exchange sort           }
  procedure RAD (lb, ub, b: integer);
                           { Modified Lomuto partioning.   }
                           {   B is bit of interest        }
    var
      i, j: integer;
      done: boolean;
    begin
    if ub > lb then
      begin
      j := lb - 1;
      for i := lb to ub do
        if bit(x[i].key, b) then
          begin
          j := j + 1;
          if i <> j then
            swap (i, j)
          end;
      rad (lb, j, b - 1);
      rad (j + 1, ub, b - 1)
      end;
    end;  { Rad }
```

```
begin  { Rsort }
rad (1, n, 15);
end;  { Rsort }
```

The third parameter in the main call to **Rad** must be big enough to accommodate the largest key that is likely to be found. Note that if the keys contain negative numbers, the negative keys will appear in sorted order at the end of the array. A simple fix to **Bit** can correct this; the details are left as a problem.

The cost of sorting an array of n b-bit numbers is $O(nb)$. If b is significantly less than $\lg n$, then the radix-exchange sort will outperform Quicksort.

The binary radix sort is a special case of a more general radix sort, in which we sort on larger portions of the key than just individual bits. For a specific example, suppose we have keys of the form (j, k), where j is one of the letters $A \dots F$ and k is a digit. We can distribute the keys into seven lists, one for each letter, and then sort each list on the digits. For example, suppose our keys are

A4, C3, F5, F4, B8, D2, D3, C9, B9, A5, A9, F2, D4, A6, D6,
F3, C5, B4, E9, F9, B1, E3, B3, E1, A8, F6, B7, E2, D7, C8,
B2, A3, B6, F7, C6, A1, E7, C1, E5, C4, B5, A2, D1

After we have sorted them by letters, we have the following six sublists:

A4	A5	A9	A6	A8	A3	A1	A2	
B8	B9	B4	B1	B3	B7	B2	B6	B5
C3	C9	C5	C8	C6	C1	C4		
D2	D3	D4	D6	D7	D1			
E9	E3	E1	E2	E7	E5			
F5	F4	F2	F3	F9	F6	F7		

We can think of these letters as the high-order characters of the keys, and here they function in much the same way as the high-order bits in our previous example, except for the obvious fact that they can take on more than two values. If we then sort each of these sublists by their digits, we have

A1	A2	A3	A4	A5	A6	A8	A9	
B1	B2	B3	B4	B5	B6	B7	B8	B9
C1	C3	C4	C5	C6	C8	C9		
D1	D2	D3	D4	D6	D7			
E1	E2	E3	E5	E7	E9			
F2	F3	F4	F5	F6	F7	F9		

The entire sorted array can now be found just by concatenating these sublists. It is generally awkward to do the sorting in place; it is probably best to use linked structures for the sublists. We have sorted from the leftmost part of the key to the rightmost, but if we use a stable sort, we can sort from the rightmost part to the left. (With a stable partitioning method, we can also sort from the least significant bit to the most significant bit in the binary case.)

4.9   BUCKET SORT

We have shown that any sort based on key comparisons cannot use fewer than $O(n \lg n)$ comparisons. But the bucket sort is a method that does not use key comparisons, and it runs in $O(n)$ time. It works by a trick. With most data, this trick is impractical; hence the bucket sort can be used only rarely.

Suppose we are sorting records with keys that are the numbers from 1 to 9:

```
8  3  5  4  9  1  2  6  7
```

We simply use these keys as subscripts into an array whose bounds are [1..9]:

```
var
    bucket: array [1..9] of sortrecord;
    data: array [1..9] of sortrecord;
    i, j: integer;
begin
for i := 1 to 9 do
    bucket[data[i].key] := data[i];
end;
```

The contents of the bucket array are clearly our records in sorted order. We use the key itself to tell us where to put the record. This is bound to give us the fastest possible algorithm; when we considered *hashing*, we saw another way in which we could get the key to tell us where an item goes.

We can do this any time the range of the keys is not significantly greater than size of the array itself. If there are gaps in the set of keys, we can still do it:

```
const
    empty = -1;          { Some value outside range of keys   }
for i := 1 to range do
    bucket[i] := empty;
for i := 1 to n do
    bucket[data[i].key] := data[i];
j := 0;
for i := 1 to range do
    if bucket[i].key <> empty then
        begin
        j := j + 1;
        a[j] := bucket[i];
        end;
```

The final loop packs the records from bucket back into the a array. Since the longest loops are of length range, then if we assume that range is, in general, comparable to n, the cost is $O(n)$. I should mention, however, that there may still be a hidden factor of $\lg n$, since it requires that many bits to represent n different numbers, and word length may affect the speed of integer arithmetic. But for $n <$maxint, we may take the cost of the arithmetic to be essentially constant.

4.10   SUMMARY

We have not seen the last of sorting. We have two more $O(n \lg n)$ sorts to consider; these will also come up in Chapters 5 and 6. External sorting will have a chapter to itself.

Probably the best general sorting method for arrays is Quicksort, provided it is suitably protected against $O(n^2)$ behavior. But any library of procedures should also include, at a minimum, the insertion sort and possibly also the selection sort. When sorting large arrays of large records that are clumsy to move around, remember that we can also sort them *indirectly*—that is, by sorting their *subscripts* so that the keys to which the subscripts point are in sorted order. This avoids all data movement (except moving the subscripts themselves), and once the subscripts have been sorted it is not difficult to move the records into place in a single pass that requires only n data movements. The possibility is explored in the problems.

In designing procedures to do these and similar tasks, it is important to verify that they will "do nothing" gracefully (see Kernighan and Plauger [1978]). A sorting or searching routine may be called blindly by some other program that does not have the judgment to see whether there is actually something there to sort. Any program that crashes when given an array or list of length 0 has a serious bug, and in the course of testing a procedure, it is important to consider this possibility.

4.11   PROBLEMS

4.1. Trace the operation of the selection sort on the following numbers:

   79 97   6 95 36 44 47 56 69 85 10 14

4.2. Modify the selection sort so that the sorted part grows from the beginning of the array instead of the end.

4.3. What changes have to be made in the selection sort so that the records are sorted by key in *descending* order?

4.4. Write a version of the selection sort for linked lists.

4.5. Trace the operation of the insertion sort on the data of Problem 4.1.

4.6. In Isort, we could add the following assertion at the end of the `while` loop: { `j points to proper location for temp whether found is true or false` } Prove this assertion.

4.7. Since we know that a binary search is faster than a sequential search, wouldn't it make sense to use that in finding a home for the new item in the insertion sort? Discuss.

4.8. In the insertion sort for linked lists, we didn't advance `last` to the next node if the list had to be rearranged. Why not?

4.9. We said the insertion sort was stable and the selection sort was not. One way to test this is to sort a list of words by their last letters, then by their second-last letters, and so on, working back to the first letter. If the sort is stable, the words will end up alphabetized; otherwise not. Modify `Isort` and `Ssort` to handle this and test them.

4.10. Trace the operation of the Shell sort on the following array:

49 78 69 64 94 80 90 56 43 15 46 56 55 3 82 56 17 74 19 37

Use step sizes of 7, 3, and 1.

4.11. We never considered an implementation of Shell's sort for linked lists. Would this be a good idea? Why (or why not)?

4.12. Write a version of the Shell sort in which `ISSort` is built into the procedure instead of written separately.

4.13. In discussing the choice of step sizes for the Shell sort, I said that powers of 2 were a bad choice. Why?

4.14. Try to program Hoare's partitioning algorithm for Quicksort.

4.15. Write a version of Quicksort that chooses the median of the first, middle, and last elements of each partition as the pivot. (What will you do if the partition has fewer than three elements?)

4.16. The median of a set of numbers is the one that is greater than or equal to half the numbers in the set. (If the set were sorted, the median would be the middle element.) Show a modification of Quicksort that will find the median of an array using $O(n)$ comparisons on the average.

4.17. When we use Quicksort only as long as the partition sizes are greater than some minimum value, Bentley recommends finishing the job with an insertion sort. Why not use a selection sort?

4.18. Trace the operation of Mergesort on the data of Problem 4.1.

4.19. Write a version of Mergesort for use with arrays instead of linked lists.

4.20. Modify the function `Bit` in the radix-exchange sort so that negative integer keys will be sorted correctly. Assume the integers are 16 bits long.

4.21. Write a sorting routine that uses an array of subscripts into an array of large records and performs the sort by sorting the subscripts. Then write a procedure to move the records into sorted order; this procedure should require no more than n data movements.

4.22. What sort would you choose to sort each of the following? (Assume you have code available for all the standard sorts.)

(a) An array of 20 integers.

(b) An array of 20 records. Assume that the keys are in memory, but the records themselves are on disc and slow to move.

(c) An array of 2,000 records in random order.

(d) An array of 20,000 records in random order.

(e) An array of 20,000 records 95% of which are already in sorted order.

(f) A linked list of 20 records.

(g) A linked list of 20,000 records in random order.

CHAPTER 5

BINARY SEARCH TREES

We have had several occasions to speak of linked lists. The main advantages of a linked list over an array are, first, that we do not need to know in advance how long the list will be and, second, that insertion, deletion, and moving an element are much simpler in a list than in an array. The main disadvantage is that a search, or any traversal of the list, can only be sequential. We can jump around in an array just by computing subscripts, but there is no corresponding operation with linked lists.

A structure that gives us all the advantages of a linked list, with quicker access as well, is the *tree*. In a tree, the nodes are not arranged in a straight line; instead, the starting node, called the *root*, is linked to two or more other nodes, called its *children*, and those nodes in turn are linked to other children, and so on. The order of the children is usually important. A tree thus looks as follows:

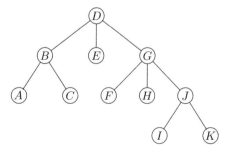

Figure 5.1

(You will see that computer trees, like family trees, grow upside-down, with the root at the top and the leaves at the bottom.) The advantage of this organization is that we can normally reach any element in a relatively small number of steps. Thus the node marked *H* is apparently the eighth one down the list (if we count from left to right), but we can reach it from the root in only two steps.

110

5.1 TREES

We must now formalize these intuitive notions. In mathematics, trees are a special kind of graph, and the study of graphs normally precedes that of trees. Because of this, trees are defined using the terminology of graphs. In particular, a tree is said to be a simple, connected graph that has no circuits.

In computer science, tree algorithms are usually considered before graph algorithms, and we must find a definition that does not rely on graph theory. As a first approach we might say that a tree consists of a node (or *vertex*) called the root which is connected by edges to one or more subtrees. This definition overlooks one important point, however: A tree can be empty. That is, a tree may have no nodes at all. Thus we must refine our definition as follows:

A tree is either

- Empty, or

- A node, called a root, which is connected to one or more other trees, called the *subtrees* of the root.

Subtrees are thus trees that are part of a larger tree. This definition implies that every tree has a special vertex identified as the root; such a tree is called a rooted tree. All the trees considered in this chapter and in Chapter 6 are rooted trees.

In Fig. 5.1, D is the root of the tree. D has three subtrees, whose roots are B, E, and G. The subtrees of B are rooted in A and C; E's subtrees are empty.

Two vertices joined by an edge are *adjacent*. These vertices are the *endpoints* of the edge that joins them. A graph in which there is at most one edge between any pair of vertices is a *simple* graph. Trees are simple graphs. In a simple graph, we can identify an edge uniquely by specifying its endpoints; thus we can speak of the edge $\{B, C\}$.

In any graph, a *path* is a series of edges connecting two vertices. In the figure, there is a path from D to K consisting of the edges $\{D, G\}$, $\{G, J\}$, and $\{J, K\}$. The *length* of a path is the number of edges on the path; thus the path from D to K has a length of 3. The *level* of a vertex is the length of the path from the root to the vertex. Notice that this means that levels are counted from the top down: the higher a vertex's level is, the further down the tree it is. The *height* of the tree is the length of the longest path from the root to a vertex.

If there is an edge connecting two vertices, the vertex nearer the root is called the *parent* (or *father*) of the other vertex and the other vertex is called the *child* (or *son*) of the parent. In our figure, D is the parent of B, E, and G, and F, H, and J are children of G. A tree in which the order of the children is important is called an *ordered tree*; in computer science, trees are usually ordered. A vertex with no children is called a *leaf*; all other vertices are called *interior vertices*. An *ancestor* of a vertex is either the vertex's parent or an ancestor of the parent. If X is an ancestor of Y, then Y is a *descendant* of X.

You can see from the foregoing that the terminology of trees is drawn in roughly equal measure from arboriculture and genealogy. Continuing in this vein, if a vertex has two children, we will find it convenient to refer to the children as brothers, siblings, or occasionally just sibs, and we will call the child of a child the grandchild. It will also be convenient to refer to grafting, pruning, chopping down, and even to tree surgery: metaphors serve to aid understanding, and we may as well make the most of these.

An *m-ary tree* is a rooted tree in which every internal vertex has at most *m* subtrees. In particular, binary trees, which we will consider in this chapter, are trees in which every internal vertex has at most two subtrees. We can also define a binary tree inductively:

A binary tree is either

- Empty, or

- A vertex with a left subtree and a right subtree, both of which are also binary trees.

To implement a binary tree in the computer, we need to define a structure for a vertex. We will do this as follows:

```
type
    treeptr = ^treenode;
    keytype = {some appropriate type};
    treenode = record
                  key: keytype;
                  data: {as needed};
                  left,
                  right: treeptr;
               end;
```

What the data field contains depends on what we are using the tree for, but there is always a distinctive item, called the *key*, that characterizes the node. We will see shortly that binary trees are frequently used for sorting and searching, and in that case the key field contains the key we use when searching or when sorting. We will normally assume that no two entries in the tree have the same key. In practice, this is nearly always true: The presence of two separate entries implies that there is something that distinguishes between them—that they are somehow different— otherwise they would have been combined into a single node. In practice, the key may be a subfield of the data field, but we will keep it separate from the other data, since that makes the programs easier to follow.

We may draw a picture of this structure as shown in Fig. 5.2. The only variable we need to access the tree is a pointer to its root; we usually name this variable **root**. If a tree pointer is **nil**, then the (sub)tree to which it points is empty.

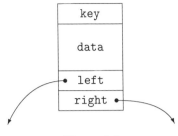

Figure 5.2

5.2 BINARY SEARCH TREES

Of the various binary trees used in computation, the most important is the *binary search tree*; here, at last, is the subject of this chapter. A binary search tree is, roughly, a binary tree in which the contents of the vertices are arranged in order. Formally, a binary search tree is a binary tree in which

- All the keys in the left subtree are less than the key in the root;
- All the keys in the right subtree are greater than the key in the root; and
- The left and right subtrees are also binary search trees.

You will notice that this is also an inductive definition. The requirement that the subtrees also be binary search trees makes the property apply "all the way down." Inductive definitions are frequently associated with recursive procedures, and this will prove to be the case with binary search trees. Figure 5.3 shows an example of a binary search tree.

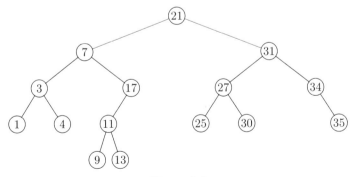

Figure 5.3

We normally label each node of the tree with the key, as we have done here. If you inspect this tree, you will see that it satisfies the definition of a binary search tree. For example, all the entries in the left subtree of 17 have keys less than 17.

We will now consider how such a tree is grown, how new nodes are added to the tree, how unwanted nodes are deleted, and how it is used.

5.3 INSERTION AND GROWTH

The first two problems are both the same, actually; we grow a binary search tree by starting with an empty tree and adding new nodes to it. To add a new node, we proceed as follows:

1. Start at the root.

2. If the tree is empty, make the new node the root.

3. Otherwise:

   - If the key of the new node is less than that of the root, insert it in the left subtree;

   - Else if the key of the new node is greater than that of the root, insert it in the right subtree.

We insert in the subtrees by invoking the insertion algorithm recursively with `root^.left` or `root^.right` as appropriate.

We can implement this as follows:

```
procedure INSERT (var newnode, root: treeptr);
   begin                           { Insertion in binary search tree  }
   if root = nil then               { Tree empty:     }
      root := newnode               {    put in root  }
   else                             { Otherwise       }
      if newnode^.key < root^.key then  {    insert in     }
         insert (newnode, root^.left)   {    left subtree }
      else
         insert (newnode, root^.right)  {    or right one }
   end; { Insert }
```

Notice that the insertion in the subtree is done by a recursive call to `Insert`. This recursive call enforces the "all the way down" property specified by the definition; it also results in a very compact and simple program.

In the form I have shown here, we assume that the new node was already created and stuffed with data in the main program. This is generally the simplest way, since otherwise we must carry all the data that go into the new node through all the recursions. Hence in the main program we would have

```
new (p);
with p^ do
   begin
   key := {whatever};
   data := {whatever};
   right := nil;
   left := nil;
   end;
insert (p, root);
```

That is all there is to inserting a new node into the tree. To grow a binary search tree, we simply do this repeatedly. If, for example, we were reading the data that go into the tree from a file, we would have something along these lines:

```
root := nil;                        { Tree initially  }
                                    {    empty        }

while not eof(inf) do
    begin
    read (inf, {data as needed});   { Get the data    }
    new (p);                        { Make a new node }
    with p^ do
        begin
        key := {whatever};          { Stuff it        }
        data := {whatever};         {    with goodies }
        right := nil;               { Subtrees are    }
        left := nil;                {   initially empty}
        end;  { with }
    insert (p, root);               { Put it in tree  }
    end;  { while }
```

It is a good idea to walk through this procedure to see how it works. At the start, the tree is empty and `root` is `nil`. Suppose we want to insert a node whose key is 37. We arrive at `Insert`; `root = nil`; so the node is attached to the root. The tree looks like this:

Figure 5.4 (*a*)

Next, suppose we have to insert a node whose key is 19. We arrive at `Insert` and this time the root isn't `nil`. (It can't be; it's pointing to that 37.) So we reach the `if`. Since `newnode`'s key is 19, that's less than 37, so the procedure calls itself to insert the node in the left subtree. On this recursive call, `Insert` thinks the root is the pointer I have labelled **r'** in Figs. 5.4 (*a*) and (*b*). Since this is `nil`, the new node is attached there.

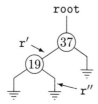

Figure 5.4 (*b*)

Now suppose the next key is 26. When we call Insert this time, it looks at the root, finds the root isn't nil, and, since the key is less than 37, it calls itself with p^.left. On this first recursion, it looks at r', which it now thinks is the root. This pointer isn't nil, either, and since the key is greater than 19, it makes a second recursive call using 19's right-subtree pointer, which I've labelled r'' in Figs. 5.4 (b) and (c). This pointer, on this last recursive call, is nil, so that's where the new node is attached:

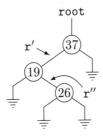

Figure 5.4 (c)

The process continues this way until there are no more nodes to be added.

5.4 SEARCHING

The structure of a binary search tree is intended to give us quick access to any item in the tree. To see how this happens, let us consider searching for a particular item. We will pass the root of the tree, together with a key, to the searching subprogram, and it will return a pointer to us. Since it is returning only a simple data object, we may as well write it as a function. If the key we're after is in the tree, the function will return a pointer to the node where it was found. (This gives the calling program direct access to the desired data.) If the key isn't found—always a possibility—then the function will return nil.

The logic of the search function is simple:

1. If the root node contains the key, the item is found.

2. If the root is nil, the item isn't in the tree.

3. Otherwise,

   - If the key we are after is less than the key in the root, search in the left subtree;

   - Else if the key we are after is greater than the key in the root, search the right subtree.

We search the subtrees by invoking the algorithm recursively with root^.left or root^.right as appropriate.

This outline leads directly to the code:

```
function TREESEARCH(key: keytype; root: treeptr): treeptr;
   begin                        { Searches a binary search tree }
   treesearch := root;          { Assume it's here or nowhere   }
   if root <> nil then
      if key < root^.key then            { Try left subtree       }
         treesearch := treesearch(key, root^.left)
      else if key > root^.key then     { Try right subtree      }
         treesearch := treesearch(key, root^.right)
   end;  { TreeSearch }
```

This function runs down the tree recursively, always selecting the correct subtree to search, until it either finds the desired item or reaches a `nil` pointer. The caller can determine whether the item was found by testing the returned value:

```
q := treesearch (root, key);
if q <> nil then
   { do something with q^ }
```

5.5 TRAVERSAL

We can use a binary search tree for sorting our data, too. To do this, we grow the tree as before and then run through it in a special way:

- Traverse the left subtree;
- Inspect the root and output its contents;
- Traverse the right subtree.

This process will output everything in the left subtree—that is, everything whose key is less than the root's key—and then will output the key (and possibly other data) in the root. Finally, it will output everything in the right subtree. This kind of traversal is called an *inorder* (or *symmetric*) traversal. It will give us the data sorted by key, *provided* we traverse the subtrees in the same way we traversed the main tree. So we refine our algorithm as follows:

- Traverse the left subtree in *inorder*;
- Inspect the root and output its contents;
- Traverse the right subtree in *inorder*.

As usual, this specification makes the inorder rule apply all the way down. The code is simple:

```
procedure INORDER (root: treeptr);
   begin                        { Inorder traversal of binary tree   }
   if root <> nil then
      begin
```

```
    inorder (root^.left);
    visit (root);
    inorder (root^.right)
    end
end;  { InOrder }
```

Inorder traversals have many uses, so I have resorted to a procedure call (`Visit`) to indicate what is to be done at the root.

One of these uses is sorting. We can outline an algorithm for sorting with a tree as follows:

- Build a binary search tree from the data;
- Traverse the tree in inorder.

The code for doing this can be assembled from our previous procedures for growing a tree and doing an inorder traversal. `InOrder` calls `Visit`; in `Visit` we output the contents of the root to whatever destination is to receive the sorted data.

This algorithm is known as Treesort. We will see presently that its costs correspond to Quicksort: best case $O(n \lg n)$, worst case $O(n^2)$. We will also see that, as with Quicksort, there are ways of avoiding the worst case. But unlike Quicksort (or Mergesort, for that matter), the tree structure used to order the data has the added advantage that records can be added or deleted relatively painlessly. Additions and deletions in a sorted array requires that we move all subsequent records, and additions or deletions in a linear linked list require a sequential traversal of the list; these are both $O(n)$ operations. We will see that the worst cost when deleting from a binary search tree depends only on the height of the tree, and we will also find that this height is $O(\lg n)$ if the tree is well balanced. (This is a big *if*; we will consider it presently.)

Since we specify this traversal by the special name, inorder, that suggests that there are other traversals as well. There are two others: *preorder* and *postorder*. The rules for these are as simple as the rule for an inorder traversal:

Preorder:

- Visit the root;
- Traverse the left subtree in *preorder*;
- Traverse the right subtree in *preorder*.

Postorder:

- Traverse the left subtree in *postorder*;
- Traverse the right subtree in *postorder*;
- Visit the root.

It's not at all obvious why we would want these other orders. Here is an example of an application of a preorder traversal. Suppose our tree contains the elements of an algebraic expression, as in Fig. 5.5:

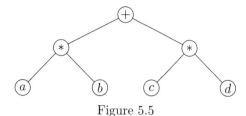

Figure 5.5

The structure of this tree tells us that the expression is basically a sum. But the two terms being added are products; one is the product of a and b and the other is the product of c and d. In conventional algebraic notation, this would be just $ab + cd$.

Now see what happens if we traverse it in preorder. Each interior node is an operator, and its subtrees are the operands it works on. When we traverse this in preorder, we get the sequence, $+ * ab * cd$. This is known as *Polish notation* or *prefix notation*. Polish notation is used as an intermediate representation of program statements in some compilers. If we traverse this tree in postorder, we get the sequence $ab * cd * +$; this is called *reverse Polish notation* or *postfix* notation. Hewlett-Packard pocket calculators normally use reverse Polish notation.

It must seem strange to see something like $a + b$ written as $ab+$, but as a matter of fact, this is how we learned arithmetic as children. We write the operands first:

$$\begin{array}{r} 5 \\ 8 \\ \hline \end{array}$$

and then we perform the operation:

$$\begin{array}{r} 5 \\ + \ 8 \\ \hline 13 \end{array}$$

—and this is the order we see in Polish notation.

Digression on Polish notation. In 1895, a brilliant mathematician named Kazimierz Twardowski received his degree in Vienna. He returned to Poland to take a chair at the University of Lwow (which was then a part of Poland). Twardowski was a logician, a member of that field that has one foot in mathematics and the other in philosophy. He found Polish philosophy amateurish and lacking in rigor. Over the course of his career, he built up a school of logicians that became the foremost in the world and that solved many important problems in mathematical logic.

What we call Polish notation was devised by Jan Lukasiewicz, a member of this school. Why he devised it is not clear, but we may surmise that it may have been for some reason along these lines: Logicians have a lot of occasions to use *propositional forms*, the things we study in discrete math, things that look like $P \wedge (Q \vee \sim R) \rightarrow (\sim S \vee T)$. When these forms get complicated enough, it could happen that two logicians are talking about the same thing without realizing it, because it can be very difficult to show whether the expressions they are using are equivalent. Lukasiewicz may have intended to attack this problem by defining a canonical representation for propositional forms. At the risk of considerable oversimplification, we can say that if two propositional forms are converted to canonical form, they should look the same if they're equivalent and different otherwise.

For another application of postorder traversal, consider the problem of getting rid of a binary search tree once we are done with it. (We may term this chopping the tree down.) One thing we don't want to do is simply set `root` to `nil`, because that would not return all the nodes in the tree to memory for possible reuse later. This could make us run out of memory if we had lots of trees to grow and destroy.

We have to chop down the tree in postorder because we dare not free a node until all its subtrees are empty. (Otherwise, we would lose access to the subtrees and wouldn't be able to chop *them* down.) But if we chop in postorder, this is exactly what happens:

```
procedure CHOP (var root: treeptr);
  begin                           { Chops down binary tree       }
  if root <> nil then
     begin
     chop (root^.left);           { Chop down left subtree    }
     chop (root^.right);          { Chop down right subtree   }
     dispose (root);              { Get rid of root           }
     root := nil
     end
  end;  { Chop }
```

Setting `root` to `nil` may or may not be necessary; some implementations of Pascal may build this operation into `Dispose` and some may not. It doesn't hurt to add the instruction, and people may thank you for it: wild pointers can do a great deal of harm.

Yet one more traversal method is *level-by-level* traversal. As its name implies, we visit the root; then we visit all the vertices one level down from the root; then all vertices two levels down; and so on. Here a recursive program won't accomplish what we are after; we must put the children of each vertex on a queue. Since a queue is a first-in, first-out structure, this means that we will not visit the vertices on level $n + 1$ until we have done all the vertices on level n. We will provide our program with a queue and four routines,

```
procedure CLEAR_QUEUE;                      { Empties queue    }
procedure EN_QUEUE (vertex: treeptr);       { Puts on queue    }
procedure DE_QUEUE (var vertex: treeptr);   { Takes off queue  }
function EMPTY_QUEUE: boolean;              { True if empty    }
```

In what follows we will treat the queue as an abstract data type: We have access to these four operations and will not worry about how they are implemented. The code looks like this:

```
procedure LEVELS (root: treeptr);        { Does level-by-level   }
   var                                    {    traversal of tree  }
      p: treeptr;
   begin
   clear_queue;
   en_queue (root);                       { Put the root on the queue   }
   repeat
      de_queue (p);                       { Take a vertex off the queue  }
      if p <> nil then
         begin
         visit (p);              { Visit it                }
         en_queue (p^.left);     { Put its children        }
         en_queue (p^.right)     {   on the queue          }
         end
   until empty_queue;
   end;   { Levels }
```

5.6   DELETION

I have postponed the issue of deleting nodes from a binary search tree because it entails a few more problems than insertion does. For brevity we will call the node to be deleted the *target*. Removing a leaf is trivial: we need access only to the leaf and its parent. We delete the leaf, normally by doing a `dispose`, and set the parent's pointer to `nil`.

If we are removing an interior node with only one subtree, the process is almost as easy. Again, we need access to the target and its parent; we splice around the target by setting its parent's pointer to the target's non-`nil` pointer, dispose of the target itself, and we are done.

The difficulty arises when we are going to remove an interior node with two subtrees. These subtrees must not be lost, but the deleted node's parent can accommodate only one of them.

There are three ways of solving this problem. They all involve finding the *immediate successor* of the node being deleted. The immediate successor is that node that would be visited next in an inorder traversal. If a node has a right subtree, then its immediate successor will be the leftmost node of the right subtree, and in that case finding the successor always entails code equivalent to the following:

```
q := p^.right;           { p points to the given node   }
while q^.left <> nil do
   q := q^.left;          { q points to its successor   }
```

These are the ways to remove an interior node:

1. Delete the target. Move the right subtree up into its place. Move the left subtree down and make it the left subtree of the target's immediate successor.

2. Find the immediate successor of the target; copy the successor's data into the target; then delete the successor instead.

3. Find the immediate successor of the target. Detach it from the tree and move it up into the target's place.

Notice that the immediate successor of the target has no left subtree. (If it had, it wouldn't be the immediate successor.) Hence, Method 2 proceeds by reducing the problem to one of the simpler cases. To be complete, I should mention a fourth way, known as "lazy deletion": mark the node to be deleted with some special code meaning "deleted" and leave it in the tree. We can get away with this if there are not many deletions and we can spare the memory.

It is most convenient to write the deletion as a Boolean function that will return a value of TRUE if the target was found and deleted and FALSE if it was not found. Hence, we can program deletion as follows:

```
function DELETE (var root: treeptr; target: integer): boolean;
                              { Removes node from tree;        }
    var                       {   returns false if not found   }
       q: treeptr;
    begin
    if root = nil then
        delete := false       { Wasn't found             }
    else if target < root^.key then
        delete := delete (root^.left, target)
    else if target > root^.key then
        delete := delete (root^.right, target)
    else
        begin                 { Found:                   }
        delete := true;
        if root^.left = nil then
            begin             { No left subtree:         }
            q := root;        {   easy case              }
            root := root^.right;
            dispose (q)
            end
        else if root^.right = nil then
            begin             { No right subtree:        }
            q := root;        {   easy case              }
            root := root^.left;
            dispose (q)
            end
        else
            begin             { Both subtrees there:   }
            ...               {   use one of the       }
            end               {   three methods.       }
        end
    end; { Delete }
```

Method 1 is in some ways the simplest, but it tends to unbalance the tree, since making the other subtree the left subtree of the successor usually moves it down the tree and therefore increases the overall height. Tests on a large number of binary search trees grown from random numbers suggest that a tree pruned by Method 1 will typically end up about half again as high as one pruned by Method 2 or 3.

Method 2 is probably the best; it is simple and straightforward. We can code it this way:

```
function DELETE (var root: treeptr; target: integer): boolean;
                                { Removes node from tree;        }
    var                         {   returns false if not found   }
        q: treeptr;
    begin
    if root = nil then
        delete := false                  { Wasn't found          }
    else if target < root^.key then
        delete := delete (root^.left, target)
    else if target > root^.key then
        delete := delete (root^.right, target)
    else
        begin                            { Found:                }
        delete := true;
        if root^.left = nil then
            begin                        { No left subtree:      }
            q := root;                   {   easy case           }
            root := root^.right;
            dispose (q)
            end
        else if root^.right = nil then
            begin                        { No right subtree:     }
            q := root;                   {   easy case           }
            root := root^.left;
            dispose (q)
            end
        else                             { Both subtrees there:  }
            begin
            q := root^.right;
            while q^.left <> nil do       { Find successor        }
                q := q^.left;
            root^.key := q^.key;          { Copy successor's key  }
            root^.data := q^.data;        {   & data             }
            delete :=
                delete(root^.right, q^.key) { Delete successor    }
            end
        end
    end;  { Delete }
```

Notice that when we delete the successor, we use the same recursive `Delete` function. This makes the recursion go clear out to a leaf, and when the recursions unwind at the end, they retrace the path back to the root. This will turn out to be a useful property later on.

Here is an example of this deletion process at work. Suppose our tree is currently as shown in Fig. 5.6 (*a*) and suppose we want to delete the node containing the key 7. `Delete` starts with r pointing to the root, where it compares 7 to the contents of the root (as indicated by the box containing "7.") The target is less than the key in the root, hence the next recursion goes to the left subtree.

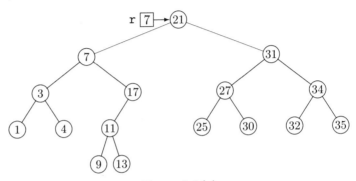

Figure 5.6 (*a*)

When it examines the next node, as shown in Fig. 5.6 (*b*), it finds a match. This is the node that must go. But it has two subtrees, so we can't simply delete it and move something up. The function now finds the successor to this node by moving q to the right subtree and thence leftward and downward until it reaches a dead end, as suggested by the dotted arrows.

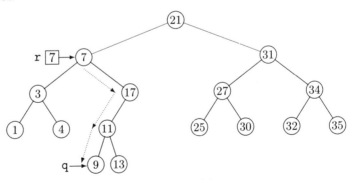

Figure 5.6 (*b*)

`Delete` now knows the successor is the node containing 9. It copies the contents of this node—except for its pointers—into the current node. (Figure 5.6 (*c*) indicates this by showing the 9 in boldface.) It then changes the target of the deletion to 9 and continues the recursive calls. As it does so, it retraces the path used to find the successor. As I said before, it pays to do this as a continuation of the recursive calls, because in some applications we will be interested in working back up the tree from the successor, and we can do this easily as the recursions unwind. The procedure ends up looking at the old node 9, as shown in Fig. 5.6 (*c*).

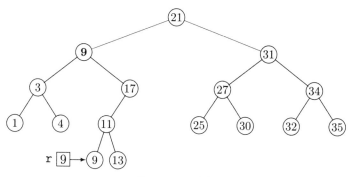

Figure 5.6 (*c*)

We can now safely delete this successor. It happens to be a leaf, so we simply remove it, and the process is done. The tree now looks as shown in Fig. 5.6 (*d*).

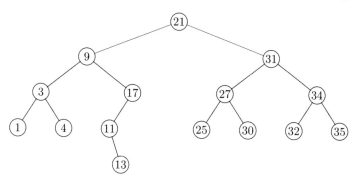

Figure 5.6 (*d*)

5.7   PERFORMANCE

We use trees in order to minimize the the distance we have to go to reach any given element. It follows from this that short, bushy trees are best for our purpose and thin, scraggly trees aren't. The ultimate in bushiness is a balanced binary tree, like the one in Fig. 5.6, where the leaves are all at the bottom level or one level up.

We learn in discrete math that a balanced binary tree containing n vertices has a height of $\lceil \lg(n + 1) - 1 \rceil$. But it is the height that determines the time needed to access any element. Hence, searching for an element is a $O(\lg n)$ process and growing the tree in the first place is a $O(n \lg n)$ process—*if* the tree is reasonably well balanced. For the time being, we will assume that it is.

Since a successful search may well terminate at some vertex fairly far up the tree, whereas an unsuccessful one will have to go all the way out to a leaf, we would expect successful searches to go faster than unsuccessful ones. We can relate the costs of these two kinds of search more precisely as follows. Let $S(n)$ be the average cost of a successful search in a tree with n vertices, and let $U(n)$ be the average cost of an unsuccessful search. (We will take the number of comparisons required as the cost of the search.) In the case of successful searching, if we systematically search for every item in the tree, we will be following the path from the root to every vertex in the tree. The number of comparisons we make along the way to each vertex is 1 more than the path length, so the number of comparisons made in this exhaustive search are n greater than the sum of the lengths of the paths to all the vertices.

When we make an unsuccessful search, we go all the way out to a `nil` pointer. We now resort to a fiction: Imagine that every `nil` pointer points to an imaginary vertex. For example, if our tree looks like Fig. 5.7 (a), then, when we draw those imaginary vertices—showing them as little dots—we get an augmented tree that looks like Fig. 5.7 (b).

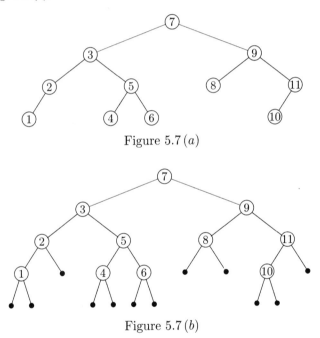

Figure 5.7 (a)

Figure 5.7 (b)

In this augmented tree, every vertex has either two children or none. Such a tree is called a *full* binary tree, and it has two properties that help us relate $S(n)$ and $U(n)$.

First, a full binary tree with n interior vertices has $n + 1$ leaves. The leaves in this augmented tree correspond to unsuccessful searches, and so there are $n + 1$ different ways in which a search may fail, depending on the imaginary vertex where it ends up. If we assume that all these different ways of failing are equally likely, then the average cost of an unsuccessful search is the sum of all the path lengths to these imaginary vertices, divided by $n + 1$.

Second, in a full binary tree, the two sums we are interested in are related. The sum of the path lengths to all the interior vertices of a full binary tree (called the *internal path length, I*) is related to the sum of the path lengths to the leaves (called the *external path length, E*) as follows:

$$E = I + 2i, \tag{5.1}$$

where i is the number of interior vertices. (This is proved in Appendix B.) Note that this equation relates the two sums we're concerned with. That's because in the augmented tree a successful search always fetches up at an interior vertex and an unsuccessful one always fetches up at a leaf. Furthermore, in our augmented tree, $i = n$. Putting this all together, we may summarize as follows:

$$
\begin{aligned}
S(n) &= 1 + \frac{I}{n}; \\
U(n) &= \frac{E}{n+1}; \\
E &= I + 2n.
\end{aligned}
$$

If we solve these three equations for $S(n)$, we get

$$S(n) = \frac{n+1}{n}\, U(n) - 1 \tag{5.2}$$

and this is the result we are after. It will be of particular importance presently; what it tells us right now is that in any large tree, the difference in average cost between a successful search and an unsuccessful one is insignificant, since when n is large, $(n+1)/n \approx 1$ and the -1 is negligible.

5.8 DEGENERATE TREES

So far I have presented binary search trees as if they were the solution to all the world's problems. They are actually a solution to a great many of them, but by no means all. Clearly a long, thin tree like the one in Fig. 5.8 is not as nice as a balanced binary tree would be. We can live with such a tree, however; we need only compare it with a linear linked list with 16 nodes. The internal path length of this tree is 57 and its external path length is 89. So the average cost of a successful search is 4.6 comparisons and that of an unsuccessful search is 5.2. It we had a linear linked list with 16 nodes, a successful search would take 8.5 comparisons on the average and an unsuccessful search would take 16.

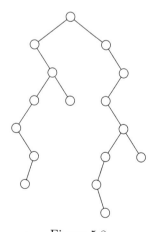

Figure 5.8

But consider what happens if we insert the following sequence of keys into a binary search tree: 3, 5, 8, 13, 21, 34, 55. Every key is greater than the one that preceded it, so every key will be inserted in the right subtree. We end up with the tree in Fig. 5.9.

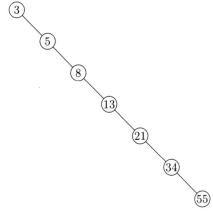

Figure 5.9

Technically, this is still a tree, but it acts just like a one-dimensional linked list. A linear structure like this completely kills the nice $\lg n$ properties we saw before, and such a tree is called *degenerate*. (Computer types, when vexed, resort to abusive language.) Note that a degenerate tree can result whenever the data are inserted in sorted order; this may happen in practical applications. There are two basic approaches to the degenerate-tree problem:

1. Hope it doesn't come up too often;

2. Make the tree "self-balancing."

The first approach is not as foolish as it sounds, especially because the second approach is difficult. We will follow up the first approach now and look at self-balancing trees later.

Degenerate trees turn out to be extremely rare if the data arrive in random order. That's a big *if*. If the data from which you are growing trees are normally stored in sorted order, then degenerate trees will be the rule. As always, you must study the application problem carefully to determine how likely this is.

But if the data do arrive in random order, degenerate trees are a great rarity. There are two ways to see this.

First, note that of all binary search trees containing n elements, there are 2^{n-1} degenerate trees. This looks like a lot, but the total number of possible binary search trees is much greater. In Appendix B, we find that the total number of distinct binary trees with n vertices is

$$b_n = \frac{1}{n+1}\binom{2n}{n} \tag{5.3}$$

This function grows much faster than 2^{n-1}, as we will see presently. Of course, degenerate trees are not the only source of inefficiency; we can also have "almost degenerate" trees in which just a few of the interior vertices have two children. Appendix B defines these precisely and provides a way of finding out how many of them there are; if we tabulate the numbers, we get the following results. (The column headed "AD" (for "Almost Degenerate") gives the sums from Appendix B, including degenerate trees; the column after it expresses these numbers as percentages of b_n.)

n	b_n	AD	% AD
1	1	1	100.
3	5	5	100.
5	42	38	90.5
7	429	284	66.2
10	16,796	5,792	34.5
15	9.695×10^6	8.816×10^5	9.09
20	6.564×10^9	1.342×10^8	2.04
25	4.862×10^{12}	2.042×10^{10}	0.420

You can see that as the number of vertices in the tree increases, the number of possible trees quickly outruns the number of trees likely to cause any problems. We are down to less than a percent when we reach 25 vertices—and remember that 25 vertices is a very small tree. The time required to search or traverse a tree as small as this is negligible, even when it is degenerate.

Second, we can estimate the probable cost of searching for an item in a tree grown at random. This proof, which may be found in Knuth [1973], assumes that all permutations of the n elements going into the tree are equally likely. As before, we let $S(n)$ be the average cost of a successful search in a tree with n vertices, and let $U(n)$ be the average cost of an unsuccessful search. We note, first of all, that if we are searching for a particular key, the cost of a successful search for it is 1 more than the cost of inserting it in the tree in the first place. This is because the process of inserting an item in the tree is identical to the process of making an unsuccessful search for it: you can see this if you examine the code for `Insert` and `TreeSearch`. The average cost of inserting the kth item is thus $U(k)$, and the average cost of searching for it is $S(k) = U(k) + 1$. If we then average over all n items, we find

$$S(n) = 1 + \frac{U(0) + U(1) + \cdots + U(n-1)}{n}. \tag{5.4}$$

But we also had another way of relating $S(n)$ and $U(n)$ from our consideration of internal and external path lengths:

$$S(n) = \frac{n+1}{n} U(n) - 1 \tag{5.5}$$

Combining these two equations and eliminating $S(n)$ between them, we get

$$(n+1)U(n) = 2n + U(0) + U(1) + U(2) + \cdots + U(n-1). \tag{5.6}$$

This is a recurrence relation; it is easiest to solve if we evaluate it at $n-1$:

$$nU(n-1) = 2(n-1) + U(0) + U(1) + U(2) + \cdots + U(n-2).$$

If we subtract these two equations, the sums cancel out and we get

$$(n+1)U(n) - nU(n-1) = 2 + U(n-1),$$

or

$$U(n) = U(n-1) + \frac{2}{n+1}, \tag{5.7}$$

with initial condition $U(0) = 0$. We get the result,

$$U(n) = 2\sum_{i=1}^{n+1} \frac{1}{n} - 2. \tag{5.8}$$

This sum is the nth *harmonic number*,

$$H_n = \sum_{i=1}^{n} \frac{1}{n}. \tag{5.9}$$

(See Appendix A for a detailed discussion of harmonic numbers.) Thus we end up with the following expressions for the costs of unsuccessful and successful searches:

$$U(n) \;=\; 2H_{n+1} - 2 \tag{5.10}$$

$$S(n) \;=\; 2\left(\frac{n+1}{n}\right)H_n - 3. \tag{5.11}$$

As we can see from Appendix A, the harmonic numbers are very similar to logarithms, and indeed $H_n \approx \ln n$. Converting this approximation to base-2 logs, we get

$$U(n) \;=\; 2\ln 2 \, \lg(n+1) - 2 \tag{5.12}$$

$$S(n) \;=\; 2\left(\frac{n+1}{n}\right)\ln 2 \, \lg n - 3. \tag{5.13}$$

We must not allow the math to distract us from what we are looking for. As usual, we are mostly concerned with large n; in such cases the ratio of $n+1$ to n approaches 1, the difference between -2 and -3 becomes negligible, $\lg(n+1) \approx \lg n$, and the cost of searching is roughly $1.39 \lg n$ whether we find what we're after or not. This gives us a measure of how bad things are apt to get, and the factor of 1.39 tells us they don't get very bad, on the average. Notice the similarity to the numbers we had for Quicksort, except for the extra factor of n in the latter: best performance $\lg n$; average performance $2\ln 2 \lg n$; worst-case performance $O(n)$.

Again, remember that this assumes that all permutations of the data are equally likely. It is a valid and reassuring analysis as long as this assumption is justified. The gross deviations usually arise from a situation where you are inserting a new item in a list or file in which the other items are already stored in sorted order. But files frequently *are* stored in sorted order, and if they are, the permutations are anything but equally likely, and in this case our whole analysis goes out the window. Engineers have a saying, "Know your materials"; we could use a similar saying, "Know your data!"

5.9   BALANCING BINARY SEARCH TREES

We have shown that trees grown from random data are pretty well balanced. But much of what we do in data processing involves imposing order on data, and so it is safest to regard random data as the exception rather than the rule. If we know our data have a high probability of giving us a degenerate tree, and if the tree is going to be large enough for this to make a difference, then we it would be highly desirable to have a way of rebalancing the tree in the course of making insertions and deletions.

Suppose we are growing a tree with the keys 10, 20, and 30. If we insert them in that order, we get a tree like Fig. 5.10 (*a*).

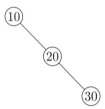

Figure 5.10 (*a*)

An unbalanced tree with three nodes is nothing to worry about, but there may be more keys coming, and if we are going to fix up the tree, now is the time to do it. We could rebalance it if only we could make 20 the root, as in Fig. 5.10 (*b*). This kind of fixup is known as a *rotation*, and, as we will see, it is not difficult to carry out.

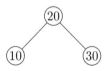

Figure 5.10 (*b*)

Rotations affect subtrees, not just individual nodes. A rotation like the one in Fig. 5.10 (*b*) raises the rightmost subtree (in this case 30) and lowers the leftmost one (in this case 10's empty left subtree). This gives us just what we want, because balance is an issue that concerns subtrees as well. Our general strategy is this: After inserting into (or deleting from) a self-balancing tree, we work our way back to the root as we return from the recursions, and while doing so, we check the balance of the subtrees at each step and make the necessary rotations to correct them.

We must start out by considering general cases. First, suppose we have the structure of Fig. 5.11 (*a*), in which **r** is currently the root of the tree.

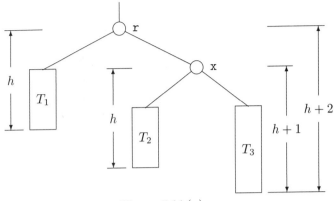

Figure 5.11 (*a*)

The boxes labelled T_1, T_2, and T_3 represent the subtrees of **r** and **x**. (In our previous example, T_1 and T_2 were empty, **r** held 10, **x** held 20, and T_3 was 30.) The dimensions h, $h+1$, and $h+2$ give the heights of the various subtrees. The tree is out of balance because T_3 makes **r**'s right subtree higher than its left. We can fix this up by making **x** the root instead of **r**, as shown in Fig. 5.11 (*b*).

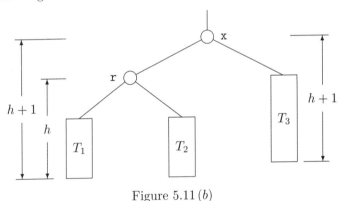

Figure 5.11 (*b*)

We call this process a *left rotation*, because we rotate nodes **r** and **x** counterclockwise from the position $\searrow$ to the position $\nearrow$.

What does it cost us to do this? It costs us three pointer movements:

1. Change the root pointer from **r** to **r^.right**;

2. Change **x^.left** from T_2 to **r**;

3. Change **r^.right** from **x** to T_2.

Thus to rotate the tree, we rotate the three pointers tt **r**, **r^.right**, and **x^.left**. Pointer operations aren't free, but they're normally among the cheapest things we can do in a computer; hence, this operation is quick and painless. It also preserves the ordering of the tree contents: If we had a binary search tree before rotation, we will have one afterwards. This is because the outer two subtrees are unchanged: T_1 was **r**'s left subtree before, and it still is after, the rotation. Similarly, T_3 was x's right subtree before, and it still is after. T_2 was in between r and x before the rotation, and it still is afterward. Thus the ordering of the subtrees, and hence of the keys, is unchanged.

This explanation also gives us a good way to remember how to do rotations when working through an example on paper, for example, in debugging—or in an examination. First, rotate the two nodes in question (here r and x). Next, remember that *the outside subtrees stay the same*: the left subtree of the left node is still the left subtree of the left node after rotation, and the same with the right subtree of the right node. This leaves only the middle subtree for which we must find a new home. But there's only one place for it to go, because its keys must still lie between r and x.

The rotation we have looked at here is a left rotation. When T_1 is the offending subtree, we must do a right rotation; the code for a right rotation is the mirror image of what we just saw. If we define the type `direction` in the main program as

```
type
    direction = (left, right);
```

then we can code these procedures as follows:

```
procedure ROTATE (var root: treeptr; d: direction);
    var                      { Rotates subtree left or right }
        temp: treeptr;
    begin
    if d = left then
        begin                      { Left rotation }
        temp := root^.right;
        root^.right := temp^.left;
        temp^.left := root;
        root := temp
        end
    else
        begin                      { Right rotation}
        temp := root^.left;
        root^.left := temp^.right;
        temp^.right := root;
        root := temp
        end
    end;  { Rotate }
```

Figure 5.12 shows an example of the way rotation works on an actual binary search tree. Here the subtree rooted in 9 is too far down, and a left rotation of 4 and 7 will correct it.

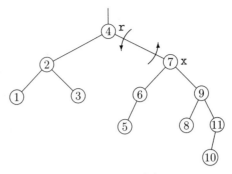

Figure 5.12 (*a*)

After the rotation, the tree looks as shown in Fig. 5.12 (*b*). You should observe that, as we said before, the outside subtrees are the same before and after the rotation and that the middle subtree (the one containing the keys 6 and 5) has been placed where it will keep the elements in order.

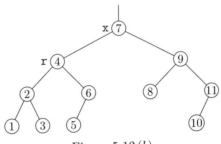

Figure 5.12 (*b*)

What we have seen takes care of the situation where one of the outer subtrees is the one that is too high. If the offending subtree is in the middle, we must do two rotations. Figure 5.13 shows an example:

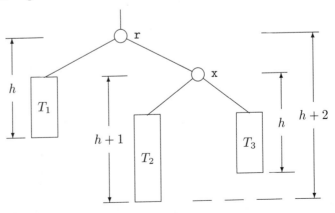

Figure 5.13

Rotations change the heights of the outside subtrees but not the height of the middle one; so here, if we do the same kind of rotation we did before, we end up with the same problem: the middle subtree is too far down. (The result will be approximately the mirror image of Fig. 5.13, with the middle subtree as bad as it was before.)

The correct solution proceeds in two stages. To show this more clearly, we will display the contents of T_2 explicitly: it must consist of a root **w** and two subtrees, which we will call T_2a and T_2b. So now we have Fig. 5.14 (a):

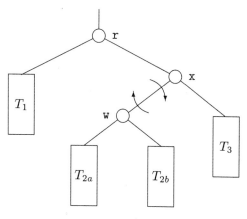

Figure 5.14 (a)

First, we do a right rotation on **w** and **x**, as indicated by the arrows in Fig. 5.14 (a); this gives us the tree shown in Fig. 5.14 (b).

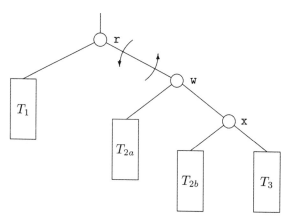

Figure 5.14 (b)

Now the middle subtree is all right, and the problem has been shifted over to node **x**. But we know how to fix this; we do a left rotation on **r** and **w**, as indicated by the arrows in Fig. 5.14 (b). The result of this second rotation is as shown in Fig. 5.14 (c):

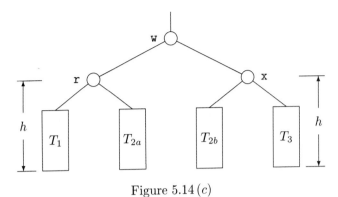

Figure 5.14 (*c*)

Rotations provide an attractive solution to the problem of balance; they give us an easy way to restore the balance of the tree without disturbing the order of its contents. The trick is to know when and where to do them. This means detecting when a tree is going out of balance and applying the corrective rotation(s) at the right place. There are two important approaches to this: AVL trees and red-black trees. (AVL stands for two (not three) Russian mathematicians named Adel'son-Vel'skiĭ and Landis [1962].)

Neither of these methods produces perfect balance, but they produce pretty good balance cheaply, and in programming we will nearly always prefer the cheap, pretty good method to the expensive, perfect method. In any case, binary search trees work so well that all we are really concerned with is keeping the worst horrors off. Both these approaches prevent degenerate trees with more than two vertices and almost-degenerate trees with more than four vertices. We will see that an AVL tree with n vertices has a height of at most $1.44 \lg n$ and that a red-black tree with n vertices has a height of at most $2 \lg(n + 1)$ and typically much less.

We will start by considering AVL trees. The AVL algorithm is the older of these two, and is now mostly of historical interest, since red-black trees are easier to implement and offer comparable performance. Nevertheless, the AVL algorithm is still important, and it is a little more clear how this algorithm achieves the desired result.

5.9.1   AVL Trees

An AVL tree is one in which

- The heights of the left and right subtrees differ by at most 1, and

- The right and left subtrees are also AVL.

You will see that this is yet another recursive definition; as usual, the second clause of the definition makes the property apply all the way down. Figure 5.15 shows some AVL trees:

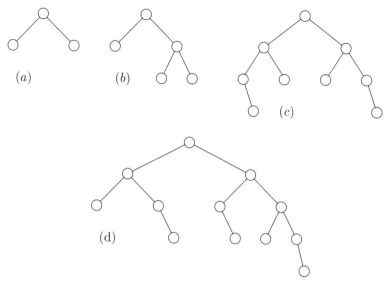

Figure 5.15

The one in Fig. 5.15 (d) is as badly unbalanced as an AVL tree ever gets; it should be clear that we can live with that.

The AVL algorithm must determine when rebalancing is necessary. It also will help if the tree surgery can be done locally; that is, we don't want a minor adjustment at one corner of the tree to propagate into a major reorganization that involves the entire tree. The AVL algorithm meets these requirements (as does the red-black algorithm). The overhead for data storage is small; the amount of code necessary to maintain the tree is considerable. This is one of the few exceptions to the otherwise general rule that recursive procedures tend to be compact. This code is not compact, but its long-windedness consists mostly of conditional branches, and on any one insertion or deletion only a small fraction of the code is ever actually executed. This is an important consideration, because if the balancing act itself were time-consuming, it would defeat the purpose of the AVL structure.

To determine whether the tree needs to be rebalanced, we place a balance indicator in each node. This indicator can take on three values:

1. *Left-high*: The left subtree's height is 1 greater than the right subtree's height.

2. *Balanced*: The two subtrees have equal heights.

3. *Right-high*: The right subtree's height is 1 greater than that of the left.

In drawings of AVL trees, we will use the symbols -1, 0, and 1 to indicate these cases, respectively.

This indicator (which we will call a *balance flag*)[1] is the only extra storage we need. We can declare the AVL node as follows:

```
type
    treeptr = ^avl_node;
    balance = -1..1;
    keytype = {some appropriate type};
    avl_node = record
                    bflag: balance;
                    key: keytype;
                    data: {some appropriate type};
                    left,
                    right: treeptr;
               end;
```

Insertions.   An empty tree is AVL, and a tree consisting of a single node with empty subtrees is AVL. So we can always start out with an AVL tree; the trick is to make sure the tree grows in such a way that it keeps on being AVL, and to do this in such a way that doesn't cost unreasonable amounts of overhead. Perhaps the best way to illustrate the problems that arise is with the following example: Suppose the tree is as shown in Fig. 5.16 (*a*), and suppose the new node ends up being inserted as the left child of node *b*.

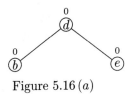

Figure 5.16 (*a*)

Then we must note these consequences:

1. Node *b* changes from balanced to left-high.

2. The subtree rooted in *b* has become taller.

3. Because the subtree rooted in *d* has become taller, node *d* is now left-high.

So now the tree looks like Fig. 5.16 (*b*).

---

[1]This is also called a balance *factor*; but since a factor is normally a multiplier, it seems more proper to refer to it as a flag.

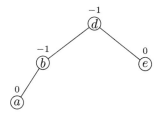

Figure 5.16 (b)

Now suppose another node is inserted, this time b's right child. Then node b becomes balanced, but since this insertion didn't change the height of the subtree rooted in b (or of that rooted in d), the balance flag of d doesn't change. So we have Fig. 5.16 (c):

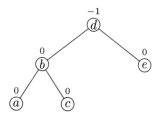

Figure 5.16 (c)

From this we see that we must modify our insertion procedure to keep track of the balance flag and to note whether adding the new node has made the subtree higher or not. We need an additional parameter, **higher** (a Boolean), to tell whether the insertion has made the current subtree taller or not. So we need something along the following lines:

1. If root empty, insert the node and set **higher** to true;

2. Otherwise:

    a. If contents of node < contents of root, then

        i. Insert in left subtree;

        ii. Check balance and correct if necessary

    b. else

        i. Insert in right subtree;

        ii. Check balance and correct if necessary

To see how we handle the balance issue, consider insertion in the left subtree:

If left subtree was made taller by the insertion, then

    If balance flag is

        Left-high: rebalance;

        Balanced: change to left-high and make **higher** TRUE;

        Right-high: change to balanced and make **higher** FALSE.

Here is the reasoning behind this: If the insertion didn't change the height of the left subtree, the balance flag of the current node doesn't change; in fact, nothing changes at this level. That explains the first *if*.

But if the left subtree became higher because of the insertion, then this will change the current subtree's balance and may change its height. If the current subtree was already left-high, it is now *more* left-high; in fact, it's in violation of the AVL requirement, and we have to do a rebalancing operation. (How this is done we will take up later.) If the current subtree used to be balanced, the higher left subtree now makes it unbalanced, and furthermore it is higher. (We saw this in the previous example.) But if the current subtree *was* right-high, it is now balanced, and its height doesn't change. (We saw that above, too.) So that is why we have the rules in the second *if*.

We must now consider how to do the balancing acts. We saw at the very start that we sometimes need a single rotation and sometimes a double rotation. The double rotation comes about when the middle subtree is causing the problem. So our fixup rule reads as follows:

1. If root is right high, check balance of the right subtree.

   a. If the right subtree is also right high, do a left rotation at the root.

   b. If the right subtree is left high, do a right rotation at the subtree's root and then do a left rotation at the main root.

   In either case, set **higher** to FALSE.

If the imbalance is in the opposite direction—that is, if the left subtree is too high—then we have the opposite solution:

2. If the root is left high, check the balance of the left subtree.

   a. If the left subtree is also left high, do a right rotation at the root.

   b. If the left subtree is right high, do a left rotation at the root of the subtree and then do a left rotation at the main root.

   In either case, set **higher** to FALSE.

The one point not covered here is the need to update the balance flags in the various cases; this makes the programs a little more long-winded than they might otherwise be.

This looks as if we have added a lot of extra work to the program. It's true that the balancing acts add a lot of code—I said this was one notorious exception to our rule that recursive programs with linked storage are short—but it won't be used much. On any insertion, we need to do only one rotation or, at worst, two rotations. This is because these rotations are necessary only if balancing is necessary. But the balance procedures are called only if **higher** is TRUE (and not always then), and you will note that one of the things the balance procedures do in every case is set **higher** to FALSE. Therefore, if at some level of recursion either balancing act has been called, **higher** will be FALSE on all higher levels of recursion, and we will never need to call the balance procedures again on that insertion.

Deletions. In deleting nodes, the logic is a little more complicated, because we may have to delete a node with subtrees, but the balancing procedure is similar. The programs now require a boolean variable called `shorter`. One approach is this: Find the target by the usual recursive search. If the target has only one nonempty subtree, just splice out the target and return with `shorter` = TRUE. If the target has two nonempty subtrees, locate the target's successor, copy the successor's data into the target, and delete the successor instead. To delete the successor, we continue the recursive search, just as we did in `DeleteNode`. This means that the chain of recursions will trace the path to the successor by way of the target. Then as we return from the recursions, we will retrace this path and can check the balance at each stage and correct it as necessary.

Height of AVL Trees. As we have seen, the efficiency of computation depends on the height of the tree. Since AVL trees are not always the shortest trees possible, we don't necessarily get the best performance out of them. How bad do they get? In particular, is the improvement worth all this trouble?

We answer this question by trying to get the worst possible imbalance in a tree and still have it meet the AVL requirements. Then we will find an approximate formula giving the height of this tree as a function of the number of nodes it has. We will find the formula by showing that the relationship of these worst-case trees has a familiar form and making use of that fact.

We can make the worst-case tree making every interior node left-high; this makes every part of the tree as badly balanced as possible, and the resulting tree will have the fewest nodes possible for a given height, h.

Let A_h be such a tree with height h. I claim that the following recurrence relation holds among such trees:

$$(|A_h| + 1) = (|A_{h-1}| + 1) + (|A_{h-2}| + 1), \tag{5.14}$$

in which $|A|$ means the number of nodes in the tree A.

Proof: Suppose we want to build A_h. We can create this tree as follows: Make a new root, make a left subtree that is also a worst-case, left-high AVL tree of height $h - 1$, and make a right subtree that is also a worst-case, left-high AVL tree of height $h - 2$. (This makes the new root left-high, but not enough to violate the AVL requirement. It also guarantees the minimum number of nodes, because its subtrees are already minimal.) But that means that the left subtree is A_{h-1} and the right subtree is A_{h-2}. Then the number of nodes in this new tree, $|A_h|$, is $|A_{h-1}|$ (left subtree) + $|A_{h-2}|$ (right subtree) + 1 (the new root). So we have

$$|A_h| = |A_{h-1}| + |A_{h-2}| + 1.$$

If we add 1 to both sides of this equation, we have our desired result:

$$|A_h| + 1 = (|A_{h-1}| + 1) + (|A_{h-2}| + 1).$$

With the initial conditions, $|A_0| = 1$ and $|A_1| = 2$, we can work this recurrence relation out for any desired height. For example:

h	$|A_h|$
0	1
1	2
2	4
3	7
4	12
5	20
6	33

But we need a formula for this, because we want to solve for the height as a function of the number of nodes: given $|A_h|$, find h. Some sharp-eyed researcher noticed that the numbers in the second column were all 1 less than the Fibonacci numbers. (Indeed, trees of the sort we are constructing here are called Fibonacci trees.) So now we have

$$|A_h| + 1 = F_{h+3}$$

and that's a lucky break, because it happens that we *have* a formula for F_h:

$$F_h \approx \frac{\phi^h}{\sqrt{5}} \tag{5.15}$$

or

$$|A_h| + 1 = F_{h+3} \approx \frac{\phi^{h+3}}{\sqrt{5}}$$

Where ϕ is a special number, $(\sqrt{5}+1)/2 = 1.618033989\cdots$. Since h appears in an exponent, we must take logs to solve for it.

$$\lg(|A_h| + 1) \approx (h + 3)\lg\phi - \tfrac{1}{2}\lg 5$$

or

$$h\lg\phi \approx \lg(|A_h| + 1) + \tfrac{1}{2}\lg 5 - 3\lg\phi$$

or

$$h \approx \frac{\lg(|A_h| + 1) + \tfrac{1}{2}\lg 5 - 3\lg\phi}{\lg\phi}. \tag{5.16}$$

Now with a pocket calculator we can make some numbers: We get

$$h \approx 1.44\lg(|A_h| + 1) - 1.33,$$

or, roughly,

$$h \approx 1.44\lg|A_h|. \tag{5.17}$$

Now the purpose of mathematics is insight, not equations.[2] What insight do we get here? We started out by considering the worst possible AVL tree, and this equation tells us that the worst AVL tree of n nodes has a height of about $1.44\lg n$.

---

[2]This is adapted from the motto of R. W. Hamming's [1962] book: "The purpose of computing is insight, not numbers." Well worth remembering.

Is this good or bad? To answer that, we must compare AVL trees with regular binary search trees. We know that the best (perfectly balanced) binary trees have a height of roughly $\lg n$. For binary trees grown at random, we have an average search time of about $1.39 \lg n$, and we know the worst binary trees have a height of n. So the height of an AVL tree *at worst* is only about 44 percent higher than a perfect binary tree, and its *worst height* is comparable to the *average search time* of a random binary tree. It can also be shown that Fibonacci trees have an average search time of about 4 percent more than the optimum. That's not bad.

We looked at the worst case because that's mathematically tractable. Finding the average height is one of those messy problems like finding the execution time of a Shell sort, and, as with the Shell sort, researchers have tried to find the average height by experiment. These experiments show that optimally balanced trees occur surprisingly often and that worst-case trees are relatively rare. By growing large numbers of AVL trees on random data, researchers have been able to show that the average number of comparisons needed to insert the nth item is about $\lg n + 1/4$ for large n. That is very good indeed.

5.9.2 Red-Black Trees

Red-black trees are easier to balance than AVL trees are. The code is shorter, and so the red-black algorithm is now frequently considered the method of choice. We will consider it in some detail.

In a red-black tree we mark each vertex. The mark requires only one bit, although, as the name implies, we normally associate colors with this bit, so a vertex is said to be red or black. A red-black tree has the following properties:

1. Every vertex is either red or black.

2. An empty tree is black.

3. A black vertex may have children of either color, but every red vertex has two black children.

4. Every path from the root to a leaf passes through the same number of black vertices.

(There's more to it than that, because a degenerate, all-black tree would meet these conditions. We will find, however, that if we make each leaf red when we insert it and then enforce these properties, the tree will be balanced.) For example, Fig. 5.17 shows a red-black tree; in this illustration the red vertices are drawn light and the black ones dark (the links to the vertices are drawn similarly for emphasis). You can see that this tree conforms to these properties; in this case every path from the root to a leaf passes through exactly two black vertices (three if you count the root itself).

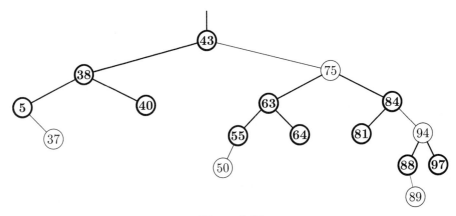

Figure 5.17

These rules tell us a fair amount about the balance of the tree. At the global level, it should be clear that in any path from the root to a leaf will never encounter two red vertices in a row; otherwise, there would be a red vertex with a red child. This in turn tells us that if the level of the highest leaf on the tree is k, then the level of the lowest leaf will be at most $2k + 1$. This can happen when the path to the highest leaf is all black and the path to the lowest leaf is alternating red and black, as is the case with the paths to the leaf 40 and that to the leaf 89 in the figure. This in turn puts a limit on the maximum amount of imbalance in the tree.

These rules also mean that the height a red-black tree with n vertices is at most $2\lg(n+1)$. To prove this, let $b(k)$ be the number of black vertices in the path from an interior vertex k to a leaf, not including k itself. We will call this the *black height* of the leaf. Then the subtree rooted in k contains at least $2^{b(k)} - 1$ vertices. We can show this by induction on the height of k. If the tree consists of a single node, its height is 0, $b(k) = 0$, and $2^0 - 1 = 0$. Next, suppose k is an internal node with two children x and y, as shown in Fig. 5.18.

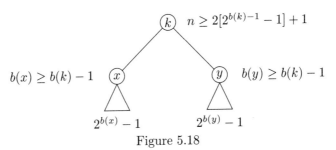

Figure 5.18

(In this figure the triangles represent the subtrees rooted in x and y. We are not showing the colors of these nodes; they may be any legal combination.) The inductive hypothesis is that the subtrees rooted in x and y contain at least $2^{b(x)} - 1$ and $2^{b(y)} - 1$ vertices, respectively, as shown by the expressions under the subtrees. But if k is red, then $b(x) = b(y) = b(k)$, and if k is black, then $b(x) = b(y) = b(k) - 1$. So each of these subtrees contains at least $2^{b(k)-1} - 1$ vertices, and the subtree rooted in k contains at least $2[2^{b(k)-1} - 1] + 1$ vertices. (The final $+1$ is for k itself.) But this is $2^{b(k)} - 1$, and that completes the inductive step. But in that case, if the entire tree, with root r, has a height of h, then $b(r) \geq h/2$. Therefore the entire tree has $n \geq 2^{h/2} - 1$ vertices; solving this for h gives us $h \leq 2 \lg(n + 1)$. This is not as nice as the $1.44 \lg n$ figure we had for AVL trees, but the difference is not enough to worry about, and in fact this is a very loose upper bound; in most cases the height is a good deal less. (We will come back to this point at the end of this section.)

At the local level, the color of a vertex and its children tell us about the balance of the subtrees, and these are what we use to tell us when and how to rotate. In particular, a red node can be thought of as an excess node, since any path through it to a leaf will be longer than the minimum-length path, and two red nodes in succession may result in a path that is longer than the maximum permissible. All we have to do is make sure that the subtree where we did the insertion or deletion obeys the rules, all the way back up to the root, and this alone is sufficient to keep the tree balanced.

Insertions. Our insertion procedure is the usual recursion for inserting a new node in a binary search tree. Every time we insert an item in the tree, it is added to the tree as a leaf, as usual, and colored red. Coloring it red forces the program to do any necessary rotations and avoids the degenerate case. It also means the new leaf's black height is the same as that of all other leaves. If its parent is black, there is no violation of the rules, since a black parent may have children of either color and since the new leaf does not change the number of black vertices in the path. But the parent itself may be red. If this is so, then we must adjust the parent and grandparent. But the grandparent is invisible to us at this point; we will not be able to make an adjustment until we have backed up two levels of recursion.

We handle this as follows. The levels of recursion correspond to levels on the tree. At each level we fix the child and grandchildren, if necessary; then if anything needs to be done at this level, we pass the word to the next level up.

Specifically, I will call the insertion procedure `RB_Insert`; its parameters will be the root of the tree (or subtree), the new node to be inserted, and a pointer I will call `excess_red`. After a recursive call to `RB_Insert`, this pointer lets the current root know whether any of its grandchildren have misbehaved. If so, we take corrective action at this level. The corrective action will ensure that the children and grandchildren obey all the conditions. After this has been done, we check the colors of the current node and its child. If all is well, we set `excess_red` to `nil`; otherwise we make `excess_red` point to the offending node, and this is passed back to the previous recursion for *it* to take corrective action.

This gives us the first approach to the insertion procedure. In the main program we declare

```
type
   hue = (red, black);
   treeptr = ^rbnode;
   rbnode = record
               key: integer;    { or whatever }
```

```
            data: {as appropriate};
            color: hue;
            left,
            right: treeptr
         end;
```

Then the insertion program takes the following general form:

```
function RB_INSERT (var r, x, excess_red: treeptr): boolean;
            { Red-black tree insertion.  r is current root; }
            {   x is node to be inserted; excess_red either }
            {   is nil or points to a red grandchild.        }
            {   Returns true if insertion successful,        }
            {   false in case of duplicate key.              }
   begin
   if r = nil then                    { Empty tree: insert at root }
      begin
      r := x;
      r^.color := red;
      excess_red := nil;
      rb_insert := true
      end
   else if x^.key = r^.key then { Duplicate key: error          }
      begin
      excess_red := nil;
      rb_insert := false
      end
   else if x^.key < r^.key then
      begin                           { Insert in left subtree     }
      rb_insert := rb_insert (r^.left, x, excess_red);
      if excess_red <> nil then
            { ==> take corrective action here    }
                              { Now check children              }
      if (r^.color = red) and (r^.left^.color = red) then
         excess_red := r^.left  { Pass the word up to the      }
      else                      {    next generation            }
         excess_red := nil
      end
   else
      begin                     { Insert in right subtree       }
      rb_insert := rb_insert (r^.right, x, excess_red);
      if excess_red <> nil then
            { ==> take corrective action here    }
                              { Now check children              }
      if (r^.color = red) and (r^.right^.color = red) then
         excess_red := r^.right { Pass the word up to the      }
      else                      {    next generation            }
```

```
        excess_red := nil
    end
end;  { RB_Insert }
```

Notice that this is the usual recursive insertion algorithm with only minor changes. As usual, `newnode` is allocated and stuffed with data in the calling program. Notice also that the process divides neatly into three phases: In making the recursions, we are searching for a place to insert the new node; on the last recursion, we insert the node; and returning from the recursions, we correct the balance as we work back up the tree to the root. This is essentially what we did with AVL trees.

For example, suppose we have just added a leaf z to the following tree:

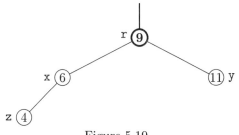

Figure 5.19

The children of z are both `nil`; these are considered black, so there is no problem at that level and we set `excess_red` to `nil`. Returning to the previous recursion, we find `excess_red` = `nil` and no corrective action need be taken. But at this level we find that x and z are both red; hence we send word of this up to the top generation by making `excess_red` point to z.

At r, we can get color information about r, x, and y directly, and we have access to z by way of `excess_red`. We are thus in a perfect position to correct these four nodes as needed. (In this particular case it is enough to change r to red and x and y to black.) All other cases are handled similarly, but the repairs may be more complicated and in some cases involve single or double rotations.

The other cases generally arise in the course of working back up the tree after the recursive calls. There are six cases in all, but three of them occur after making an insertion into the right subtree and are the mirror images of the ones that may occur after insertion into the left subtree. For brevity, then, we will consider only the latter. As in our previous example, we will refer to the current root as r and call its children x and y; the vertex at fault is z. In all cases x and z are both red. Then the three cases we must consider are:

1. x and y are both red.

2. y is black and z is the left child of x.

3. y is black and z is the right child of x.

The colors from x on up are the same as they were before insertion, so they are correct. The colors from z on down are correct, because they were corrected as we worked up the recursions from the leaf. Hence, the problem we must deal with is local to x and z. We must correct this problem in a way that leaves all the black heights unchanged.

We have seen Case 1 in Fig. 5.19, but here it is again in greater generality. The dark nodes are black and the light nodes red; the little triangles indicate the subtrees rooted in the various nodes. Note that if x is red, r and q must be black, because at this level the tree was all right before the insertion was made. If we make r red and x and y black, we have corrected the problem without changing the number of black nodes in the path from r to any leaf. (Making y black doesn't violate any of our rules, because a black vertex may have children of either color.)

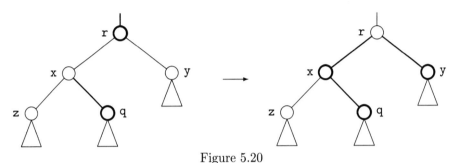

Figure 5.20

Two consecutive red nodes are normally a danger sign. In this case they are a false alarm; we were able to correct the black height of z's leaves without doing a rotation.

In Case 2 (y black, z the left child of x), the rules about color guarantee that r and q will both be black. If we change the colors as we did the time before, we will violate Condition 4. The only way we can handle this is by doing a right rotation on x and r, as shown; then we can safely make the new root x black and its children z and r red:

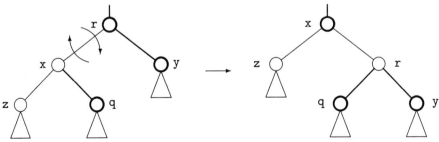

Figure 5.21

This makes the tree comply with the conditions. The two consecutive red nodes were the sign that the leftmost subtree was too high, and the rotation corrected this.

Case 3 (y black, z the right child of x) looks as shown in Fig. 5.22. Since x is red, q must have been black; similarly since z is red, z_1 and z_2 must be black. This is the case that requires a double rotation. As usual, the preliminary rotation is one level down, between x and z, as shown in Fig. 5.22 (a).

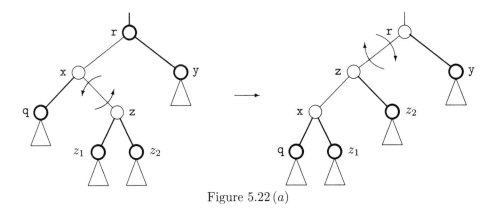

Figure 5.22 (a)

We will not make any color changes until after the second rotation, which is between **r** and **z**. When this rotation has been done, all the black vertices are grandchildren; hence, we can now make **x** and **r** red and **z**, the new root, black.

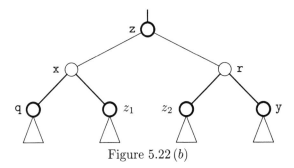

Figure 5.22 (b)

Notice that it wasn't any global examination of the tree that told us to make the double rotation, but only the presence of two consecutive red nodes and the position of **z**. If the colors are right, then the tree will be right. You should verify that if **q** and its subtree were all right before the double rotation, and if **x**, **y**, and **z** were all right, then the result in Fig. 5.22 (b) conforms to all the rules.

We can now fill in the missing blanks in the code. We have an auxiliary procedure, `Set_Colors`, which sets the colors of the root and its children:

```
procedure SET_COLORS(var root: treeptr; rootcolor, kidcolor: hue);
   begin
   if root^.left <> nil then
      root^.left^.color := kidcolor;
   if root^.right <> nil then
      root^.right^.color := kidcolor;
   root^.color := rootcolor;
   end;  { Set_Colors }
```

Then the main insertion procedure is as follows:

```
function RB_INSERT (var r, x, excess_red: treeptr): boolean;
              { Red-black tree insertion.  r is current root; }
              {   x is node to be inserted; excess_red either }
              {   is nil or points to a red grandchild.        }
              {   Returns true if insertion successful,        }
              {   false in case of duplicate key.              }
begin
if r = nil then                    { Empty tree: insert at root }
   begin
   r := x;
   r^.color := red;
   excess_red := nil;
   rb_insert := true
   end
else if x^.key = r^.key then { Duplicate key: error           }
   begin
   excess_red := nil;
   rb_insert := false
   end
else if x^.key < r^.key then
   begin                          { Insert in left subtree     }
   rb_insert := rb_insert (r^.left, x, excess_red);
   if excess_red <> nil then { Both kids red: color flip  }
      if r^.right^.color = red then
         setcolors (r, red, black)
      else if excess_red = r^.left^.left then
         begin                    { Single rotation            }
         rotate (r, right);
         setcolors (r, red, black);
         end
      else
         begin                    { Double rotation            }
         rotate (r^.left, left);
         rotate (r, right);
         setcolors (r, black, red)
         end;
   if (r^.color = red) and (r^.left^.color = red) then
      excess_red := r^.left  { Pass the word up to the    }
   else                         {   next generation           }
      excess_red := nil
   end
else
   ...                          { Mirror image for insertion }
                                { in right subtree           }
```

```
end;  { RB_Insert }
```

This code is considerably more economical and concise than is the code for AVL insertion.

It is helpful to see the entire process at work. Here are the stages in the growth of a red-black tree; the keys are 91, 2, 75, 65, 45, 40, 47, 77, 97, 38, 8, inserted in that order:

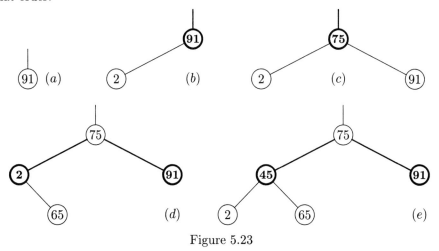

Figure 5.23

After insertion of 40, 47, 77, and 97:

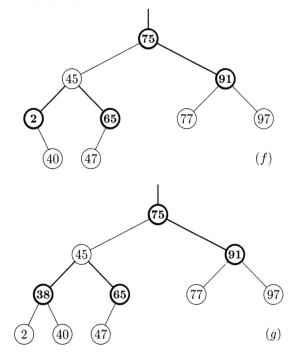

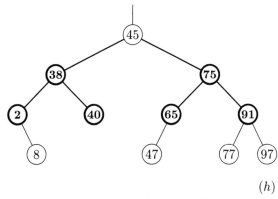

(h)

Figure 5.23 (continued)

Notice that in rebalancing after insertion, we may have to continue doing color changes all the way up to the root of the tree; hence, the time complexity of this process is $O(\lg n)$. But color changes are simple operations, and once we have performed rotations at any level, the root at that level is left black, and the process terminates. Hence, the number of actual structural alterations required is $O(1)$.

Deletions. In deletion, we follow the usual recursive algorithm, patching around the target if it has only one subtree, or copying and deleting its immediate successor if it has two subtrees.

As with insertions, we check the local correctness of the tree as we return from each recursive call. In insertion, the principal concern was that no red node should have a red child. In deletion, we must make sure the number of black nodes in each path is not changed. If the vertex deleted is red, there is no problem, since deleting a red vertex will not change the black height of any of its descendants.

If the vertex deleted is black, then we are shy one black vertex on the paths to all its descendants. We must then correct its ancestors until all black heights are the same over the entire tree. It may help to think of the parent of the deleted vertex as having to be "doubly black" in order to keep all the black heights equal. But it's *impossible* for a vertex to be doubly black; hence, we must make corrections farther up the tree that will absorb that excess blackness and enable the node at fault to revert to "single blackness."

We can make these corrections as the unwinding recursions take us back up the tree. We will use a variable of type **hue** called **testcolor** to indicate what the color of the deleted vertex was and thus whether corrections need to be made. If the deleted vertex was red, then **testcolor** has the value RED and nothing need be done. If the deleted vertex was black, then **testcolor** is likewise BLACK. This variable will also be passed up the tree as the recursions unwind and corrections continue until **testcolor** becomes RED. We will see that the corrections do not generally continue for very long.

Tarjan [1983] identifies two cases that can arise when **testcolor** is BLACK. In both these cases, the vertex that has been deleted has changed the black height of the subtree rooted in a vertex we will call **v**. Vertex **v** is the one at fault, the one that is "doubly black." The parent of v we will call u, and it is when the unwinding recursions have brought us back to u that we make the corrections. We will consider only the case where v is u's left child; the treatment when v is the right child is the mirror image of what we describe here. The other subtree of u is rooted in w, and the cases depend on the colors of w and its children. Note that u may be either red or black.

In Case 1, w is black. This case has three subcases, depending on the colors of w's children; these are shown in Fig. 5.24 (*a–c*). (The little triangles represent the subtrees of the various vertices, as usual.) In Case 1*a*, w's children x and y are both black.

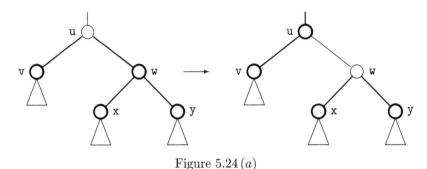

Figure 5.24 (*a*)

In this case, it is necessary only to make w red and u black. (Since x and y are both black, we can safely make w red.) This restores the black heights in the subtree rooted in v without disturbing those in w's subtree. I have shown u as red and the correction has made it black. If u was already black at the start, then it is now "doubly black" and the corrections must continue up the tree.

In Case 1*b*, w's right child is red. In this case, we must rotate u and w left to correct the tree, as shown in Fig. 5.24 (*b*).

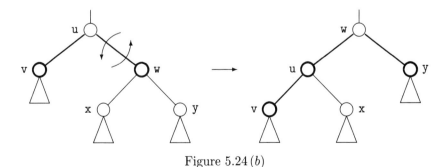

Figure 5.24 (*b*)

Here the rotation has moved an additional black vertex into the path to v so that v needs now be only singly black. I have shown vertex x as red here, but it may be red or black; in either case its color remains unchanged. In these rotations, w inherits u's color. Thus the color of the root is unchanged and the corrections terminate.

In Case 1*c*, **w**'s left child is red. This means that the problem lies in the middle subtree, and we must make two rotations, first rotating **w** and **x** to the right and then rotating **u** and **x** to the left, as shown in Fig. 5.24 (*c*).

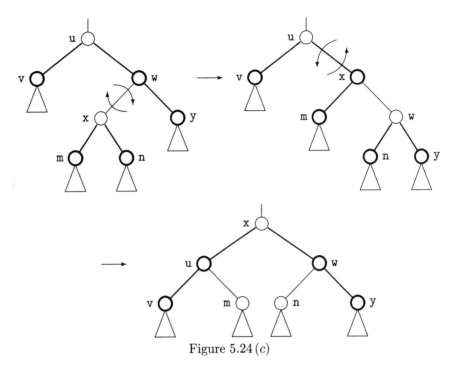

Figure 5.24 (*c*)

Here again the color of the root is unchanged and the process terminates.

In Case 2, vertex **w** is red. This requires two operations: first, we rotate **u** and **w** to the left. Vertex **w** inherits **u**'s color, but vertex **u** is made red, as can be seen in Fig. 5.25.

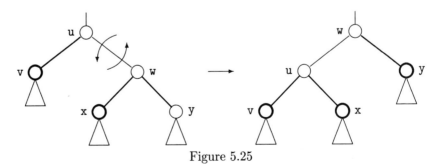

Figure 5.25

This hasn't solved the problem, however, because **v** is still "doubly black." Hence, we complete the process by applying Case 1 to **u** in its new position. Since **u** is initially red, Case 1*a* will always terminate when applied to **u**.

The algorithm for deletion takes the following form:

1. If root is `nil`, indicate failure and set `testcolor` to `nil`

2. Else if key is less than `root^.key`, delete from left subtree. If, after deletion, `testcolor` is BLACK, call **Rebalance**.

3. Else if key is greater than `root^.key`, delete from right subtree. If, after deletion, `testcolor` is BLACK, call **Rebalance**.

4. Else if no left subtree, splice around vertex to be deleted. If vertex and right child both black, set `testcolor` to BLACK, otherwise to RED.

5. Else if no right subtree, splice around vertex to be deleted. If vertex and left child both black, set `testcolor` to BLACK, otherwise to RED.

6. Else find successor, copy successor's data fields, and delete successor instead. If after deletion `testcolor` is BLACK, call **Rebalance**.

Rebalance is the procedure that handles Tarjan's two cases; we will consider this later.

This leads to the following implementation:

```
function RB_DELETE (var r: treeptr; var testcolor: hue;
                            kk: keytype): boolean;
                    { Red-black deletion             }
                    { Attempts to delete record with key }
                    {   kk.  Returns true if deleted,    }
                    {   false if not found.          }
   var
      q: treeptr;   { for finding successor }
   begin
   if r = nil then
      begin
      rb_delete := false;        { Wasn't found        }
      testcolor := red           { No fixup            }
      end
   else
      if kk < r^.key then        { Delete from left    }
         begin                   {   subtree           }
         rb_delete := rb_delete (r^.left, testcolor, kk);
         if testcolor = black then
            rebalance (r, testcolor, left)
         end
      else if kk > r^.key then   { Delete from right   }
         begin                   {   subtree           }
         rb_delete := rb_delete (r^.right, testcolor, kk);
         if testcolor = black then
            rebalance (r, testcolor, right)
         end
```

```
              else                          { Found                    }
          if r^.left = nil then
              begin                         { No left subtree:          }
              q := r;                       {   easy case               }
              r := r^.right;
              if r = nil then
                  testcolor := q^.color { Empty tree is black       }
              else
                  testcolor := red;
              if r <> nil then
                  r^.color := black;
              dispose (q);
              rb_delete := true
              end
          else if r^.right = nil then
              begin                         { No right subtree:         }
              q := r;                       {   easy case               }
              r := r^.left;
              if r = nil then               { Empty tree is black       }
                  testcolor := q^.color
              else
                  testcolor := red;
              if r <> nil then
                  r^.color := black;
              dispose (q);
              rb_delete := true
              end
          else                              { Has two subtrees          }
              begin
              q := r^.right;
              while q^.left <> nil do        { Find successor            }
                  q := q^.left;
              r^.key := q^.key;              { Copy successor's key      }
              r^.data := q^.data;            {   & data                  }
              rb_delete :=                   { Delete successor          }
                  rb_delete (r^.right, testcolor, q^.key);
              if testcolor = black then
                  rebalance (r, testcolor, right)
              end
      end;   { RB_Delete }
```

Rebalance handles Tarjan's two cases. We use `testcolor` in two ways here; it is set to BLACK in Case 1*a* if the repairs must continue up the tree. This makes `RB_Delete` call Rebalance again as it returns from the next recursion. In the other cases, the repairs terminate at the current generation, and we set `testcolor` to RED to prevent further calls as `RB_Delete`'s recursions unwind.

Here is the code: We have declared a type direction to be (left, right), and the parameter dir informs Rebalance which child of u is "doubly black."

```
procedure REBALANCE (var u: treeptr; var testcolor: hue;
                          dir: direction);
                 { Corrects red-black tree after deletion      }
      var              { u is parent of node at fault   }
         w,            { w is sib of node at fault      }
         x, y: treeptr; { x, y are w's kids             }
      begin
      if dir = left then
         begin
         w := u^.right; { Select sib    }
         x := w^.left;  {   & kids       }
         y := w^.right
         end
      else  { dir right }
         begin
         w := u^.left;
         x := w^.right;
         y := w^.left
         end;
      if w^.color = black then           {  ===== Case 1 =====   }
                                         { NB: nil is black       }
         if ((x = nil) or (x^.color = black)) and
                     ((y = nil) or (y^.color = black)) then
            begin                        { Case 1a         }
            testcolor := u^.color;       { Remember u's color   }
            u^.color := black;           { Color flip    }
            w^.color := red
            end
         else if y^.color = red then
            begin                        { Case 1b         }
            w^.color := u^.color;
            rotate (u, dir);             { Single rotation       }
            u^.left^.color := black;
            u^.right^.color := black;
            testcolor := red             { Terminates    }
            end
         else
            begin                        { Case 1c         }
            x^.color := u^.color;
            u^.color := black;
            if dir = left then           { Double rotation       }
               rotate (u^.right, right)
            else
```

```
                    rotate (u^.left, left);
                rotate (u, dir);
                testcolor := red              { Terminates    }
                end
        else  { w is red }
           begin                              {  ===== Case 2 =====   }
           w^.color := u^.color;
           u^.color := red;
           rotate (u, dir);                   { Single rotation       }
           if dir = left then                 { Apply Case 1  }
              rebalance (u^.left, testcolor, dir)
           else
              rebalance (u^.right, testcolor, dir);
           testcolor := red                   { Terminates    }
           end
   end;  { Rebalance }
```

The recursions will always go from a leaf back up to the root of the tree; hence, in a tree with n vertices, the time complexity of the deletion process is $O(\lg n)$, as it was for insertion. But most of the work consists of doing rotations and adjusting colors, and it should be clear that, since the process terminates at any level at which we do rotations, we require at worst three rotations for any deletion. The worst case arises if Case 2 is followed by Case 1c. Hence the number of structural alterations needed on any deletion is $O(1)$, as in the case of insertions.

Comparisons. Knuth [1973] describes an exhaustive test of AVL trees made from seven keys in every possible permutation. Of the 5,040 trees that resulted, 2,160 were perfectly balanced and the rest were of height 3. Hence, for trees of this size the average height is 2.57. Duplicating this experiment with red-black trees we find 1,584 perfectly balanced trees and the rest of height 3; the average height is 2.69. In no case do we find the theoretical maximum height of $2\lg 8 = 6$. Trees this small do not yield very persuasive results. For trees with 8 and 9 keys, both the AVL and red-black algorithms yield trees of height 3 for all permutations of the keys. The next really meaningful size is probably 12 keys, the size of the next larger Fibonacci tree; but 12 keys have 479,001,600 permutations, and one's patience runs out at that point.

5.10   SUMMARY

Binary search trees give us the flexibility of a linked data structure with the ease of access we associate otherwise only with sorted arrays. In a well-balanced tree, the search time is competitive with binary search. We have seen a sorting procedure based on binary search trees, but in a sense this is superfluous, since we could argue that the data in a binary search tree are essentially sorted already.

The main weaknesses of binary search trees are the possibility of degenerate trees and problems with deletion. The only way we will know whether we must worry about degenerate trees is by studying the application for which the tree is being used. If we know the size of the tree will always be small (*e.g.*, fewer than 100 nodes), or if we know the data will arrive in random order, then a degenerate tree is generally not worth worrying about. Otherwise, it is prudent to use a red-black tree to avoid the problem.

Deleting data is nearly always troublesome. This is true even of arrays; only in an unordered linear linked list can we delete an element without having to fuss around to make sure everything is left as it should be. (Stacks and queues are also structures in which deletion is simple.) Fortunately, there are many tree applications in which deletions are rarely or never necessary.

5.11 PROBLEMS

5.1. Trace the growth of a binary search tree when the following keys are inserted in the order given:

    (a) 1, 23, 6, 11, 46, 32, 18, 4.

    (b) 23, 5, 82, 51, 34, 15, 7, 66.

    (c) 4, 14, 23, 34, 42, 51, 59, 66, 72.

5.2. Trace the steps when searching the tree of Problem 5.1 (a) for the keys 23, 32, and 19.

5.3. List the nodes in the following trees when traversed in preorder, inorder, and postorder:

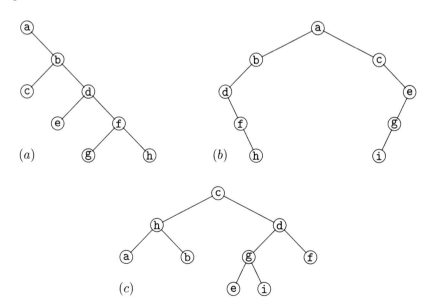

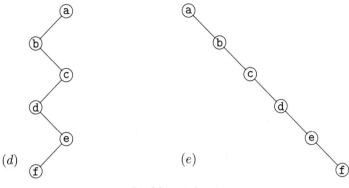

Problem 5.3

5.4. Trace the level-by-level traversal of the tree in Problem 5.3 (*c*).

5.5. Write a procedure that will count the nodes in a binary search tree.

5.6. Since the recursions we use when inserting a node come at the very end of the procedure, these are tail recursions. It should thus be relatively easy to find a nonrecursive version of the procedure. Do so.

5.7. (a) Trace the steps when deleting the node **g** in the following tree. (b) Trace the steps when deleting the node **a** using method 1. (c) Trace the steps when deleting the node **j**. (d) Trace the steps when deleting the node **c** using method 1.

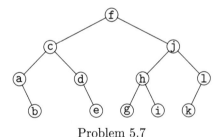

Problem 5.7

5.8. If we delete any arbitrary vertex A from a binary tree, using method 2, and then delete any arbitrary vertex B, will the tree end up with the same shape as if we had deleted B first and then A?

5.9. (a) Using the tree shown in Problem 5.7, trace the steps when deleting the node A using method 2. (b) Trace the steps when deleting the node C using method 2.

5.10. Write a deletion procedure that implements deletion method 1 (moving the right and left subtrees).

5.11. Write a deletion procedure that implements deletion method 3 (moving the successor into the target's place).

5.12. Write a procedure that will replace a binary search tree by its mirror image (so that an inorder traversal will list the keys in *descending* order).

5.13. It can be very helpful to be able to display a binary tree stored in computer memory. If you have a graphics capability on your computer and are handy with it, write a procedure that will do this.

5.14. In the absence of a display capability, the following strategy is a crude substitute for drawing a picture of a tree: List the contents of the left subtree within a pair of parentheses, then list the root, and then list the contents of the right subtree within a pair of parentheses. In listing the subtrees, apply this principle "all the way down," so that, for example, the tree

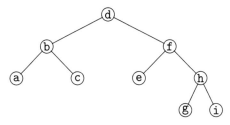

Problem 5.14

is listed as

```
((a)b(c))d((e)f((g)h(i))).
```

(Notice that empty trees do not get parentheses.) Write a procedure to do this.

5.15. Another way to draw a tree is to use the outline form as a model. An outline looks like this:

   I. First Part
      A. One Subsection
      B. Another Subsection
         1. One Subsubsection
         2. Another Subsubsection
  II. Second Part
 III. Third Part

... and so on. Outlines and trees are, in fact, isomorphic if we ignore the fact that the outline omits the root of its tree. We can take advantage of this correspondence to list a graph, omitting the Roman and Arabic numbers and using only indentation. The outline representation of the graph in the previous question would then be

```
D
    B
        A
        C
    F
        E
        H
            G
            I
```

Write a procedure that will list the nodes of a binary search tree in outline form. You will need some way of keeping track of the levels of the nodes; it should not be necessary to make the level global.

5.16. A *pre*order traversal of a binary tree (not a binary search tree) yields the following sequence of keys:

> C A D G B H F I E

An *in*order traversal of the same tree yields the following sequence of keys:

> G D A H F B C I E

Draw the tree.

5.17. Write a program to solve the previous problem and display the tree.

5.18. (a) Can a tree be reconstructed from a postorder and inorder traversal? (b) Can a tree be reconstructed from a postorder and preorder traversal?

5.19. We can carry out a nonrecursive inorder traversal with the aid of a stack, as follows:

> Empty the stack.
>
> Set a pointer p to the root of the tree.
>
> Repeat
>> If the (sub)tree is not empty,
>>> Push p
>>>
>>> Go to the left subtree
>>
>> else if the stack is not empty,
>>> Pop p
>>>
>>> Visit p
>>>
>>> Go to the right subtree
>
> Until p = nil and the stack is empty.

Using this as a guide, program a nonrecursive inorder traversal.

5.20. Modify the nonrecursive algorithm in the previous problem to perform a preorder traversal.

5.21. There are $\frac{1}{5}\binom{8}{4} = 14$ binary trees with 4 nodes. But there are $4! = 24$ possible permutations of a set of four keys. So every permutation doesn't result in a different binary search tree if the keys are entered in that order. Draw the 14 different binary trees, determine which permutations result in which trees, and from that determine the probability that each tree will occur and the average height of the trees over all permutations.

5.22. Show how Eq. (5.8) follows from Eq. (5.7).

5.23. A *completely full* binary tree of height h is one all of whose leaves lie on the same level. Show (a) that the external path length of such a tree is $h2^h$ and (b) that the internal path length is $(h-2)2^h + 2$. (c) Use the results of Section 5.7 to find expressions for the average cost of a successful search and of an unsuccessful search as a function of n.

5.24. Trace the growth of an AVL tree when the following keys are inserted in the order given:

  (a) 5, 13, 33, 46, 45, 52, 58, 68.

  (b) 9, 83, 13, 79, 21, 58, 29, 46.

5.25. Trace the growth of a red-black tree when the following keys are inserted in the order given:

  (a) 5, 13, 33, 46, 45, 52, 58, 68.

  (b) 9, 83, 13, 79, 21, 58, 29, 46.

5.26. In programming AVL insertions and deletions, it is helpful to have a procedure, which we might call `AVL_Check`, that will verify that that the heights of each node's subtrees differ by at most 1 and that the balance flags are properly set. Write such a procedure. It is probably best to base it on a postorder traversal, so that when you visit the root you have the heights of the two subtrees available for immediate use.

5.27. Write a similar procedure for checking red-black trees. The procedure should verify that the number of black nodes in the path to every leaf is the same and that no red node has a red child.

5.28. Write a procedure that will determine the maximum height of a binary search tree. Use this procedure to find the maximum height of a large number of AVL trees grown from random data and compare the results with the theoretical maximum of $1.44 \lg n$.

5.29. Use the same procedure to find the maximum height of a large number of red-black trees and compare the results with the theoretical maximum of $2 \lg(n+1)$.

CHAPTER 6

GENERAL TREE ALGORITHMS

Trees are used everywhere in computer applications. Binary search trees are probably the most important kind, but there are many other kinds of trees. In this chapter, we consider some of the more important ones and their applications.

6.1 MULTIWAY TREES AND FORESTS

The obvious alternative to the binary tree is a tree in which nodes may have more than two children. We will encounter some specific trees of this kind later in the chapter; here we consider such trees in general and how they may be stored in memory. The method we show can be adapted to store sets of trees as well.

6.1.1 Multiway Trees

There are many applications in which we need to provide a vertex with more than two subtrees. Figure 6.1 illustrates such a tree.

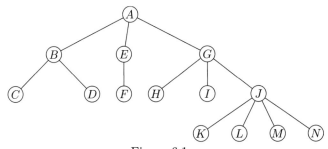

Figure 6.1

If we took the implementation of binary trees as our starting point, we might be tempted to declare nodes for such a tree with something like

```
type
    treeptr = ^treenode;
    treenode = record
```

```
               key: {whatever};
               data: {whatever};
               sub1,
               sub2,
               sub3,
               sub4: treeptr;
           end;
```

The obvious problem with such an approach is that we are locked into exactly four subtrees for each vertex. In some cases, this restriction is acceptable, but in general, if only a few vertices have this many children, most of that space goes to waste, and if even one vertex requires five children we are out of luck.

A much simpler and more flexible structure provides a pointer to the eldest (leftmost) child and a link to that child's younger brother, as shown in Fig. 6.2.

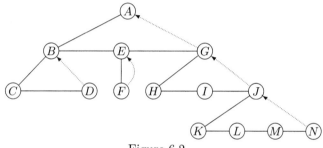

Figure 6.2

For this more economical structure, we can use the following declarations:

```
type
   treeptr = ^treenode;
   treenode = record
                key: {whatever};
                data: {whatever};
                eldest,
                next: treeptr;
            end;
```

This is clearly capable of indefinite expansion. The **next** field of the last vertex in any horizontal chain is normally set to **nil**, although for purposes of working back up the tree without recursion, it may sometimes be made to point back to the parent, as suggested by the dotted arrows in Fig. 6.2.

Another possible solution to the problem of multiple children is simply to provide each node with a pointer to its parent instead of pointers to its children. So a tree like that in Fig. 6.3 (*a*) can be replaced by one like that in Fig. 6.3 (*b*). Whether this is practical depends, of course, on how the tree is to be used. Normally, we start at the root and work down, and in this case we need pointers to the children. We will see an application that uses paternal pointers in Section 6.3.

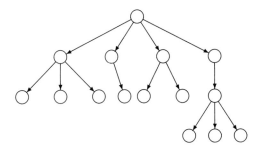

Figure 6.3 (*a*)

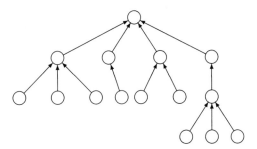

Figure 6.3 (*b*)

6.1.2   Forests

A graph may occasionally consist of two components, each of which is a tree. In that case, we call the collection of trees a *forest*. (If the ordering of the trees is important, they are sometimes called an *orchard.*) Figure 6.4 shows a forest.

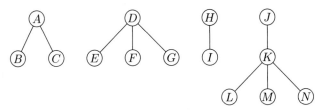

Figure 6.4

Again, we would like to use our more flexible eldest-child/younger-brother structure for these trees. In addition, however, it may be convenient to link the trees together, especially if they form an orchard. We can do this by making the root of each tree after the first one the younger brother of the root immediately to its left, as shown in Fig. 6.5.

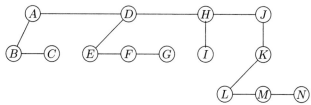

Figure 6.5

What we have ended up with as a result of this transformation is isomorphic to a binary tree. Indeed, if we could grasp that forest by vertex *A* and shake it gently, we would get the binary tree shown in Fig. 6.6.

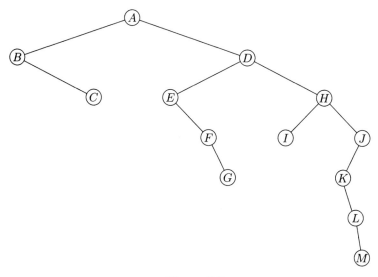

Figure 6.6

The programming equivalent of shaking the tree is nothing more than changing the eldest-child pointers to *left*-child pointers and the younger-brother pointers to *right*-child pointers.

The similarity to a binary tree goes beyond this structural resemblance, however. We can extend the definition of a preorder traversal of such a forest to mean traversing the trees from left to right and, in each tree, visiting the root before traversing any of the subtrees in preorder. There is a surprisingly simple way to do this, which takes advantage of this isomorphism: We just adapt our ordinary binary traversal procedure, doing nothing more than changing `left` to `eldest` and `right` to `next`:

```
procedure PREORDER (root: treeptr);
   begin                           { Preorder traversal of forest  }
   if root <> nil then
      begin
      visit (root);
```

```
        preorder (root^.eldest);
        preorder (root^.next)
        end;
    end;  { PreOrder }
```

The same thing can be done with a postorder traversal. The parallel breaks down in the case of an inorder traversal, since it is not clear when we would want to visit the root when there are more than two subtrees. A level-by-level traversal uses a queue, as in the case of a binary search tree, but in order to handle each level, we put only the eldest children on the queue and take care of the younger brothers with a while loop:

```
procedure LEVELS (root: treeptr);
                            { Does level-by-level traversal }
    var                     {    of forest                  }
        p: treeptr;
    begin
    clear_queue;
    en_queue (root);              { Root goes on queue       }
    repeat
        de_queue (p);             { Take vertex off queue  }
        while p <> nil do         { Visit it & next of kin }
            begin
            visit (p);
            en_queue (p^.eldest); { Eldest goes on queue    }
            p := p^.next
            end;
    until empty_queue;
    end;  { Levels }
```

The Clear_Queue, En_Queue, De_Queue, and Empty_Queue operations are the familiar ones used with the queue ADT.

6.2 HEAPS AND PRIORITY QUEUES

A *heap* is a binary tree with some special properties:

1. All the leaves are on the bottom level or one level up.

2. All the leaves on the bottom level are as far to the left as possible.

3. There is no ordering between left and right children.

4. The key in any node is at least as large as the keys of its children (if any).

Notice that where the ordering in a binary search tree is between left and right subtrees, here the ordering is between generations. Because there is no ordering between left and right children, heaps are sometimes called *partially ordered trees*.

(If this reminds you of partially ordered sets, you are on the right track: A Hasse diagram is *not* a heap (in fact, it frequently isn't even a tree), but it shares with the heap the property that there is an implicit ordering between parents and children but none between brothers, cousins, nieces, third cousins once removed, and so forth.)

This organization is of interest because it is easy to create and easy to maintain, because it is a balanced binary tree with a height of only $\lceil \lg(n+1) - 1 \rceil$ (where n is the number of elements), and because we can store a heap in an ordinary array instead of using linked storage. Figure 6.7 shows a heap, drawn as a tree:

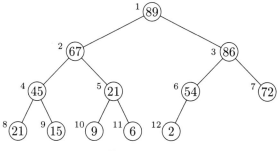

Figure 6.7

To place this heap into an array, we number the nodes horizontally from left to right. (In Fig. 6.7, these numbers are the small ones next to each node.) The numbers give us the positions in the array in which the nodes go, and they tell us something else as well: If a node is in position i in the array, then its left child will be in position $2i$, its right child will be in position $2i + 1$, and its parent will be in position $\lfloor n/2 \rfloor$. This is the reason for the first two properties previously listed: they are what let us use this handy way of climbing up and down the tree, and the heap fills the array without any gaps.

Figure 6.8 shows that same heap drawn as an array:

1	2	3	4	5	6	7	8	9	10	11	12
89	67	86	45	21	54	72	21	15	9	6	2

Figure 6.8

Notice that looking at the array tells you nothing; you have to redraw the array as a tree, using the numbering scheme I have described, to see that it is actually a heap.

This method of storage gives us two things: (1) It stores the tree in an array as compactly as possible, and (2) it gives us an easy way to find the children or the parent of any node without the use of pointers. These two things are important in creating and maintaining a heap.

In many applications, it is important to find the greatest (or smallest) element in a hurry. A heap is ideal for this, because the greatest element is always at the start of the array. If we need to find the smallest element, we can invert property

4 above and make the key in the parent *less* than the keys in either of its children. (We may call such a heap a heap of losers.)

Heaps have two natural applications. We can use them to maintain priority queues and we can use them for yet another sorting method. In an ordinary queue, elements leave the queue in the order in which they arrived: first in is first out. In a priority queue, elements leave the queue in the order of their importance. A high-priority item, entering at the tail, pushes its way up to the head of the queue and will be bumped down to a lower position only if some other element with an even higher priority arrives. Priority queues are elitist.

We may define the ADT `Priority_Queue` as follows:

A priority queue is a data structure each of whose elements has an associated value, which we may call a priority. There are two basic operations associated with a priority queue:

- Insert a new element.
- Retrieve the element having the highest priority, unless the queue is empty.

Since we have already used `En_Queue`, and so forth, for regular queues, we will name these operations `Insert_Heap` and `Delete_Heap`, respectively. The importance of the heap structure is that it enables us to perform the second operation quickly. We could use an ordinary unsorted array to implement a priority queue, but locating the element with the highest priority would then require a sequential search, which costs $O(n)$ comparisons if there are n elements in the queue. We will see that the cost of retrieving the highest-priority element from a heap is $O(1)$ and that the cost of maintaining the heap property is $O(\lg n)$.

Priority queues are used in multitasking operating systems, in which different users' jobs have different priorities and where the high-priority jobs must be served first. Heaps are ideal for this purpose; they require no more complexity than an array, and the algorithms we will outline for maintaining the heap property will automatically move high-priority requests up the queue until they land in their proper place. The server can then pick the highest-priority request in the queue just by removing the first element of the array. When this has been done, the remaining items can be moved up the queue by restoring the heap property.

We will encounter priority queues when we consider external sorting, where we will want to select the smallest of a group of input records to be written to the output file; in graph algorithms, where they will control the order in which the various vertices of the graph are handled; and in Huffman coding, where we need to find the smallest and second-smallest elements of large arrays repeatedly.

For internal sorting, a priority queue will clearly speed up the logic of the selection sort. You will recall that the selection sort finds the greatest unsorted element and swaps it into its proper place. We had to do a sequential search to find that greatest element, but if we kept the unsorted elements in a heap, this wouldn't be necessary. Of course, after swapping the greatest element into place we must then restore the heap property, but we will find that even this costs less than the sequential search would have cost.

6.2.1   Creating and Maintaining a Heap

When you add a new element to a priority queue, you must first move it, and possibly other elements, around until they make a heap. This has been called "heapifying," and that's what I will call it.

Heapifying.   The general idea is this: We grow the heap one element at a time. If a new element violates the heap requirement (*i.e.*, has a greater priority than its parent), then we swap the two elements. After every swap, we have to compare the parent and grandparent the same way and swap if necessary, working this way back to the root. We call this *sifting up*. We add a new element to the heap simply by putting it at the end of the array and sifting up. In the code that follows, we assume that we have the following declarations in the main program:

```
const
   heapsize = 64;  { or whatever: capacity of the heap}
type
   keytype = {some appropriate type};
   heaprecord = record
                   key: keytype;
                   {other things as needed}
                end;
   heap = array [1..heapsize] of heaprecord;
```

The key field will contain the priority associated with each record.

Then our procedure for inserting in a heap is as follows. The parameters are a, the heap itself, x, the record being inserted, and n, the current size of the heap.

```
procedure INSERT_HEAP (var a: heap; x: heaprecord;
           var n: integer);    { Inserts x in a heap cur-  }
   begin                       {    rently holding n records }
   n := n + 1;
   a[n]  := x;
   siftup (a, n);       { Restore heap property }
   end;  { Insert_Heap }
```

Before we look at the code for SiftUp, let us consider what it is supposed to do. We can see this best with an example. In the following diagrams, the data are shown as an array across the top, and the heap grows just underneath. The array subscripts are written above the corresponding boxes in the array and next to the tree nodes. I will use an arrow to show the element to which the subscript i is pointing.

Initially, the array is empty. Suppose the first element inserted has the key 53. Then the heap looks like Fig. 6.9 (*a*).

Figure 6.9 (*a*)

A single element is always a heap, so no adjustment is necessary and we go on to add the second element. Suppose its key is 32; this gives us Fig. 6.9 (*b*)

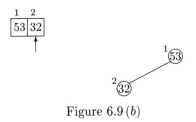

Figure 6.9 (*b*)

The heap requirement is that each parent be at least as big as both its children; here $53 \geq 32$, so this is still a heap. Now suppose the third element has the key 85, as shown in Fig. 6.9 (*c*).

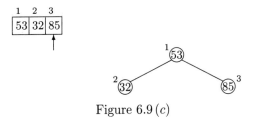

Figure 6.9 (*c*)

This violates the heap requirement, because $85 > 53$. So we swap the two, as in Fig. 6.9 (*d*).

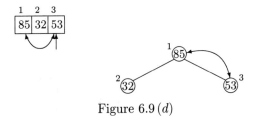

Figure 6.9 (*d*)

We now see what `SiftUp` is for: Its job is to restore the heap property, if necessary, after each new element is added.

We now add the fourth element. Suppose its key is 19; then we have Fig. 6.9 (*e*).

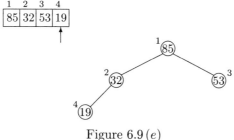

Figure 6.9 (*e*)

This time, the new element has a key less than that of its parent, so that the heap property is preserved and no adjustment is necessary. Adding a fifth element with the key 97 gives us:

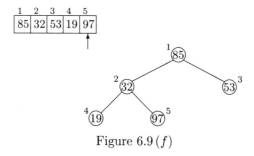

Figure 6.9 (*f*)

Now 97 > 32, so we must swap up. But when we swap 97 with 32, we still don't have a heap, because 97 > 85, too. So there's a second swap, bringing the 97 to the top of the heap:

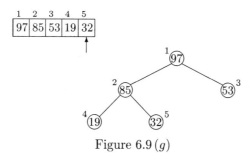

Figure 6.9 (*g*)

This should be enough to convey the general idea. Notice that swapping a child with its parent doesn't affect the heap property with its brother. If we had a heap before adding the new child, then the parent was greater than the brother. Since the new element is greater than the parent, it will certainly be greater than its brother. After inserting the keys 8, 53, 19, and 46, we have the heap shown in Fig. 6.9 (*h*).

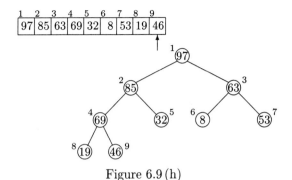

Figure 6.9 (h)

These examples should make the following algorithm for heapification clear:

While child is not the root and child's priority is greater than parent's:

a. Swap parent and child;

b. Move up one generation.

We may implement SiftUp as follows:

```
procedure SIFTUP (var a: heap; c: integer);
                         { Heapifies ancestors of a[c]   }
    var
        p: integer;    { Parent subscript       }
    begin
    while c > 1 do              { Invariant: a[1] through a[c]  }
        begin                   {    form a heap               }
        p := c div 2;
        if a[p].key < a[c].key then
            begin                  { If invariant violated,       }
            swap (a[p], a[c]);  {    correct it                }
            c := p                 {    & go up one generation    }
            end
        else
            c := 0         { Quick exit       }
        end
    end;  { SiftUp }
```

The while loop moves up the tree, swapping as it goes, until it encounters a pair of keys in the correct order or until it reaches the root. Notice how the div 2 operation makes it simple to find each node's parent. If we want a heap in which the *least* element is at the top, we need only change the test in the while loop to a[p].key > a[c].key. (Swapping is done in the usual way, and in a program as short as this it could be written in line instead of as a procedure call; as usual, it is written as shown for greater clarity.)

There is a particularly neat recursive form of SiftUp:

```
procedure SIFTUP (var a: heap; c: integer);
                           { Heapifies ancestors of a[c]   }
   var                     { (Recursive version)           }
      p: integer;
   begin
   if c > 1 then
      begin
      p := c div 2;
      if a[p].key < a[c].key then
         begin                        { If out of order,   }
         swap (a[p], a[c]);           {    correct         }
         siftup (a, p);               {    & recurse       }
         end
      end
   end;  { SiftUp }
```

The duration of the **while** loop (or the depth of the recursions in the recursive version) depends on how far we are down the heap. If the depth of a[c] is d, then there will be at worst d passes through the loop. (This worst case occurs when the loop goes clear back to the root of the heap.) The *worst* worst case arises when we are at the bottom of the heap—that is, when we are inserting items in the latter half of the array. At this point, the heap has reached its full height of $\lceil \lg n \rceil$, where n is the capacity of the heap (the constant we named **heapsize**). In the first half of the array, the height of the heap will be less. Hence, we can say that the cost of sifting up is at most $\lg n$.

Reheapifying. We have seen insertion into a heap. When we take something off the heap, we must somehow remove it from the heap. The easiest way to do this is to swap it off to the end of the heap just before decrementing the counter that keeps track of the size of the heap. (This will be particularly convenient in implementing **HeapSort**.) Of course, the swap will destroy the heap property, and we must do a series of additional swaps to restore it. We may term this *reheapifying*; it will be done by a procedure **SiftDown**, whose logic we will examine presently. In the meantime, here is the code for deleting from a heap:

```
procedure DELETE_HEAP (var a: heap; var n: integer;
         var x: heaprecord); { Removes & returns x from a }
                           {    heap currently holding     }
   begin                   {    n records                  }
   x := a[1];           { Pick greatest element }
   swap (a[1], a[n]);
   n := n - 1;          { Heap is smaller       }
   siftdown (a, 1, n); { Restore heap property }
   end;  { Delete_Heap }
```

The algorithm for reheapifying is essentially a mirror image of the `SiftUp` procedure:

1. Start at the root.

2. While parent is not a leaf and greater child has a priority greater than that of parent:

    a. Swap parent and greater child;

    b. Move down one generation.

We select the child with the greater priority for swapping because, when it becomes the new parent, its priority will also be greater than that of its unswapped sibling. There is only one complication in this algorithm: In finding the larger child, we must take care not to run off the end of the heap.

We can illustrate this process with the following example. Suppose we have the heap we had before and wish to remove the largest element (that is, the one with the highest priority). The largest element is in position 1; we copy that element to its destination; then we swap it with the element at the end of the array, as shown in Fig. 6.10 (a).

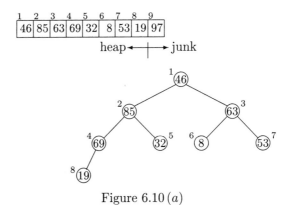

Figure 6.10 (a)

When we swap in this way, the heap shrinks. The heap (as the figure suggests) is now only elements 1 through 8, and this is why the tree in the figure has lost a leaf.

Swapping has placed the highest-priority element past the end of the heap, where we want it, but it has destroyed the heap property; that 46 is too high. We must swap it back down again, and that is the responsibility of `SiftDown`. `SiftDown` must move 46 down by swapping it with the larger of its children. Why the larger? Because that's the largest element remaining in the subtree, and swapping it will move it to the top, where we want it. Now, of course, 46 and 69 are out of order, so we must swap those, too. The end result is as shown in Fig. 6.10 (b):

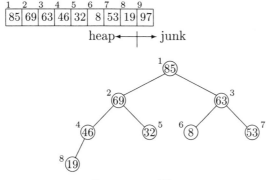

Figure 6.10 (*b*)

Here is the code for `SiftDown`:

```
procedure SIFTDOWN (var a: heap; p, k: integer);
                    { Re-heapifies elements a[p]..a[k]      }
    var
       c: integer;      { Child subscript         }
    begin
    c := 2*p;
    while c <= k do               { Invariant: a[p] through a[k]  }
                              {    form a heap.                  }
       begin
       if c + 1 <= k then              { Find greater child    }
          if a[c + 1].key > a[c].key then
             c := c + 1;
       if a[p].key < a[c].key then
          begin             { If invariant violated      }
          swap (a[p], a[c]);  {   fix it                   }
          p := c;             {   & go down one generation }
          c := 2*p;
          end
       else
          c := k + 1  { Quick exit     }
       end
    end; { SiftDown }
```

The code is complicated by the need to find the child with the greater key and by the need to avoid running off the end of the heap. The procedure guesses that the child will be the left son of `a[p]`. It then looks to see whether there is a right son (that is, whether `c + 1` is still part of the heap) and, if there is, compares it with the left son. Having identified the desired offspring, it then makes the comparison and exits the loop (by setting `c` to `k + 1`) if they are in order. Otherwise, it swaps them and loops back.

`SiftDown` can also be written recursively:

```
procedure SIFTDOWN (var a: heap; p, k: integer);
                    { Re-heapifies elements a[p]..a[k]    }
                    { (Recursive version)                 }
   var
      c: integer;    { Child subscript }
   begin
   c := 2*p;
   if c < k then                        { Find greater child   }
      if a[c + 1].key > a[c].key then
         c := c + 1;
   if (c <= k) and (a[p].key < a[c].key) then
      begin                             { If out of order      }
      swap (a[p], a[c]);                {    correct           }
      siftdown (a, c, k)                {    & recurse          }
      end
   end; { SiftDown }
```

6.2.2   Heapsort

As I mentioned in Section 6.2, we can improve the performance of the selection sort by maintaining the unsorted part of the array as a heap. When we make this change, we have *Heapsort*. Now the largest element will always be at the root of the tree, which is in position 1 of the array. The cost of the swap is only $O(1)$. Of course, if we swap a[1] with the last element in the array, we no longer have a heap. So then we must reheapify, just as we did with DeleteHeap. Once we have done that, we can again swap, this time swapping a[1] with the second-last element, and so forth. The advantage of Heapsort over the selection sort is that it takes only $O(\lg n)$ time to reheapify, whereas it takes $O(n)$ time to find the largest element in the selection sort. (We measure the cost here by the number of comparisons required.) We will see that the duration of the outer loop is still $O(n)$. As a result, while the selection sort is $O(n^2)$, Heapsort is $O(n \lg n)$.

Every time we do a swap, the heap becomes one element smaller and the sorted part, which grows from the end of the array backwards, becomes one element bigger. We're using the array space in two ways here, as shown in Fig. 6.11; the low end is a heap, the high end is the sorted array:

Figure 6.11

As in the selection sort, all elements in the sorted part are greater than or equal to the elements still in the heap.

Suppose the array size is n. Then we have the following skeleton of a procedure:

```
{ heapify; }
```

```
for i := n downto 2 do
   begin
   swap a[1] and a[i];
   { reheapify }
   end;
```

We will see that the initial heapification is simply a series of calls to `SiftDown`, and the reheapification is likewise done by a call to `SiftDown`.

We may now write the code for the entire Heapsort. We will save some trouble here by nesting `SiftDown` inside `HeapSort`, so that we don't have to pass as many parameters to it.

```
procedure HEAPSORT (var a: heap; n: integer);
                              { Sorts the array A; n is      }
        var                   {    the length of the array   }
           i: integer;

        procedure SIFTDOWN (p, k: index);
              ... etc., as before ...

        begin  { HeapSort }
        for i := n div 2 downto 1 do        { Heapify        }
           siftdown (a, i, n);
        for i := n downto 2 do
           begin
           swap (a[1], a[i]);
           siftdown (a, 1, i - 1)           { Restore heap  }
           end
        end;  { HeapSort }
```

When the array is already in place, we can heapify faster if we call `SiftDown` as shown. Since `SiftDown (p, k)` heapifies all descendants of `a[p]`, and since all elements of `a` past `a[n div 2]` are leaves, there is no need to heapify the latter half of `a`. Furthermore, the other calls to `SiftDown` will be short. Let n be the number of elements in the array. Let j be the distance of any element from the bottom of the tree, so at the bottom level, j is 0; the next level up, it is 1; and so on. Then for all $j > 0$, there will be $n/2^{-(j+1)} = (n/2)2^{-j}$ elements and the cost of the call (measured by the number of iterations of the `while` loop or by the number of recursions in the recursive version) will be at most j. In that case, the total cost of heapifying is

$$C \le \frac{n}{2} \sum_{j=0}^{\lg n - 1} j\, 2^{-j}.$$

All the terms in this sum are positive; hence clearly

$$C < \frac{n}{2} \sum_{j=0}^{\infty} j\, 2^{-j}.$$

But this infinite sum is shown to be 2 in Appendix A; hence, the cost of heapifying is less than n.

Heapsort will make $n - 1$ calls to `SiftDown`. On any call, the worst cost occurs when `SiftDown` has to go from the root all the way down to a leaf. Since the height of the tree is $\lceil \lg n \rceil$, the cost of the `while` loop, which dominates the cost of `SiftDown`, will be at most $\lceil \lg n \rceil$. So we conclude that the sorting loop has a cost of $O(n \lg n)$. Since this is greater than the cost of heapification, we conclude that the cost of the entire sorting algorithm is $O(n \lg n)$.

We thus have an $O(n \lg n)$ algorithm for sorting arrays. Quicksort, which we saw previously, is also $O(n \lg n)$, but only on the average over all permutations of the input keys. Heapsort, on the other hand, is completely immune to the $O(n^2)$ problem we noted with Quicksort; it is *always* $O(n \lg n)$. Why isn't it used more often, then? Some people are apparently put off by the fact that, while both algorithms may be $O(n \lg n)$, the constant multiplier for Heapsort is greater than that for Quicksort. A typical implementation of Heapsort can be expected to take roughly two to three times as long as a suitably protected Quicksort. It is a robust algorithm, however, and optimal, and the various clever tricks that have been devised to protect Quicksort are unnecessary.

6.3   REPRESENTING SETS WITH TREES

In small applications, sets are normally implemented with *bit vectors*. A bit vector is one or more bytes of computer memory in which each bit corresponds to an element that *might* be in the set. For example, if we declare

```
var
   x: set of char;
```

then most implementations of Pascal will set aside 32 bytes of computer memory. These 32 bytes comprise 256 bits; the first bit of the first byte corresponds to the character whose ASCII code is 0; the next bit, to the character whose code is 1; and so on. The last bit of the last byte corresponds to the character whose code is 255. The language implementation will allocate a similar bit vector for every set the user declares.

Set operations using such a representation are very simple; the union of two sets is found by doing a bitwise OR between the corresponding bit vectors; intersection is found by a bitwise AND; and other operations are implemented in similar ways.

The main problem with this representation is that the data type has to have a limited range of values. A single byte can take on 256 values, just as a single character can; hence, a set of `byte` or `char` can be handled with a bit vector 32 bytes long, and we will never find an element that can't be put into the set. But if we needed a `set of integer`, we would run into a serious difficulty: A 16-bit integer can take on $2^{16} = 65{,}536$ possible values, and any one of those values might be an element of the set; hence, our bit vector would require 65,536 bits, or 8,192 bytes. This is almost always unacceptable, particularly because, in practice, sets of this type may well contain many fewer than 65,536 elements, so most of those bytes will go to waste.

One alternative way to represent sets is to use a tree. The empty set will be an empty tree; to add an element to a set, we will add it to the tree for that set. To see whether an element belongs to a set, we will see whether it is in that set's tree. We can take the union of two sets by grafting one set's tree onto the other set's tree. The only limitation of this approach is that it is troublesome to delete elements and very difficult to find intersections. In many applications, this is no great problem.

The element at the root of a set's tree will be used to identify that set. We are thus representing the entire set by one of its elements, and we will call that element the *representative* of the set. If we need to associate some particular name with the set, we will create an association between that name and the set's representative. Since the element at the root is thus all-important, we need a way of reaching the root from anywhere in the tree; hence, our tree nodes will have pointers to their parents rather than to their children. The root will have a parent of `nil`. This solves an additional problem for us, because the interior vertices of the tree may have more than two children; using parental pointers makes this trivial to handle, as we observed back at the beginning of this chapter.

Figure 6.12 shows some sets represented this way. Set S comprises $\{2, 45, 13, 6, 54\}$; set T comprises $\{19, 64, 27, 44\}$. Note that the shape of the tree is not significant; set T' is equal to set T, even though its tree has a different shape.

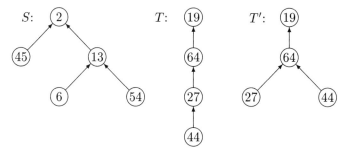

Figure 6.12

I have drawn the edges in these trees as arrows to emphasize the fact that they are pointers to parents, not children.

We can declare the data type for these nodes as follows:

```
type
    etype = integer;      { or whatever: element type    }
    setptr = ^setnode;
    setnode = record
                element: etype;
                pa: setptr;
            end;
```

We need three operations: we must be able to create a set, we must be able to find whether an element is in the set, and we must be able to construct the union of two sets. (Since the two main operations this representation supports are finding elements and forming unions, these trees are sometimes known as the *find-union* data type.)

To create a set, we need only make a single node, put the element in the node, and make its parent `nil`:

```
procedure MAKE_SET (var p: setptr; x: etype);
   begin                                { Makes a set con-      }
   new (p);                             {   taining only x; p   }
   p^.element := x;                     {   points to the set   }
   p^.pa := nil
   end;   { Make_Set }
```

It should be clear that the cost of `Make_Set` is $O(1)$.

There are two ways to construct the union of two sets; one is more clever than the other, but it requires a modification of our data type, so we will start with the simple-minded way. We will form the union by grafting one tree onto the other; since the root is the representative of the set, we will graft onto the root. The code goes as follows:

```
procedure UNION (var s, t: setptr);     { Makes t^            }
   begin                                {   a subset of s^    }
   t^.pa := s
   end;   { Union }
```

The cost of finding the union is obviously independent of the sizes of the two sets, and its cost is also $O(1)$. For example, if we find the union of the sets S and T' of Fig. 6.12, we get the tree shown in Fig. 6.13. The thick arrow shows where T' was grafted onto the root of S.

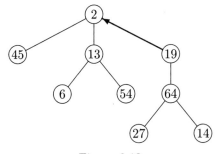

Figure 6.13

If we wish to add a new element to a set, we make a set containing only the new element and then form the union of that new set and the existing one. Note that this is essentially the same as what is done with the regular Pascal `set` data type:

```
s := s + [5];
```

Using trees, we would write

```
make_set (t, 5);
union (s, t);
```

For finding whether an element is in a set, we will provide an auxiliary function that is useful in itself: Find finds the set to which an element s^ belongs:

```
function FIND (s: setptr): setptr;        { Finds root of tree   }
   begin                                   {    containing s^     }
   while s^.pa <> nil do
      s := s^.pa;        { Climb up tree }
   find := s
   end;   { Find }
```

The function returns a pointer to the representative element of the set. Then to determine whether s^ is in a set t we can write

```
in_set := find(s) = t;
```

The cost of Find, measured by the duration of the while loop, depends on where we enter the tree. In the worst case, the tree will be degenerate, in which case its height is one less than the cardinality of the set. If the tree contains n elements, then the worst-case cost is $O(n)$. If all elements have an equal likelihood of being accessed, then the average cost of searching such a degenerate tree, over all possible elements, will be $n/2$, which is also $O(n)$. We will see a somewhat better way of handling Find in a moment.

The reason these are not the best possible ways to do unions and finds is that the union operation can create unbalanced trees. Our concern here is to minimize the amount of time it will take to do a Find for any element in the resulting union; hence, instead of concentrating on the heights themselves, we will consider the number of elements in each set and will always graft the tree with fewer nodes onto the other one. To do this efficiently, we must know the number of nodes in each tree, which we will call the *weight* of the tree, and it is best to maintain these weights as we go along. To this end we will change our node declaration as follows:

```
type
   etype = integer;      { or whatever: element type    }
   setptr = ^setnode;
   setnode = record
                element: etype;
                pa: setptr;
                weight: integer;
             end;
```

We now modify Make_Set and Union as follows. The only change in Make_Set is to set the weight of the tree to 1:

```
procedure MAKE_SET (var p: setptr; x: etype);
   begin                                   { Makes a set          }
   new (p);                                {    containing only x  }
   p^.element := x;
   p^.pa := nil;
   p^.weight := 1
   end;   { Make_Set }
```

Union determines which tree is lighter and makes that the subtree of the heavier tree:

```
function UNION (var s, t: setptr): setptr;
   begin                                    { Returns root of tree }
   if s^.weight >= t^.weight then        {    containing union    }
      begin
      t^.pa := s;
      s^.weight := s^.weight + t^.weight;
      union := s
      end
   else
      begin
      s^.pa := t;
      t^.weight := t^.weight + s^.weight;
      union := t
      end
   end;   { Union }
```

Using this form of Union, we will get generally wide, bushy trees. To see this, note that if we build up a set an element at a time, by creating a new set for each element and then adding it to the existing set with the Union procedure we just saw, the tree will end up looking like Fig. 6.14.

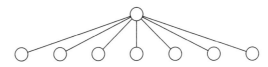

Figure 6.14

We could get this same structure from our first versions of Make_Set and Union, but only by carefully choosing the order of the operands in the calls to Union; here the order doesn't matter, because the lighter tree will always be grafted onto the heavier one.

We can modify Find to make the trees still shorter by doing something that bears a distant relation to the self-organizing storage we mentioned back in Section 2.1. Suppose we have found the union of four sets, resulting in the tree in Fig. 6.15 (a).

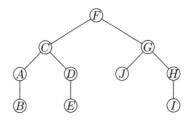

Figure 6.15 (a)

Suppose we call **Find** to identify the set to which E belongs. **Find** will work its way from E up to the root, passing through nodes D, C, and F. Now, if we have looked at E once, we may very well look at it, or one of the other members of its set, again. So in order to save time the next time around, we will attach D and E to the root as we come to them, as shown in Fig. 6.15 (b).

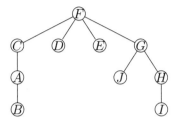

Figure 6.15 (b)

This will not make the current **Find** any faster; in fact, it will slow it down a little. But the next time we do a **Find** with either one of these elements, it will be significantly faster. Since the path lengths from D to F and from E to F were reduced to 1, we call this process *path compression*. You can see the similarity to self-organizing storage here: There, too, the search was slowed down slightly by moving the record that was retrieved to the head of the list, and there, too, doing so tended to speed the search the next time that record was accessed.

The code for **Find**, modified to provide path compression, is as follows:

```
function FIND (s: setptr): setptr;       { Finds root of tree    }
   var                                    {    containing s^.     }
      p,                                  { Does path compression }
      r: setptr;
   begin
   r := s;
   while r^.pa <> nil do        { Find root as before   }
      r := r^.pa;
   find := r;
   while s <> r do
      begin
      p := s^.pa;               { Make every node       }
      s^.pa := r;               {    on path a child     }
      s := p                    {    of r                 }
      end
   end;  { Find }
```

In reckoning the cost of these methods, we must average the cost over a great many **Unions** and **Finds** so that the savings resulting from weighting and path compression will be taken into account. (The cost over many operations is known as the *amortized cost*.) The analysis of the cost is extravagantly complicated, and I will simply state the result: The cost of building a tree with n edges with these operations is $O(n\alpha(n))$. I won't define $\alpha(n)$, but it is a function that grows so slowly with n that we can regard it as essentially a constant. (For example, consider 2^{65536}; written out in decimal, this is a 19,729-digit number. It can be shown that $\alpha(2^{65536}) = 6$.) We can thus say that the average cost is essentially $O(n)$.

6.4 RADIX TREES

Up to now we have used the entire key to determine how to grow or search a tree. But it is possible to use pieces of the key as well. This is similar to the way we used pieces of keys in the radix-exchange sort, and we term trees formed from pieces of the key *radix trees*. With only a couple of exceptions, these methods cannot handle duplicate keys, so in this section we will assume that all the keys are always distinct.

6.4.1 Digital Trees

As our first example of radix trees, suppose we are storing the keys (75, 70, 37, 90, 13, 2, 15). Then we use the following algorithm:

1. Set $n = 0$.

2. If the root is empty, insert the new node at the root.

3. Otherwise, while n is less than or equal to the number of bits in the key:

    a. Test the nth bit of the key.

        If the bit is 0, insert the node in the left subtree.

        If the bit is 1, insert the node in the right subtree.

    b. Increment n.

(As I mentioned in Section 3.3, there is no agreement on how to number bits; some people number them from left to right and some from right to left; some people start numbering from 0 and some from 1. Just now we will number them from right to left, starting with 0; in Section 6.4.3 we will need to number them from left to right.)

As usual, we allocate and stuff the new node in the calling program. In our example, we start out with 75. The root is empty, so it receives 75. The next key is $70 = 1000110_2$. The root isn't nil, and the 0th bit is 0. (The low-order bit is bit 0.) So 70 goes in the left subtree. The third key is $37 = 100101_2$. The root isn't nil, and this time bit 0 is a 1, so 37 goes in the right subtree. The fourth key is $90 = 1011010_2$. The root isn't nil, bit 0 is 0, so 90 goes in the left subtree. But the root of the left subtree isn't nil, either (it contains 70), so we test bit 1 of 90. This is a 1, so 90 goes in 70's left subtree.

Continuing this way, we end up with the tree of Fig. 6.16.

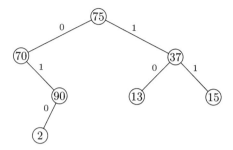

Figure 6.16

In this structure, the bit pattern of the key determines where the record shall
go in the tree. You can work through the key from left to right or from right to left.
If you work from left to right, you must know what the longest key will be and set
n initially to the leftmost bit position. In most programming languages, it is easier
to test the rightmost bit, and we can shift the key one position to the right instead
of maintaining the bit counter n. If we assume the following declarations,

```
type
    treeptr = ^treenode;
    keytype = integer;
    treenode = record
                    key: keytype;
                    left,
                    right: treeptr
               end;
```

then the code for insertion is as follows:

```
procedure R_INSERT (var root: treeptr; p: treeptr; key: keytype);
    begin                           { Inserts p^ into radix tree    }
    if root = nil then
        root := p
    else
        begin
        if odd(key) then          { Test low bit  }
            insert (root^.right, p, key div 2)
        else
            insert (root^.left, p, key div 2)
        end
    end;  { R_Insert }
```

This is clearly a minor modification of our regular insertion procedure. The parameters include the key so that we can keep shifting it to the right by the div 2
operation without destroying the information contained in the node we want to
store.

Searching is nearly as easy. We modify the usual searching function so that
it uses the bit pattern to choose which subtree to search. Since we are going to

compare with the key (to see whether the current root contains it) and also shift it in order to access other bits, we will need two copies, one kept unspoiled for the comparison and one that we can mutilate as we wish. The function looks like this:

```
function R_SEARCH (root: treeptr; target, n: keytype): treeptr;
    begin                    { Searches radix tree for target}
    search := root;
    if root <> nil then
        if root^.key <> target then
            if odd(n) then          { Test low bit  }
                search := search(root^.right, target, n div 2)
            else
                search := search(root^.left, target, n div 2)
    end;  { Search }
```

The parameters `target` and n contain the same value at the start of the recursions; on each new activation of `R_Search`, key still contains the original key while n contains the shifted version. The main program would call this as follows:

```
p := r_search (root, key, key);
if p = nil then
    { not found }
else
    { whatever }
```

Notice that there is a sharp limit on the height of the tree, no matter how it is grown, since if the longest key stored is b bits long, the length of the path to that key cannot be greater than $b - 1$. Thus the tree is guaranteed to be bushy if a large number of keys are stored, and even a degenerate tree will not be very high. Hence, we conclude that the cost of searching a digital tree containing n items is at worst $b - 1$.

If the keys are character strings, the shifting and bit testing will be more complicated, since we must take into account the number of bits per character (seven or eight?), and we must contrive somehow to shift the entire string by one character when we reach the end of a character. We will see another way of handling character strings in the next section.

6.4.2 Tries

An alternative structure stores the keys only in the leaves of the tree. This form is known as a *trie*. (This term was suggested by E. Fredkin [1960]; he took it from the middle of the word "re*trie*val," which suggests that it would be pronounced "tree." That would never do, so it is the custom to pronounce it "try.")

Except for this one difference, a trie is essentially the same as a digital tree, at least in theory. In practice, it is apt to be considerably different, because the pieces of the key with which we will work are commonly letters of the alphabet. If we ignore case, this means every node will have 26 children instead of just two. We can picture the node as looking something like the structure shown in Fig. 6.17.

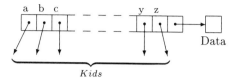

Figure 6.17

The node consists of nothing but pointers. The first 26 are an array; the little letters over each pointer to the kids indicate the subscripts. The last pointer points to a record containing data. (This is the leaf in which the item is stored.)

We organize the contents of the trie as follows:

1. All words beginning with a are grouped together, then all words beginning with b, ..., and so on.

2. Under the group of a-words, all words whose second letter is a are grouped together; then all words whose second letter is b, ..., and so on; and similarly for all words beginning with the other letters of the alphabet.

3. Under each subgroup of letters whose second letter is a are grouped all words (if any) whose third letter is a, ..., and so on.

There is a dummy root node (if we were going to store the null string, this is where it would go), and when we group the words beginning with a, we put them in the subtree rooted in the pointer whose subscript is a.

It's hopeless to try to draw a trie with all 26 pointers in the nodes. Figure 6.18 shows a mini-trie in which the nodes have pointers only for the letters a, b,..., e. This trie contains the words a, abe, dad, cede, dead, and deed. The lines between nodes show how the trie is linked together, and empty boxes represent nil pointers.

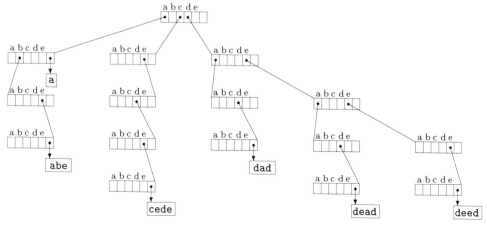

Figure 6.18

To retrieve an entry from the trie, we use the individual letters of the key to find our way through the trie. For example, to find a word like dead, we would look at the group whose first letter is d (by using the d as a subscript into the array of pointers in the root); then in this group, at the subgroup whose second letter is e; then in that subgroup, for the words whose third letter is a; and so on. As we go through the key letter by letter, we go down the trie level by level.

This is a little like a set of filing cabinets, or the card catalogue of a library (back in the days when libraries still had card catalogues). You look in the D cabinet (that's the top level of the trie); find the E drawer (the next level down); inside that drawer you find the index tab with an A on it (the level after that); and so on. Of course, in this analogy, these shortcuts give out at some point, and you end up thumbing through individual cards.

In programming trie insertion and searching, we will use the following declarations:

```
const
    first = 'a';        { Range of characters        }
    last = 'z';         {    of interest             }
type
    letter = first..last;
    tstring = string[maxlength];
    itemptr = ^item;
    item = record
                key: tstring;
                { other data as needed }
            end;
    trieptr = ^node;
    node = record                    { Typical trie node       }
                kids: array [letter] of trieptr;
                data: itemptr;
            end;
var
    root: trieptr;        { Root of trie (obviously)      }
```

The record that will end up as a leaf of the trie is defined by the type item. For brevity, I have given it only one field, containing the key; in practice, there would normally be other data. For example, if our trie were to contain a dictionary, there would be fields for the pronunciation, the etymon, the definition, and so on.

The algorithm for searching for an entry in the trie follows the general outline I sketched above:

1. Set $i = 0$.

2. Point to the root.

3. While the pointer isn't nil and i is less than the length of the key k:

   a. Increment i;

   b. Set the pointer to the k_ith element of the kids array.

4. If the pointer is `nil`, or if the `data` field of the current node is `nil`, the entry isn't in the trie.

5. Otherwise, the `data` field is pointing to the desired entry.

This translates directly into the following implementation:

```
function T_SEARCH (root: trieptr; key: tstring): itemptr;
   var                          { Searches trie for key }
      p: trieptr;
      i: integer;
   begin
   i := 0;
   p := root;
   while (p <> nil) and (i < length(key)) do
      begin                     { Work down the trie   }
      i := i + 1;
      p := p^.branch[key[i]];
      end;
   t_search := nil;             { Assume the worst     }
   if p <> nil then             { Anything there?      }
      if p^.data <> nil then    { Data there?          }
         t_search := p^.data    {   --yes: success     }
   end;   { T_Search }
```

This code assumes string handling similar to Turbo Pascal's, where a `length()` function is available for finding the length of the string. In standard Pascal, where strings must be implemented as arrays of characters, some sort of makeshift will be necessary. It may be feasible to terminate the string with a `nul` character (ASCII code 0) and use a test `key[i] <> nul` in the `while`.

Insertion is more difficult, but it is patterned on the search procedure. Again we work down the trie level by level, guided by the characters in the key. But when we enter a key like **deed**, we need a set of nodes that will provide a path to the leaf containing the key. Initially, such a path may not exist; hence, we build it as we go along. If there is no root, we must make a root. If part of a path already exists, the main loop in the insertion procedure follows it. If it reaches a dead end before the end of the key, then it must create new nodes to make the rest of the path.

When we create a new node, we set all its pointers to `nil`. You will notice that, in the main loop, the new node is created by passing `p^.kids[item.key^[i]]` to the `new` procedure; this automatically grafts the new node onto the correct place in the trie.

```
function T_INSERT (var root: trieptr; item: itemptr): boolean;
           { Inserts Item in trie;  Returns true if       }
           {   insertion successful, false if word is      }
           {   duplicate.                                   }
      var
         i: integer;     { Character counter     }
```

```
      p: trieptr;     { Goes down trie       }
      ch: letter;     { Subscript for kids   }
begin
if root = nil then
   begin
   new(root);                       { Create a root & set   }
   for ch := first to last do       {   pointers to Nil     }
      root^.kids[ch] := nil;
   root^.data := nil;
   end;
p := root;
for i := 1 to length(item^.key) do { Main loop: over key   }
   begin
   if p^.kids[item^.key[i]] <> nil then
      p := p^.kids[item^.key[i]]    { Follow trie           }
   else                             {   to dead end         }
      begin
      new (p^.kids[item^.key[i]]);  { Dead end: make new    }
      p := p^.kids[item^.key[i]];   {   child node, point   }
      for ch := first to last do    {   to it, & make       }
         p^.kids[ch] := nil;        {   kids & data nil     }
      p^.data := nil
      end { else }
   end;  { of loop over key }
if p^.data <> nil then              { End of word: if word  }
   t_insert := false                {   already there, error }
else
   begin
   p^.data := item;                 { Else insert it        }
   t_insert := true
   end
end;  { T_Insert }
```

Suppose the root is already in place; then as we work our way through the key, we create nodes that correspond to d, de, dee, and finally the node that holds deed. If it should happen later on that we need to enter a key deb, we will then find that there is a path out to de and need only attach a new node for deb. Similarly, if we find we must enter a record with the key de, the path already exists and we need only hang the data record on the node for de.

We cannot tolerate duplicate keys in a trie, so before inserting the new entry, we make sure that there is nothing there by testing p^.data at the end of the main loop. If this pointer isn't nil, then the word is already in the trie and we return a value of FALSE to warn the calling program that the item was not inserted.

Deletion from a trie is reasonably straightforward. If the key is in part of a path leading to other keys, we need only delete the data node containing the key and its associated data. If the key is at the end of a path, then we must retrace our

steps back up the path and delete the path itself until we come to a node whose
data field is not nil. If we delete recursively, we can easily find our way back as
the recursions unwind. The code is as follows:

```
function T_DELETE (var root: trieptr; key: tstring): boolean;
                        { Attempts to delete an entry from a    }
                        {   trie.  Returns true if found,        }
     var                {   otherwise false.                     }
        cc: char;
        busy: boolean;
     begin
     t_delete := true;          { Always the optimist            }
     if root = nil then         { Nothing there: give up         }
        t_delete := false
     else
        begin
        if length(key) > 0 then        { Recurse                 }
           t_delete := t_delete (root^.kids[key[1]],
                    copy(key, 2, 255))
           else                        { End of road:            }
              if root^.data = nil then { No entry:               }
                 t_delete := false     {   give up               }
              else
                 begin
                 dispose (root^.data); { Get rid of entry        }
                 root^.data := nil     { Make sure Pascal        }
                 end;                  {   knows it's gone        }

        busy := false;                 { Now check for           }
        cc := first;                   {    path deletion        }
        while not busy and (cc <= last) do    { Is this node     }
           if root^.kids[cc] <> nil then      {   busy?          }
              busy := true                    {   (i.e., any     }
           else                               {   kids?)         }
              cc := succ(cc);
        if not busy and (root^.data = nil) then
           begin
           dispose(root);                     { No further       }
           root := nil                        {    need for      }
           end                                {    this node     }
        end  { else }
     end;  { T_Delete }
```

In this procedure, a node is busy if it has children. If it isn't busy and has no
attached entry, it can safely be deleted. This test comes after deletion has been
done, so it will be made upon returning from a recursive call; in this way, the path
will be removed in an orderly and simple manner as we return.

It is easier to see the relation between a trie and a digital tree if we imagine a trie for storing binary data. In this case, the `kids` array requires only two pointers, one for 0 and one for 1. In that case, we might as well rename them `left` and `right`, and at that point the similarity between the two structures should become clear.

There's an obvious problem with a trie of this sort: The pointer-to-data ratio is very high. With one set of test words, I obtained a trie that needed 705 nodes to hold 207 distinct words. If we really provide the nodes with 26 pointers, we are making provision for words like "dhcmrlchtdj" and "zmqclrv" as well as words like "the," "philippic," and "syzygy." If we have a really large number of very long words, we may easily run out of memory. Hence, we will probably use a trie as a part of a hybrid structure, carrying it only a few levels down and then going to some other organization, just as, in our card catalogue example, we end up thumbing through the individual cards.

6.4.3 Patricia

There is yet another method for retrieving character strings by means of a tree. This method, due to Morrison [1968] is named *Patricia*, an acronym for "**P**ractical **a**lgorithm **t**o **r**etrieve **i**nformation **c**oded **i**n **a**lphanumeric." A Patricia tree is a digital tree modified to minimize the number of tests needed to move about the tree. The text to be searched is not contained in the tree; it is stored elsewhere, either as a long string in memory or in a file, and the Patricia tree contains pointers to keys in the text. A match is found if there is a string anywhere in the text whose prefix is the key. Note that this means, in effect, that a matching substring can extend from the part matching the key clear out to the end of the text string. It also means, however, that no key may be a prefix of any other key already pointed to by the tree.

In searching with a Patricia tree, there is never any need to refer to the text string until the search is complete; at that point the searching algorithm returns a subscript, or a pointer of some kind, into the text string. If the key is there, Patricia will find it; if the key isn't there, she will normally return a subscript pointing to a near miss. Only at this point, when the search is over, is it necessary to verify, by means of a single comparison, that the subscript actually points to what is wanted. This is a consequence of the fact that the structure of the tree reflects that of the text to be searched. From this it follows, in turn, that the tree is thus customized for a particular body of text; you can't take a Patricia tree grown from one file and use it to search a different file.

It is best to approach Patricia trees by gradual stages. We can start by thinking of them a streamlined digital trees. In a digital tree, we frequently have nodes with only one child; at those points, there is only one way to branch, but we must take time to test and make the branch anyway. For example, Fig. 6.19 (a) shows a digital tree formed from the keys (e, h, l, c, g, o, n, s, m, d, k, z). In this tree, six of the nodes have only one child.

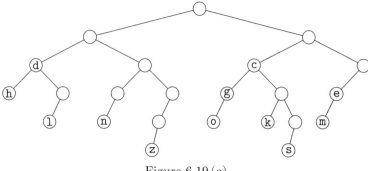

Figure 6.19 (*a*)

These one-way nodes are needed because the level of the node tells the program which bit to test. But in finding **z**, for example, there is no point in testing bits 3 and 4, because there is only one way to branch at these nodes. We could do away with one-way nodes like these if we could mark every node with the number of the bit to be tested at that point. Thus, we could construct a tree like that of Fig. 6.19 (*b*).

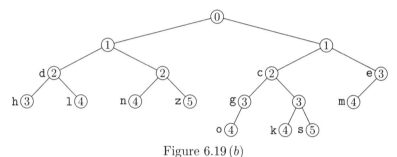

Figure 6.19 (*b*)

Here every node contains the number of the bit to be tested as well as the key. We have eliminated the two redundant nodes on the path to **z** and have moved it up in the tree. This and similar shortcuts save us a number of nodes on the tree and a number of comparisons when searching.

This shows the main idea behind a Patricia tree, but it can't be the whole story, because in this modification the keys are still in the nodes. But there are no keys in the Patricia tree; in a sense, the keys are built into the structure of the tree instead of stored explicitly. Furthermore, Patricia never does any key comparisons. In that case, how does she know when to stop searching? We will find the answer as we develop the algorithms for searching and for growth.

The Patricia tree consists of a root node and as many vertices as are required. We may declare a vertex as follows:

```
type
    patptr = ^patnode;
    patnode = record
                keysub,                  { Subscript into string }
                bitno: integer;          { Bit to examine        }
```

```
        left,                  { Pointers              }
        right: patptr
    end;
pstring = {some suitable string representation}
```

This same structure can be used for the root as well; in the root, only **keysub** and **left** are used.

As her name implies, Patricia was designed as a text-searching algorithm. Morrison said she was "for constructing an index into a binary coded library," and that description emphasizes the fact that she is well adapted to searching huge text strings. In modified forms, however, she can search for any other data that can be represented by bit strings. The example I will show here searches for keys in a text string, however. Thus the **keysub** field holds the subscript into the string where the key begins. The **left** and **right** fields are the pointers, of course, but we will find that the pointers may point back to an ancestor node as well as to a child, somewhat like a threaded tree. This means that the Patricia tree is a tree by courtesy only, because the existence of upward pointers implies the existence of circuits. But the structure is used as a tree, for the most part, and we will continue to refer to it as a tree.

Searching. It is probably best to start by showing a Patricia tree and explaining how we search it for a key; the searching procedure will make clear some of the funny details of the tree. In Fig. 6.20, the text string, **Practical algorithm to retrieve data coded in alphanumeric** is shown on the right. Each node contains a pointer to one of the keys. The text string is treated as an array of characters, and the pointer is the subscript of the first character in the key.

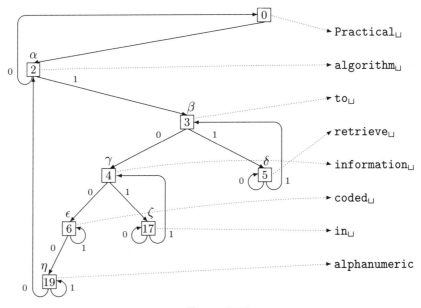

Figure 6.20

Each node is labelled with the number of the bit to be considered in deciding which way to branch. (This is the `bitno` field; the Greek letters are for identification only.) The dotted arrows indicate the keys to which the nodes point. The ␣ after each key is the blank that separates it from the following word. (If we didn't include the blank, then `in` would be a prefix of `information`; Patricia would consider that a duplicate key and we would not be able to store it.)

Suppose we are going to search for the key `algorithm`. The search proceeds in a rather curious way. The root is a special case; the only place we can go from the root is left. When we arrive at node α, we are told to look at bit 2 of the key. Bit 2 of `algorithm` is the third bit from the left in the initial a. (Notice that we are now numbering bits from left to right and the leftmost bit is bit 0.) Since the ASCII code for a is 011̲00001, bit 2 (underlined) is a 1. The right link from node α takes us to node β, where we are to examine bit 3. But that is very strange, because in fact node α is the one we want; it points to `algorithm`␣.

Nevertheless, we have gone on to β, and since bit 3 is a 0, we go left to node γ, where we are to test bit 4. Bit 4 is also a 0, so we go left again to node ϵ, where we are to test bit 6. This bit is also a 0, so we end up at node η, where we must test bit 19. The key is `algorithm` and its first three characters, in ASCII, are the bit string 01100001 01101100 011̲00111. Then bit 19 is the fourth bit from the left in the g. This bit is a 0, so we take the left pointer; and if this doesn't bring us right back to node α... ! That bit 19 is the bit that distinguishes the g of `algorithm` from the p of `alphanumeric`, and the pointer is so arranged as to take us back to the node where we should have gone in the first place.

The reasons for this peculiar mode of proceeding are, first, that we didn't have enough information about the key the first time we visited node α, and second, that the search ends the first time it follows an upward pointer. If we had been searching for `alphanumeric`, the bit in the p would have taken us on the upward pointer right back to node η, and there we would have stopped. (A self-loop pointer is considered an upward pointer.)

So we can outline the algorithm for searching as follows:

1. Start at the root and take the left pointer.

2. Repeat:

   > Test the indicated bit; take the left pointer if it is 0 and the right pointer if it is 1.

   Until the last pointer taken points up the tree.

This leads to the following implementation:

```
procedure PAT_SEARCH (root: patptr; key: pstring; lgth: integer;
        var p, c: patptr);        { Searches Patricia tree        }
                                  {   for key.                     }
                                  { c points to node where found  }
    begin                         { p points to that node's pa    }
    if root = nil then
       c := nil  { Don't search empty tree        }
```

```
      else
         begin
         p := root;
         c := root^.left;
         while (c^.bitno > p^.bitno) and (c^.bitno < lgth) do
            begin
            p := c;
            if bit(key, c^.bitno) then
                c := c^.right      { Bit is 1: go right    }
            else
                c := c^.left       { Bit is 0: go left     }
            end   { while }
         end   { else }
   end;   { Pat_Search }
```

The structure of a Patricia tree is such that the `bitno` field of a child will always be greater than that of the present node; hence, to test for an upward pointer we need only compare `c^.bitno` and `p^.bitno`. This procedure returns a pointer to the node containing the pointer to the key (if the key is found), but it also brings back the pointer to that node's parent as well; we will need this when growing the Patricia tree. In growing the tree, we will also need to be able to terminate the search prematurely, which is why the parameter `lgth` is included. In any ordinary search, we set `lgth` to something harmless like `maxint`.

This procedure requires the ability to test any bit in the key; this ability is provided by the function `Bit`:

```
function BIT (key: pstring; n: integer): boolean;
                                   { Returns true if bit n }
      var                          {    of key is a 1.     }
         i, j: integer;            {    (Leftmost bit is   }
                                   {    bit 0.)            }
      begin
      i := n div 8 + 1;    { Character to examine }
      j := n mod 8;        { Bit position         }
      bit := (ord(key[i]) and ($80 shr j)) <> 0
      end;   { Bit }
```

Since the bit number n may be greater than 7, we must first select which character to examine; that is the reason for the first statement. The `$80 shr j` creates a mask that is all 0's except for a 1 in the jth bit position, and that is how we select the bit to be tested.

Insertion and Growth. To grow the tree in the first place, we must decide where to put each new node. If there is no tree, then we make a root node and put the key information in it; otherwise, we will use our searching procedure to guide us, as usual.

In installing a new key, we search the tree for that key. This search will normally be unsuccessful, unless we are trying to insert a duplicate key. The search will return to us the node pointing to a near miss; this is usually something that begins like the key and then diverges from it at some point. We need to locate the first position in which the bits differ. This location will be the `bitno` field of the new node, and it also guides a second search, telling it to terminate before it reaches the differing bits. We now know where to put the new node: it will lie between the pointer returned and its parent. (That's why we wrote `Pat_Search` to return these two pointers.)

One of the children for this node will be the node itself; this is the path we want to take if we find a match, because this pointer will be an upward pointer pointing to the new node. The other child will be the node pointed to by `Pat_Search`. Thus, if the new bit didn't indicate a match, we will go to where we would have gone if the node had never been inserted. This is how those pointers to distant ancestors are obtained: In our example in Fig. 6.20, the one from node η back to node α started out in life as β's left-son pointer; but when nodes γ, ϵ, and η were added, each of these went between a parent and a child, and in every case that child was α. We will see this in greater detail presently when we trace the first few steps in growing a Patricia tree.

As a result of all this, the algorithm for insertion is fairly complicated. We may summarize it as follows:

1. If root is `nil`, new node is root.

2. Else search for pattern.

3. If search returns pointer to match of key, key is duplicate; quit.

4. Else find location of first differing bit.

5. Repeat search, truncating before differing bit. Parent node returned by search will be parent of new node; child node returned will be child of new node.

6. Make new node:

   a. `bitno` is location of first differing bit.

   b. `keysub` is location of key in text string.

   c. New node is one of its own children; child returned by search is the other.

7. Make new node child of parent returned by search.

We can implement this insertion algorithm as follows. It is written as a Boolean function; its return value tells the caller whether the insertion was successful or not.

```
function PAT_INSERT (var root: patptr; key: pstring): boolean;
                    { Inserts new node for key in Patricia  }
                    {   tree.  Returns true if insertion    }
                    {   successful, false if key a dupli-   }
                    {   cate or prefix of an existing key.   }
```

```
var
   p,                      { New node's parent    }
   c,                      { New node's child     }
   r: patptr;              { New node             }
   j: integer;             { First different bit  }
begin
pat_insert := true;    { Assume no duplicate   }
if root = nil then
   begin
   new (root);                      { No tree: present key  }
   with root^ do                    {    becomes the root   }
      begin
      keysub := pos(key, textstr);
      bitno := 0;
      left := root;
      right := root;
      end
   end
else
   begin
   pat_search(root, key, maxint, p, c);
                     { c points to nearest matching key      }
   j := strmatch(key, copy(textstr, c^.keysub, 255));
                     { j is bit # of first different bit      }
   if j = 8*length(key) then      { Do all bits match?   }
      pat_insert := false          { --yes: duplicate key }
   else
      begin
      pat_search (root, key, j + 1, p, c);
                  { p & c now point to correct parent & child      }
      new (r);
      with r^ do
         begin
         keysub := pos(key, textstr); { Subscript for key     }
         bitno := j;
         if bit(key, j) then              { Check differing bit  }
            begin
            right := r;              { 1: r is own right son }
            left := c                { Left points to parent }
            end
         else
            begin
            left := r;               { 0: r is own left son  }
            right := c               { Right points to parent}
            end
         end;
```

```
          if c = p^.left then              { Find where to attach  }
              p^.left := r                 {    new node           }
          else
              p^.right := r
          end  { else (not duplicate) }
      end  { else (root not nil) }
  end;  { Pat_Insert }
```

In order to find the first bit position in which the two strings differ, we call the function `StrMatch`. `StrMatch` looks like this:

```
function STRMATCH(str1, str2: pstring): integer;
    var                              { Returns b for which first b  }
        i,                           {   bits of str1 same as first }
        j,                           {   b bits of str2.            }
        k,           { Mask for bit comparisons }
        b: integer;
    begin
    i := 1;
    b := 0;
    while (i < length(str1)) and (str1[i] = str2[i]) do
        begin                        { Count matching characters    }
        i := succ(i);
        b := b + 8                   { (8 bits per character)        }
        end;
    k := $80;                        { 1 in leftmost bit of mask     }
    j := ord(str2[i]);
    i := ord(str1[i]);
    while (k <> 0) and ((i and k) = (j and k)) do
        begin                        { Count matching bits           }
        b := b + 1;                  {    in first nonmatching chars  }
        k := k shr 1                 { Shift mask for next bit       }
        end;
    strmatch := b
    end;  { StrMatch }
```

`StrMatch` tells how many matching bits there are, and since we are numbering bits from 0, that result is also the number corresponding to the position of the first pair of nonmatching bits.

The program may be more clear if we watch it in action. We will use the same test phrase as in our previous example. Consider the point after `Practical` and `algorithm` have been inserted and we are about to add the key `to`. The situation before insertion is as shown in Fig. 6.21 (*a*). The search comes back with p and c both pointing to node α. (In the search, p pointed to α directly and c was α's right-son pointer, which points to α.)

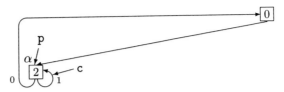

Figure 6.21 (a)

Then the new node is inserted between p and c, as shown in Fig. 6.21 (b). The procedure doesn't know initially whether c is supposed to be the new node's left child or right child, but a check on the test bit will tell it. Similarly, at the end of the insertion procedure, it tests p and c to see whether the new node should be p's left or right child. In this case, it finds that α is β's left child (because the test bit is 1) and that β is α's right child (because c was p's left child). This explains the pointers in Fig. 6.21 (b).

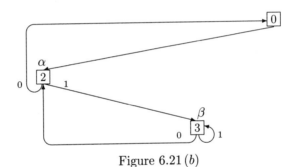

Figure 6.21 (b)

For a second example, consider the shape of the tree a few steps later. Here the key `retrieve` has been inserted and we are about to insert the key `information`. At this point, the tree looks as shown in Fig. 6.21 (c). This time the search comes back with p pointing to node β and c pointing to node α.

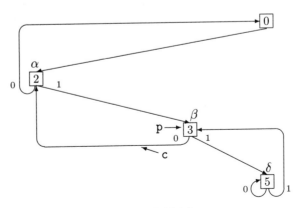

Figure 6.21 (c)

So the new node, γ, will lie between β and α. Because c was β's left-son pointer, γ becomes β's left child; because the test bit was 0, the pointer to α is now γ's left-son pointer.

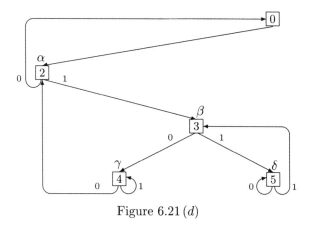

Figure 6.21 (d)

Notice how these successive insertions move the upward pointer to α down the tree; at the end of the process, we have the tree shown in Fig. 6.20.

Patricia trees tend to be generally well balanced (if you ignore the fact that the root has no right subtree). A complete analysis of Patricia is too difficult for us to consider here, but if the trees are well balanced, clearly the cost of searching is $O(\lg n)$. It is worth observing, however, that we are counting bit tests here, not key comparisons. If we have an easy way to select and test bits, this is an extremely attractive method.

6.5 SUMMARY

After arrays, trees may well be the most useful data structures in computer science. They offer nearly as much convenience as arrays without the clumsiness that attends insertion in arrays, and they avoid the sequential searching necessary with linear linked lists. They are well adapted to modeling hierarchical organizations of data, and their structure is suited to the test-and-branch operations that characterize so many programs. We can implement many tree operations with simple, compact recursive algorithms.

The main drawback to trees is that deletion tends to be awkward. There are usually complications that are, in some way, analogous to deletion from an array. This drawback is generally outweighed, however, by the versatility and power trees offer us.

Of all the different types of trees (and there are others we have not discussed in these chapters), the binary search tree is by far the most useful. But the trees we have seen in this chapter are also important and well worth knowing about. We will see applications of some of them—particularly priority queues—in subsequent chapters.

6.6 PROBLEMS

6.1. Convert the following forest to the isomorphic binary tree:

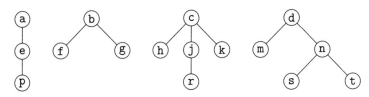

Problem 6.1

6.2. Convert the following binary tree to the isomorphic forest:

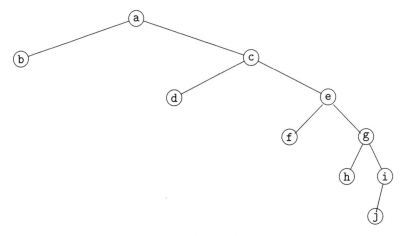

Problem 6.2

6.3. Trace the growth of a heap as the following keys are entered, in the order given: 1, 16, 4, 6, 23, 29, 13, 21, 7, 22.

6.4. Modify `SiftUp` and `SiftDown` to implement a heap of losers.

6.5. We could use a priority queue as an all-purpose queue *if* elements with equal priorities would always leave the queue in the same order as that in which they entered it. Will they?

6.6. Trace the operation of Heapsort on the following array: (4, 26, 14, 21, 55, 51, 8, 10, 2, 3, 13, 56).

6.7. In the selection sort, we found we were able to put the sorted part at the beginning of the array if we searched for the minimum element in the unsorted part. Why would this be a bad idea in Heapsort?

6.8. Show the tree that results from the following set operations, using the weighted `Union` procedure:

```
make_set (a, 1);    make_set (b, 2);
make_set (c, 3);    make_set (d, 4);
make_set (e, 5);    make_set (f, 6);
make_set (g, 7);    make_set (h, 8);
union (a, b);
union (c, d);
union (c, a);
union (e, f);
union (g, h);
union (e, g);
union (a, e);
```

6.9. Trace the growth of a digital tree when the following keys are inserted, in the order given: (24, 17, 36, 82, 19, 38, 15, 45).

6.10. Does the digital tree lend itself to being listed in sorted order?

6.11. Modify the trie of Fig. 6.19 to include the words *abed, cad, be*, and *bead*.

6.12. Draw a trie containing the following words: *a, add, an, dad, dna, nada*, formed from the alphabet, {a, d, n}.

6.13. Suppose we need to construct a trie for words over the alphabet, {a, b, c, d}. Write a Pascal **type** statement to describe the structure of a trie node.

6.14. Write a procedure for traversing a trie so that its contents will be printed in alphabetical order.

6.15. Is the shape of a trie independent of the order in which the keys are inserted? Why/why not?

6.16. Is the shape of a digital tree independent of the order in which the keys arrive? Why/why not?

6.17. Trace the growth of a Patricia tree as the keys **a**, **b**, **an**, **any**, and **by** are inserted.

6.18. Is the shape of a Patricia tree independent of the order in which the keys are inserted? Why/why not?

6.19. We never discussed deletion from a Patricia tree. Why doesn't this concern us?

6.20. Does the Patricia tree lend itself to being listed in sorted order?

CHAPTER 7

EXTERNAL SEARCHING

In Chapter 2, we assumed that the data to be searched were all in memory. In some cases, however, we may need to search for data in a file on some external device like a magnetic tape or a disc. If the file is small enough to fit into memory, then the solution is simple: read the entire file into memory and carry out the search using one of the methods we have already seen.

In many cases, however, the file may be too big to fit into memory. The actual searching must still be done in memory, but we will have to process the file in small chunks, each chunk being of a size that will fit conveniently into memory. When this happens, time required to read a record from an external device will affect the time required for the entire process and may, in fact, dominate it. It is true that, as costs have declined, memory has become more and more abundant. Some personal computers now have more memory than many mainframes of 25 years ago. But files can be huge, too, and occasions will always arise when it is necessary to search a file that is too big to fit into even the vast expanses of memory that are now commonplace.

Where we previously searched by accessing memory, we must now access something stored on disc; and while comparisons can be done in millionths of a second, disc access normally takes perhaps hundredths of a second—10,000 times as long, and that's on a hard disc; floppy discs are even slower.

The reason for this disparity lies in the fact that operations within the computer are electronic, whereas magnetic discs and tapes are mechanical. Electronic operations are limited by the time it takes the control signal or the information to get from one place to the other and by the speed with which the various devices operate. These are all short times: Electrical signals travel at essentially the speed of light, and present-day electronic devices typically have response times measured in nanoseconds. (One nanosecond is 10^{-9} second.) But to access a record on a disc, you must move the read–write heads to the correct track and wait for the desired sector to pass under the heads. At this writing, hard-disc access times typically take somewhere between 15 and 30 milliseconds. Magnetic tape is slower still; the time required to access a record on tape is measured in seconds or, occasionally, minutes.

The most important consequence of this is that we must now consider algorithms that organize the storage of data in such a way as to minimize the number of disc or tape accesses required. In this chapter we will discuss two such organizations: B-trees and extendible hashing.

7.1 B-TREES

When we are searching for an item in external storage, the rules change, as I have explained. Our interest has been focussed on the number of comparisons made in memory. But when we search an external file, we must also concern ourselves with the time it takes to find and read the data in the file, and this can easily swamp the time we spend making comparisons.

We can see this from a simple example. Suppose we had a tree in memory in which every node had k children. Let us call this a k-tree. A balanced k-tree containing n elements has $O(\log_k n)$ levels. At each level, we must do some kind of search among the pointers to find which child we want to inspect next. The best search we can do is a binary search, which costs $O(\log_2 k)$ comparisons, as we know. Hence the cost per level is $O(\log_2 k)$, and the total cost is thus

$$C \text{ is } O(\log_2 k \log_k n).$$

But $\log_2 k \log_k n = \log_2 n$; hence, the cost is independent of k.

But suppose we are dealing with external storage. Now we must count levels much more heavily than comparisons. In external searching, we normally don't read in just one or two bytes. First, it's impossible to pick out a selected byte from a physical block on a disc; disc controllers are built to find a physical block (usually a sector) and read the entire sector. Second, if we *could* read just a couple of bytes, it would take just as long as it does to read an entire sector. So the norm is, slow access times and many data items per access.

In this case, if each node contains the data from a physical block and each level corresponds to a disc access, a search tree with multiway branches begins to make a lot of sense. We will get a lot of data to examine per access, typically a whole sector's worth and certainly enough to make a choice among several branches. Furthermore, the comparison time is negligible relative to the access time. Suppose each comparison costs one unit of time and each access costs T units; then at each level we require $T + \log_2 k$ units of time. (This is a simplification, since the access time may also depend in part on the amount of data to be read in. But this dependency is hard to predict, since it depends, in part, on the way the operating system does disc accesses. We will make the easiest assumption and treat it as a constant.) Since there are still $\log_k n$ levels, our average cost now becomes

$$(T + \log_2 k) \log_k n = T \log_k n + \log_2 n,$$

which is $O(T \log_k n)$. In Big-O notation, we normally treat all logs as equivalent and ignore constant multipliers; but here T is so huge that we must include it and may ignore the second log. The following numbers will bear this out. Suppose $T = 10{,}000$ and $n = 1000$; then $\log_2 n = 9.97$, and for the other term we have

k	Levels	$T \log_k n$
2	9.96	99,668
10	3.00	30,010
50	1.77	17,668
100	1.50	15,010
200	1.30	13,048
500	1.11	11,125

Now, when we considered multiway trees at the beginning of Chapter 6, we ruled them out because a node might not have enough pointers to accommodate all its children. So we are going to have to find a way around this: and we will.

If each node of a multiway search tree has a maximum of m children, we say it is of order m. The number of data items that can be held in any node is $m - 1$. To see this, look at a typical node of a 7-way tree, as shown in Fig. 7.1.

Figure 7.1

(The numbers in the boxes are subscripts, not actual values.) Here, pointer 0 points to a subtree containing items with keys less than that of item 1; pointer 1 points to a subtree containing items with keys greater than that of item 1 but less than that of item 2; and so on; and pointer $m - 1$ points to a subtree containing items with keys greater than that of item $m - 1$.

B-Trees (Bayer and McCreight, 1972) are balanced multiway trees. The exact definition is:

An order-m B-tree is an m-way tree in which

All leaves are on the same level (this is the balance requirement);

All internal nodes except the root have from $\lceil m/2 \rceil$ to m children;

The root has either 0 or 2 to m children (0 if the root is also a leaf);

The number of keys in each internal node is one less than the number of children.

This definition is set up so as to give us an efficient structure that is easy to maintain. The requirement that all nodes except the root have at least $m/2$ children guarantees that the tree will not only be balanced but at least approximately symmetrical.

Before we start going into detail about the creation and maintenance of B-trees, let us look at one. Figure 7.2 shows an order-5 B-tree.

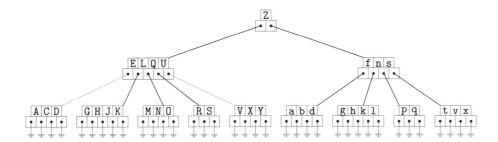

Figure 7.2

You can see how this fits our description: It is order 5, and every node holds at most four keys. Notice also that every key in a node is bracketed by the contents of the nodes pointed to by the adjacent pointers. For example, the pointer just left of the key L points to a node containing the keys G, H, J, K, and the pointer just to the right points to a node with the keys M, N, O. An order-5 tree, which is all we can put on the printed page, is actually too small to be realistic; B-trees typically have orders of 100 or more. The power of B-trees lies not in their order, however, but in their balance, which stems from the requirement that no node be more than half-empty.

7.1.1   Searching

Growing a B-tree is complicated, so we will begin by describing how to search one. Once we have seen the search logic, the growth is less difficult to describe. The algorithm for searching is as follows:

1. Set p equal to the root.
2. If p is nil, the item is not in the tree.
3. Otherwise, look for the key in this node.
4. If found, we are done.
5. Otherwise, look for the keys in this node that bracket the key we are looking for. Set p to the pointer in between these keys and return to Step 2.

In implementing this, we will assume the following declarations:

```
const
   order = 7; { or whatever: number of kids    }
   max = order - 1;    { Number of records    }
   min = order div 2;  { Minimum # of records }
type
   keytype = integer;   { or whatever         }
   datarec = record
```

```
              key: keytype;
              { other stuff }
          end;
nodeptr = ^node;
node = record
          count: integer;
          data: array [1..max] of datarec;
          next: array [0..max] of nodeptr;
      end;
```

We need the `count` field in the node to keep track of how many data entries the node currently holds. I showed a typical node before; here it is again, partly filled with data:

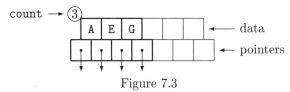

Figure 7.3

The empty boxes are unused locations in the node. There are only three records currently stored in the node, so `count` stands at 3.

The searching procedure is best divided into two parts, one managing the movement between levels and the other searching the current node for the key. We will implement the latter as a binary search; for the small trees we must use for our examples, this is overkill, but real B-trees may be of order 100 or more, in which case a binary search is reasonable.

We can implement the first part recursively as follows:

```
procedure B_SEARCH (target: keytype; p: nodeptr; var found:
          boolean; var node: nodeptr; var location: integer);
                          { Searches B-tree for target;   }
                          {    target; reports success or  }
                          {    failure in Found; returns   }
  begin                   {    node and location if found  }
  if p = nil then
     found := false
  else
     begin
     nodesearch (target, p,   { Try current node         }
          found, location);
     if found then
        node := p             { Return root as node      }
     else                     { Make recursive call      }
        b_search (target, p^.next[location], found,
           node, location);
     end;
end;  { B_Search }
```

To locate the target, we must specify the node containing it and the location of the target within that node; hence, B_Search returns two parameters, **node** and location. The call to NodeSearch searches the current node; it combines Steps 3 and 5, since it returns the location of the target, if it is there, or the subscript of the pointer to be followed in the recursive call if the target is not there.

We can use our usual binary search for NodeSearch, except that we must modify it so that if the key isn't found, location will indicate the proper pointer for the recursive call:

```
procedure NODESEARCH (target: integer; node: nodeptr;
                      var found: boolean; var location: integer);
    var                            { Searches node        }
       first, mid, last: integer;  {   for target         }
    begin
    found := false;
    location := -1;
    with node^ do
       if count > 0 then           { Don't search empty list   }
          begin
          first := 1;
          last := count;
          while last > first do    { Usual binary search  }
             begin
             mid := (t + first) div 2;
             if target > data[mid] then
                first := mid + 1
             else
                last := mid
             end;  { while }
          location := last;
          if target < data[last] then
             location := last - 1   { Adjust subscript     }
          else if target = data[last] then
             found := true;         { Indicate success     }
          end;  { if, with }
    end;  { NodeSearch }
```

The subscripts first, mid, and last are the same subscripts we saw in the binary search, and last takes its initial value from node^.count. If last ends up pointing to the key (here called target), then we have found the record. Otherwise, last points to one of a pair of array elements that bracket target. If target is greater than node^.data[last], then location will direct the calling program to the correct subtree; if it is less, then we have to decrement target. The first if at the end of the while loop determines which of these conditions holds and sets the return value properly.

7.1.2   Insertion and Growth

The growth of B-trees is peculiar in that they grow at the top instead of the bottom. We grow the tree, as usual, by successive insertions. If there is no tree, then we create a root, and as records are added, the root gradually fills up. But then when it is full, instead of sprouting a leaf, it *splits*. The two halves resulting from the split become leaves of a new root. This is shown in Fig. 7.4. In Fig. 7.4 (*a*), an order-5 node has just filled up and we are about to add the key 75.

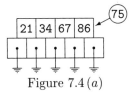

Figure 7.4 (*a*)

If the node could accommodate all those records, they would go in the sequence (21, 34, 67, 75, 86). Since there isn't room for all these records, the node splits, a new root is created, and the record with the key that would have been in the middle (in this case 67) pops up into that new root, as shown in Fig 7.4 (*b*).

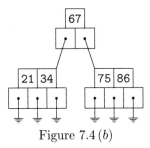

Figure 7.4 (*b*)

The next time one of the lower nodes fills up, there will be no need to create a new root; the node splits and one record moves up to the existing parent node. This can always be done, and when the parent node fills up as a result of these moves, *it* splits and spawns a fresh root. Examples of this are shown in Fig. 7.5. In Fig. 7.5 (*a*), the keys 52 and 71 have been added to the tree in the previous figure.

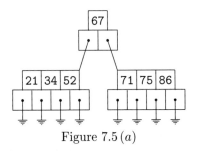

Figure 7.5 (*a*)

Figure 7.5 (*b*) shows the tree after adding the keys 17, 40, and 94:

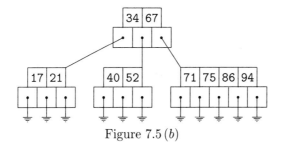

Figure 7.5 (*b*)

Here 17 and 40 overloaded the left leaf; it split, and 34 moved up to join 67 in the root.

At this point, the rightmost node is full; adding 68 will split it and make the middle record (the one with the key 75) move up to the root:

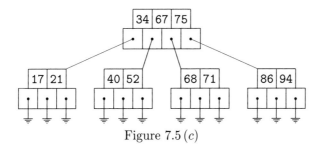

Figure 7.5 (*c*)

Adding 5, 12, 19, 28, 30, and 22 will move records successively up to the root until it overloads and splits, too. At that point the tree looks as shown in Fig. 7.5 (*d*).

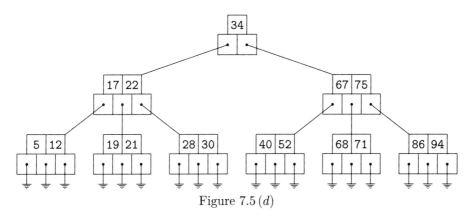

Figure 7.5 (*d*)

In programming insertion, we will go through the motions of searching for the new item. When we reach a `nil` pointer, that pointer belongs to the node in which the new record belongs. If the node is not full, we insert the new record and are finished. If the node is full, then we must manage a split. But we must be aware that moving a record up to the previous level may cause a split there, too. If we make the insertion program recursive, then we can check the status of each level as we back up from the recursions.

This leads to the following algorithm for insertion:

1. Recursively find the node where the new record goes.

2. Insert the record.

   a. If it will fit, insert it and return from the current recursion empty handed.

   b. Otherwise, split the node, insert the record, and return with the excess record for insertion the next level up.

3. Upon returning, if there is a record to be inserted, go back to Step 2.

B-trees are intended for storing and retrieving data stored on disc. This means that the code must include provision for accessing specific blocks of data on the disc; the details of this get us into the secrets of the operating system, and I must unfortunately regard those as beyond the scope of this book. In the code that follows, we pretend that the entire tree is contained in memory. This is quite unrealistic, but it enables us to see the various details of how the tree is grown. Later, I will sketch in how the code must be changed to handle a real-life situation where the nodes would correspond to blocks of data stored externally.

Insertion is best implemented with three procedures. The topmost procedure will call the next one down, which decides where to insert. After insertion, the topmost procedure will determine whether a new root is needed, and if so will create one and link it to the rest of the tree.

The second procedure will carry out Step 1, finding where to insert the new record by searching the tree recursively. If the search is successful, then we are trying to insert a duplicate, and the procedure returns with an indication that a duplicate was found. Otherwise it calls the third procedure, which inserts the new record in the proper node.

The third procedure is responsible for Step 2. It makes room for the new record and inserts it. If the node is full, then it manages the split by creating a new node and copying the latter half of the existing node into that new node.

As the recursions unwind, the second procedure also determines whether a split occurred in the level below the current one. (This is Step 3.) If so, then it calls the third procedure again to insert the record passed up from the split.

The code for the top-level procedure is as follows:

```
procedure B_INSERT (var root: treeptr; entry: noderecord;
                    var found: boolean);
                                   { Main insertion procedure    }
            var                    {    for B-trees              }
                p, fixup: treeptr;
            begin
            fixup := nil;
            if root <> nil then         { Tree already exists:  }
               begin                    {    insert record in it }
```

```
            insert (root, entry, found, fixup);
            p := root;
            end;
        if (root = nil) or (fixup <> nil) then
            begin                       { Either no root yet    }
            p := root;                  {   or must have split  }
            new (root);
            with root^ do
                begin
                data[1] := entry;
                next[0] := p;
                next[1] := fixup;
                for i := 2 to max do   { No other kids yet      }
                    next[i] := nil
                end  { with }
            end  { if }
        end;  { B_Insert }
```

If `root` is not `nil`, then `B_Insert` calls `Insert` to install the new record. Otherwise, it creates the root and does the insertion itself. If it called `Insert` and the current root was split, it finds this out from the fact that `fixup` is not `nil`, creates a new root, and links it to the rest of the tree. You will see that the creation of the original root and the creation of a new one have enough operations in common that the code for doing these two things can be consolidated. The parameter `found` is normally false; if it is true, then there is already a record in the tree with the same key as that of the one we're trying to insert. In that case, the record is not inserted, and returning a value of TRUE alerts the caller to this fact. (This is better programming practice than displaying an error message in the middle of the insertion code.)

The code for the second level, which finds a home for the new record and manages the insertion, is as follows:

```
procedure INSERT (var root: treeptr; var entry: noderecord;
                  var found: boolean; var fixup: treeptr);
                            { Main procedure for entering   }
    var                     {   new item in a node          }
        i,
        loc: integer;
    begin
    nodesearch (entry.key, root,         { Look for it here        }
                found, loc);
    if not found then            { If found we're in trouble   }
        with root^ do
            begin
            if next[loc] = nil then      { At a leaf?              }
                insert_here (root, entry, loc + 1, fixup)
            else
                begin                        {   --no: recurse       }
```

```
                    insert (next[loc], entry, found, fixup);
                    if fixup <> nil then          { Insertion split node? }
                        insert_here              {  --yes: insert record}
                                (root, entry, loc + 1, fixup)
                    end
                end;
        end;   { Insert }
```

This procedure is based on the **Search** procedure we saw previously. It looks for the record in the current node; if it doesn't find it, it moves down the tree recursively, just as **Search** did. If at any level **NodeSearch** reports a successful search, then we are trying to insert a duplicate record and the process terminates.

You will see that there are two calls to the third-level procedure, **Insert_Here**. The main one is the one that follows the **else**: When we reach a leaf, next[loc] is **nil**, and this fact tells us to insert the record here. Insertion may result in splitting the node, however, and that fact has to be passed back to the previous recursion. If a split occurred, **fixup** points to the new node, and the fact that it isn't **nil** is what tells **Insert** that a record was passed back up; this is the reason for the second call to **Insert_Here** after the recursive call. You will notice that **entry** is a variable parameter; it does double duty, carrying the new entry down the tree for insertion and bringing the result of a split back up.

The code for the third level, which handles the actual insertion and splitting, is as follows:

```
procedure INSERT_HERE (var root: nodeptr; var entry: noderecord;
            loc: integer; var fixup: nodeptr);
                            { Inserts record in this node, splits  }
                            {   node if it overflows.  If split oc- }
                            {   curred, returns with fixup pointing }
                            {   to new node and with entry holding  }
        var                 {   record to be moved up.              }
            i,
            j,
            middle: integer;
            tempentry: noderecord;    { Overflow     }
            tempptr: nodeptr;         {   area       }
        begin
        with root^ do
            begin
            if loc > count + 1 then   { Allows caller to append       }
                loc := count + 1;     {   without knowing count       }
            tempentry := data[max];             { In case of overflow  }
            tempptr := next[max];
            for i := max downto loc + 1 do
                begin                          { Make room for entry   }
                data[i] := data[i - 1];
                next[i] := next[i - 1]
```

```
                end;
        if loc <= max then                  { Insert in node      }
            begin
            data[loc] := entry;
            next[loc] := fixup
            end
        else                                 { Save for split      }
            begin
            tempentry := entry;
            tempptr := fixup
            end;
        count := count + 1;
        if count <= max then                 { Overflow?           }
            fixup := nil
        else
            begin                            { --yes: split node   }
            middle := max div 2 + 1;
            count := middle - 1;
            new (fixup);
            fixup^.next[0] := next[middle];
            j := 1;
            for i := middle + 1 to max do
                begin                        { Copy data           }
                fixup^.data[j] := data[i];   {    & pointers        }
                fixup^.next[j] := next[i];   {     into new         }
                next[i] := nil;              {     node            }
                j := j + 1
                end;
            fixup^.data[j] := tempentry;
            fixup^.next[j] := tempptr;
            fixup^.count := j;
            for i := j + 1 to max do
                fixup^.next[i] := nil;
            entry := data[middle]            { Data to be moved up  }
            end
        end   { with }
    end;   { Insert_Here }
```

The main problem in inserting is handling overflow. If there were just one more record in the `data` array, we would be able to handle it much more easily, and a spare record is sometimes included in the array, particularly if the data fields are small. I have provided two overflow variables, `tempentry` and `tempptr`. The parameter `loc` tells `Insert_Here` where the new record goes; the first **for** loop shifts records over to make room for it. If the location is not at the end of the array, we then just drop it in; otherwise, if the node is full and the new record goes at the end, we put it in the overflow area instead.

If the node did not overflow, then we are done, and we set `fixup` to `nil` to indicate that the node wasn't split. Otherwise, we identify the middle of the array, allocate a new node, and copy everything after the middle, including the overflow data, into the new node. (If the order of the tree is odd, there will be no element exactly in the middle; in that case, we take the nearest one.)

By way of illustrating the operation of `Insert_Here`, Fig. 7.6 shows the details of the splitting operation that led from Fig. 7.5 (b) to Fig. 7.5 (c).

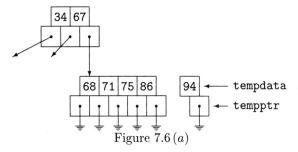

Figure 7.6 (a)

In Fig. 7.6 (a), the new record (with the key 68) has been moved into place, and the final record (with the key 94) has been moved to the overflow space.

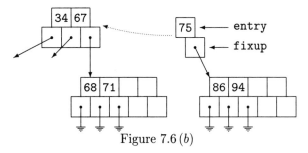

Figure 7.6 (b)

In Fig. 7.6 (b), a new node has been created; the second half of the old node has been copied into it, along with the overflow items. The middle entry (75) has been copied into the variable `entry` and the pointer to the new node is in `fixup`; these will be inserted the next level up, as suggested by the dotted arrow.

7.1.3   Deletion

Deletion poses a number of extra problems, since as usual deleting from an internal node may affect the structure of the subtrees that depend on it. We can sidestep most of these problems as we did with binary search trees, by finding the record's immediate successor, copying it, and deleting it instead. It should be easy to see that if a record isn't in a leaf, its immediate successor will be. This strategy reduces all deletions to deletions from a leaf.

Our troubles are not over, however, because of the requirement that an order-m B-tree must have at least $\lfloor (m-1)/2 \rfloor$ records. If deletion from a leaf leaves it with fewer than that number, then we must fill it up again. We will see how to handle this presently.

The idea is reasonably straightforward, but the code gets caught up in a lot of details. As with insertion, we can keep the complexity under control by sharing the work among various procedures, in this case, four of them. The first one, B_Delete, calls the second to take care of the deletion and then removes the root if the root turns out to be empty as a result of the deletion.

```
procedure B_DELETE (var root: nodeptr; key: keytype;
                        var found: boolean);
                                    { Main procedure for deletion   }
     var                           {    from a B-tree               }
        p: nodeptr;
     begin
     found := false;
     if root <> nil then           { Don't delete from empty tree  }
        begin
        remove (root, key, found);
        if root^.count = 0 then         { Root empty?               }
           begin
           p := root;                   {   --yes: next level       }
           root := root^.next[0];       {     down is root          }
           dispose (p);
           end
        end
     end;  { B_Delete }
```

The second procedure, Remove, is modelled on the recursive deletions we have seen with other trees. It calls NodeSearch to see whether the entry is in the current node or, failing that, to find what pointer to follow in the next recursion. If NodeSearch finds the key and we are in a leaf, we call the third procedure, Delete_Here, to delete the entry. If NodeSearch finds the key and we are in an interior node, then we locate the immediate successor, copy its contents, and delete the successor instead. When we return from a recursion, we decide whether any adjustments need to be made to restore balance; if so, we call the fourth procedure, Adjust.

```
procedure REMOVE (var root: nodeptr; key: keytype;
                     var found: boolean);
                                   { Recursive B-tree deletion      }
                                   {    procedure: finds node &      }
                                   {    calls delete_here for final }
                                   {    removal.                     }
     var
        p: nodeptr;
        loc: integer;
        jj: integer;
     begin
     nodesearch (key, root, found, loc);  { Look for it here         }
```

```
with root^ do
  begin
  if found then
      if next[loc - 1] = nil then    { If leaf, delete      }
        delete_here (root, loc)
      else
        begin
        p := next[loc];                         { Else find    }
        while p^.next[0] <> nil do          {    successor  }
          p := p^.next[0];
        data[loc] := p^.data[1];            { & copy        }
        remove (next[loc], data[loc].key, found)
        end
    else  { not found }                     { Recursive call  }
      if next[loc] <> nil then
        remove (next[loc], key, found);
                                            { Fix up if necessary  }
    if (next[loc] <> nil) and (next[loc]^.count < min) then
      adjust (root, loc)
  end
end;  { Remove }
```

The third procedure, **Delete_Here**, does the deletion; all it needs to do is shift the remaining entries left, wiping out the one to be deleted, and decrement the node's **count** field.

```
procedure DELETE_HERE (var root: nodeptr; loc: integer);
                            { Removes record at loc      }
  var                       {    & adjusts count         }
    i: integer;
  begin
  with root^ do
    begin
    if loc > count then     { Allows caller to access end  }
      loc := count;         {    without knowing count      }
    for i := loc to max - 1 do
      begin                             { Shift everything back }
      data[i] := data[i + 1];
      next[i] := next[i + 1]
      end;
    next[max] := nil;
    count := count - 1;                 { One item less        }
    end
  end;  { Delete_Here }
```

The fourth procedure is the one that rebalances the tree. It is complicated by a number of special cases, because in general we need to work between the leaf to be corrected and its two neighboring leaves. But if the entry of interest is at one end or the other of the parent node, there is only one neighbor to consider. We will have to test for this.

We have already seen the general scheme for balancing; here it is in more detail. If a neighboring leaf can spare a record, we can move it up to the parent node and move the parent node's record into the leaf from which we deleted, as in Fig. 7.7 (a) and (b), which shows part of an order-5 B-tree:

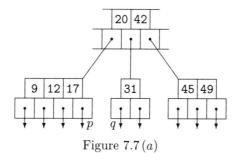

Figure 7.7 (a)

Here we have deleted a record from the middle leaf, leaving it too small. But the leaf to the left can spare a record; hence in a kind of rotation we move 20 down to the middle leaf and 17 up to the parent.

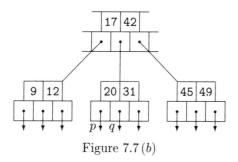

Figure 7.7 (b)

For the sake of simplicity, I have spoken of these bottom nodes as leaves, but we will find that these adjustments may have to be made further up the tree as well, and for that reason it is important to move the pointers as well. In particular, the pointer p in Fig. 7.7 (a) and (b) is the one that points to the subtree (if any) containing records with keys between 17 and 20, and it must be moved as shown to keep that subtree in the correct order.

If a neighboring leaf can't spare a record, then the number of records in the leaf and its neighbor will total less than m; hence they are small enough that they can be consolidated into a single leaf, as in Fig. 7.7 (c) and (d).

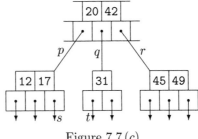

Figure 7.7 (*c*)

Here, neither adjacent leaf can spare a record. But that means that they are small enough that we can consolidate 12, 17, 20, and 31 into a single leaf.

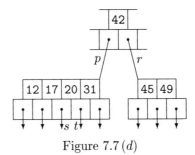

Figure 7.7 (*d*)

Again, it is important to keep the pointers in order. We will see that our `Adjust` procedure will take care of pointer *p* properly. The pointer *q* pointed to the node that was to be disposed of, and for that reason it does not appear in Fig. 7.7 (*d*).

Consolidating two leaves will remove an entry from the parent node; if the parent then has too few entries, the problem moves one level up. If we do the fix-ups upon returning from recursive calls, we can pursue the problem up the tree until it is solved or the root becomes empty. We have seen that `B_Delete` will remove an empty root.

To make these adjustments, we must be able to access the records that are to be moved, must be able to insert and delete them as required, and in the process must not misplace any pointers. We use our existing `Insert_Here` and `Delete_Here` procedures as far as possible in order to keep the procedure from being even longer than the following code:

```
procedure ADJUST (var root: nodeptr; loc: integer);
    var                         { Fixes up nodes with too few  }
      fixup,                    {   records                    }
      q, r: nodeptr;
      rec1, rec2: noderecord;
      i,
      leftcount,
      rightcount: integer;
    begin
    with root^ do
```

```
begin
if loc = 0 then                        { No left neighbor      }
   leftcount := 0
else
   leftcount := next[loc - 1]^.count;
if loc = count then                    { No right neighbor     }
   rightcount := 0
else
   rightcount := next[loc + 1]^.count;

if leftcount > min then                { Rotate right          }
   begin
   fixup := next[loc]^.next[0];
   q := next[loc - 1]^.next[leftcount];
   rec1 :=                             { Record coming up      }
        next[loc - 1]^.data[leftcount];
   rec2 := data[loc];                  { Record going down     }
   insert_here (next[loc], rec2, 1, fixup);
   delete_here (next[loc - 1], maxint);
      next[loc]^.next[0] := q;
   data[loc] := rec1;
   end
else if rightcount > min then          { Rotate left           }
   begin
   fixup := nil;
   rec1 :=                             { Record coming up      }
        next[loc + 1]^.data[1];
   rec2 := data[loc + 1];              { Record going down     }
   insert_here (next[loc], rec2, maxint, fixup);
   delete_here (next[loc + 1], 1);
   data[loc + 1] := rec1;
   end
else                                   { Merge                 }
   begin
   if leftcount > rightcount then
      loc := loc - 1;
   q := next[loc];
   r := next[loc + 1];
   fixup := r^.next[0];
   insert_here (q, data[loc + 1], maxint, fixup);
   for i := 1 to r^.count do
      insert_here (q, r^.data[i], maxint, r^.next[i]);
   dispose (r);
   r := nil;
   delete_here (root, loc + 1);
   end
```

```
      end;  { with }
   end;  { Adjust }
```

Merging is done by copying the records from the parent and from the neighbor to the right into the left leaf (for example, in Fig. 7.7, copying 20 and 31 into the node containing 12 and 17), using `Insert_Here` to manage the insertion for us. The techniques given here will handle any ordinary B-tree, but they run into trouble if the order of the tree is 4 or less, because a deletion may result in a node with no data at all, and this creates problems. But an order as small as that is unrealistic; B-trees are intended for massive amounts of data.

When a B-tree is used to organize and search records in external storage, one node is normally sized to hold an entire block read from the disc. In this case, the pointer fields hold the disc addresses of the children. These addresses may be no more than offsets from the beginning of the file. Sometimes a separate index file is used, in which case the pointer fields point to entries in the index file. In allocating a new node, instead of doing a `New`, we must consult with the operating system to get a block of unused disc space and add it to the file being worked on. One possibility is simply to append the new block to the end of the file by a `write` operation. Similarly, in freeing a node, we must advise the operating system that this block is no longer a part of the file. Alternatively, we can do "lazy deletion," in which a block on the disc is simply flagged as unused; then in a separate compaction run, we copy the entire file to a new file, omitting the unused blocks. The details of these implementations are heavily dependent on the operating system and the facilities it offers the user.

There are many variations on the B-tree theme. Sometimes the size of the nodes is made to depend on their depth. Sometimes only the leaves hold data, in which case the interior nodes hold only keys and pointers instead of full records and pointers, and the nodes we have been calling leaves so far have pointers to records instead of `nil` pointers. In that case, if we also link successive leaves to one another, we can obtain sequential access as well as access through the B-tree. Furthermore, this organization makes it easy to accommodate duplicate entries, since they need only be linked together at the leaves. Knuth [1973] proposes a B*-tree in which all nodes but the root are required to be $2/3$ full instead of half full; this requirement uses memory more efficiently and tends to make searching go faster.

7.2   EXTENDIBLE HASHING

An alternative to B-trees, *extendible hashing* represents a marriage of two techniques we have seen before: hashing and the use of radix trees. Hashing is an attractive way to get quick access to files; it should be clear that if we can hash a key, use the hash value as an subscript into an *index file* consisting of pointers to all the records, and use the index-file entry to retrieve the record, we have reduced the retrieval problem to two disc accesses. The weaknesses of hashing are that hash tables can fill up, collisions must be resolved, and chaining is a less attractive option for external storage than it is for internal storage.

Several researchers (Knott [1971], Larson [1978], Litwin [1978], and Fagin *et al.*
[1979]) have found ingenious ways around all these problems. We will follow Fagin
et al. in the material that follows. To see how they arrived at their solution, let us
forget all about hashing temporarily and consider their starting point: radix trees.
Figure 7.8 shows a radix tree adapted for use with external storage. In this tree,
the interior vertices are pointers only; the data are contained only in the leaves.
Each leaf is a record; each record is identified by the three *leading* bits of its key.

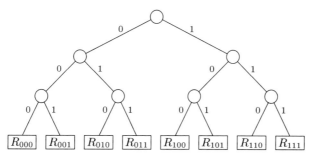

Figure 7.8

Here we have assumed exactly eight keys, whose leading bits range from 000 to
111. But clearly if we need to insert an additional record, for example, one with a
key beginning 0110, we need only split one of the leaves, as shown in Fig. 7.9, and
use four leading bits to choose between the two new leaves.

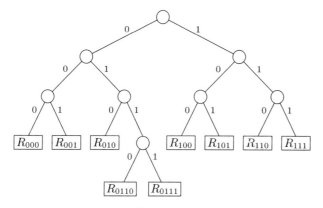

Figure 7.9

Since we can so easily split the leaves this way, this radix tree offers us an
extendible structure for storing and accessing external data. As with B-trees, however, we have one access per level on the tree, and since this is only a binary tree,
there will be many levels. (I have shown only nine records in this example; in
real applications, the number of records may be in the thousands.) Fagin's first
improvement was to squash the tree down to a 1-level array, as shown in Fig. 7.10.
Here each array element is identified by the three leading bits of the key; thus instead of having three accesses, each one on a single bit, we have a single access by
way of a 3-bit subscript.

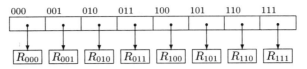

Figure 7.10 (a)

The squashed tree, shown here as an array of pointers, will be an index file. Hence, we can now access any record in two steps: read the index file, then read the record to which the directory entry points.

It looks as if we have lost the extendibility that the radix tree gave us, because if we now split a leaf, as in Fig. 7.10 (b), we will break up this pattern. We can squash the new subtree, as shown, but this has increased the number of disc accesses for the two new leaves.

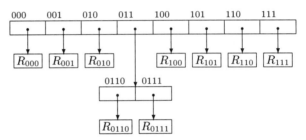

Figure 7.10 (b)

We can solve this problem as well if we are willing to make a tradeoff between space and access time. Instead of splitting a leaf, we will double the size of our index file so that there will be at least one entry for every record. When the last bit of the key is not significant, we will simply make both entries point to the same record, as shown in Fig. 7.10 (c).

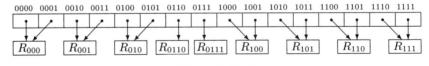

Figure 7.10 (c)

We are now beginning to approach our goal. By splitting leaves this way and occasionally doubling the index-file size, we have a two-level, expandable storage scheme. We must now face the fact that records in real life may not have keys as uniformly distributed as these are. This is the point at which hashing enters the picture; because one of the virtues of hashing is that it tends to map arbitrary keys to a more-or-less uniformly distributed set of subscripts. Hence, our next step is to apply a hashing function to the keys and use the leading bits of the hashed key to address the index file, instead of using the keys themselves. This may be hard to visualize; perhaps Fig. 7.11 will convey the general idea.

Keys:

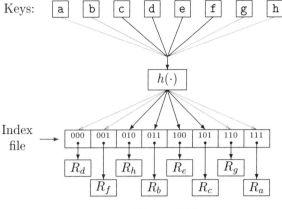

Figure 7.11

Here we envision a set of records with keys a, b, ..., h, which, in practice, may or may not actually be uniformly distributed, and a hash function $h(\cdot)$, which, for the time being at least, we will pretend ideally maps these keys to addresses whose leading three bits are 000, 001, ..., 111. These hashed addresses, which Fagin *et al.* call "pseudokeys," are subscripts into the index file.

We must now address the question of collisions. I have drawn the preceding figures as if each record were stored in a separate place on the disc. Normally, however, a block of disc space will be big enough to hold several records.[1] Hence, we can handle collisions by storing all records that hash to the same value in the same block. (Notice the similarity between this approach and hashing with chaining.)

We assumed an ideal hashing function in Fig. 7.11. To show how the scheme works with a real hashing function and storage of more than one record in a block, we will consider the following example, taken from the program we are going to describe. We start with 14 keys, a through n. We assume that each block can hold a maximum of four records. In that case, a directory size of 4 is sufficient, and to access the directory we use the leading two bits of a hash value obtained using the multiplicative hashing function of Section 2.3. This leads to the structure shown in Fig. 7.12 (*a*). The contents of the boxes at the bottom are the keys, stored in sorted order, with the leading 8 bits of their hashed values, in hexadecimal. (These are unsigned integers.)

If we now add the key o, the leading two bits of its hash function are 10, so its record should go in the block containing b, g, j, and l. But that is more than the block can hold. We deal with the overflow problem by splitting the block into two new blocks and, in this case, doubling the size of the index file. (We assume that disc space is plentiful but that access time must be kept short. Furthermore, index-file entries, since they are only disc addresses, are small.) When we double

---

[1]What I am calling "blocks" are also known as pages. A block is normally the smallest amount of disc space that can be accessed in a single read operation, typically a sector.

the index-file size, we make its addresses depend on the leading 3 bits of the hash value.

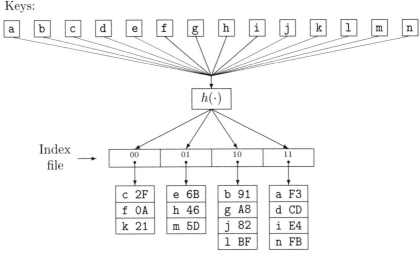

Figure 7.12 (*a*)

It may seem as if doubling the index-file size is going to require a complete reorganization of the records we access; but in fact this won't be necessary. The blocks that aren't split will simply have redundant entries, and hashing to either of these entries will find the appropriate block. (This is the policy we adopted back in Fig. 7.10.) The result after splitting the block and doubling the index-file size is shown in Fig. 7.12 (*b*).

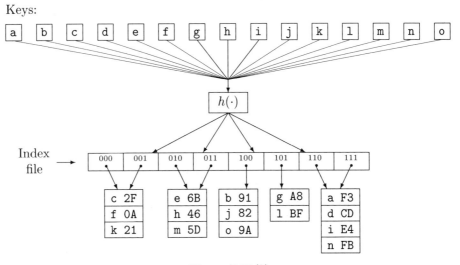

Figure 7.12 (*b*)

The key to extendible hashing is that *we are not using the entire hashed address,*
but only as many of its leading bits as we need. Hence, if we run out of block space,
we can simply split that block and use one extra bit to distinguish between the two
new blocks.

If we need to access record c, we hash its key. When we stored this record, we
took the two leading bits 00 of its hashed address and used these to decide where it
went. When we retrieve it, we will now be looking at the three leading bits; but it
doesn't matter whether the extra bit turns out to be 0 or 1; the redundant index-
file entries will direct us to the correct block. Once we have read that block into
memory, it is a small matter to search its contents for c. The records in each block
may be stored sequentially in sorted order, if sequential processing is important
to the application; alternatively, if every block contains very many records, it may
be better to use hashed storage within the block, using the remaining bits of the
hashed address and resolving collisions at this level in some convenient way.

As usual, it is not practical to show code for dealing with disc storage; we will
simulate the blocks on the disc with records in memory. We need the following
declarations:

```
const
    max = 32;      { Maximum size of index file (power of 2) }
    capacity = 4; { or whatever: records/block                }
type
    keytype = string[12];
    datarec = record                  { Individual data item  }
                 key: keytype;
                 data: { as needed }
              end;
    block = record                    { Storage block         }
               blockdepth,            { Bits for this block   }
               count: integer;        { Number of items stored}
               recs: array[1..capacity] of datarec;
            end;
    blockptr = ^block;
    directory = record                { For index file        }
                   depth,             { Number of bits used   }
                   last: integer;     { Current file size     }
                   data: array[0..max] of blockptr;
                end;
var
    dir: directory;    { Index file }
    newitem: datarec;
    key: keytype;
```

We simulate the index file with the record dir; it contains the number of hash bits
currently being used and the length of the file; the rest of the file is an array of
pointers, which, in an actual application, would be disc addresses. We use the type
block to simulate a block of disc storage; it is configured as an array of records and

is provided with a `count` field giving the current number of records stored. We can use `count` to determine whether a block has room for another record. The `depth` field indicates how many high-order bits of the hashed key will be used to form the subscript into the `dir.data` array, and `blockdepth` tells us how many bits are relevant for this particular block.

For our hashing function we will use the multiplicative form described in Section 2.3 as follows:

```
function HASH (var key: keytype): word;
    const
        n = maxint;
        phi = 0.618034;
    var
        i: integer;
        sum: word;
    begin
    sum := 0;
    for i := 1 to length(key) do
        sum := sum + ord(key[i]);
    hash := trunc(2.0*(n + 1)*frac(phi*sum))
    end;  { Hash }
```

Scaling the hash value to `2.0*(maxint + 1)` gives us a full 16-bit result from which we can select as many leading bits as we need.

7.2.1   Searching

It is probably best to show the code for searching first, since insertion uses the hashed key in much the same way. In this implementation, we assume the records are stored in sorted order, and `Access` takes advantage of this fact:

```
procedure ACCESS (key: keytype; var sub, loc: integer;
                          var found: boolean);
                                    { Finds record with given key   }
                                    { Returns block no. in Sub &    }
                                    {   position where found (or,    }
                                    {   if not found, where should  }
                var                 {   be) in Loc.                  }
        temp: block;
        i,
        k: integer;     { Hashed key    }
    begin
    k := hash(key);
    sub := k shr (16 - dir.depth);          { Isolate high bits     }
    found := false;
    i := 1;
    if dir.data[sub] <> nil then            { If there's a block,   }
```

```
     begin                        {   read it into memory }
     temp := dir.data[sub]^;
     while (i <= temp.count)       { Sequential search     }
           and (temp.recs[i].key < key) do
        i := i + 1;
     found := (i <= temp.count) and (temp.recs[i].key = key)
     end;
   loc := i
   end;  { Access }
```

`Access` hashes the subscript and then shifts it to the right to isolate the required number of bits; this is the pseudokey. If the record is there at all, it will be in the block pointed to by `dir.data[sub]`, so this block is read into memory. Since our blocks hold only four records, a sequential search is fast enough for us. If the block held hundreds of records, we would access them by hashing if they were stored that way, or by a binary search if they were sorted by key when entered. The function returns the record and, for good measure, the subscript of the index file that pointed to its block.

7.2.2 Insertion

Insertion must add the new record to the correct block. We can summarize the algorithm as follows:

> Find where the record should go. There are then four possibilities:
>
> 1. Item already present: return with duplicate indicated.
> 2. No block for this item: create one and insert the record.
> 3. Room for record in block: insert the record.
> 4. No room for record: Split block and insert record:
>   a. If we can foresee that the directory must be doubled, and if the directory is full, return with "full" indicator.
>   b. Save existing contents of block. Split the block.
>   c. If directory size must be doubled, double it.
>   d. Distribute saved records and new record between blocks.

We use `Access` to find the correct block and also to guard against duplicate entries. If there is no block, it allocates one; we simulate this with a call to `New`. If there is a block and it is not full, it simply inserts the record. For our example, we insert the records in sorted order; hence, if the block is not empty, we will shift the subsequent records over to make room for the new record. So the code so far looks like this:

```
procedure INSERT (item: datarec; var dup, full: boolean);
                                { Stores record in file using  }
        var                     {   extendible hashing         }
          temp: block;
          q: blockptr;
```

```
    bdepth,            { Block depth            }
    i, j,
    loc,               { Location where found }
    blkno: integer;    { Block where found    }
    junk,              { Unused results        }
    found: boolean;
begin
full := false;
                            { Find where record should go      }
access (item.key, blkno, loc, dup);
                            { Case 1: Already there: quit      }
if dup then
    exit;
                            { Case 2: No block: create & insert}
with dir do
    if data[blkno] = nil then
        begin
        new (data[blkno]);          { Make new block          }
        data[blkno]^.recs[1] := item; { Store item            }
        data[blkno]^.count := 1;    { Only one so far         }
        data[blkno]^.blockdepth := dir.depth
        end
                            { Case 3: Room in block: insert    }
    else if data[blkno]^.count < capacity then
        with data[blkno]^ do
            begin
            count := count + 1;
                                     { Shift to make room      }
            for i := count downto loc + 1 do
                recs[i] := recs[i - 1];
            recs[loc] := item        { Drop record in          }
            end { else, with }
                            { Case 4: No room: split & insert  }
    else ...
                            { ... (worry about this presently) }
```

If the block is full, we must split it. To do this, we copy all the entries in the block to a temporary area temp. If the number of hash bits currently used for this block is less than the depth of the index file itself, then we must have two or more redundant index-file entries pointing to this block. In that case, we do not need to double the index-file size; we need only delete all index-file entries pointing to this block and re-insert the contents of temp using one more bit from the hashed address. Using one more bit will properly redistribute the records among the redundant entries. But first we must predict whether we will have to double the index file size and see whether we can do so. Hence, our code continues as follows (we are still in the with dir here):

```
                              { Case 4: No room: split & insert  }
                                   { Will we have to double}
                                   {  & if so, can we?      }
else if (data[blkno]^.blockdepth = depth)
      and (last >= max - 1) then
    full := true                     { Will have to & won't  }
                                     {  be able to: give up. }
  else
     begin
     data[blkno]^.blockdepth :=
        data[blkno]^.blockdepth + 1;
     bdepth :=                       { Need 1 more hash bit  }
        data[blkno]^.blockdepth;
     temp := data[blkno]^;           { Copy block to be split}
     q := data[blkno];
     for i := 0 to dir.last do           { Delete entries}
        if data[i] = q then              {    pointing to }
           data[i] := nil;               {    this block  }
     dispose (q);                    { Delete the block      }
     q := nil;
                          { Double index file if necessary   }
     if depth < bdepth then ...
                          {  ... (worry about this later)  }
                     { Split complete: insert items in temp  }
     for i := 1 to capacity do
        insert(temp.recs[i], junk, full);
     insert (item, junk, full);      { Insert new item       }
     end  { else, with dir }
  end;  { Insert }
```

Finally, we must worry about doubling the index-file size. We will need to do this only if the number of bits needed in splitting the block is greater than the current depth of the index file, because, in that case, there are no redundant entries for the block we are going to split. We double the index-file size as follows:

```
                          { Double index file if necessary   }
  if depth < bdepth then
     begin
     j := last;                   { Point to old end      }
     last := 2*(last + 1) - 1;
     depth := depth + 1;
     for i := last downto 1 do
        begin                        { Copy entries          }
        data[i] := data[j];
        if not odd(i) then
           j := j - 1
        end
```

```
      end;  { if }
                      { Split complete: insert items in temp   }
       for i := 1 to capacity do
          insert(temp.recs[i], junk, full);
       insert (item, junk, full);     { Insert new item       }
       end  { else, with }
    end;  { Insert }
```

We work from the end of the index file backwards, copying all entries as we go. We copy every entry twice so that every other entry is redundant; that's why j is decremented only every other pass through the **for** loop. These redundant entries will be correct except in the case of the ones pointing to the block to be split; but the insertions that follow will correct those.

We must also consider how to set things up initially in the main program. We need do only the following:

```
    dir.last := 0;     { Only one entry at start;     }
    dir.depth := 0;    {   hence no bits needed        }
    for i := 0 to max do
       dir.data[i] := nil;
```

7.2.3 Deletion

To delete an entry we locate it and remove it; the details of removal depend on whether the individual records within the block are hashed or sorted; in the case of sorted records, we can simply shift all subsequent records back one position, overwriting the one to be deleted. Managing the blocks and the index file is essentially the reverse of what we did when storing: If the total number of records in a block and its mate is less than **capacity**, then the two blocks can be merged. If as a result of the merger all pairs of even–odd index-file entries point to the same block, then all blocks have redundant entries and we can halve the length of the index file. The deletion procedure is not difficult; it is left as an exercise.

Notice that the code we ended up with had nothing whatever to do with a radix tree. The radix tree was a preliminary model that allowed Fagin *et al.* to work toward the final algorithm; it was like a ladder that is thrown away once a stairway has been built. I have followed their development because I like it and because if it worked for them, then perhaps it has worked for us, too. Notice, again, that the key to extendible hashing is that the hashed address has more bits than we need to access entries in the index file. It follows from this that if we are eventually going to store n records, the hashed address must be at least $\lg n$ bits long.

Fagin's analysis of extendible hashing, which takes the radix tree as its starting point, is difficult. Simulations show that extendible hashing provides faster insertion and access times than do B-trees. Access and insertion is about 10 percent faster for a database of 40,000 records, and the difference increases with the size of the index file and is roughly proportional to the log of the database size. In view of the relative simplicity of the code for extendible hashing, this represents a particularly attractive alternative to B-trees. On the other hand, B-trees, since they are a natural extension of the binary search tree, are better adapted to sequential processing, although storing records in sorted order, as we did in the example above, partially overcomes this drawback in the case of extendible hashing.

7.3 SUMMARY

The main consideration in internal searching is minimizing the number of comparisons that must be made. In external searching, our main concern is arranging and handling data in external storage so we can access them quickly; in particular, so as to minimize the number of disc accesses we need to get hold of an item. We have seen B-trees and extendible hashing; in both techniques, we impose a structure on the data to make them quick to access. These techniques both draw on materials we have seen before: multiway trees, hashing, and radix trees.

7.4 PROBLEMS

7.1. Show the stages in the growth of an order-4 B-tree when the following keys are inserted in the order given: 84, 82, 29, 99, 65, 12, 50, 28, 58, 71, 92, 75, 79, 19, 55.

7.2. Show how the B-tree in the preceding problem changes when the following keys are deleted, in the order given: 28, 50, 75, 29, 65, 58.

7.3. Repeat Problems 7.1 and 7.2 with an order-5 B-tree.

7.4. If a record in a B-tree isn't in a leaf, then its immediate successor will be. Why?

7.5. In the definition of an order-m B-tree, we said that each node except the root had to have at least $\lceil m/2 \rceil$ children. In discussing deletion we said that each node except the root had to contain at least $\lfloor (m-1)/2 \rfloor$ records. This doesn't seem consistent, somehow: How did we arrive at that? How did that ceiling ($\lceil\ \rceil$) become a floor ($\lfloor\ \rfloor$)?

7.6. Write a procedure that will list the records in a B-tree in sorted order.

7.7. Write, compile, and test a main program for extendible hashing using the procedures shown in Section 7.2.

7.8. For the preceding problem, it is useful to have a procedure for displaying the current contents of the directory and individual blocks. Write one.

7.9. Write the procedure for deleting a record from a block using extendible hashing, (a) without merging blocks and halving the index file, (b) including code for merging blocks, (c) including code for merging blocks and halving the index-file size.

CHAPTER 8

EXTERNAL SORTING

External sorting has this in common with external searching: the actual work is done in memory, and our concern is to make a large sorted file out of many small subfiles, each of which has been read into memory, sorted there, and then written out to external storage. A second concern, as with external searching, is to minimize the number of reads and writes from and to external storage.

8.1 MERGING

The most straightforward solution to external sorting is a natural extension of Mergesort: We read as many records as will fit into memory, sort them, and write the sorted records out to a temporary file. We continue doing this until the input file is used up. We then merge the contents of the temporary files to obtain a completely sorted output file.

We can illustrate this as follows: We will represent the file to be sorted, which I will call the *source file*, by a string of boxes, as in Fig. 8.1 (*a*). Each box represents a record, and the contents of the boxes are the keys. Since our space, time, and patience are all limited, we will use a small example, but it should be clear that the technique is applicable to any size file and any amount of available memory. In our case, we will assume that memory can hold five records.

Source | 18 | 36 | 11 | 25 | 3 | 34 | 12 | 17 | 30 | 7 | 26 | 5 | 10 | 20 | 31 | 14 | 2 | 8 | 37 | 21 | 15 | 22 |

Figure 8.1 (*a*)

We read the first five records—the ones with keys 18, 36, 11, 25, 3—into memory and sort them there. We write them in sorted order to an output file which we will call Temp1. We do the same with the next five records, writing them to a second output file, Temp2; and so on. We end up with the situation shown in Fig. 8.1 (*b*).

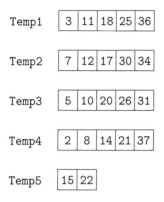

Figure 8.1 (*b*)

Each of these temporary files now contains five records, sorted into ascending order. We will be talking about these subsets of sorted records a lot in what follows; in the literature they have come to be called *runs*, and that is what we will call them here.

We now do a five-way merge among these five files. We read the first record of each file and compare their keys. We select the lowest one—in this case, the one with the key 2—and write it to the output file. Since that record came from the file `Temp4`, we replace it with the next record from that file and repeat the process. This time we select the one with the key 3 (since the one with the key 2 is gone), append it to the output file, and replace it with the next record from `Temp1` (since that is where that record came from). Continuing in this way, we end up with a sorted file, as shown in Fig. 8.1 (*c*).

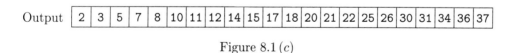

Figure 8.1 (*c*)

If the source file contains n records and the capacity of memory is m records, we require $\lceil n/m \rceil$ temporary files. We must read and write each record twice, once during the sorting phase and once during the merging phase. If we can safely assume that the cost of the input/output operations will completely swap the cost of sorting, so that we can measure the cost of the process by the total number of reads we must do, then the cost is $2n$.

This is the basic idea behind virtually all external sorting procedures. Everything else is trimming on the cake: The merging passes are what take most of the time, particularly when we are sorting files stored on tape, and we will consider, for the most part, ways of minimizing the number of passes made in merging. When working with tape, we must also work with a limited number of temporary files and must consider how to get the most out of the available files.

8.2 BALANCED MERGING

Most disc storage systems can handle large numbers of temporary files. When we must use magnetic tapes, however, we do not have this flexibility, because it is not practical to have more than one temporary file on a tape, and the number of available tape drives is usually limited. (It isn't practical because of the time lost as the tape shuttles back and forth between one file and the other.) We can get by with as few as four tapes in the following algorithm (and in fact we could make do with three). A similar problem could arise when the temporary files are on disc if the $\lceil n/m \rceil$ records that must be compared when merging are too many to fit in memory, so that we must use fewer temporary files. This is unlikely, but the following algorithms can handle that eventuality, too.

If the number of tapes is limited in this way, we must make more passes over the data. We will start as we did before, except that this time we will assume that memory can accommodate only four records (since this results in a simpler example). Let us assume that we mount the tape containing the source file on drive 4 and mount two scratch tapes, for holding the temporary files, on drives 1 and 2. (We will refer to these tapes as tape 1 and tape 2, respectively.) We read four records from the source tape, sort them, and write them out to tape 1 as a run of four records. We read the next four input records, sort them, and write them as a run to tape 2. We read four more, sort them, and write them as a run to tape 1. We continue this way, writing the sorted blocks alternately onto tapes 1 and 2, until the source file has been exhausted.

We now have the situation in Fig. 8.2 (a). Tape 1 has three runs of four records each, and tape 2 has two runs of four records each and a final run of two records. (The runs are shown as separate boxes in the figure.)

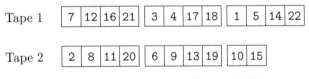

Figure 8.2 (a)

To merge these tapes, we do the following: We remove the source tape and mount two more scratch tapes on drives 3 and 4. (We will call these tape 3 and tape 4.) We merge the first run from tape 1 with the first run from tape 2, writing the output as a run of *eight* records on tape 3, as shown in Fig. 8.2 (b). We then merge the second run on tape 1 with the second run on tape 2 and write these as a run of eight on tape 4. We then merge the third runs similarly and put their output on tape 3. In this example, with its limited amount of data, the second pass is now done, but it should be clear that with larger files we would continue merging corresponding runs from tapes 1 and 2 and writing the merged outputs alternately to tapes 3 and 4.

Tape 3 | 2 | 7 | 8 | 11 | 12 | 16 | 20 | 21 | 1 | 5 | 10 | 14 | 15 | 22 |

Tape 4 | 3 | 4 | 6 | 9 | 13 | 17 | 18 | 19 |

Figure 8.2 (b)

We now repeat this process with the new, larger runs on tapes 3 and 4, putting the outputs on tapes 1 and 2, as shown in Fig. 8.2 (c).

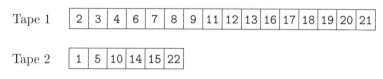

Tape 1 | 2 | 3 | 4 | 6 | 7 | 8 | 9 | 11 | 12 | 13 | 16 | 17 | 18 | 19 | 20 | 21 |

Tape 2 | 1 | 5 | 10 | 14 | 15 | 22 |

Figure 8.2 (c)

In this example, it remains only to merge the contents of the two tapes and write the sorted output to the tape that is to receive it. For larger files, we would continue making passes back and forth between the two pairs of drives until we reached the point where each scratch tape contained only one run, as in Fig. 8.2 (c), at which point we would merge the two scratch tapes onto the output tape.

It should be clear that if we are endowed with a generous number of tape drives, we could use more than two pairs of scratch tapes. Since all scratch tapes receive approximately the same number of records, this is termed a *balanced multiway merge*. If the source file comprises n records and the memory capacity is m records, then on the first pass we will have $\lceil n/m \rceil$ runs distributed over the tapes. On the next pass we will have approximately half that many runs, since each run has doubled in length. By induction, on the kth pass we will have approximately $\lceil n/2^k m \rceil$ runs. When we reach the point where there is only one run containing all n records, we are done. If we ignore the ceilings on these expressions, we can say that the number of passes is given by

$$\frac{n}{2^k m} \approx 1;$$

The process thus takes about $\log_2(n/m)$ passes to get down to a single run; since we read all n records on each pass, the total cost is $n \log_2(n/m)$ reads. This is for four tape drives; if we had $2d$ drives, then on the kth pass we would have a total of $\lceil n/d^k m \rceil$ records, and the total cost would be approximately $n \log_d(n/m)$ reads.

The example here uses four scratch tapes. This is just fine if your installation has that many tape drives, but in general with a little fancy footwork you can get by with as few as three by writing the outputs of the merge phase onto a single tape and then distributing the contents of that tape to the temporary tapes between passes. This also means that if you have N drives in all, you can use $d = N - 1$ drives for the temporary files. Because $\log_d(n/m)$ gets smaller and smaller with increasing d, the more tapes you can use, the better.

We can outline the procedure for carrying out a multiway merge as follows. We will simulate the scratch tapes with an array of temporary files on disc. There is clearly going to be a lot of interchanging of input and output files, so we use an array of files in order to be able to exchange the rôles of the various temporary files by manipulating subscripts. Hence, we declare (among other things)

```
const
   ntapes = 6;
   halfn = ntapes div 2;
   bufsize = 128;
   infinity = maxint;    { or whatever: end-of-run sentinel }
type
   keytype = integer;    { or whatever                }
   datarec = record      { Input record type          }
               key: keytype;
               { other things as needed       }
             end;
   sortarray = array [1..bufsize] of datarec;
   ints = array [1..ntapes] of integer;
   recfile = file of datarec;
   temparray = array [1..ntapes] of recfile;
var
   count: ints;          { Output record counts }
   fsize,                { Source file size     }
   firstin, lastin,      { Input & output       }
   firstout, lastout,    {   tape subscripts     }
   temp: integer;        { For swapping         }
   done: boolean;        { False: stay in loop  }
   inf: recfile;         { Source file          }
   tape: temparray;      { Temporary files      }
```

Balanced merging can be done with an odd number of tapes, but the code is simpler if we make **ntapes** even, and that is the only condition we will consider here.

In the main program, we open the input file and set up the temporary files (giving them names nobody is likely ever to use):

```
write ('Input file: ');                 { Preliminaries }
readln (infname);
assign (inf, infname);
reset (inf);
for i := 1 to ntapes do
   assign (tape[i], 'zxcvbnm' + chr(i + ord('0')));
```

We then make the first pass over the source file, reading it in small chunks that will fit into memory. The size of the chunks is set by **bufsize**.

```
reset (inf);                             { Initial read & sort  }
for i := 1 to halfn do
```

```
      rewrite (tape[i]);
   distribute (inf, tape, fsize, count);
   for i := 1 to halfn do
      close (tape[i]);
   close (inf);
```

The `rewrite` and `close` loops run to `halfn` because we are using the first $n/2$ tapes as our initial scratch tapes. We will discuss `Distribute` below.

We then enter the main merging loop. This loop is controlled by the Boolean `done`. Every pass through this loop merges the contents of the input temporaries to the output temporaries. The input files will be `temp[firstin]` through `temp[lastin]` and the outputs will be `temp[firstout]` through `temp[lastout]`. At the end of each pass through the main loop we swap the values of `firstin` and `firstout` and of `lastin` and `lastout` in order to reverse the rôles of the temporaries for the next time around.

The data must be merged one set of runs at a time; in our example, this was one pair at a time. The main program pushes the actual work of merging the temporary files onto the procedure `Merge`; it is `Merge`'s responsibility to understand about the run lengths and to make sure the files are merged completely. The main program simply calls `Merge` repeatedly until both input temporaries are used up. Picking up the code where we left off before, we have

```
   done := false;
   firstin := 1;
   lastin := halfn;
   firstout := lastin + 1;
   lastout := ntapes;
   repeat
      for i := firstin to lastin do
         reset (tape[i]);
      for i := firstout to lastout do
         rewrite (tape[i]);
      merge (tape, firstin, lastin, firstout, lastout, count);
      ... [decide whether done] ...
      for i := 1 to ntapes do
         close (tape[i]);
      if not done then
         begin                      { Swap input & output tapes    }
         swap (firstin, firstout);
         swap (lastin, lastout)
         end
   until done;
```

We are `done` when all the records are on one output tape. We can determine this simply by looking at the `count` array, which contains the record counts for the output tapes:

```
      j := halfn;                   { j counts empty tapes          }
```

```
for i := firstout to lastout do
   if count[i] = 0 then
      j := j - 1
   else
      iout := i;           { Note where output went      }
done := j = 1;
```

We will need to know which scratch tape contains the final merged output after we are done, so we use this loop to tell us that, too.

That is the heart of the main program; we are now ready to look at the procedures that do the real work. The business of reading chunks from the source file, sorting each chunk, and writing them as runs to the initial temporary files is taken care of by Distribute. Its operation is reasonably straightforward; we can outline it as follows:

1. Set the output tape counter j to 1.

2. While there are more input data:

   a. Read a chunk;

   b. Sort it;

   c. Write it to output tape j;

   d. Advance j; if it is greater than half the number of scratch tapes, set it back to 1.

Sorting is done by a call to QSort, a regular Quicksort. (For a block size of 128 this is overkill, but it wouldn't be for a more realistic size. Bear in mind also that if we are sorting data, large portions of which are already sorted, we will want to protect Qsort against $O(n^2)$ behavior. We will return to this question in Section 8.3.) The parameter fsize counts the source records; this isn't essential, but it is considerate to the user to state how many records were read. (In programming, it is much more important to be user considerate than to be user friendly.)

We can implement this as follows; here I am using outtape for j:

```
procedure DISTRIBUTE (var inf: recfile; var tape: temparray;
                      var fsize: integer; var count: ints);
                          { Reads input file in blocks of length  }
                          {   rsize, sorts the blocks, & writes    }
                          {   them by turns to tape[1]             }
              var         {   through tape[ntapes].                }
         buffer: sortarray;
         i,
         n,
         outtape: integer;
      begin
      outtape := 1;
      fsize := 0;                       { Input record count    }
      for i := 1 to halfn do           { Output record counts  }
```

```
        count[i] := 0;
    while not eof(inf) do
      begin
      n := 0;
      while (n < bufsize) and not eof(inf) do
        begin                        { Read a block  }
        n := n + 1;
        read (inf, buffer[n]);
        fsize := fsize + 1
        end;
      qsort (buffer, n);             { Sort it       }
      for i := 1 to n do             { Write it out  }
        begin
        write (tape[outtape], buffer[i]);
        count[outtape] := count[outtape] + 1
        end;
      buffer[1].key := infinity;     { Write         }
      write (tape[outtape], buffer[1]); {    sentinel  }
      count[outtape] := count[outtape] + 1;
      outtape := outtape mod halfn + 1 { Go to        }
      end                            {    next tape  }
    end;  { Distribute }
```

Merging these temporary files is handled by the procedure `Merge`. Merging files is apt to be a tricky business. We can avoid most problems by terminating each run with a *sentinel record*, one whose key is greater than any key that will ever be found in the file to be sorted. In the code, we call this sentinel value `infinity`. You will have noticed that we tacked one of these sentinels onto the end of every run in `Distribute`; we will now use these sentinels to control `Merge`. Notice that because of these sentinel records, `Merge` doesn't need to know the current run length. We will find that because of this we can use `Merge` without alteration with replacement selection (discussed in Section 8.3), where the run lengths are unpredictable. (This will leave a sentinel record at the end of the final scratch tape; we can remove it when we copy the scratch tape to the tape that is to receive the sorted data.)

The main loop in `Merge` is similar in spirit to the merging procedure in Merge-sort, except that it works with input and output file records instead of having to fuss with linked-list nodes. Each time through the main loop it selects the record with the smallest key, writes it out, and tries to replace it. If the input tape from which that record came is exhausted, it puts a dummy key of `infinity` into the record. Similarly, if the input tape is at the end of a run, it will read the sentinel record, which also has a key of `infinity`. Since the selection loop selects the smallest key, and since the initial value of `minkey` is set to `infinity`, it will automatically reject records from inputs that have terminated. When all inputs have been terminated, $imin = 0$, and that fact tells us we are done.

```
procedure MERGE (var tape: temparray; firstin, lastin,
```

```
                    firstout, lastout: integer; var count: ints);
                       { Balanced merging                       }
                       {   Firstin, lastin: input tapes         }
                       {   Firstout, lastout: output tapes      }
                       {   Count: output record counts          }
       var
          work: array [1..ntapes] of datarec;
          i,
          outtape,        { Output tape number           }
          imin: integer;  { Record with smallest key     }
          minkey: keytype;  { Smallest key               }
          run_over,
          done: boolean;
       begin
       for i := 1 to ntapes do
          count[i] := 0;
       outtape := firstout;
       done := false;
       while not done do
          begin
          for i := 1 to ntapes do
             work[i].key := infinity;
          for i := firstin to lastin do
             if not eof(tape[i]) then
                read (tape[i], work[i]);
          run_over := false;
          while not run_over do
             begin
             imin := 0;
             minkey := infinity;                    { Find          }
             for i := firstin to lastin do          {   record with }
                if work[i].key < minkey then        {   smallest key}
                   begin
                   imin := i;
                   minkey := work[i].key
                   end;
             if imin = 0 then                { All keys were infinity}
                run_over := true
             else
                begin
                write (tape[outtape], work[imin]);  { Write it out  }
                count[outtape] := count[outtape] + 1;
                work[imin].key := infinity;         { Replace it if }
                if not eof(tape[imin]) then          {   possible    }
                   read (tape[imin], work[imin])
                end
```

```
            end;
        work[1].key := infinity;
        write (tape[outtape], work[1]);
        count[outtape] := count[outtape] + 1;
        done := true;
        for i := firstin to lastin do
            if not eof(tape[i]) then
                done := false;
        outtape := outtape + 1;
        if outtape > lastout then
            outtape := firstout
        end  { while }
    end;  { Merge }
```

If you fill out the rest of the main program and want to test it, one possibility is to declare

```
type
    datarec = record
                    key: char;
                end;
```

and use the program to sort a text file. In a dump of the output file, you will then normally find a bunch of line-feed and carriage-return characters at the beginning, followed by lots of blanks, and then other ASCII characters in the usual collating sequence.

The only weakness of the code as shown here is that it leaves the sorted output on one of the temporary files. We can get the main program to tell us which file that was, and we may find it convenient to obtain our final sorted file simply by renaming that temporary file to the desired name of the output file. If your version of Pascal can delete files from the directory from within the program, it is user considerate to get rid of the unneeded temporary files. (If this program actually used tapes, these details wouldn't be necessary.) It is probably worth noting that this program will sort a file whose size is less than the initial block length and that it works correctly with a file containing 0 records.

8.3 REPLACEMENT SELECTION

In the distribution procedure, I specified a Quicksort. I said that this may not be such a good idea, because frequently a program like this may be used to sort files that are already largely sorted, and in that case Quicksort is not a good choice. Since we are going to use large buffers to hold the data, memory is going to be at a premium and we would rather not have the overhead needed for pointers in a Mergesort. Thus our minds turn naturally to Heapsort.

Our first guess would be simply to change the line `qsort (buffer, n)` to say `heapsort (buffer, n)`, but there is a better way. We will read the input records directly into the heap as they arrive and reheapify on each new record. We will make this a heap of losers—that is, a heap in which the record with the *least* key appears at the top—and the top element in the heap will be the next one to be written to the output tape. This technique is called *replacement selection*. If the input buffer size is m and there are n records to be sorted, the cost of this is $O(n \lg m)$. This is no worse than Quicksort, because in that case sorting the buffer will cost $O(m \lg m)$, but this must be done $\lceil n/m \rceil$ times, so the cost is essentially the same in either case—unless Quicksort degenerates to $O(n^2)$. It is true that Heapsort runs somewhat more slowly than Quicksort, but we will see presently that this approach offers an offsetting advantage.

There are a couple of problems to be resolved. First, we must fill the heap at the start of the process. Second, we must make sure that the heap is emptied at the end of the process. We will see that these two problems are easy to handle, but the third problem is trickier: We must be careful in managing the heap if records are going to be put into it as they are read. Specifically, suppose we have read a bunch of records and have output a sequence of keys (2, 7, 13, 18, 25, 27, 36). Now we read a new record, and its key happens to be 12. We can't output that as a part of the current run; it's too late. But if we just insert it into the heap and `SiftDown`, that key will bubble up to the top of the heap and will be the next one selected.

Things like this are bound to happen. We deal with this by tagging each record in the heap with a run number. Every time we read a new record, we compare its key with the most recent key written out. If the new record's key is greater or equal to the most recent key, it is not too late to include the new record in this run, and we tag it with the current run number. If the new key is less, then it must go in the next run, and we tag it with the current run number plus 1. For example, suppose we are in the middle of run 7 when we have the sequence in our previous example. In the heap these keys were marked as follows: (7, 2); (7, 7); (7, 13); (7, 18); (7, 25); (7, 27); (7, 36)—although not necessarily in that order. When we read the record with the key 12, it's too late to put it into run 7, so we tag it with the run number 8: (8, 12).

The procedures for maintaining the heap must take these tags into account. In particular, we will declare

```
type
   keytype = char;  { or whatever }
   datarec = record     { Input record type     }
               key: keytype
               { other fields as needed }
            end;
   heaprec = record     { For priority queue     }
               run: integer;   { Run number     }
               data: datarec;
            end;
   heaparray = array [1..bufsize] of heaprec;
   ints = array [1..ntapes] of integer;
```

```
recfile = file of datarec;
temparray = array [1..ntapes] of recfile;
```

We need a different record type for the heap, because the records in the file don't carry run numbers. When we pass the heap array to SiftDown, this procedure must compare the run numbers as well as the keys. The code for SiftDown will thus be as follows:

```
procedure SIFTDOWN (var a: heaparray; p, k: integer);
                                 { Re-heapifies descendants     }
      var                        {    of A[p]                   }
         c: integer;       { Child subscript        }
         temp: heaprec;
         done: boolean;
   begin
   done := false;
   while not done do
      if 2*p > k then
         done := true
      else
         begin
         c := 2*p;
         if c + 1 <= k then
            if (a[c + 1].run < a[c].run)         { Compare runs   }
               or (a[c + 1].run = a[c].run)   { as well as keys}
                  and (a[c + 1].data.key < a[c].data.key) then
               c := c + 1;
         if (a[p].run < a[c].run) or (a[p].run = a[c].run)
               and (a[p].data.key < a[c].data.key) then
            done := true
         else
            begin
            swap (a[p], a[c]);
            p := c
            end
         end;
   end;  { SiftDown }
```

We can outline our new Distribute procedure as follows:

1. Set the run counter *nruns* to 0.
2. Fill the priority queue and heapify.
3. Set the output tape counter *j* to 1.
4. While there are more input data:
   a. While the current run isn't over:
      i. Take a record off the top of the heap and write it to tape *j*.

ii. Read a new input record if possible.

iii. If you couldn't read a new input record, set the run number to `maxint`.

iv. If you could read a new input record, and if its key is greater than or equal to that of the record just written, then set its run number to *nruns* + 1; otherwise, set it to *nruns*.

v. Put the new record at the top of the heap and reheapify.

b. Advance *j*; if it is greater than half the number of scratch tapes, set it back to 1.

To fill the heap initially, we do

```
nruns := 0;                          { Run count      }
for i := 1 to bufsize do
   begin
   if not eof(inf) then              { Fill buffer    }
      begin
      read (inf, indata);
      work[i].data := indata;
      work[i].run := nruns;
      end
   else
      work[i].run := maxint;
   end;
for i := bufsize div 2 downto 1 do   { Heapify        }
   siftdown (work, i, bufsize);
```

This is similar to the beginning of Heapsort. The main difference is that if the file ends before the buffer fills up, the excess records are tagged by making their file number `maxint`. (It is highly unlikely that this would ever happen, but a good programmer protects the user against highly unlikely eventualities.)

In the distribution process itself, we use that `maxint` tag to detect the end of data; hence, the outer `while` loop does not terminate when the end of file is reached but rather when the heap is empty. You will see that reading an input record is guarded by an end-of-file test, and when the end is reached, the records going into the heap are again tagged with a run number of `maxint`. The `SiftDown` procedure will automatically put these records near the bottom of the heap, and when a record so tagged appears in `work[1]`, we know all the input data have been sorted and written out. Similarly, we know we have reached the end of a run when the run number at the top of the heap is no longer the current one.

The entire `Distribute` procedure is then as follows:

```
procedure DISTRIBUTE (var inf: recfile; var tape: temparray;
                      var fsize: integer; var count: ints);
                                  { Distribution with replacement }
   var                            {   selection                   }
      work: heaparray;
```

```
      indata,
      outrec: datarec;
      i,
      outtape,   { Output tape number     }
      nruns,     { Current run number     }
      outtape: integer;
begin
for outtape := 1 to halfn do { Output record counts  }
   count[outtape] := 0;
fsize := 0;                     { Input record count    }
nruns := 0;                     { Run count             }
for i := 1 to bufsize do
   begin
   if not eof(inf) then              { Fill priority queue   }
      begin
      read (inf, indata);
      fsize := fsize + 1;            { Count input records   }
      work[i].data := indata;
      work[i].run := nruns;
      end
   else
      work[i].run := maxint;
   end;
for i := bufsize div 2 downto 1 do   { Heapify               }
   siftdown (work, i, bufsize);
outtape := 1;                     { Initial scratch tape  }
while work[1].run <> maxint do
   begin
   while work[1].run = nruns do       { Do a run             }
      begin
      outrec := work[1].data;
      write (tape[outtape], outrec); { Write the record      }
      count[outtape] := count[outtape] + 1;
      if not eof(inf) then
         begin
         read (inf, indata);
         fsize := fsize + 1;          { Count input records   }
         work[1].data := indata;
         if indata.key >= outrec.key then   { Can it still  }
            work[1].run := nruns              {   go in run? }
         else                                 { --no: belongs }
            work[1].run := nruns + 1          {   in next run }
         end
      else
         work[1].run := maxint;                 { Sentinel value}
      siftdown (work, 1, bufsize);   { Re-heapify            }
```

```
        end; { of this run }

    outrec.key := infinity;
    write (tape[outtape], outrec);    { Mark end of run        }
    count[outtape] := count[outtape] + 1;
    nruns := nruns + 1;
    outtape := outtape mod halfn + 1; { Go to next output tape}
    end; { of input data }
  end;   { Distribute }
```

The inner **while** loop determines when a run has ended from the fact that the run number at the top of the heap is no longer equal to the current run number. This works exactly the same way as the end-of-data test: As long as the heap contains any records for the current run, SiftDown will place all records for the following run below them.

Replacement selection gives us another advantage besides protection against slow sorts, because on the average the run length will be longer than the size of the buffer. You can think of the boundary line between the current run and the next one as working gradually through the heap array from the end back to the beginning, while if the keys come in at random, they will go into random positions in the heap. Then when the buffer is (say) half full of records for the current run, then with probability $1/2$ the next incoming key will be great enough that it can still be included in the current run. This suggests that, if the keys arrive at random, the run length will be about twice the heap size, and this can be proved, although the proof is more subtle than this hint seems to imply. In practice, the run length is rarely less than $1\frac{1}{2}$ times the heap size, and if the file is already largely sorted, the runs will generally be much greater than the heap size. Longer runs tend to mean fewer merges, so replacement selection should give us a quicker program.

8.4 POLYPHASE MERGING

The drawback of balanced merging is that it uses many tapes. If we want to do a p-way merge, we need, ideally, $2p$ tapes. I said that we could get by with $p + 1$ tapes by writing all the output onto a single tape and then distributing that output onto the other p tapes, but the distribution requires yet another pass through the data, and passes through the data are the very thing we want to minimize.

Suppose we had three tapes, T_1, T_2, and T_3, at our disposal and consider the following sequence of steps:

1. Sort and distribute the records onto T_1 and T_2.

2. Merge T_1 and T_2 onto T_3, leaving something on T_2.

3. Merge T_2 and T_3 onto T_1, leaving something on T_3.

4. Merge T_3 and T_1 onto T_2, leaving something on T_1.

5. Merge T_1 and T_2 onto T_3, leaving something on T_2.

    ... and so on ...

This sequence always leaves us with two source tapes, since we leave some runs behind on one of the tapes. This means we never have to distribute any output files. We would like to arrange the leftovers so as to minimize the amount of reading we must do, and of course when we reach the last merging pass, we want each input tape to contain exactly one run, so that all the data will converge on the output tape in a single sorted run.

For example, suppose the source file is 13 times as long as the largest chunk that will fit into memory. (The reason for using this lucky number will emerge presently.) In describing the sizes of the runs written on the tapes, I am going to use the *chunk* as a unit of measurement; this will simplify the material that is to come. A chunk is the number of records that can be accommodated in computer memory for internal sorting in the sort-and-distribute step. In our example, this initial pass will put five runs of length 1 (that is, of one chunk each) onto T_1 and eight runs of length 1 onto T_2.

In each merge pass, we will merge all of the tape with fewer runs (call it T_x) with an equal number of runs from the other source tape (call it T_y), leaving some unmerged runs behind on T_y. For example, the first merge pass will merge everything on T_1 with five runs from T_2; we end up with five runs of length 2 on T_3 and three runs of length 1 *left over* on T_2. We continue in this way, as shown in Fig. 8.3, until one tape contains the entire sorted file. In the figure, each box is a run and the number inside the box is the length of the run (in chunks).

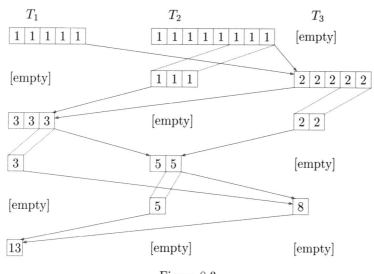

Figure 8.3

This requires five passes. A four-tape balanced merge requires four passes for this many records; it appears at first glance as if we have paid for saving one tape with an extra pass. But notice that passes in the balanced merge go through all the data, whereas passes in our three-tape algorithm went through only part of the data, since on every pass but the last something was left behind. If you count the number of runs read in both algorithms, the balanced merge reads $4 \times 13 = 52$

runs, whereas our three-tape method reads $10 + 9 + 10 + 8 + 13 = 50$ runs. So we have saved one tape and two runs. (The cost of the initial sort-and-distribute step is the same in both cases.)

This kind of merging is called *polyphase merging*. The trick is to get the right initial distribution on the sort-and-distribute step. After that, everything follows automatically, since exactly the right number of runs is left behind on each pass. The explanation of the trick should become clear if you examine the numbers of runs at each level of Fig. 8.3: these are all Fibonacci numbers. (That's why I chose a file with 13 runs as my example; 13 is a Fibonacci number.) Clearly, the number of runs in the output is going to be the sum of the numbers of runs in the two input files; but one of those numbers must also be the sum of the numbers in *its* input files... and so on. But this is what the definition of the Fibonacci numbers gives us:

$$F_n = \begin{cases} 0, & n = 0, \\ 1, & n = 1, \\ F_{n-1} + F_{n-2} & \text{otherwise} \end{cases} \qquad (8.1)$$

So for a two-way merge using three tapes, if the length of the file to be sorted is F_n for some n, then in distributing the sorted runs, we put F_{n-1} runs onto one of the tapes and F_{n-2} runs onto the other. Because of this association with Fibonacci numbers, polyphase merging is sometimes also called Fibonacci merging.

This leaves three unanswered questions: What if the source file is not exactly F_n runs long? What if we have more than three tapes? How do we do the merges when the runs we are merging are of unequal length (as they will be on every pass but the first)?

The answer to the first question is so simple that it's hard to believe we can get away with it: We expand the output of the sort-and-distribute step to the next Fibonacci number with dummy records of length 0. We will discuss how this is done in more detail when we start looking at code.

To see how to merge with more than three tapes, it's best to start with the desired end result and work backwards. We can do this with a table; each row of the table corresponds to a pass through the merging process, and the entries in each row give the total number of runs on each tape. For example, suppose we are merging with four tapes. Here we are doing 3-to-1 merges. It's obvious that we want to end up with everything in a single run on one tape; it's also obvious that in the pass before this, we want one run on each of the other three tapes, so they can be combined with a single 3-to-1 merge. This gives us the first two rows of the table:

T_1	T_2	T_3	T_4	
1	0	0	0	(desired end result)
0	1	1	1	

Now, how could we have arrived at the arrangement in that second row? One of those 1's must have resulted from a 3-to-1 merge; suppose it's T_2. Then T_2 must have been empty the time before. Furthermore, if T_3 and T_4 have one run left over now, they must have had two runs the time before, since they both contributed one run to the merge. So the third row of the table must be

$$\begin{array}{cccc} T_1 & T_2 & T_3 & T_4 \\ 1 & 0 & 2 & 2 \end{array}$$

We now follow the same reasoning. T_3 has two runs on it; it must have gotten those from a merge of the other three tapes; hence, the time before T_3 must have been empty and the other tapes must have had two more runs than they have now. If we continue this way, we get the following results. (This table includes the sums across each row; the sum gives the largest file size that can be distributed using this set of numbers.)

T_1	T_2	T_3	T_4	Sum
1	0	0	0	1
0	1	1	1	3
1	0	2	2	5
3	2	0	4	9
7	6	4	0	17
0	13	11	7	31
13	0	24	20	57

...and so on. The row whose sum is greater than or equal to the number of runs in our input file gives the distribution of the initial runs from the sort-and-distribute pass.

If we permute the rows cyclically so that the empty tape is always the last one, we get the following modified table, from which we can derive a way to construct the table on the fly, as we are reading in records:

$$\begin{array}{cccc} 1 & 0 & 0 & 0 \\ 1 & 1 & 1 & 0 \\ 2 & 2 & 1 & 0 \\ 4 & 3 & 2 & 0 \\ 7 & 6 & 4 & 0 \\ 13 & 11 & 7 & 0 \\ 24 & 20 & 13 & 0 \end{array}$$

From this we see that we can obtain every new row by shifting everything one position to the left, adding the largest element in the preceding row to all the other elements in the preceding row, and setting the last element to 0. For example, if row n contained

$$\begin{array}{cccc} a & b & c & d \end{array}$$

(where d is always 0), then row $n+1$ would contain

$$\begin{array}{cccc} a+b & a+c & a+d & 0. \end{array}$$

We will pursue this method of constructing the table further when we get to the code; for the time being, we will pretend that we must scan the sums in the completed table and select the row whose sum is the least upper bound of the size of the file to be sorted.

For example, consider merging a source file 17 chunks long using four tapes. By a fantastic stroke of luck, the sum of the fifth row in our table just happens to be 17. So, following the numbers in the row whose sum is 17, we distribute 7 runs on T_1, 6 runs on T_2, and 4 runs on T_3. (When we can fill all the row entries in a table this way with no need for dummy records, we say we have a *perfect* distribution.) Initially, we do a three-way merge as follows: We merge one run from each of T_1, T_2, and T_3 and put it on T_4. We continue this way until T_3 is used up; this results in four 3-chunk runs on T_4, as shown in the second row of Fig. 8.4. Notice that we now have leftover data on *two* of the input tapes.

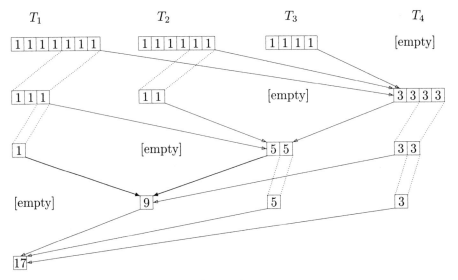

Figure 8.4

We then do a three-way merge from tapes T_1, T_2, and T_4 onto tape T_3. We are now merging one-chunk runs from each of the first two tapes with three-chunk runs from T_4; each output run will thus contain 5 chunks. The result is shown in the third row of Fig. 8.4. As we continue, we end up with all 17 records converging on T_1, as shown.

Again, some comparisons are in order. If we merged a 16-run file using four tapes, merging would require four passes through the data, reading all the data each time, which is a cost of 64 runs. The 17-run example we have just shown requires four passes, too, but again only the last pass reads all the data; the cost is $12 + 10 + 9 + 17 = 48$ runs.

The numbers that appear in this table are obtained from *generalized* Fibonacci numbers. The order-p Fibonacci numbers are defined as follows:

$$F_n^{(p)} = \begin{cases} 0, & 0 \le n \le p - 2 \\ 1, & n = p - 1 \\ F_{n-1}^{(p)} + F_{n-2}^{(p)} + \cdots + F_{n-p}^{(p)} & \text{otherwise.} \end{cases} \qquad (8.2)$$

So every order-p Fibonacci number is the sum of the preceding p order-p Fibonacci numbers. The ordinary Fibonacci numbers we all know and love are $F^{(2)}$.

These numbers get into the table as follows: First, note that the greatest number in any row is the sum of the two greatest numbers in the preceding row. For example, in our previous table, 24, the greatest number in the seventh row, is the sum of 11 and 13, the two greatest numbers in the sixth row. But the second-greatest number in any row is the sum of the greatest and *third*-greatest numbers in the preceding row; and the third-greatest is the sum of the greatest and *fourth*-greatest in the row before that; and so on, until at some point the nth-greatest number turns out to be 0. In a table of $p + 1$ columns, like our previous example, we will hit that zero $p + 1$ rows back. But that means that as we trace the ancestry of the greatest number in any row, it turns out to be equal to the sum of the greatest numbers in the previous p rows. If we consider how the table begins, it should be clear that the greatest number in every row is an order-p Fibonacci number. In our 4-tape table, for example, $24 = 13 + 7 + 4 = F_7^{(3)} + F_6^{(3)} + F_5^{(3)}$. In general, we may write,

$$\text{Largest number in row } n = F_{n-2}^{(p)} + F_{n-1}^{(p)} + F_n^{(p)} + \cdots + F_{n+p-2}^{(p)}.$$

That is, it is the sum of a sequence of p $F^{(p)}$-numbers beginning with $F_{n-2}^{(p)}$.

The other table entries are also obtainable from the same generalized Fibonacci numbers. For example, the second-greatest number is the sum of the $p - 1$ greatest numbers in the previous rows; so

$$\text{Largest number in row } n = F_{n-1}^{(p)} + F_n^{(p)} + \cdots + F_{n+p-2}^{(p)}.$$

That's the sum of a sequence of $p - 1$ $F^{(p)}$-numbers beginning with $F_{n-1}^{(p)}$. We can obtain the entire table this way, but this is largely a matter of mathematical interest. It is easier to construct the run table by the procedure to be outlined presently than to go to the labor of computing the appropriate set of generalized Fibonacci numbers and adding subsets of them to obtain the table entries. These mathematical properties are of more interest in obtaining expressions for the performance of a polyphase merge.

We are now ready to consider some code. The sort-and-distribute procedure that follows is freely adapted from Knuth's Algorithm D [1973, p. 170f]. In this procedure, we will build the run table row by row, computing each new row as we need it. Only the current row is of interest, so we store only that row. The current row gives the number of runs that are to go onto each scratch tape. For example, if the current row is

(24, 20, 13, 0),

then we want 24 runs on the first scratch tape, 20 runs on the second, and 13 runs on the third. The fourth entry corresponds to the tape onto which they will be merged, so of course it is zero, since we always merge onto an empty tape.

In general, the size of our file is not going to give us a perfect distribution, so we will need to allow for a number of dummy runs. Knuth's algorithm is designed to distribute the dummy runs over all the output tapes.

We know that the first row of the table will always be $(1, 1, 1, \ldots, 1, 0)$. We construct the row entries before we have obtained the runs that will fill them, so we maintain an array of dummy counts that indicate how many dummy records will be needed to fill the row. We approach the dummy question pessimistically in that we set the dummy counts to $(1, 1, 1, \ldots, 1, 0)$, too, as though we feared the entire row was going to be filled with dummies. Then every time we distribute a run to a particular tape, we subtract 1 from that tape's dummy count. When all the dummy counts are 0, that row of the table has been filled. That is, enough runs have been read and distributed that the contents of each scratch tape correspond to the entries in the row. If there are more data to come, we then compute the next row of the table.

In computing the next row, we follow the rule given for the permuted table given above: We add the largest count in the existing row to all the other counts for that row. Since the first entry in the row is always the largest, we can simply use that as the largest count.

Bear in mind that when we generate the new row, the previous row has been filled. So the number of dummies needed will now be the *difference* between the old row entry and the new one. If the row is held in the array `run_count` and the dummy counts are in `dummy`, then the code for updating these arrays goes like this:

```
rmax := run_count[1];
for j := 1 to ntapes - 1 do
   begin                        { Dummies needed =      }
   dummy[j] :=                  {    delta (run_count)  }
      rmax + run_count[j + 1] - run_count[j];
   run_count[j] := rmax + run_count[j + 1]
   end;
```

So much for updating the arrays. We use the `dummy` array to control the distribution of the runs among the files. The idea is this: We start by writing runs to the first scratch tape. Every time we write a run, we decrement that tape's dummy count. As long as the current dummy count is less than the next one, we keep writing runs to the current scratch tape. If it is less then the next one, we start writing runs onto the next scratch tape; otherwise, we return to the first scratch tape. When we run out of input data, the process stops. This strange-sounding procedure has the effect of distributing the runs over the three scratch tapes so that the first scratch tape holds the largest number of runs, the second, the second-largest number, and so on, and so that any remaining dummy records are more-or-less evenly distributed over the tapes. When all the dummy counts have been reduced to 0, the current row of the table has been filled and it's time to generate a new row and a new set of dummy counts.

As with the balanced multiway merge, we simulate the scratch tapes with an array of temporary files; these are passed as a parameter `temp` to the distribution procedure, along with the source file. (The array of temporary files is of type `filearray`.) We return the row count, the dummy counts, and an array giving the total number of files written; these numbers will be used to control the merge passes.

```
procedure DISTRIBUTE (var inf: recfile; var temp: filearray;
          var dummy, run_count: ints; var row: integer;
          var fsize: word);   { Reads, sorts, & distributes  }
                              {   input chunks among output   }
                              {   files.  Returns run &       }
                              {   dummy counts & input        }
                              {   file size.                  }
   var
      work: sortarray;   { Holds input chunk     }
      rmax,              { Maximum row entry     }
      i,
      j,                 { Tape subscript        }
      n: integer;        { Input record count    }
   begin
   for j := 1 to ntapes do      { Preliminaries:        }
      begin                     {   Open files &        }
      rewrite (temp[j]);        {     set up            }
      dummy[j] := 1;            {     arrays            }
      run_count[j] := 1;
      end;
   fsize := filesize(inf);
   run_count[ntapes] := 0;
   dummy[ntapes] := 0;
   row := 1;
   while not eof(inf) do
      begin
      j := 1;
                                         { Loop (on rows)        }
      while (dummy[j] <> 0) and not eof(inf) do
         begin
         n := 0;
         while (n < runsize) and not eof(inf) do
            begin                        { Read a chunk          }
            n := n + 1;                  {   of data             }
            read (inf, work[n]);
            end;
         if n > 0 then
            begin
            qsort (work, n);             { Sort it               }
            for i := 1 to n do           { Write it out          }
               write (temp[j], work[i]);
            work[1].key := infinity;     { Write end-of-run      }
            write (temp[j], work[1]);    {   marker              }
            dummy[j] := dummy[j] - 1;    { One less dummy needed }
            end;
                              { Invariant: number of runs       }
```

```
                                    {   on temp[j] + dummy[j]      }
                                    {      = run_count[j]           }
            if dummy[j] < dummy [j + 1] then
                j := j + 1                     { Cycle tape subscript  }
            else
                j := 1
            end;  { while (dummy }

        if not eof(inf) then        { More to come?                 }
            begin
            row := row + 1;         { Yes: new row:                 }
            rmax := run_count[1];          { Update dummy counts    }
            for j := 1 to ntapes - 1 do    {    & run counts        }
                begin                      { Dummies needed =       }
                dummy[j] :=                {    delta (run_count)    }
                    rmax + run_count[j + 1] - run_count[j];
                run_count[j] := rmax + run_count[j + 1];
                end
            end
        end;  { while not eof }

    for i := 1 to ntapes do
        close (temp[i])
    end;  { Distribute }
```

The procedure as shown does not use replacement selection. The program will run faster if we use replacement selection, and it is not difficult to incorporate it; modifying the procedure to do so is left as an exercise.

In the main program, we identify the source file and give the temporaries outlandish names; then we call Distribute:

```
write ('Input data file: ');          { Preliminaries:           }
readln (fname);
assign (inf, fname);
for i := 1 to ntapes do
    assign (temp[i], 'zmxqrv' + chr(i + ord('0')));

reset (inf);                           { Sort & distribute        }
distribute (inf, temp, dummy, run_count, level, fsize);
close (inf);
```

Level receives the number of rows that had to be generated in Distribute. We can use this number to determine the number of merges that will be needed. The main program continues,

```
target := ntapes;
smallest := target - 1;
```

```
for i := 1 to ntapes do
   if i <> target then
      reset (temp[i]);

while level > 0 do                    { Merge tapes           }
   begin
   rewrite (temp[target]);
   polymerge (temp, dummy, run_count, level, smallest, target);

   rmin := run_count[smallest];       { Back run counts down  }
   for i := 1 to ntapes do
      run_count[i] := run_count[i] - rmin;
   run_count[target] := rmin;

   close (temp[target]);              { Cycle tapes           }
   close (temp[smallest]);
   if level > 0 then
      begin
      reset (temp[target]);
      target := smallest;
      smallest := smallest - 1;
      if smallest = 0 then
         smallest := ntapes
      end;
   end;  { while }

for i := 1 to ntapes do               { Wrapup                }
   if (i <> smallest) and (i <> target) then
      close (temp[i]);
```

In this code, `target` is the scratch tape to which the current tapes are to be merged. The variable `smallest` identifies the tape with the fewest runs on it; this will be the target tape the next time around. Immediately after each merge pass, we back the run-length table down to the previous row; the code for doing this is essentially the opposite of the next-row code in `Distribute`.

Merging is complicated by the fact that the runs on the various scratch tapes are generally not of the same length. Besides the fact that the merging process itself creates longer runs on the output tape, the presence of dummy records means that these longer runs themselves are not necessarily of uniform length; furthermore, the length of the input file itself may not be an integer number of runs. We address this problem by marking the end of each run with a sentinel value, as we did with balanced merging; you will notice that `Distribute` added a sentinel record at the end of each run. (As before, `infinity` is a constant set to be larger than any key that will ever be found in a file.)

To see what we do about dummy records, let us look at an example. We return to the example of Fig. 8.5, assuming this time that the source file was only 13 chunks long. In that case, there will be four dummy runs; `Distribute` will put them in the places marked with an × in the top row of Fig. 8.5.

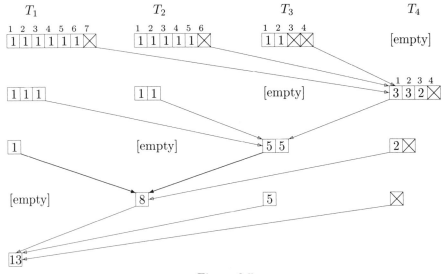

Figure 8.5

I have numbered the runs so that we can track them. We would ordinarily merge run 1 from T_1, run 1 from T_2, and run 1 from T_3 to obtain run 1 on T_4, and the same for runs 2, 3, and 4. But run 3 on T_3 is a dummy; we will merge dummies by ignoring them.

Furthermore, we can save ourselves some work by writing only *three* runs to T_4, filling it up with one dummy run. So we will merge runs 1, 2, and 3 as originally proposed, but for the fourth output run we will pretend we are merging run 7 from T_1, run 6 from T_2, and run 4 from T_3. But merging three dummies is a purely imaginary act: in fact, we *do nothing* and simply say that the fourth run on T_4 is a dummy.

This has used up all the input dummies. As a result of this, we end up with three runs and a dummy on T_4, as shown in the figure, and no dummies in any of the leftover runs on the other tapes. (The length of the third run on T_4 is only two chunks because one of the input runs was a dummy.) The rest of the merges proceed similarly, as shown in the figure.

The rule for doing this in the program is as follows: find the smallest number of dummy runs on any of the input tapes. (Call this `dmin`.) Make the number of dummies on the output tape equal to `dmin` and subtract `dmin` from the dummy counts on all the input tapes in order to find the new dummy counts.

It is probably best to handle the merging process with two procedures. In the main procedure, a loop over the number of runs to be merged calls a secondary procedure whose job is to merge one run from each input tape to the output tape. The main procedure, which I have named `PolyMerge`, goes like this:

```
procedure POLYMERGE (var temp: filearray; var dummy,
```

```
                    run_count: ints; var level: integer;
                    smallest, target: integer);
    var                 { Does one level of polyphase merge      }
        dmin,      { Smallest dummy count  }
        i, j,
        lim: integer;
    begin
    dummy[target] := 0;
    dmin := maxint;                          { Find tape with fewest }
    for j := 1 to ntapes do                  {    dummies            }
        if j <> target then
            begin
            if dummy[j] > run_count[j] then
                dummy[j] := run_count[j];
            if dummy[j] < dmin then
                dmin := dummy[j]
            end;
    lim := run_count[smallest] - dmin;   { Find number of passes }
    for j := 1 to lim do
        merge_runs (temp, target, level);         { Now merge      }
    for j := 1 to ntapes do
        dummy[j] := dummy[j] - dmin;       { Update dummy counts   }
    dummy[target] := dmin;
    level := level - 1;                   {    & level             }
    end;  { PolyMerge }
```

Most of `PolyMerge`'s work involves managing the counts of dummy records and finding out how many runs are to be merged at this level. It finds this out by subtracting `dmin` from the run count of the smallest input file. Once it knows the number of runs to be merged, it calls `Merge_Runs` to merge them.

`Merge_Runs` uses an array `work` to hold the input records to be compared. It fills this array at the beginning; if any tape has been used up, it puts the sentinel value `infinity` into the corresponding record. It then enters the usual loop, finding the record with the smallest key, writing that record to the output tape (identified by the parameter `target`), and replacing it with a new record from the input tape from which we obtained the one just written out. Since the keys can appear in any order, we must use a sequential search to find the smallest key; but since the number of tapes will always be small, this is acceptable.

The sentinel value solves the problem of unequal run lengths. Initially, records are read from any tape that isn't at an end of file. Eventually one of the replacement reads will get the sentinel record, and that marks the end of a run. Since the corresponding `work` array element is set to the sentinel value, the loop that looks for the smallest record will never consider it; hence, no further records from that tape will be merged until the next time `Merge_Runs` is called.

The main loop continues until the `work` array contains nothing but sentinels; at this point `imin` will be 0, meaning that all tapes are used up. The Boolean `done`, which controls the main loop, is set to TRUE, and we are done.

```
procedure MERGE_RUNS (var temp: filearray; target,
                    level: integer);
    var                           { Merges tapes for PolyMerge      }
        work: array[1..ntapes] of datarec;
        i,
        imin: integer;      { Record with smallest key      }
        min: keytype;       { Smallest key                  }
        done: boolean;
    begin
    for i := 1 to ntapes do                 { Read initial contents }
        begin                               {   of work array       }
        work[i].key := infinity;
        if i <> target then
            if not eof(temp[i]) then
                read (temp[i], work[i]);
        end;
    done := false;
    count := 0;
    while not done do                       { Main loop             }
        begin
        imin := 0;                          { Find smallest key     }
        min := infinity;
        for i := 1 to ntapes do
            if work[i].key < min then
                begin
                imin := i;
                min := work[i].key
                end;
        if imin > 0 then                    { Write it out          }
            begin
            write (temp[target], work[imin]);
            if not eof(temp[imin]) then      { Replace it    }
                read (temp[imin], work[imin])   {   if possible }
            else
                work[imin].key := infinity
            end
        else  { imin was 0 }
            done := true;
        end;  { while }
    work[1].key := infinity;                { Write end-of-run      }
    write (temp[target], work[1])           {   sentinel           }
    end;  { Merge_Runs }
```

At the end of the merge, Merge_Runs writes a sentinel record for use on the next pass.

The performance of any external sort is hard to estimate, since so much depends on details of the data, the length of the runs, and things we haven't considered, like the time it takes for a tape to rewind between passes. For the polyphase merge, Knuth [1973], who is, as usual, encyclopædic, gives expressions for the number of passes for various numbers of tapes; the results are all of the form $\alpha \ln n + \beta$, where n is the length of the data (measured in chunks). The constants α and β depend on the number of tapes; α varies from about 1.5 for three tapes to about 0.76 for seven tapes, and β is a small number typically less than one. To get the total cost, we must multiply these numbers by n and add the cost of the initial sort-and-distribute phase. The main result is that polyphase merging is an $O(n \lg n)$ process. We also learn that it does not pay significantly to use more than seven tapes.

The results given here ignore a number of practical considerations, like the details of starting and stopping a tape, which affect the speed with which we can read or write, and the time required to rewind a tape back to the load point. Most of the more sophisticated sorting algorithms take these times into consideration (*e.g.*, merging some tapes while others rewind); on the other hand, the availability of massive amounts of disc storage for temporary files tends to make these clever tricks a little less important than they once were.

8.5 SUMMARY

The main consideration in internal sorting is minimizing the number of comparisons and, in some cases, the amount of data that must be moved around. In external sorting, our main concern is minimizing the number of passes we must make through the data. This is more important when sorting data stored on tape than when sorting data stored on disc. Since tapes are still used for mass storage of data, however, these concerns are still relevant.

8.6 PROBLEMS

8.1. Trace (by hand) the execution of the basic merge process of Section 8.1 on a file containing the following keys:

   97 47 90 55 29 84 51 36 63 62 9 77 81 30 49 58 10 42 92 84 79

Assume that memory can hold five records.

8.2. Using the same data as in the previous problem, trace the operation of a balanced merge. Assume that memory can hold five records and that there are four tape drives available.

8.3. Complete and test the balanced sorting program outlined in Section 8.2.

8.4. When writing external sorting programs, it is useful to have a program that will verify (a) that the unsorted and sorted files are the same length and (b) that the sorted file really is sorted. Write such a verification program.

8.5. It's difficult to trace the operation of a polyphase merge without using large amounts of data, since each run consists of enough records to fill the `work` array, and this array is normally large. We can fake it for hand tracing by starting with runs of only one record. Do this, using the data of Problem 8.1

8.6. Suppose we want to do a polyphase sort of a file 125 runs long. Draw up a table for finding the initial distribution, assuming we have six tapes available.

8.7. Modify the polyphase sorting program to use replacement selection in the distribution phase.

CHAPTER 9

GRAPH ALGORITHMS

We have already looked at those specialized graphs known as trees; we now consider graphs and graph algorithms in general.

It may be worth a moment to consider why we care about graphs. The main reason is probably because graphs are models of connectivity—what things are connected to what other things. Diagrams showing the routes of an airline are an example, and so are road maps and railway and subway maps. For convenience and intelligibility, such maps are usually drawn to match the actual geography, roughly, but the connection information could be conveyed without any reference to geography at all. Graphs are also used to represent the flow of information in signal processing and to represent electrical networks. Indeed, a typical circuit diagram can be thought of as a sort of modified graph, and part of the foundations of network analysis is the theory of graphs. Here the independence of geography is particularly apparent: When drawing a circuit diagram, one normally pays absolutely no attention to where the components are physically located. If the system is a doorbell, the transformer may be in the basement, the button at the front door, the bell in the third-floor apartment, but the circuit diagram for this system is just

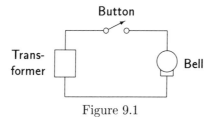

Figure 9.1

But graphs are also useful models for more abstract things:

- Corporate structures
- Social hierarchies and relationships
- Family trees
- Flow of work in a project (or in a factory)

- Project planning and management
- Delivery routes
- Finite-state machines
- Representation of chemical compounds
- Moves in a game (or in negotiations)
- Steps in solving a problem

Because of that last item, an ability to work with graphs and to solve problems with their aid is a basic skill in artificial intelligence.

A graph is a picture, after all; it takes something intangible and abstract and lays it out before us so that we can look at it and point to it. Most of us are much better at dealing with pictures than we are at dealing with abstractions, and the graph frequently points the way to a programmable solution to our problem.

So if I show an edge between two vertices, you must consider the possibility that one vertex is a lathe and the other vertex is a milling machine and that the edge represents the fact that work done on the lathe goes next to the milling machine (or vice versa); or that one vertex is the main office and the other vertex is the St Louis office and that the edge represents the company mail that goes between these two offices.

We will discuss how graphs are represented in the computer, and we will look at some common tasks that the computer must be able to carry out in using graphs as an analytical tool. But initially we will briefly review some of the elementary things you may have been taught about graphs in discrete math.

9.1   FUNDAMENTALS

A graph is a set of *nodes* (or *vertices*) that may be joined by *edges* (or *arcs*). (We will use the terms vertex and node interchangeably, except when we are referring to linked data structures in the computer, in which case we will use node for the record in the computer and vertex for the graph.) Every edge is associated with exactly two vertices, called the *endpoints* of the edge. (You can have vertices without edges but not edges without vertices.)

Figure 9.1 shows some graphs: We draw the vertices as circles and the edges as lines between the circles.

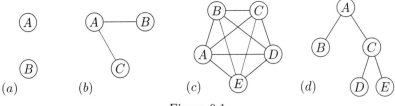

Figure 9.1

If there is an edge from vertex A to vertex B, we say that A and B are *adjacent*. If a certain vertex is an endpoint of an edge, we say the edge is *incident* on the vertex.

A graph in which there is no more than one edge between any pair of vertices is called a *simple* graph.

Note that, unless specified otherwise, the only thing that matters in a graph is who is connected to whom. The edges can be straight, curved, or wiggly; they can follow any route in going between their endpoints. The only thing that matters is who is connected to whom. When it also matters *how closely* they are connected, we will put weights on the edges, but we aren't ready to talk about that yet.

Writers on graph theory sometimes identify a graph by writing $G = (V, E)$ (or occasionally $G(V, E)$). Here V is the set of vertices and E is the set of edges. For a complete specification, we must also list the contents of the sets V and E. In a simple graph, edges can be specified by giving their endpoints, for example, $\{A, C\}$. Since V and E are sets, $|V|$ is the number of vertices and $|E|$ the number of edges.

Every vertex has a *degree*: this is the number of edges incident on that vertex. If there are $|V|$ vertices in a graph, and $|E|$ edges, then the sum of the degrees of all the vertices is $2|E|$. This follows because each edge has two ends and each end adds 1 to the total.

As we saw in Chapter 5, a *path* is a sequence of edges and vertices that leads from some starting vertex to some final vertex. All other vertices on the path are called *interior vertices*. The length of the path is the number of edges in the path. If no two vertices on a path are the same, we call it a *simple* path.

If the path begins and ends on the same vertex, (*i.e.*, the final vertex is the same as the starting vertex) then it is called a *circuit* (or *cycle*). If no two interior vertices on a circuit are the same, and if no interior vertex is the same as the starting vertex, we call it a *simple* circuit. In Fig. 9.1 (*c*), the path $ABCDA$ is a simple circuit. If the graph contains no circuits, it is a tree.

A vertex j is *reachable* from some other vertex i if there is a path from i to j. An undirected graph is *connected* if every vertex is reachable from every other vertex. The graphs in Fig. 9.1 (*b*), (*c*), and (*d*) are connected; the graph in Fig. 9.1 (*a*) isn't. If it is not connected, then it consists of two or more connected pieces called *components*. In an undirected graph, it is easy to see that reachability is an equivalence relation. We know from discrete math that an equivalence relation partitions a set into equivalence classes; in this case the classes are the components. (This is not true if the graph is directed, since in that case reachability is not symmetric.)

A graph in which there is an edge between every pair of distinct vertices is called complete; it is easy to show that if $|V| = n$, then the number of edges in a complete graph is $\frac{1}{2}n(n-1)$. A graph in which there are very few edges is said to be *sparse*.

Digraphs. In an ordinary graph, the endpoints can be written in any order: we may define an edge as $\{A, B\}$ or as $\{B, A\}$. But sometimes the order is important, and an edge (A, B) is considered different from (B, A). Such a graph is called a *directed* graph (or a *digraph* for short); when we draw a digraph we indicate the directions with arrowheads on the edges.

Much of what we said about graphs in general can be extended to directed graphs. The main differences are:

1. We must now distinguish between edges arriving at a vertex and edges departing from a vertex. The *indegree* of a vertex is the number of edges pointing to the vertex, and the *outdegree* is the number of edges pointing away from the vertex.

2. An edge may start and end on the same vertex; this is commonly called a self-loop.

3. When we consider paths and circuits, we must treat the edges as one-way streets. In particular, in this digraph,

there is no path from A to C (or from C to A).

4. A digraph is *strongly* connected if there is a path between every pair of vertices. It is *weakly* connected if the undirected graph that results when we remove the arrowheads is connected.

9.2   REPRESENTATION IN MEMORY

There are two principal ways to represent a graph in a computer:

1. We can use a table, an array of Booleans, called an *adjacency matrix*, where a[i, j] is TRUE if vertices i and j are adjacent and FALSE otherwise.

2. For each vertex, we can list the vertices that are adjacent to the given vertex. The adjacent vertices can go in an array, in a set, or in a linked list. The linked list is probably the most common choice; in that case we refer to the set of adjacent vertices as an *adjacency list*.

9.2.1   Adjacency Matrices

When we study graphs in discrete math, we learn about representing them by adjacency matrices. An adjacency matrix has a 1 in row i, column j, if there is an edge between vertices i and j, and 0 otherwise; 1 and 0 correspond to TRUE and FALSE, respectively.

For example, suppose we have this graph:

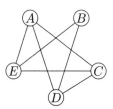

Figure 9.2

This graph has five vertices, and its adjacency matrix is thus of order 5:

$$
\begin{array}{c c}
 & \begin{array}{c c c c c} A & B & C & D & E \end{array} \\
\begin{array}{c} A \\ B \\ C \\ D \\ E \end{array} &
\left[
\begin{array}{c c c c c}
0 & 0 & 1 & 1 & 1 \\
0 & 0 & 0 & 1 & 1 \\
1 & 0 & 0 & 1 & 1 \\
1 & 1 & 1 & 0 & 0 \\
1 & 1 & 1 & 0 & 0
\end{array}
\right]
\end{array}
$$

(The letters are for convenience and not part of the matrix.) If the graph is undirected, as this one is, the adjacency matrix is symmetric.

An adjacency matrix is also a natural way to represent a graph inside the computer. In the computer, we nearly always make this a Boolean array: If there is an edge between i and j, then a[i, j] = TRUE. Thus, in Pascal, we would declare an adjacency matrix as follows:

```
const
    maxnodes = 5;   { or whatever: largest graph accommodated }
type
    node = 1..maxnodes;
    a_matrix = array [node, node] of boolean;
```

This is usually the method of choice, provided the graph is not too big. (We will see some algorithms that run faster with other representations, however.) On the other hand, adjacency matrices tend to be wasteful of memory, because most of their entries are usually zero. (Such a matrix is called *sparse*.) For small graphs this is no problem, but for really big graphs it is crucial, and in practice the really big graphs tend to be the ones with the sparsest matrices.

9.2.2 Adjacency Sets and Lists

For that same graph, the adjacency sets are

Node	Set
A	$\{C, D, E\}$
B	$\{D, E\}$
C	$\{A, D, E\}$
D	$\{A, B, C\}$
E	$\{A, B, C\}$

Pascal includes the **set** data type; for adjacency sets we can thus declare

```
type
    node = 1..maxnodes;
    a_set = set of node;
    a_list = array[node] of a_set;
```

Adjacency sets may be more useful if they are represented by linked lists. Adjacency lists take various forms, depending mostly on the application; the two most important forms are probably pure linked and a hybrid structure based on an array of pointers to lists. Since we speak of nodes in linked lists and nodes in graphs, we had better call the ones in the graph vertices, in order to avoid confusion.

Pure linked.   For the graph of Fig. 9.2, the adjacency list would look as shown in Fig. 9.3.

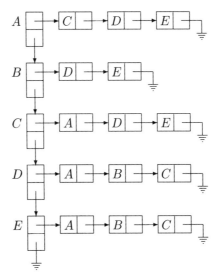

Figure 9.3

Here the vertices are represented by nodes in a linked list (running down the left side in Fig. 9.3), and each vertex's adjacency set is contained in a linked list attached to the node for that vertex. (In the nodes on the left, we could include a field containing the identity of the vertices, but we don't need to; they are defined by their order: the first is A, the second, B, and so on.)

The big advantage of the linked structure is the saving in memory. This is hard to appreciate in school, because in order to save time, we have to keep our examples simple and this means using small graphs for which the linked structure doesn't buy us anything. But in real applications, the graphs are often very large and saving memory becomes a vital issue.

Mixed form.   The drawback of the linked structure is its relative clumsiness. If we need to jump about this list, we are going to have trouble; we can crawl along linked lists but not jump about in them. If we need to jump, we must use an array. We can effect a compromise, with an array for the vertices and linked lists for the adjacencies, as shown in Fig. 9.4.

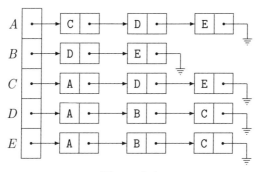

Figure 9.4

This form represents an attractive compromise between the convenience of an array and the economy of a linked list, and we will use this representation whenever we consider implementations of graph algorithms based on adjacency lists instead of adjacency matrices. We will declare

```
type
    listptr = ^listrec;
    listrec = record
                node: integer;   { Node number            }
                next: listptr
            end;
    alists = array [1..maxnodes] of listptr;
var
    graph: alists;
```

Now that we know how to represent a graph inside the computer, we will consider a number of problems that occur when applying graphs in real applications.

9.3   PATHS

Numerous graph applications involve getting from one node in a graph to some other node. Sometimes the other node may be only one edge away from where we are now (an adjacent node); other times it may be more distant and we may want to know how to reach it from where we are, or whether we can reach it at all—whether there is a path to that node. Sometimes there may be many possible paths to our destination and we want the shortest one.

Suppose we want to discover whether we can get there from here. With the simple graphs we look at here, inspection tells us; but (a) a computer can't inspect a graph the way we can and (b) if the graph has several hundred nodes, maybe we can't tell, either—particularly if the graph is directed.

To find whether a node is reachable, we use Warshall's [1962] algorithm. This takes the adjacency matrix, $\mathbf{A}$ as its input and computes the *reachability matrix* $\mathbf{W}$. For any two nodes i and j, $\mathbf{W}_{ij}$ is TRUE if there is a path *of any length* from node i to node j.

The general idea is this: Suppose we are considering whether we can get from node i to node j. We can make the following statements:

1. If $\mathbf{A}_{ij}$ is TRUE, then there is an edge from i to j and hence a path of length 1.

2. Suppose we know all paths (from any node to any other node) whose interior nodes are drawn only from the set $\{1, 2, \ldots, k-1\}$. (That's the first $k-1$ nodes in the graph.) For brevity, I will call such a path a $(k-1)$ path. Here the induction is on the pool of nodes over which we can find the path. Then there is a k path from i to j (*i.e.*, one whose interior nodes are drawn from the first k nodes) if

   a. we already have a $(k-1)$ path from i to j, or if

   b. there is a $(k-1)$ path from node i to node k and a $(k-1)$ path from node $k+1$ to node j.

(Statement 2a follows from the fact that any $(k-1)$ path is also a k path.)

The idea behind this reasoning is that we can build the reachability matrix in stages, starting out with the adjacency matrix and adding interior nodes one by one. We do the induction on k because the procedure's outermost loop will be on k and we have to be sure we can get away with that. This reasoning isn't the easiest thing in the world to follow; an example is a great help. Suppose the graph is as shown in Fig. 9.5.

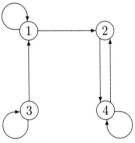

Figure 9.5

Then its adjacency matrix is

$$A = \begin{bmatrix} 1 & 1 & 0 & 0 \\ 0 & 0 & 0 & 1 \\ 1 & 0 & 1 & 0 \\ 0 & 1 & 0 & 1 \end{bmatrix}$$

Now initially $\mathbf{W}$ contains only the paths with no interior nodes at all; these paths are of length 1 and consist simply of the edges in the given graph. So $\mathbf{W}$ is initially equal to $\mathbf{A}$. We will call this initial form $\mathbf{W}^{[0]}$.

When we allow paths to use node 1 as an interior node, we can now get from 3 to 2 (the path is $3 \rightarrow 1 \rightarrow 2$, as can be seen from the graph). Since we are now including node 1, I will call this $\mathbf{W}^{[1]}$. (*Note* that the [1] superscript isn't an exponent. We aren't raising $\mathbf{W}$ to a power here; it's just a way of keeping track of the node subset considered so far.)

$$\mathbf{W}^{[1]} = \begin{bmatrix} 1 & 1 & 0 & 0 \\ 0 & 0 & 0 & 1 \\ 1 & \boxed{1} & 1 & 0 \\ 0 & 1 & 0 & 1 \end{bmatrix}$$

(The new path is marked with a box.)

When we allow paths to use node 2 (as well as node 1) as an interior node, we can now get from 1 to 4. We can also get from 3 to 4. Notice that this is an illustration of Statement 2b: there was a 1 path from 3 to 2 and a path from 2 to 4; by adding 2 to the list of eligible interior nodes, we found a 2 path from 3 to 4. So now our version of $\mathbf{W}$ (still preliminary) is

$$\mathbf{W}^{[2]} = \begin{bmatrix} 1 & 1 & 0 & \boxed{1} \\ 0 & 0 & 0 & 1 \\ 1 & 1 & 1 & \boxed{1} \\ 0 & 1 & 0 & 1 \end{bmatrix}$$

When we allow node 3 as an interior node, there is no change. So $\mathbf{W}$ is now just

$$\mathbf{W}^{[3]} = \begin{bmatrix} 1 & 1 & 0 & 1 \\ 0 & 0 & 0 & 1 \\ 1 & 1 & 1 & 1 \\ 0 & 1 & 0 & 1 \end{bmatrix}$$

Finally, when we allow node 4 as an interior node, we can now find a 4 path from 2 to 2. This is the only new path. So the final version of $\mathbf{W}$ is

$$\mathbf{W}^{[4]} = \begin{bmatrix} 1 & 1 & 0 & 1 \\ 0 & \boxed{1} & 0 & 1 \\ 1 & 1 & 1 & 1 \\ 0 & 1 & 0 & 1 \end{bmatrix}$$

The reason for finding new paths in this peculiar way is that it allows us to find them using a loop on k. Statement 2a says that there is a path using only the first k vertices as interior vertices. But since those are a subset of the first $k+1$ vertices, then that also qualifies as a $(k+1)$ path. Statement 2b says that there is a path in which the only new interior vertex is vertex $k+1$ and that you can reach $k+1$ from i, and j from $k+1$, by k-paths.

To keep track of those k-paths, let $\mathbf{W}^{[k]}$ be a Boolean matrix such that $\mathbf{W}^{[k]}_{ij}$ is TRUE if there is a k-path from vertex i to vertex j. Our desired reachability matrix is then $\mathbf{W}^{[order]}$, where *order* is the order of $\mathbf{A}$—that is, $|V|$. Then our two statements 2a, 2b are

2. $\mathbf{W}^{[k]}_{ij}$ is TRUE iff

a. $\mathbf{W}_{ij}^{[k-1]}$ is TRUE or

b. $\mathbf{W}_{ik}^{[k-1]}$ is TRUE and $\mathbf{W}_{kj}^{[k-1]}$ is TRUE.

Or, briefly,

$$\mathbf{W}_{ij}^{[k]} = \mathbf{W}_{ij}^{[k-1]} \vee (\mathbf{W}_{ik}^{[k-1]} \wedge \mathbf{W}_{kj}^{[k-1]}).$$

To program this, we do not need to use separate matrices for $\mathbf{W}^{[k-1]}$ and $\mathbf{W}^{[k]}$. We used those in the derivation simply to be able to distinguish among the different $\mathbf{W}$'s; in the program, we can safely overwrite the old values with new values as follows:

```
procedure WARSH (var a, w: a_matrix; order: integer);
    var                         { Transitive closure of graph   }
        i, j, k: integer;
    begin
    w := a;                              { Statement 1   }
    for k := 1 to order do
        for i := 1 to order do
            for j := 1 to order do
                w[i, j] := w[i, j]        { Statement 2a  }
                    or w[i, k] and w[k, j]; { Statement 2b  }
    end;   { Warsh }
```

where order and a_matrix are defined as in Section 9.2.1.

Before we enter the loops, w contains all paths with *no* interior vertices—that is, w is $\mathbf{W}^{[0]}$, which is just the same as a, the adjacency matrix. At the end of each pass through the outer loop, w is now $\mathbf{W}^{[k]}$, and at the end of the entire procedure, w is $\mathbf{W}^{[order]}$, which is our desired reachability matrix.

Notice the simple procedure that results from this difficult reasoning. (That's the whole justification for the reasoning, of course.) This is no more expensive than an ordinary matrix multiplication. And of course it tells us a great deal, since it tells us whether *any* given vertex is reachable from *any* other given vertex. Because it consists of three nested loops, each of length $|V|$, its time complexity is $O(|V|^3)$.

Some discrete math texts introduce Warshall's algorithm in graph theory; others introduce it to carry out an equivalent operation on relations. In the latter case, what we get is called the *transitive closure* of the relation, and occasionally you will hear the reachability matrix being called the transitive closure of the graph, as it was in the code.

9.4   TRAVERSAL AND SEARCHING

Warshall's algorithm tells us whether a path to some specified vertex exists, but not what that path is. There may be more than one path, but it tells us nothing about that, either. We now consider ways of finding a specific object (*i.e.*, vertex) in a graph in ways that can be made to yield the path as well.

We will consider searching as a special case of a more general problem, that of *traversing* a graph. Just as traversing a tree or a linked list was visiting all the nodes of the tree or the list in some specified way, so traversing a graph is visiting all its vertices. If we are searching for a particular item, then visiting the vertex consists of looking at it to see whether that's what we're looking for, and the traversal stops when and if we find it. If the graph is connected and undirected, we can start a traversal from any desired vertex. If the graph is directed, some vertices may not be reachable from the vertex at which we start, in which case we will have to try more than one unvisited vertex. Similarly, if the graph is not connected, we will have to take more than one starting point.

There are two general strategies for traversing a graph. One strategy starts by branching out as widely as possible from each vertex. We call this a *breadth-first* search. The other strategy starts out by going just as far away from the starting vertex as it can, until it hits a dead end; then it backs up and tries other edges and does the same with those. This is called a *depth-first* search. Each strategy is good for certain applications and not for others.

9.4.1 Breadth-First Traversal

I said that in a breadth-first traversal we would fan out as widely as possible from the current vertex. This means going out on an incident edge until we hit its other endpoint (the adjacent vertex). We then visit that adjacent vertex (for example, look at it to see whether it's the thing we're after). Then we return to our current vertex, go on to the next incident edge, and ride out that one to have a look at that adjacent vertex. When we've visited all the adjacent vertices, we've finished with the current vertex. This is illustrated in Fig. 9.6 (*a*), in which *A* is our current vertex and we have fanned out to *B*, *C*, and *D*.

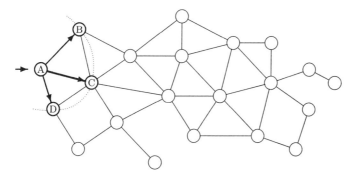

Figure 9.6 (*a*)

We then go to each of those adjacent vertices and fan out from them the same way. In Fig. 9.6 (*b*), we have taken *B* as our current vertex and visited *E*; then, taking *C* as our current vertex, we have visited *F* and *G*. (Since *E* has already been visited, we can't visit it again.) Finally, taking *D* as our current vertex, we have visited *H*. In this way, we have a "frontier" that gradually moves out from the initial vertex into unexplored territory, as suggested by the dotted lines in Fig. 9.6 (*a*) and (*b*).

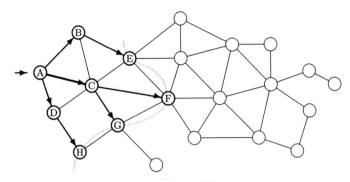

Figure 9.6 (*b*)

In doing breadth-first traversal, the idea is thus to visit (a) the starting vertex; (b) all vertices one edge away from the starting vertex; (c) all vertices two edges away from the starting vertex; (d) all vertices three edges away, and so on. Since it's troublesome to keep track of how many edges away a vertex is, we implement this slightly differently:

1. Visit the starting vertex and mark it.

2. For all unmarked vertices adjacent to that vertex, visit and mark those vertices.

3. For every vertex you visited in Step 2, repeat Step 2.

4. Repeat Steps 2 and 3 until there are no more vertices to visit.

That summary is our starting point, but we will have to refine it. Suppose we visit a vertex. Then we must do two things: (1) we must make a note that we've visited that vertex (so we don't visit it again later); and (2) we must make a note to branch out from that vertex later on.

To keep track of the vertices that have been visited, we provide a Boolean array, `visited`, and when we visit vertex j, we set `visited[j]` to TRUE.

Since we must proceed level by level, the process takes on the following organization:

For the current vertex (say, 1), visit all unmarked vertices one edge away; remember these vertices (say, 2, 4, 5).

For the first of the remembered vertices (*i.e.*, 2), visit all unmarked vertices one edge away and remember these vertices (say, 3, 6, 7).

Now we have remembered 2, 4, 5, 3, 6, 7, in that order. The procedure clearly has to be iterative, running through the remembered vertices. But these remembered vertices fall into two categories:

$$(\underbrace{2, 4, 5,}_{\text{distance}=1} \quad \underbrace{3, 6, 7}_{\text{distance}=2})$$

But this means that the first vertices remembered must be the first ones processed. Hence, our memory must be a *queue*, since this has the first-in, first-out organization we require. (You will notice the correspondence between breadth-first traversal of a graph and level-by-level traversal of a tree.) Using the queue makes the computer work outward level by level: we don't start visiting the next level until the first level is done, so that those vertices don't enter the queue until all the first-level vertices have been queued.

And in fact, the program runs off that queue. We pick each vertex off the queue and use it as our working vertex—the one we're going to fan out from. We fan out from that vertex, and when we're done, we pick the next vertex off the queue. The program terminates when the queue is empty.

So we can write the skeleton of the program this way:

```
mark all vertices as unvisited; { Preliminaries          }
empty the queue;

visit the starting vertex;      { This gets us started }
mark it as visited;
put it on the queue;
*done := false;

while (queue isn't empty)        { Main loop              }
           *and not done* do
    begin
    take working vertex off queue;
    for all vertices adjacent to working vertex do
       if the adjacent vertex isn't marked then
          begin
          visit it;
 *        if this vertex is the target then
 *           done := true;
          mark it as visited;
          put it on the queue
          end
    end; { while }
```

This process works equally well with a directed or undirected graph. What I've shown here is a *search* of the graph; this version visits every vertex in the graph that is reachable from the starting vertex until it finds the target. To make it into a traversal, we need only omit the starred statements and the starred **and not done** in the **while** statement.

Here is an implementation of a breadth-first traversal, using an adjacency matrix to represent the graph.

```
procedure B_FIRST (adjac: a_matrix; order: integer);
   var                           { Breadth-first traversal      }
       visited: array [1..maxnodes] of boolean;
       this_node,  { Node from which we fan out  }
       j,          { Adjacent node subscript     }
```

```
                n: integer;
            begin
            for n := 1 to order do
                visited[n] := false;
            clear_queue;
            for n := 1 to order do              { Loop on separate parts}
                if not visited[n] then
                    begin
                    en_queue (n);
                    repeat
                        de_queue (this_node);       { Pick a node off queue }
                        if not visited[this_node] then      { Fan out      }
                          begin
                          visit (this_node);
                          visited[this_node] := true;
                                                  { Put unmarked adjacent }
                          for j := 1 to order do  {   nodes on the queue  }
                              if adjac[this_node, j] then
                                  if not visited[j] then
                                      en_queue (j)
                        end { if }
                    until empty_queue
                end; { if not visited }
            end; { B_First }
```

Clear_Queue, En_Queue, De_Queue, and Empty_Queue are the usual procedures and functions for the ADT queue. In this version, our goal is traversal, and so the outer loop (on n) tries all unmarked vertices, in case there were some vertices that were not reachable from the first vertex. If we know the graph will be undirected and connected, this loop is unnecessary.

When we are using this algorithm for searching, we must associate with each vertex a number giving the vertex from which it was visited. (We can call this the *predecessor* of the vertex.) We can then work backwards from the target, using these numbers, to determine the path from the starting vertex to the target.

It should be clear that the path found by the breadth-first search will be the shortest possible. To see this, note that at any level k we visit all the vertices reachable by a path of length k. (The starting vertex is at level 0.) Next, suppose we found the target at level k and suppose there were a shorter path to the target vertex, of length $j < k$. But then we would have found the target when we reached the jth level, and we would never have had to go on out to the kth level.

If we mark all the edges along which we moved in visiting the various vertices, those marked edges will form a tree. This is because the only way we could have a circuit in those edges would be if some vertex had been visited from two different working vertices. But our visited array, and the if not visited[j] test guarantees that no vertex will ever be visited twice.

If we do a full traversal instead of just a search, and if the graph is undirected and connected, then the tree will include all the vertices in the graph. We say that the tree *spans* the graph, and such a tree is called a *spanning tree*. Every undirected, connected graph has a spanning tree, and in fact unless the graph itself is a tree, it will have more than one spanning tree. Any spanning tree we get from a breadth-first traversal is called a *breadth-first* spanning tree. If the graph is directed, it may take more than one tree to span the graph, in which case we speak of a spanning forest; the same thing is true if the graph isn't connected.

To see the time complexity of a breadth-first traversal, note that the length of the `repeat` loop is determined by the number of vertices on the queue. But every vertex goes on the queue exactly once; hence, the length of this loop is $|V|$. The inner loop on j also has length $|V|$; thus the time complexity, using an adjacency matrix, is $O(|V|^2)$. If we represent the graph with adjacency lists, then the inner loop traverses the list for each vertex. The cost of the two loops is thus $|V|$ for the dequeueing operations in the `repeat` loop plus the sum of the lengths of the lists of the various vertices; but this is clearly $O(|E|)$; hence, for a graph represented by adjacency lists the time complexity is $O(|V| + |E|)$.

9.4.2   Depth-First Traversal

In going depth first, we want to go out as far as possible from the current vertex. So the general procedure is: Go on from edge to edge, moving away instead of fanning out, until you hit a dead end. (You hit a dead end when you've arrived at a vertex with no unvisited adjacent vertices.) Then back up to the most recent fork in the road and take one of the other edges and follow *that* up.

Thus, the procedure begins by finding a path that goes out to the bitter end, as suggested by the heavy arrows in Fig. 9.7 (a).

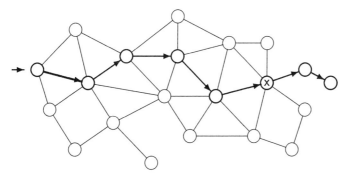

Figure 9.7 (a)

Once it has reached a dead end, it backs up until it finds another possibility—*e.g.*, one of the other edges incident on the vertex marked x—and follows that new path until *it* dead-ends, as in Fig. 9.7 (b).

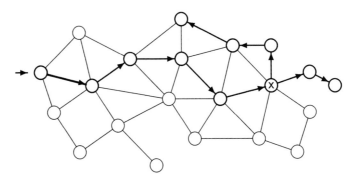

Figure 9.7 *(b)*

The traversal continues this way until it has visited all reachable vertices.

Now as soon as we see that phrase, "back up," that should immediately say one of two things to us: *stack* or *recursion*. And indeed, to do a depth-first search or traversal, we will either manage it with a stack ourselves or get Pascal to handle it for us by means of recursions.

The recursive way is probably a little easier to see. (The nonrecursive form uses a stack in exactly the way B_First used a queue; a problem at the end of this chapter investigates this implementation.) Recall that the way to understand a recursive program is to take it on faith that the recursive call will function properly and consider only the current level. So we look at it this way: Eventually we want to follow up all incident edges from where we are right now (*e.g.*, from the vertex marked x). But we don't want to follow up edge number 2 until we've traced edge number 1 to the bitter end, as in Fig. 9.7 *(a)*. So to trace edge number 1 to the bitter end without losing our place, we will do it recursively. When we return from the recursive call, we *will* have traced edge number 1 all the way out and we can now go on to edge number 2, as in Fig. 9.7 *(b)*.

The depth-first search program has the following skeleton:

```
procedure D_FIRST (this_vertex: integer);
   begin
 *if this_vertex is the target then return;
   visit this vertex;
   mark this_vertex as visited;
   for all vertices adjacent to this_vertex do
      if the adjacent vertex isn't marked then
         d_first (adjacent vertex);
   end;  { D_First }

begin  { Calling procedure }
mark all vertices as not visited;
for all unmarked vertices do
   d_first (vertex);
end;
```

To begin, we mark all vertices as unvisited and then call `D_First` with the starting vertex as a parameter. As written here, the program will do a search; that is, it will visit every vertex in the graph reachable from the starting vertex until it has found the target. To make it into a traversal, we need only delete the starred statement.

You are aware that every recursive program requires a safety net to prevent infinite recursion. It's not obvious where the safety net is in this case. But clearly once every vertex is marked, then the recursions will stop, because the `if` statement in the `for` loop will prevent any further recursive calls.

Here is a Pascal implementation of a depth-first traversal:

```
procedure DEPTH (a: a_matrix; order: integer);
                              { Depth-first traversal        }
     var                      {    (recursive)               }
        visited: array [1..maxnodes] of boolean;
        i: integer;

     procedure D_FIRST (node: integer);   { Recursive part        }
        var
           j: integer;
        begin
        visited[node] := true;
        for j := 1 to order do
           if a[node, j] then
              if not visited[j] then
                 begin
                 visit (j);
                 d_first (j);      { Forge ahead   }
                 end;
        end;   { D_First }

     begin   { Depth }
     for i := 1 to order do
        visited[i] := false;
     for i := 1 to order do        { Loop on separate parts}
        if not visited[i] then
           d_first (i);
     end;   { Depth }
```

As with the breadth-first procedure, this considers every unvisited vertex as a possible starting point; that's the reason for the second loop on i in the body of **Depth**. As with the breadth-first procedure, if the graph is undirected and connected, this loop will not be needed.

The time complexity of a depth-first traversal depends on how the graph is represented in memory. In any case, we assume that **Visit** requires $O(1)$ time. We call `D_First` for every unmarked vertex and, in each call, mark the vertex; hence. `D_First` is called $|V|$ times. If we use an adjacency matrix, then to find the vertices adjacent to vertex k within `D_First` requires going through a row of the matrix;

this is the loop on j, whose length is $|V|$. But we must do this for every vertex; hence, the total cost is $O(|V|^2)$.

If we use adjacency lists, then all we can find the vertices adjacent to vertex k by traversing the list for vertex k. To do the entire graph, we must traverse all the adjacency lists. But all the adjacency lists taken together comprise $2|E|$ entries. Thus, the cost is $|V|$ for the calls to D_First plus $2|E|$ for the adjacency-list entries, and so the time complexity in this case is $O(|V| + |E|)$.

Is this an important difference? It depends on the graph. If the graph is so sparse that $|E| + |V| \ll |V|^2$, there can be a considerable saving in time if we use an adjacency list. If the graph is complete, or nearly so, then there are $O(|V|^2)$ edges, and adjacency lists don't buy us anything. (But if the graphs we are working with are known to be that crowded, we probably wouldn't use adjacency lists in the first place.)

Again, since every vertex is visited only once, we end up with a tree, and again, if the graph is undirected and connected, this tree spans the graph; we call it a depth-first spanning tree.

9.4.3   Connectivity

If an undirected graph consists of more than one component, we will realize this when we discover that there is no one spanning tree but only a spanning forest. A more subtle question is whether the graph is *biconnected*. A graph is biconnected if there is no vertex whose removal would break up the graph into two or more connected components. This can be an important consideration when the graph represents a communications network. If the network is biconnected, then an equipment failure at any node will not prevent the other nodes from communicating, since they can find a path that does not go through the node that is down.

The graph in Fig. 9.8 is not biconnected, since the removal of vertex F would break the graph into two components. A vertex like F is called an *articulation point*. Articulation points divide the graph into *biconnected components*, which are joined only by the articulation points. (Note that a subgraph consisting of only a single vertex or of only two vertices is considered to be a biconnected component.) The articulation points are bottlenecks; if Fig. 9.8 represents a communications network, then not only does the reliability of the network as a whole depend crucially on that of node F, but that node must carry a particularly heavy load of messages, because it is the only link between the two biconnected components.

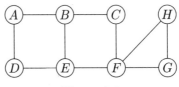

Figure 9.8

We approach the problem of biconnectivity indirectly by finding the set of articulation points; if the set is empty, then the graph is biconnected. In a graph as simple as this one, we can identify the articulation point by inspection, but for large graphs the problem may not be so easy. Since each articulation point is a bottleneck, we will base our search for articulation points on a consideration of alternative paths between vertices.

The same graph is shown in Fig. 9.9. This representation is based on a depth-first spanning tree originating at vertex A. The thick edges are the tree; the edges that do not belong to the tree are the thin ones; we call these *back edges*.

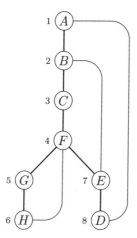

Figure 9.9

We have numbered the vertices in the course of doing the depth-first traversal, giving each vertex a number as we get to it. It should be clear that we have a direct route from any vertex n to any lower-numbered vertex: We need only go back up the tree. For example, we have a direct route from C to A by way of the path CBA. But we also have an alternative route that goes *down* the tree and takes a back edge to get back up: this is the path $CFEDA$. It should also be clear that a graph is biconnected if there is at least one alternative route from every vertex to every vertex further up the tree.

The point of using a depth-first spanning tree is that it allows us to number the vertices, and we can use those numbers both to implement a systematic test for alternative routes and to identify any articulation points. (In what follows, "vertex n" refers to the vertex that has been numbered n by the traversal, and similarly for other vertices.) Specifically, let $low(n)$ be the *lowest*-numbered vertex that can be reached from any vertex n by an alternative path: that is, a path that doesn't go through n's parent and that contains at most one back edge. If $low(n) = q$ and $q < n$, then such a path provides an alternative route from n to q.

If a vertex i isn't the root of the tree, it is an articulation point if, for some descendant j, $low(j) \geq i$. We can say this because if i isn't the root, there are vertices in the graph whose numbers are lower than i, and if $low(j) \geq i$, then clearly j can't reach those lower-numbered vertices by an alternative route. For example, in Fig. 9.9, F (for which $i = 4$) has descendants G and H, and $low(G) = low(H) = 4$; thus, we find the F is an articulation point.) Hence, to program this, we need only find a way of computing $low(i)$ for every vertex i in the graph. Then the algorithm consists of two parts: number the vertices from the depth-first spanning tree and find $low(i)$ for all i on the tree.

We can find $low(i)$ by noting that it is the minimum of three numbers:

$$low(i) = \min \begin{cases} i \\ low(j : j \text{ is child of } i) \\ low(j : \text{the edge from } i \text{ to } j \text{ is a back edge}) \end{cases} \tag{9.1}$$

It's easy to identify the back edges, because if we are finding $low(i)$ in the course of a traversal, then an edge from i to j is back edge if j has already been numbered. We will be putting the numbers into an array, and when we program the traversal, we will use that array instead of a `visited` array. So our traversal algorithm will take the following form, which does everything for us:

1. Give the current vertex p a number $d(p) = n$.

2. Set $low(p) = n$.

3. Increment n.

4. For every vertex q adjacent to p:

    a. If q isn't numbered, traverse recursively from q. Then when we return,

        i. if $low(q) \geq d(p)$, then p is an articulation point;

        ii. if $low(q) < low(p)$, then make $low(p) = low(q)$.

    b. Else if q isn't p's parent, then (p, q) is a back edge; if $d(q)$ is less than $low(p)$, then $low(p) = d(q)$.

(This algorithm is due to Hopcroft; see Aho *et al.*, 1974.) The counter n is set to an initial value of 1 by the calling program. Step 4.a.i comes about this way: Step 4.a.ii guarantees that, at the end of Step 4, $low(p)$ will be as small as the smallest *low* value of any of its descendants. But that also means that when we come back from the recursive call in Step 4.a, $low(q)$ will be as small the smallest *low* value of any of *its* descendants. But that is just what we need to know in order to find out whether p is an articulation point; hence, the test comes right on the heels of the recursive call.

We can write the traversal from this outline as follows. First we must declare

```
const
    maxnodes = 16; { or whatever: size of biggest graph }
type
    a_matrix = array [1..maxnodes, 1..maxnodes] of boolean;
    ptype = array [1..maxnodes] of integer;
    aset = set of byte;
var
    adjac: a_matrix;        { Adjacency matrix      }
    apts: aset;             { Articulation points   }
    dfnum,                  { Depth-first numbers    }
```

```
low,                  { Lowest reachable node }
preds: ptype;         { Predecessor nodes     }
nodes,                { Number of nodes       }
num: integer;         { Depth-first number    }
```

Then the depth-first traversal looks like this:

```
procedure DF (this: integer);            { Depth-first traversal }
                                         {   for biconnectivity  }
                                         {   (preliminary version)}
   var              { "This" is current node p }
      next,         { Adjacent node q           }
      min: integer; { Possible value of low     }
   begin
   dfnum[this] := num;                        { Step 1           }
   min := num;                                { Step 2           }
   num := num + 1;                            { Step 3           }
   for next := 1 to nodes do                  { Step 4           }
      if adjac[this, next] then
         if dfnum[next] = 0 then              { Not visited      }
            begin
            preds[next] := this;
            df (next);                        {   Step 4.a       }
            if (low[next]                     {     Step 4.a.i   }
                   >= dfnum[this]) then
               apts := apts + [this];
            if low[next] < min then           {     Step 4.a.ii  }
               min := low[next]
            end
         else
            if next <> preds[this] then       {     Step 4.b     }
               if dfnum[next] < min then
                  min := dfnum[next];
   low[this] := min;
   end;  { DF }
```

The variable `num` contains the number to be assigned to each vertex; the `dfnum` array contains the depth-first numbers $d(\cdot)$ assigned to the vertices; the array `low` holds the *low* values for the vertices; and the array `preds` contains the predecessors (*i.e.*, the parents) of the vertices on the tree. As we find the articulation points, we put them into the set `apts`.

We start by setting `min` to the number assigned to `this`, the current node. When we come back from the recursive call, we also know what `low[next]` is, and we compare `min` with that. But at this point `low[next]` holds the smallest *low* value for anything in the subtree of `next`; hence, we make the articulation-point test right here. Finally, we compare `min` to the number of any back edge, and the resulting minimum becomes `low[this]`, in accordance with Eq. (9.1).

DF is nested inside another procedure, which provides the variables num, preds, low, dfnum, and the parameter apts. It looks like this:

```
procedure BICON (start: integer; adjac: a_matrix;
                        var apts: aset);
                                { Finds articulation points     }
                                {   of an undirected graph       }
        var                     {   (preliminary version)        }
            dfnum,
            low,
            preds: array [1..maxnodes] of integer;
            i,
            num: integer;

        procedure DF (this: integer);
            { ... as above ... }

    begin { Bicon }
    for i := 1 to order do          { Preliminaries }
        dfnum[i] := 0;
    apts := [];  { No articulation points yet     }
    num := 1;
    df (start);                     { Do traversal  }
    num := 0;
    apts := apts - [start];         { Remove root   }
    for i := 1 to order do          { Check root     }
        if i <> start then          { Count children}
            if preds[i] = start then
                num := num + 1;
    if num > 1 then                 { More than 1:  }
        apts := apts + [start];     {    put it back }
    end;  { Bicon }
```

The parameter start is the starting vertex for the traversal and hence also the root of the spanning tree. The call to DF will list the root as an articulation point whether it actually is or not. Therefore, after we return, we remove the root from the list and then enter a loop that counts the root's children by scanning the preds array; it should be clear that if the root has more than one child, it is also an articulation point.

What we have so far are procedures that find the articulation points but not the biconnected components themselves. (This is why we have labelled them "preliminary version.") We can modify DF to list the components as follows: We will push each new edge onto a stack. Then when we detect an articulation point, we will pop the stack until the last edge popped is the current edge. For example, consider the graph of Fig. 9.10.

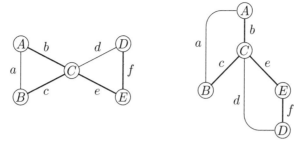

Figure 9.10

The graph is on the left; the depth-first spanning tree is on the right. As the procedure grows the tree, it puts the edge b on the stack when it moves from A to C; then as it moves from C to E, it puts the edge e on the stack; and finally, it pushes f as it moves from E to D.

As the procedure returns from the last recursion, nothing happens to the stack; but when it returns to the recursion from C to E, it discovers that C is an articulation point. At this point, it pops edges from the stack until the edge e is popped. These edges—f and e—and their endpoints are sufficient to identify the biconnected component $G_1 = (\{C, D, E\}, \{d, e, f\})$.

At this point, the stack contains only b. Still at node C, the procedure now goes to B and puts edge c onto the stack. After the remaining recursions unwind, it finds itself at node A, looking at C. Now A is falsely identified as an articulation point. We will have to correct this when we return to Bicon, but at the moment it has the effect of popping c and b off the stack, and this identifies the other biconnected component $G_2 = (\{A, B, C\}, \{a, b, c\})$.

Since the different biconnected components tend to appear at different levels on the tree, the edges in these components go in consecutive levels on the stack, as did f and e. It should be clear that the lowest articulation point in the tree will be the first to be identified. Hence, when we find such a point, we pop everything down to the first edge in the component, inclusive. Since the edge that DF is currently contemplating was the first to be pushed, it will be the last to be popped and thus can be used to stop a repeat loop. This leaves edges in the next component at the top of the stack. When we popped that first component G_1, one of the edges b was left on the stack; this was an edge belonging to the other component, and the next recursion from C put the other edge c onto the stack.

Here are the procedures, modified to incorporate these changes. First, we add these declarations:

```
const
    maxcomps = 16;          { Maximum number of components  }
type
    comparray = array[1..maxcomps] of aset;
var
    comp: comparray;        { Biconnected components        }
    ncomps: integer;        { Number of components          }
```

(Each component will go in a set comp[i].) Our procedures now look like this:

```
procedure BICON (start: integer; var apts: aset;
                 var comp: comparray; var ncomps: integer);
                                    { Finds articulation points    }
                                    {   & biconnected components    }
          var                       {   of an undirected graph      }
             dflow,
             dfnum: array [1..maxnodes] of integer;
             i,
             num: integer;

          procedure DF (this: integer);   { Depth-first traversal    }
                                          {   for biconnectivity      }
               var       { "This" is current node }
                  next,  { Adjacent node          }
                  n,     { Popped                 }
                  t,     {   endpoints            }
                  min: integer;
               begin
               min := num;
               dfnum[this] := num;              { First possibility    }
               num := num + 1;
               for next := 1 to order do        { For all adjacent     }
                  if adj[this, next] then        {   nodes,             }
                     if dfnum[next] = 0 then
                        begin                    { If not visited then  }
                        push (this);             {   push and recurse   }
                        push (next);
                        preds[next] := this;
                        df (next);
                        if dflow[next]<min then { Second possibility:  }
                           min := dflow[next];  {   child of This       }
                                                { Articulation point    }
                                                {   test                }
                     if dflow[next] >= dfnum[this] then
                        begin                    { Found one            }
                        apts := apts + [this];
                        ncomps := ncomps + 1;
                        repeat
                           pop (n);          { Pop edges          }
                           pop (t);          {   & add to set      }
                           comp[ncomps] := comp[ncomps] + [n] + [t]
                        until (n = next) and (t = this);
                        end
                  end
```

```
          else                        { Third possibility:   }
            if next <> preds[this] then   { back edge       }
              if dfnum[next] < min then
                min := dfnum[next];
      dflow[this] := min;
      end;  { DF }


  begin { Bicon }
  for i := 1 to order do        { Preliminaries }
     dfnum[i] := 0;
  apts := [];                   { No points yet }
  for i := 1 to maxcomps do     { No components }
     comp[i] := [];             {    either      }
  ncomps := 0;
  num := 1;
  clear_stack;
  df (start);                   { Do traversal  }
  num := 0;
  apts := apts - [start];       { Remove root   }
  for i := 1 to order do
     if i <> start then         { Check root    }
        if preds[i] = start then
           num := num + 1;
  if num > 1 then
     apts := apts + [start];    { Put it back   }
  end;  { Bicon }
```

The execution time of `Bicon` is dominated by the loop on `i` after the call to `DF`; this loop is $O(n)$ if the graph has n vertices. The modifications to `DF` do not change its cost, so its execution time is the same as that for a regular depth-first traversal: $O(|V|^2)$ if we use an adjacency matrix, and $O(|V| + |E|)$ if we use an adjacency list. The procedure `DF` is virtually the same in the latter case; writing this version is left as an exercise.

9.5 SHORTEST-PATH PROBLEMS

Consider the map in Fig. 9.11. Suppose we wish to go from New York to Washington. Clearly the quickest route is by way of Philadelphia and Baltimore; but since the path by way of San Francisco has only two edges, a breadth-first search will tell us to go clear out to San Francisco and then from there to Washington, which is ridiculous. San Francisco is something like 3,000 miles away, and the search is telling us to go 6,000 miles to reach a city that's 220 miles away.

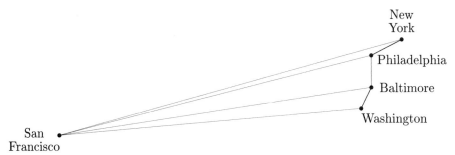

Figure 9.11

So although there are many applications where all that matters in a path is the number of edges, there are others where the *cost* of going along an edge is important. We indicate such situations by labelling each edge with a *weight*. The weight gives us some measure of what it costs to go down that edge—in our example here, the mileage. Such a graph is called a *weighted graph*, and with weighted graphs we need different kinds of searches if we are interested in minimizing the cost, that is, the sum of the weights along the selected path.

We can include the weights in the adjacency matrix by entering the weights instead of 1s and 0s. A *weighted* adjacency matrix is defined as follows:

$$a_{ij} = \text{ weight of edge from vertex } i \text{ to vertex } j.$$

If there is no edge between i and j, we specify a weight of infinity.

For example, the graph in Fig. 9.12 has this weighted adjacency matrix:

$$
\begin{bmatrix}
-- & 6 & \infty & 3 & \infty \\
\infty & -- & 9 & \infty & \infty \\
5 & 3 & -- & \infty & \infty \\
\infty & \infty & 8 & -- & 1 \\
2 & \infty & \infty & 7 & --
\end{bmatrix}
$$

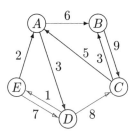

Figure 9.12

What goes on the main diagonal depends on the graph. Usually, if the graph is undirected, the main-diagonal entries are 0, since if we are at vertex k already, it costs us nothing to go to vertex k. If the graph is directed, we usually assume that we cannot go from vertex k to vertex k unless there is a self-loop on the vertex. In this case, the main-diagonal entries will be ∞ unless there is a self-loop on a vertex, in which case the entry will be the weight on the self-loop. In general, however, the treatment of the main-diagonal entries depends on the application for which the graph is being used.

We will get to the shortest-path problem eventually, but before we do, there is a related problem we will consider first, because it is important in its own right and because it makes the shortest-path algorithm easier to follow.

9.5.1 Minimal Spanning Tree

We spoke of depth-first and breadth-first spanning trees, but with a weighted graph it is sometimes important to know what is the least-cost spanning tree—the tree for which the sum of the weights of its edges is a minimum. This is called a *minimal* (or sometimes *minimum*) spanning tree. For conciseness, we will refer to edges with minimal weight as *shortest* edges, although in practice the weights could clearly reflect some cost other than length.

We will present two well-known algorithms for finding a minimal spanning tree. Both of these algorithms depend on the following principle: Given a graph $G = (V, E)$, let A and B be any partitioning of V. If the graph is connected, there must be at least one edge connecting some vertex in A to some vertex in B. We will call any such edge a *bridge* between A and B. (Any spanning tree, whatever its cost, has to include one of these bridges; otherwise, it would not span G.) These bridges will have various lengths (*i.e.*, weights); let e be the shortest bridge. Then there is a minimal spanning tree that includes e.

We can prove this indirectly as follows: Suppose there is no minimal spanning tree including e. Then there is some minimal spanning tree T that *doesn't* include e, as in Fig. 9.13. One edge in T must be a bridge e' between A and B. If we remove e' from T and substitute e, we will have a new spanning tree T'. Because of the way we chose e, its length is no greater than that of e'; hence the cost of T' is no greater than that of T. But now T' is a minimal spanning tree that includes e; this contradicts our assumption that there was no such tree.

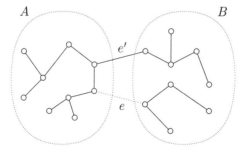

Figure 9.13

Finding a minimal spanning tree can thus be reduced to assembling it from minimal-weight edges like e for various partitionings of V. The two algorithms we present simply do the partitionings in different ways.

Prim's Algorithm.   The following algorithm, due to Prim [1957], finds the minimal spanning tree of a connected, weighted, undirected graph G, starting from a given vertex.

1. Initially, the tree consists only of the given vertex.

2. While the tree does not include all the vertices in G:

   > Examine all the edges in G with one endpoint in the tree and the other endpoint not in the tree. Find the shortest one of these edges and add it (and its other endpoint) to the tree.

In each step in this algorithm, the partition A comprises as much of the tree as has been grown so far and B comprises the rest of the vertices. In the body of the loop, we are searching for the shortest (lowest-weight) bridge between A and B. Since every edge added to the tree is a minimum-weight bridge, the tree is minimal.

In implementing this, we will call the weighted adjacency matrix cost. If our starting vertex is named start, then we might be tempted to write something like this:

```
tree := [start];
repeat
   jmin := 0;
   mincost := HUGE;
   for i := 1 to order do
      if i in tree then
         for j := 1 to order do
            if not (j in tree) then
               if cost[i, j] < mincost then
                  begin
                  jmin := j;
                  mincost := cost[i, j]
                  end;  { for; if; for; if; if }
   if jmin <> 0 then
      tree := tree + [jmin];
until jmin = 0;
```

(HUGE is some number guaranteed to be greater than the sum of all the weights in the matrix.)

This is not the best we can do, however. If there are $|V|$ vertices, then the loop on j makes $O(|V|)$ passes and the loop on i makes $|V|$ passes. But the repeat loop will run until all $|V|$ vertices are in the tree, so that is also $O(|V|)$. Since these loops are nested, the total time is $O(|V|^3)$.

The problem is that it takes $O(|V|^2)$ time to search a $|V| \times |V|$ matrix for the minimum value and we have to do this search $|V|$ times because of the outer loop. We could speed this up if we had an array dist giving the shortest distance to any vertex in the tree for all the vertices in the graph. Then we could simply do a sequential search of this array in order to select the next vertex to be added. We would have to set this array up initially, of course, and we would have to update it every time a new vertex is added to the tree, but the cost of those operations will be only $O(|V|)$.

In addition, we need a more explicit representation of the tree than just a set. At the end, the set will just contain all the nodes, and that tells us little or nothing. We will use an array `preds` that will hold the predecessor of every node in the tree. (If the spanning tree were rooted, `preds[i]` would indicate the parent of node i.) For example, if our graph is as in Fig. 9.14, with the spanning tree originating in node A marked by the dark lines,

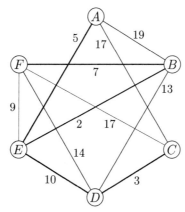

Figure 9.14

then the predecessor array is

Node	A	B	C	D	E	F
Predecessor	–	E	D	E	A	B

(Since A is our starting vertex, it has no predecessor.) With this array, we can trace out the tree by working backwards from the various vertices.

The code for doing all this is as follows. (The `dist` and `preds` arrays are of type `ptype = array[1..maxnodes] of integer`. The weighted adjacency matrix is of type `c_matrix = array[1..maxnodes, 1..maxnodes] of integer`.)

```
procedure MIN_SPAN (start, nodes: integer; var cost: c_matrix;
                    var preds, dist: ptype);
                                     { Minimal spanning tree;       }
                                     {    Prim's algorithm.  Uses   }
         var                        {    weighted adjacency matrix  }
             i, n,
             imin,
             mincost: integer;
             in_tree: array [1..maxnodes] of boolean;
         begin
         tcost := 0;                            { Preliminaries }
         for i := 1 to nodes do
            begin
```

```
          dist[i] := cost[start, i];
          preds[i] := start;
          in_tree[i] := false
          end;
      preds[start] := 0;
      dist[start] := 0;
      in_tree[start] := true;

      for n := 2 to nodes do
         begin
         imin := 0;
         mincost := infinity;               { Find         }
         for i := 1 to nodes do             {    shortest  }
            if not in_tree[i]               {    edge      }
                  and (dist[i] < mincost) then
               begin
               imin := i;
               mincost := dist[i]
               end;
         if imin <> 0 then
            begin
            in_tree[imin] := true;          { Add to tree  }
            for i := 2 to nodes do
               if not in_tree[i] and (cost[imin, i] < dist[i]) then
                  begin
                  preds[i] := imin;         { Update preds }
                  dist[i] := cost[imin, i] {    & dist     }
                  end;                      {    arrays    }
            end { if imin <> 0 }
         end { for n }
      end; { Min_Span }
```

This takes some explanation. Initially, the vertex specified by **start** is the only one in the tree, so we simply set **dist[i]** to **cost[start, 1]**. This costs $O(|V|)$. Next, within the loop on **n**, we select the vertex for which **dist[i]** is the smallest and add it to the tree.

Now updating the **dist** array is simple. When we enter the updating loop, **dist[i]** gives the lowest cost for getting to i from any vertex in the tree as it was before we included **imin**. But now maybe it's cheaper to go by way of **imin**. So we compare **dist[i]** to the cost of coming from **imin**. If it's no cheaper, we leave **dist[i]** unchanged; if we can make a better deal with **imin**, then we update **dist[i]** and **preds[i]** to reflect the better deal.

Finding **imin** requires a scan of the **dist** array, which costs $O(|V|)$. Updating the **dist** array likewise costs $O(|V|)$. So the inside of the main loop is $O(|V|)$. The main loop (on **n**) multiplies this by $|V| - 1$, so that the total cost is now only $O(|V|^2)$.

Notice that this algorithm simply grabs the shortest edge with no further consideration—that is, it doesn't consider the possibility that, later on, this choice might be a mistake. People who grab the shortest thing without taking further thought are called greedy, and an algorithm that does the same is called a *greedy algorithm*. It would be nice if all problems could be solved by greedy algorithms, but unfortunately they can't.

If we use an adjacency list representation, the code does essentially the same thing, but it looks quite different. We will use an array of pointers to the heads of these lists. Thus we have the declarations,

```
type
   listptr = ^listrec;
   listrec = record
                node,            { Node number        }
                cost: integer;   { Cost to reach it    }
                next: listptr
             end;
   alists = array [1..maxnodes] of listptr;
   dist_array = array [1..maxnodes] of integer;
var
   cost: alists;
   dist,
   preds: dist_array;
```

Note that `listrec` includes a `cost` field: these are *weighted* adjacency lists. For the graph in Fig. 9.14, the `cost` array and its lists would look as shown in Fig. 9.15.

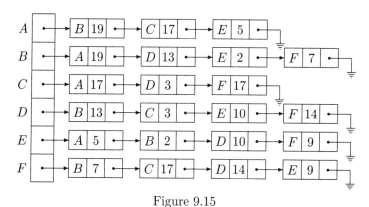

Figure 9.15

In addition, we will decrease the execution time still further by using a priority queue to control the choice of vertices. This is essentially the same structure we used in Heapsort, but we must make a few changes to make it suitable for our application. First, this will be a heap of losers: We wish to put the vertex with the *least* distance at the top of the heap, so our comparisons will be the reverse of what they were in Heapsort.

Second, we must handle duplication in the heap. When we looked at the matrix version, we saw that we would frequently have to update a `dist` entry. We must now find an easy way to handle this using a priority queue. We must be able to detect when an entry is already in the queue, and we must be able to find it quickly without having to look through the entire queue for it. We do this with a cross-reference array `xref` that will tell us where every current entry is to be found. We will set the entries in this array to 0 in `Clear_Queue`.

Finally, the comparisons will be based on the contents of the `dist` array. But the nested indexing implied by `if dist[queue.data[p]] > dist[queue.data[c]] then ...` is clumsy; hence, we will add an array indicating the relative priority of every entry; we will call this `rank` and will pass each entry's priority along with its value when we put it on the queue. All this means that we must declare the queue as follows:

```
const
   queuemax = 64; { Or whatever   }
   maxnodes = 32; { Or whatever   }
var
   queue: record
             last: integer;
             data,
             rank: array [1..queuemax] of integer;
             xref: array [1..maxnodes] of integer;
          end;
```

This entails some revision of our queue-handling procedures. `SiftDown` and `SiftUp` are essentially the same as in previous examples, except that the comparisons are reversed to produce a heap of losers and the comparisons are done on the `rank` array. But when we swap entries, we must swap their ranks and cross-references as well; so `Swap` looks like this:

```
procedure SWAP (a, b: integer); { Swaps queue entries  }
   var                           {   at a and b          }
      a_temp, b_temp: integer;
   begin
   with queue do
      begin
      a_temp := data[a];
      b_temp := data[b];
      data[a] := b_temp;              { Swap data     }
      data[b] := a_temp;
      xref[a_temp] := b;              { Swap cross    }
      xref[b_temp] := a;              {   references  }
      a_temp := rank[a];
      rank[a] := rank[b];             { Swap ranks    }
      rank[b] := a_temp
      end
```

```
   end;  { Swap }
```

The En_Queue procedure uses `queue.xref` as follows:

```
procedure EN_QUEUE (x, y: integer);      { Adds x to queue       }
   begin                                 {   with priority y      }
   with queue do
      if last < queuemax then
         begin
         if xref[x] = 0 then      { New entry:              }
            begin
            last := last + 1;     {   add to queue          }
            data[last] := x;
            rank[last] := y;
            xref[x] := last        {   note where it went   }
            end
         else                      { Old entry:              }
            rank[xref[x]] := y;  {   update rank           }
         siftup (xref[x]);          { Restore order           }
         end
   end;  { En_Queue }
```

The test against `queuemax` avoids overflow; normally there would be some kind of error handling associated with this test. The parameter `x` must not go onto the queue a second time if it is already there; this is guarded by the test on `xref`. But if it is not put in the queue, its priority will probably have changed, so we use `xref` to find the entry and update the corresponding `rank` entry.

The only change needed in De_Queue is to remove x from `queue.xref` when it is taken off the queue:

```
procedure DE_QUEUE (var x: integer);     { Retrieves x from queue}
   begin
   with queue do
      if last > 0 then
         begin
         x := data[1];            { Remove top entry      }
         xref[x] := 0;             { No longer there       }
         if last <> 1 then
            begin
            data[1] := data[last];    { Move last          }
            rank[1] := rank[last];    {   entry up          }
            xref[data[last]] := 1
            end;
         last := last - 1;
         siftdown (last);          { Restore order           }
         end
   end;  { De_Queue }
```

The end result of all this code is that we are replacing each $O(|V|)$ scan of the dist array with an $O(\lg|V|)$ heapification.

The logic of the procedure is otherwise the same as it was when we used the weighted adjacency matrix. Instead of scanning the dist array for the minimum entry, we will take the corresponding vertex off the queue. We then use this vertex as a basis, just as before. Since we are going through a linked list, we will work with a pointer p. When we find a place where we can change the dist entry, we do so, but we also put that vertex on the queue. Hence our implementation looks like this:

```
procedure MIN_SPAN (cost: alists; var dist, preds: dist_array;
                    nodes,                  { Number of vertices  }
                    start: integer);        { Starting vertex     }
                                  { Minimal spanning tree         }
                                  {   Prim's algorithm.  Uses     }
                                  {   weighted adjacency lists     }
    var
        in_tree: array [1..maxnodes] of boolean;
        p: listptr;
        k: integer;
    begin
    for k := 1 to nodes do       { Preliminaries           }
        begin
        dist[k] := maxint;
        preds[k] := 0;
        in_tree[k] := false;
        end;
    clear_queue;                 { Initialize queue        }
    preds[start] := 0;
    dist[start] := 0;
    in_tree[start] := true;
    en_queue (start, 0);

    while not empty_queue do
        begin
        de_queue (k);                        { Takes place of search of dist }
        in_tree[k] := true;
        p := cost[k];                        { Point to head of list          }
        while p <> nil do
            begin
            with p^ do
                if not in_tree[node] and (dist[node] > cost) then
                    begin
                    preds[node] := k;
                    dist[node] := cost;
                    en_queue (node, cost)    { For possible updating }
```

```
              end;
          p := p^.next
          end
      end
  end;  { Min_Span }
```

(`Clear_Queue` sets `queue.last` to zero and zeroes out `queue.xref`. The function `Empty_Queue` returns a value of TRUE if `queue.last` is zero.)

The cost of this process depends on the two **while** loops. Since every vertex will go onto the queue, the length of the outer loop is $O(|V|)$.

Inside this loop we have a call to `De_Queue`, which costs $O(\lg |V|)$ because of the need to call `SiftDown`. Then the inner **while** loop goes over all the vertices adjacent to the one specified by `cost[k]`, so if there are m_k adjacent vertices, this loop repeats m_k times. The cost of this loop depends on whether we must call `En_Queue` (which also costs $O(\lg |V|)$ because of the need to call `SiftUp`). If we make the pessimistic assumption that it will always call `En_Queue`, then the cost of this inner **while** is $O(m_k \lg |V|)$.

In that case, over the entire outer **while**, the cost is $O\big(\sum_{k=1}^{|V|} (1 + m_k) \lg |V| \big)$. Since $\sum_{k=1}^{|V|} m_k = 2|E|$, the overall cost is thus $O\big((|V| + |E|) \lg |V|\big)$. In a sparse graph, where $|V| \gg |E|$, this reduces to $O(|V| \lg |V|)$.

That's the good news. The bad news is the extra code required to manage the priority queue. As usual, there is a trade-off between costs and benefits. As we have seen before, $O(n \lg n)$ algorithms tend to come into their own when working with large bodies of data. But large graphs are precisely the ones most likely to be represented by adjacency lists; the two versions of the algorithm thus live in different worlds. It would be possible to use a priority queue to control the adjacency-matrix version as well. (A problem at the end of this chapter addresses this.) If the graph is large and yet dense enough to justify using an adjacency matrix, this is an attractive possibility.

Kruskal's Algorithm.   A second approach to finding a minimal spanning tree is this algorithm, due to J. B. Kruskal [1956]:

1. Partition V into $n = |V|$ subsets, each containing one vertex of G.

2. Initially, the spanning tree is empty.

3. Then, while the tree is incomplete and you haven't run out of edges,

   a. Find the shortest edge not yet considered.

   b. If its endpoints are in different subsets T_i and T_j, then add it to the tree and replace T_i and T_j by their union.

In effect, we are starting with a forest of $|V|$ trees, each one containing only a single vertex. When we add an edge between two trees, its endpoints become part of a single tree; thus each edge added consolidates two existing trees into a single larger one. (We will represent these trees as sets of vertices, so we can consolidate two trees by simply forming the union of their sets.) When we are left with only one tree, the algorithm terminates and we have the minimal spanning tree. This is another greedy algorithm, because it simply grabs the shortest legal edge (legal in the sense that it won't make a cycle) and uses it. The test on the endpoints is necessary because each subset corresponds to a tree, and if both ends of a new edge are in the same tree, adding that new edge will make a circuit.

Kruskal's algorithm uses the shortest-bridge property; every time an edge is selected, it is the shortest bridge between the two trees it connects. If these trees themselves contain more than one node, they have likewise been made up of shortest bridges. Hence, the spanning forest, as its trees are gradually consolidated, is made up entirely of shortest bridges. When it finally becomes a single tree spanning the entire graph, it is thus minimal. Notice that this algorithm, in a sense, is the reverse of Prim's: Both algorithms use the shortest-bridge property, but where Prim examines all edges known to be bridges and selects the shortest one, Kruskal examines all edges known to be the shortest and not yet considered and selects one that can be a bridge.

In the worst case, we will have to examine all the edges; the cost of the loop is thus $O(|E|)$ times the cost of finding the shortest edge and finding whether it will make a cycle.

The trick is to determine whether the new edge will make a cycle in the tree; if there is an easy way to do this, we have an efficient algorithm. But any new edge will make a cycle only if both of its endpoints are in the same tree. So for every new edge, we need only verify that its endpoints are in different trees. As we continue, the trees are merged and, at the end, we have a single tree, which is the desired minimal spanning tree.

It helps to see an example. Suppose our graph is as in Fig. 9.16 (a). Initially, the forest (represented as sets of vertices) looks as shown under the graph; every vertex is a single tree of height 0.

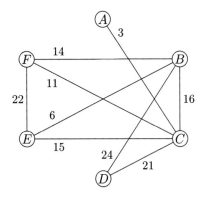

Trees: $\{A\}, \{B\}, \{C\}, \{D\}, \{E\}, \{F\}$

Figure 9.16 (a)

The shortest edge is $\{A, C\}$, so we make this edge and its endpoints a tree. This means that A and C are now in the same tree, as shown in Fig. 9.16 (*b*).

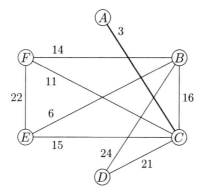

Trees: $\{A, C\}, \{B\}, \{D\}, \{E\}, \{F\}$

Figure 9.16 (*b*)

Notice that the tree $\{A, C\}$ is now represented by the union of the sets $\{A\}$ and $\{C\}$.

The shortest remaining edge is $\{B, E\}$. The endpoints are in different trees, so it's safe to make a tree of these, after which B and E will be in the same set, as shown in Fig. 9.16 (*c*).

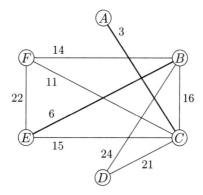

Trees: $\{A, C\}, \{B, E\}, \{D\}, \{F\}$

Figure 9.16 (*c*)

Now the shortest edge is $\{C, F\}$. Again, the endpoints are in different trees, so it is safe to add this edge. Similarly, we can add the edge $\{B, F\}$. The result is shown in Fig. 9.16 (*d*).

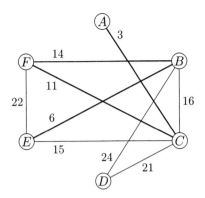

Trees: $\{A, B, C, E, F\}, \{D\}$

Figure 9.16 (d)

Now the shortest remaining edge is $\{C, E\}$. But when we consult the trees, we find that both endpoints are in the same tree. If we were to add this edge, we would get the circuit *BECFB*. So we reject it. After this edge, the shortest is $\{B, C\}$. That also has both endpoints in the same tree, so we reject it as well. The next edge is $\{C, D\}$; this has endpoints in different trees. When we add it, we have the complete minimal spanning tree, shown in Fig. 9.16 (e).

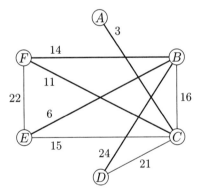

Tree: $\{A, B, C, D, E, F\}$

Figure 9.16 (e)

To find the shortest edge, we will put the edges in a priority queue in which the shortest edge will be at the top of the heap. Then the cost of finding the shortest edge is only the cost of reheapifying, which is $O(\lg |E|)$, and that makes the total cost $O(|E| \lg |E|)$.

We have seen that the trees are sets; we will represent the sets with the union-find structure of Chapter 6. We do this because our principal task in looking for legal edges is finding whether the two endpoints are in the same set or different sets, and the **Find** function of Section 6.3 does this efficiently.

We will assume the graph is represented by a weighted adjacency matrix, and we will use the following declarations:

```
const
    order = 6;               { Size of graph          }
    maxsq = order*order; { Number of edges        }
type
    alist = array [1..order, 1..order] of integer;
    setptr = ^setnode;
    setnode = record
                    v,          { Vertex            }
                    weight: integer;
                    pa: setptr
                end;
    edge = record
                    end1,
                    end2: setptr;
                    cost: integer
                end;
    edgearray = array[1..maxsq] of edge;
    forest = array[1..order] of setptr;
var
    costs: alist;            { Weighted adjacency matrix     }
    edges: edgearray;
    trees: forest;
    span: edgearray;         { Spanning tree }
    ntree,                   { Size of tree  }
    qsize: integer;          { Size of queue }
```

The first thing we must do, after reading in the graph, is to construct the forest and to put the edges into the priority queue. We do this as follows:

```
procedure MAKE_FOREST (var costs: alist; var edges: edgearray;
                var trees: forest; var qsize: integer);
                                    { Makes forest for      }
                                    {   Kruskal's algorithm }
    var
        i, j: integer;
    begin
    for i := 1 to order do          { Make the forest       }
        make_set (trees[i], i);
    qsize := 0;
    for i := 1 to order do
        for j := i + 1 to order do
            begin                   { Put the edges         }
            qsize := qsize + 1;     {   in a priority queue }
            with edges[qsize] do
```

```
            begin
            end1 := trees[i];
            end2 := trees[j];
            cost := costs[i, j]
            end
        end;
    for i := qsize div 2 downto 1 do      { Heapify      }
        siftdown (edges, i, qsize);       {   the queue  }
    end;  { Make_Forest }
```

The call to Make_Set puts vertex *i* into a set by itself. In order to access these sets easily, we put them in an array of setptrs named trees. In this procedure, the graph is undirected; the nested loops on i and j identify the edges and put them into the edges array. Since we will be needing to find whether or not the endpoints are in the same tree, we associate the endpoints with the corresponding trees entries.

We are now ready to find the tree:

```
procedure MIN_SPAN (var edges, span: edgearray;
                    var ntree: integer);     { Kruskal's algorithm   }
    var
        p, q: setptr;      { Endpoint sets }
        this_edge: edge;   { Working edge  }
    begin
    ntree := 0;
    while (qsize > 1) and (ntree < order - 1) do
        begin
        de_queue (edges, this_edge);        { Cheapest edge }
        p := find (this_edge.end1);         { Find endpoint }
        q := find (this_edge.end2);         {   sets        }
        if (this_edge.cost < infinity) and (p <> q) then
            begin
            ntree := ntree + 1;
            span[ntree] := this_edge;       { Add to tree   }
            p := union (p, q);
            end
        end;
    end;  { Min_Span }
```

The while loop depends on two things: Is the queue empty and is the spanning tree complete? We need both tests, because it might happen that the graph has no spanning tree, in which case we will find out when the queue empties. Otherwise, when the tree contains order − 1 edges, it is complete.

The function Find(p) determines the set to which p belongs. If p is the same as q, both endpoints of this_edge are in the same tree and we must reject it. (Similarly, we reject nonexistent edges, betrayed by the cost of infinity.) Otherwise, we add this_edge to the spanning tree span. The call to Union puts both endpoints in the same tree.

9.5.2 Shortest Path

This is the problem with which we started—going from New York to Baltimore. Finding the shortest path is almost like finding the minimal spanning tree; it's another greedy algorithm, due to Dijkstra [1959]. Like the minimal spanning tree algorithm, it comes in two versions, depending on whether we use an adjacency matrix or an adjacency list.

Here is Dijkstra's algorithm for finding the shortest path from vertex x to vertex y:

1. Mark vertex x; make all other vertices unmarked.

2. For all vertices, set `dist = cost[x, i]`.

3. Repeat

   a. Find the unmarked vertex for which `dist[]` is a minimum. (Call it `imin`.)

   b. [Failure] If all unmarked vertices have `dist[]` = ∞, give up: y is not reachable.

   c. [Success] else if `imin = y`, we're done.

   d. Else mark `imin`.

   e. For all unmarked vertices, update `dist` array:
   ```
   if dist[i] > dist[imin] + cost[imin, i] then
        dist[i] := dist[imin] + cost[imin, i];
   ```
   until [failure] or [success].

4. If `imin = y` then total cost $=$ `dist[y]`.

This algorithm is applicable to either directed or undirected graphs, but it is perhaps most useful with directed graphs.

Initially, only vertex x is known, and the distance table is copied from the weights. After a new vertex is added to the known set, there may be new, shorter, paths to other unknown vertices by way of this new vertex, so we compare the existing path length with this new possibility and update the distance table if the new possibility is shorter. This update procedure is clearly similar to the updating procedure we used for the minimal spanning tree.

Here is an example. Suppose we are given the following graph and need to find the shortest path from A to H:

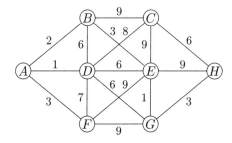

Figure 9.17 (*a*)

The weighted adjacency matrix for this graph is

$$
A = \begin{array}{c c c c c c c c c}
 & A & B & C & D & E & F & G & H \\
\left[\begin{array}{c c c c c c c c}
\infty & 2 & \infty & 1 & \infty & 3 & \infty & \infty \\
2 & \infty & 9 & 6 & 3 & \infty & \infty & \infty \\
\infty & 9 & \infty & 8 & 9 & \infty & \infty & 6 \\
1 & 6 & 8 & \infty & 6 & 7 & 6 & \infty \\
\infty & 3 & 9 & 6 & \infty & 9 & 1 & 9 \\
3 & \infty & \infty & 7 & 9 & \infty & 9 & \infty \\
\infty & \infty & \infty & 6 & 1 & 9 & \infty & 3 \\
\infty & \infty & 6 & \infty & 9 & \infty & 3 & \infty
\end{array}\right] & \begin{array}{c} A \\ B \\ C \\ D \\ E \\ F \\ G \\ H \end{array}
\end{array}
$$

We start by marking out starting vertex A and copying the entries from row A of the adjacency matrix into the dist array to determine the costs of the other vertices. (We will show the dist entries next to their corresponding vertices on the figure.) Since vertices B, D, and F, which have finite costs, are reached from A, we will darken the edges from A so that we know what these vertices' predecessor is. As we continue with the algorithm, we will show the predecessors of any new finite-cost vertices similarly. It will occasionally turn out that we can get a lower cost by choosing a different predecessor, in which case we will change the emphasized edge to show this.

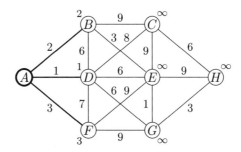

Figure 9.17 (b)

Pick D and mark it. Update costs to C, E, and G:

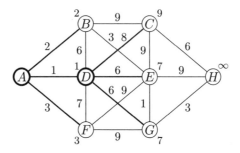

Figure 9.17 (c)

Pick B and mark it. It is now cheaper to reach E by way of B than by way of D; update E's cost accordingly:

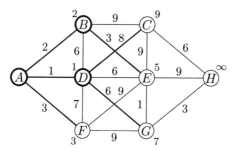

Figure 9.17 (*d*)

Pick F and mark it. (This choice does not change the costs of reaching any of the unmarked vertices.)

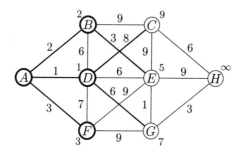

Figure 9.17 (*e*)

The lowest-cost unmarked vertex is now E. Pick it, mark it, and update the costs of G and H:

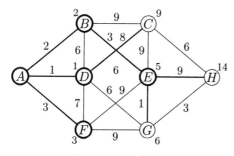

Figure 9.17 (*f*)

Pick G, mark it, and update the cost of H:

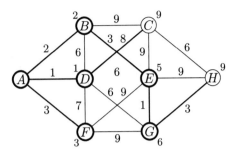

Figure 9.17 (*g*)

At this point, vertices *C* and *H* are tied for the lowest cost. We may pick either one; to make a long example short, suppose we pick *H*. This is our target, and we now have the shortest path: *A–B–E–G–H*.

Since every vertex has a unique predecessor, the emphasized edges form a tree. This tree gives the lowest-cost paths to all the vertices it includes. In this case, we happened to update every vertex in the course of finding the shortest path to *H*, with the result that the tree spanned the graph; but this doesn't always happen.

If we use a weighted adjacency matrix for our graph, the code takes the form shown here. We must specify the starting node (`start`) and the node to be found (`target`). The array `dist` contains the distances that we wrote next to the vertices in our example; the array `preds` will show the immediate predecessor of each vertex; this conveys the information we showed by emphasizing edges in Fig. 9.17. Since we will probably want the actual path as well as its cost, we include the array `preds` among the parameters. The procedure returns the total cost and the `preds` array. As usual, `HUGE` is a stand-in for infinity, *i.e.*, some constant guaranteed to be greater than any actual cost that will be encountered. If the target node was unreachable, the total cost will be `HUGE`.

```
procedure MIN_PATH (var cost: c_matrix; start, target: integer;
                    var preds: ptype; var total_cost: integer);
                                   { Dijkstra's algorithm.  Finds  }
                                   {   shortest path from start    }
        var                        {   to target.                  }
           marked: array [1..order] of boolean;
           dist: ptype;      { Array of distances        }
           i,
           imin,                 { Index of min. dist entry }
           mincost: integer; { Cost of min. dist entry  }
           done: boolean;
        begin
        for i := 1 to order do        { Preliminaries }
           begin
           dist[i] := cost[start, i];
           marked[i] := false;
           preds[i] := start;
```

```
      end;
   marked[start] := true;
   done := false;
   total_cost := HUGE;
   repeat
      imin := 0;
      mincost := HUGE;                { Search for vertex    }
      for i := 1 to order do          {   with lowest dist   }
         if not marked[i] and (dist[i] < mincost) then
            begin
            imin := i;
            mincost := dist[i]
            end;
      if (imin = 0) or (imin = target) then
         done := true           { Success or failure: quit   }
      else
         begin
         marked[imin] := true;        { Mark this vertex      }
         for i := 1 to order do       {  & update dist, preds }
            if not marked[i] then
               if word(mincost + cost[imin, i]) < dist[i] then
                  begin
                  preds[i] := imin;
                  dist[i] := mincost + cost[imin, i]
                  end;
         end  { if imin <> 0 }
   until done;
   if imin = target then                { Success: return    }
      total_cost := dist[imin]          {    total cost       }
   end;  { Min_Path }
```

In the main program, we can recover the path itself with a loop like this:

```
i := target;
repeat
   writeln (preds[i], ' -> ', i);
   i := preds[i];
until i = start;
```

We can trace the execution of this program on the graph of Fig. 9.17. Starting from node *A* we have the following initial arrays. (Marked nodes are underlined.)

	A̲	B	C	D	E	F	G	H
dist	∞	2	∞	1	∞	3	∞	∞
preds	A	A	A	A	A	A	A	A

The procedure chooses imin = 4, which corresponds to vertex *D*, since the cost of getting to that vertex is only 1. Now that node *D* is available as a predecessor, however, we revise the `dist` and `preds` tables:

	A	B	C	D	E	F	G	H
`dist`	∞	2	9	1	7	3	7	∞
`preds`	A	A	D	A	D	A	D	A

Now B has the lowest cost; this changes the cost of E, and B becomes the predecessor of E:

	A	B	C	D	E	F	G	H
`dist`	∞	2	9	1	5	3	7	∞
`preds`	A	A	D	A	B	A	D	A

At this point, the unmarked vertex with the lowest cost is F:

	A	B	C	D	E	F	G	H
`dist`	∞	2	9	1	5	3	7	∞
`preds`	A	A	D	A	B	A	D	A

Now we pick E; this changes the costs of G and H, which now have E as their predecessor:

	A	B	C	D	E	F	G	H
`dist`	∞	2	9	1	5	3	6	14
`preds`	A	A	D	A	B	A	E	E

Now we choose G:

	A	B	C	D	E	F	G	H
`dist`	∞	2	9	1	5	3	6	9
`preds`	A	A	D	A	B	A	E	G

Again, as in Fig. 9.17 (g), we have a choice of C and H, and again for brevity we will assume the algorithm selects H. (You should verify that the result will be the same if it picks C and then H.)

	A	B	C	D	E	F	G	H
`dist`	∞	2	9	1	5	3	6	9
`preds`	A	A	D	A	B	A	E	G

At this point, the algorithm is finished. If we go through the `preds` array, working backward from H, we get the sequence

$$A, B, E, G, H,$$

and this is our shortest path.

The main difference between this and the spanning-tree algorithm is the way in which we update the `dist` array. As in the spanning-tree algorithm, the time complexity is $O(|V|^2)$.

If we are using an adjacency-list representation, it is more generally convenient to arrange for it to find the shortest paths to *all* reachable vertices in the graph. The program is similar to the list version of the spanning-tree procedure. The priority queue and the declarations for the graph are the same. Thus, the code takes the following form:

```
procedure MIN_PATHS (graph: alists; nodes, start: integer;
```

```
                          var dist, preds: dist_array);
                                  { Finds shortest paths          }
                                  {    from start to all nodes    }
        var                       {    in graph                   }
           p: listptr;
           k: integer;
        begin
        clear_queue;
        for k := 1 to nodes do
           begin
           dist[k] := HUGE;
           preds[k] := 0;
           end;
        preds[start] := 0;
        dist[start] := 0;
        en_queue (start, 0);

        while not empty_queue do
           begin
           de_queue (k);       { Takes place of search of dist }
           p := graph[k];
           while p <> nil do
              begin
              with p^ do
                 if dist[node] > dist[k] + cost then
                    begin
                    preds[node] := k;
                    dist[node] := dist[k] + cost;
                    en_queue (node, dist[node])
                    end;
              p := p^.next
              end
           end
        end;  { Min_Paths }
```

(Recall that `alists` is an `array [1..maxnodes] of listptr`.)

The procedure returns the costs of the shortest paths in the `dist` array; as with the adjacency-matrix version, the path to any given node can be reconstructed from the `preds` array. Again, the main difference is in the way we handle the `dist` array. The analysis of this algorithm parallels that of the list-based spanning-tree procedure and yields a time complexity that is $O\big((|E| + |V|) \lg |V|\big)$.

Notice the versatility of the modified priority queue we have been using for these algorithms. We can pass any integer to `En_Queue` in the second (rank) parameter, after all. For Prim's algorithm, we passed `p^.cost`; for Dijkstra's algorithm, we passed `dist[k] + p^.cost`. But furthermore, as Sedgewick [1988] observes, if we number each vertex as we come to it and just pass that number, we will get a breadth-first traversal, and if we use a heap of winners instead of losers (or, alternatively, if we pass $|V|$ minus the vertex number), we will get a depth-first traversal.

9.5.3   All Shortest Paths

If we wish to know the lengths of the shortest paths between all pairs of distinct nodes, we can use a variant of Warshall's algorithm, known as Floyd's [1962] algorithm. The guiding principle of Warshall's algorithm can be stated as follows:

> There is a k path between nodes i and j if there is a $(k-1)$ path between them *or* if there's a $(k-1)$ path from node i to node k and a $(k-1)$ path from node k to node j.

For finding the shortest paths, we can say almost the same thing:

> The shortest k path from node i to node j is either the shortest $(k-1)$ path from i to j *or* the sum of the shortest $(k-1)$ paths from i to k and from k to j if that happens to cost less.

This means we can loop on k just as we did in Warshall's algorithm; the only differences are that we use a weighted adjacency matrix and that the central statement of the loop is changed to reflect our observation. So we have the following procedure:

```
procedure FLOYD (a: c_matrix; var w: c_matrix);
                              { Finds costs of shortest paths }
        var                   {    between all pairs of nodes  }
          i, j, k: integer;
        begin
        w := a;
        for k := 1 to order do
           for i := 1 to order do
              for j := 1 to order do
                 if w[i, j] > w[i, k] + w[k, j] then
                    w[i, j] := w[i, k] + w[k, j];
        end;   { Floyd }
```

At the conclusion of the loops, w[i, j] contains the cost of the shortest path from node i to node j.

9.6   DIRECTED ACYCLIC GRAPHS AND TOPOLOGICAL SORTING

A cycle is another name for a directed circuit. An acyclic digraph (or a directed acyclic graph—DAG for short) is a digraph with no cycles. A DAG *may* be a tree, but it doesn't have to be. Figure 9.18 is a DAG.

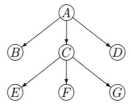

Figure 9.18

But so is Fig. 9.19.

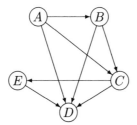

Figure 9.19

We can tell this from its reachability matrix. This graph has the adjacency matrix,

$$A = \begin{array}{c} \\ \\ \\ \\ \\ \end{array} \begin{array}{ccccc} A & B & C & D & E \\ \end{array}$$

$$A = \left[\begin{array}{ccccc} 0 & 1 & 1 & 1 & 0 \\ 0 & 0 & 1 & 1 & 0 \\ 0 & 0 & 0 & 1 & 1 \\ 0 & 0 & 0 & 0 & 0 \\ 0 & 0 & 0 & 1 & 0 \end{array} \right] \begin{array}{c} A \\ B \\ C \\ D \\ E \end{array}$$

(Here the diagonal elements are 0 since there are no self-loops.) And Warshall's algorithm gives us the reachability matrix:

$$W = \left[\begin{array}{ccccc} 0 & 1 & 1 & 1 & 1 \\ 0 & 0 & 1 & 1 & 1 \\ 0 & 0 & 0 & 1 & 1 \\ 0 & 0 & 0 & 0 & 0 \\ 0 & 0 & 0 & 1 & 0 \end{array} \right]$$

If there were a cycle, then at least one vertex would be reachable from itself and hence, there would be at least one 1 on the main diagonal.

A vertex all of whose incident edges are departing is called a *source* (its indegree is 0, and its column in the adjacency matrix is all 0's); a vertex all of whose incident edges are arriving is called a *sink* (its outdegree is 0, and its row in the adjacency matrix is all 0's). (We picture the graph as if it were a flow, coming out of the source as if it were a faucet and running down the sink as if it were a drain.) Every DAG must have at least one source and at least one sink.

It is possible to number the vertices in a DAG so that every path passes through its vertices in ascending numerical order. This is called *topological sorting*. It should be clear that this can always be done; to see this, it is only necessary to outline the method for doing it:

1. Set $n = 1$;

2. Repeat

 a. Find a source and label it n; then remove it (and its incident edges) from the DAG.

 b. Set $n := n + 1$.

 until no vertices are left.

Note that when you remove a vertex and its edges from a DAG, what's left will still be a DAG. (It's clearly still directed, and the only way you could introduce cycles would be to add edges, not take them away.) Hence, what's left will still have at least one source and you can still find one of them. Indeed, since you may have many sources among which to choose on each pass through the repeat loop, the topological sort is not necessarily unique.

Once you have relabelled the graph, you have a version in which no edge goes from a higher number to a lower number. Now, in an adjacency matrix, any element above the main diagonal corresponds to an edge going from a lower-numbered vertex to a higher-numbered vertex, and any element below the main diagonal corresponds to the opposite case. Hence, when you write the new adjacency matrix for this graph (using the new labels), it will be an upper-triangular matrix.

These observations give us a fine pencil-and-paper way to do a topological sort:

1. Set $n := 1$;

2. Repeat

 a. Pick an all-zero column in the adjacency matrix.

 b. Number that vertex n.

 c. Cross out that column and the corresponding row.

 d. Set $n := n + 1$.

 until all the columns are crossed out.

But crossing out rows and columns and finding all-zero columns are both clumsy to do in the computer; furthermore, we would like a method that is less dependent on using an adjacency matrix.

We will consider two procedures for topological sorting, one based on a depth-first traversal of the graph and one based on a breadth-first traversal. As you might expect, the depth-first version is recursive and the breadth-first version uses a queue. If there is an edge from vertex A to vertex B, we will say that B is the *successor* of A and that A is the *predecessor* of B.

The depth-first version turns our previous method around backwards:

1. Set $n := |V|$.

2. Repeat

    a. Find a sink; label it n; remove that vertex and its edges from the
       DAG.

    b. Set $n := n - 1$.

until no vertices left.

This method finds sinks and puts them into the list in reverse order.

We can adapt our existing depth-first traversal for this. The idea is to find a vertex that has no successors and put that at the end of the list. If you make a depth-first traversal of a DAG, the first time you reach a dead end, you will be at a sink. So you can label that n. Instead of removing the vertex from the list, we will mark it as visited. Then we know the depth-first algorithm will never look at this vertex again.

After that first time, when the process dead-ends, the vertex will be either a sink or a vertex whose successor has been marked (*i.e.*, is, is already in the list). In either case, this vertex is ready to go into the list, again working backwards from the end. So we end up with a procedure that is virtually identical to a depth-first traversal. We assume we have an array, `top`, which will contain the sorted list of vertices. Then we have

```
procedure DEPTH_SORT (this_vertex: integer);
   begin
   for all vertices adjacent to this_vertex do
      if the adjacent vertex isn't marked then
         depth_sort (adjacent vertex);
   mark this_vertex as visited;
  *top[topindex] := this_vertex;
  *topindex := topindex - 1;
   end;  { Depth_Sort }

begin  { Calling program }
mark all vertices as not visited
topindex := |V|;
for all vertices not visited do
   depth_sort (vertex);
end;
```

So this is virtually the same procedure as a simple depth-first traversal, except for the two starred statements. Notice that if we happen to call `Depth_Sort` from a vertex that is neither a source nor a sink, it doesn't matter; any vertices added to the list will inevitably go into the list in the correct order, just the same.

Can we similarly modify a breadth-first traversal to give us a breadth-first topological numbering? Yes, but it isn't quite as simple, because this time we must fan out from sources only.

Sources are those vertices with no predecessors. But we have another point to consider: As vertices are removed from the graph, some of their successors will also become sources. We can handle both problems at once by maintaining a *predecessor count* for every vertex. Any vertex with 0 predecessors is a source. But when it comes time to remove a vertex, what we will actually do is decrement the predecessor counts of all its adjacent vertices. When the predecessor count for any vertex becomes zero, then we know it is now a source.

With that background, the procedure becomes a little more clear. We start by putting all sources onto the queue. We then have a loop that terminates when the queue is empty. We take a vertex off the queue, just as we did when we were doing a breadth-first traversal, and put its label onto the sorted list. We visit all the adjacent vertices and decrement their predecessor counts, since our current vertex is being removed. Any vertices that become sources are put onto the queue. Our algorithm is thus as follows:

1. Find predecessor counts of all vertices;

2. Put sources onto the queue;

3. Repeat

    a. Take working vertex off the queue;

    b. Put the working vertex onto the sorted list;

    c. For all vertices adjacent to working vertex:

        i. Decrement predecessor count;

        ii. If predecessor count = 0 then put the vertex onto the queue.

    until queue empty;

We can implement this as follows. The vertices, sorted topologically, go in the array top; vlist is an `array[1..maxnodes] of integer`.

```
procedure B_SORT (graph: alists; nodes: integer; var top: vlist);
                              { Breadth-first topological    }
                              {    sort of DAG represented    }
    var                       {    by adjacency lists         }
        p: listptr;
        preds: vlist;    { Predecessor counts    }
        this_node, next_node,
        n,
        topindex: integer;
    begin
    for n := 1 to nodes do
        preds[n] := 0;
    for n := 1 to nodes do                      { Find predecessor    }
        begin                                   {    counts            }
        p := graph[n];
        while p <> nil do
            begin
            preds[p^.node] := preds[p^.node] + 1;
            p := p^.next
            end
```

```
        end;
    clear_queue;
    topindex := 0;
    for n := 1 to nodes do              { Put sources on queue  }
        if preds[n] = 0 then
            en_queue (n);
    repeat
        de_queue (this_node);           { Pick source off queue }
        p := graph[this_node];
        while p <> nil do
            begin                       { Visit adjacent nodes  }
            next_node := p^.node;
            preds[next_node] := preds[next_node] - 1;
            if preds[next_node] = 0 then    { If next_node source,  }
                en_queue (next_node);       {    put on queue        }
            p := p^.next
            end;  { while }
        topindex := topindex + 1;       { Put source onto queue }
        top[topindex] := this_node;
    until empty_queue;
    end;  { B_Sort }
```

Applications. Probably the first question that would occur to anyone studying these methods would be, "Why would anyone want to do this?" I will mention three applications.

One example is the writing of program documentation and particularly users' manuals. If you have to understand X before you can understand Y, then the section dealing with X has to come before the section on Y. If we represent this by an edge from X to Y, then we can draw a graph of all the topics. (If this graph has any cycles, then we have problems. In that case, we have to try subdividing the topics in such a way that the new assortment of topics doesn't have any cycles.) Any topological sort of the resultant graph will yield a satisfactory sequence of sections.

Second: Topological sorting of graphs is sometimes used in the optimization phase of a compiler. I can't go into this in much detail, but the general idea is this: Once the compiler has broken the user's program down into little pieces, it needs to remove any accumulated deadwood in the code. This deadwood may come from the user, but some of it also comes from the way the compiler does the breaking down. The compiler constructs a DAG from these little pieces in such a way that the deadwood is automatically excluded. Then it must put the results back together to make a version that still does what the user wants.

Now, certain instructions depend on others. For example, if the programmer wrote

```
i := i + 1;
x[i] := y;
```

it's important that these instructions be executed in that order. Now we are back to the same situation we saw in the textbook-writing example: Certain things depend on other things and must come after them. So the compiler does a topological sort of the DAG, and out of this comes one or more sequences of instructions that conform to the prerequisites implicit in the code.

A similar problem arises in recalculating a spreadsheet. The contents of some cells will frequently be expressions that take the contents of other cells as their operands. But the cells providing the operands may themselves be expressions that depend on still other cells, and so on. So when the spreadsheet updates itself after the user has changed some value, it must know the dependencies among the various cells and the updating must proceed from the known to the unknown. These dependencies can be represented by a digraph, and a topological sort of this digraph will yield the required order of computation. If the digraph has cycles, then the user has created *circular references*, in which *a* depends on *b*, which depends on *c*, which depends on . . . , which depends on *a* again. (Spreadsheets frequently include the ability to handle circular references, because such constructions can be useful in iterative calculations, but then there must be some limit on the number of trips around the cycle.)

Third: In industry, large projects are frequently managed with the aid of a DAG called a PERT diagram. (PERT stands for Program Evaluation and Review Technique.) It is a way of analyzing the dependencies among parts of the project so that each part can be started at such a time that the whole project will be finished in the shortest possible time. A PERT chart has one source (the start of the project) and one sink (the end of the project). Edges correspond to the parts of the project and are weighted by the time it will take to complete the part. The vertices are topologically sorted and the chart is drawn left-to-right so the vertices appear in topological (and therefore chronological) order.

In any such chart you can find the most expensive (the most time-consuming) path from source to sink. This is known as the *critical path*; it determines how long the entire project is going to take. It's critical because any delay along that path will cause the entire project to slip, because time slippages tend to increase the cost, and, finally, because time and cost overruns are bad.

Sometimes there may be more than one critical path, if by coincidence two paths happen to take the same time. If there is only one critical path, then any speedup along the critical path will speed the entire project. Sometimes when you've shortened the critical path, it turns out that it isn't critical any more, and you have a new critical path to worry about. (Finding the critical path is a problem in *dynamic programming*; this is a topic for another chapter.)

9.7   SUMMARY

Graphs are of importance in many programming problems; we will encounter an unexpected application of the shortest-path problem in Chapter 11. We have seen a few of the most important tools for doing common operations on graphs. Our survey has not been exhaustive; Even [1979] offers a more detailed survey of graph algorithms.

Graph algorithms are also of considerable theoretical interest, especially since some classical problems—for instance, the Hamiltonian circuit problem—are of at least exponential complexity and hence have been extensively studied as paradigms of certain classes of particularly costly algorithms.

9.8 PROBLEMS

9.1. Show that reachability in an undirected graph is an equivalence relation.

9.2. Suppose a graph is represented in a file as an adjacency matrix. For example, such a file might look like this:

```
6
1  0  1  0  0  0
0  1  0  0  0  0
0  0  1  0  1  0
1  0  0  0  0  0
1  0  0  1  0  0
0  1  1  0  0  1
```

The first line gives the order of the matrix and the remaining lines show the matrix itself. Write procedures that will read this matrix and construct (a) an adjacency matrix; (b) an array of adjacency lists.

9.3. Suppose a graph is represented in a file by adjacency lists. For example, such a file might look like this:

```
6
2   1 3
1   2
2   3 5
1   1
2   1 4
3   2 3 6
```

The first line gives the number of vertices; each following line gives the outdegree of the vertex and the numbers of its adjacent vertices. Write procedures that will read this file and construct (a) an adjacency matrix; (b) an array of adjacency lists.

9.4. In the derivation of Warshall's algorithm, why is a $(k-1)$ path also a k path?

9.5. Use Warshall's algorithm to find the reachability matrix of the graph whose adjacency matrix is as given in Problem 9.2.

9.6. Let the relation R on the set $A = \{a, b, c, d, e\}$ be $R = \{(a, e), (b, a), (b, d), (c, a), (d, b), (e, c)\}$. Represent this relation by a matrix and use Warshall's algorithm to find its transitive closure.

9.7. Trace the breadth-first traversal of the graph given by the following adjacency matrix:

$$\begin{bmatrix} 0 & 1 & 0 & 1 & 0 & 1 & 0 \\ 1 & 0 & 0 & 1 & 1 & 0 & 0 \\ 0 & 0 & 0 & 0 & 0 & 1 & 0 \\ 1 & 1 & 0 & 0 & 1 & 0 & 1 \\ 0 & 1 & 0 & 1 & 0 & 0 & 1 \\ 1 & 0 & 1 & 0 & 0 & 0 & 1 \\ 0 & 0 & 0 & 1 & 1 & 1 & 0 \end{bmatrix}$$

9.8. Rewrite the procedure **B_First** to do a breadth-first search instead of a traversal.

9.9. Modify the procedure **B_First** to traverse graphs represented by adjacency lists.

9.10. Trace the depth-first traversal of the graph given by the following adjacency matrix:

$$\begin{bmatrix} 0 & 0 & 1 & 1 & 1 & 1 & 1 \\ 0 & 0 & 1 & 0 & 0 & 0 & 0 \\ 1 & 1 & 0 & 0 & 0 & 1 & 0 \\ 1 & 0 & 0 & 0 & 0 & 1 & 0 \\ 1 & 0 & 0 & 0 & 0 & 1 & 0 \\ 1 & 1 & 1 & 1 & 1 & 0 & 0 \\ 1 & 0 & 0 & 0 & 0 & 0 & 0 \end{bmatrix}$$

9.11. Rewrite the procedure **D_First** to do a depth-first search instead of a traversal.

9.12. Modify the procedure **D_First** to traverse graphs represented by adjacency lists.

9.13. Write a nonrecursive procedure for a depth-first traversal of a graph, using a stack to handle the backtracking.

9.14. Actually, a nonrecursive depth-first traversal can be carried out without a stack if we use the **preds** array to find our way back to previous vertices. Program this and compare the procedure to that written for the previous problem.

9.15. Define a relation R on the edges of a connected graph such that for any two edges e_1 and e_2, $e_1 R e_2$ iff $e_1 = e_2$ or e_1 and e_2 are both in the same circuit. (a) Show that R is an equivalence relation. (b) Show that the equivalence classes are the biconnected components of the graph.

9.16. Verify Eq. (9.1).

9.17. (a) Show that a connected graph with k vertices must have at least k edges to be biconnected (*i.e.*, to consist of a single biconnected component). (b) What is the largest number of biconnected components a connected graph with k vertices can have?

9.18. In `Bicon`, the call to `DF` always decides that the root is an articulation point. (a) Why is this? (b) Why is the root an articulation point only if it has more than one child?

9.19. Given the following graph, with the spanning tree shown in dark lines,

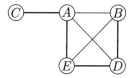

Problem 9.19

Trace the execution of `Bicon` (using the first version of `DF`). Show how the graph is numbered and note the tests upon each return from a recursive call.

9.20. Using the same graph as in the preceding problem, trace the execution of `Bicon` (using the second version of `DF`), showing the contents of the stack at each step.

9.21. Write a version of `Bicon` that uses an adjacency-list representation of the graph.

9.22. Trace Prim's algorithm for the following graph. Take vertex A as the starting point.

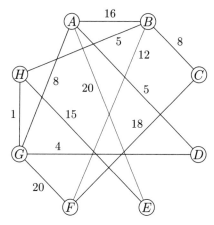

Problem 9.22

9.23. Write a version of Prim's algorithm using an adjacency matrix to represent the graph and a priority queue to select the shortest edge.

9.24. Trace Kruskal's algorithm with the graph of Problem 9.22.

9.25. We noted that, using our priority queue with priority and cross-index arrays, we can implement Prim's algorithm, Dijkstra's algorithm, breadth-first traversal, or depth-first traversal just by selecting what to pass to the second argument of `En_Queue`. Verify this by writing a general-purpose graph algorithm that will do any of these. (Use a parameter to select which function it is to carry out. Note that the choice of function must control the test for enqueuing as well as the choice of the second argument.)

9.26. Use Dijkstra's algorithm to find the shortest path from node C to node F in the following graph:

$$
\begin{array}{c}
A \\ B \\ C \\ D \\ E \\ F \\ G \\ H
\end{array}
\begin{bmatrix}
\infty & \infty & \infty & 13 & 27 & \infty & \infty & \infty \\
\infty & \infty & 8 & 28 & \infty & \infty & \infty & \infty \\
8 & \infty & \infty & \infty & \infty & \infty & 39 & 4 \\
\infty & \infty & \infty & \infty & \infty & 28 & 1 & 2 \\
14 & 6 & 3 & \infty & \infty & 30 & 22 & 10 \\
\infty & \infty & 22 & \infty & 10 & \infty & \infty & \infty \\
\infty & \infty & 7 & 30 & 23 & 15 & \infty & 8 \\
\infty & \infty & \infty & \infty & \infty & \infty & \infty & \infty
\end{bmatrix}
$$

9.27. Trace the all-pairs shortest-path algorithm on the following graph:

$$
\begin{array}{c}
A \\ B \\ C \\ D \\ E
\end{array}
\begin{bmatrix}
0 & 15 & 7 & \infty & \infty \\
13 & 0 & \infty & \infty & 18 \\
\infty & \infty & 0 & 16 & 19 \\
\infty & 1 & 13 & 0 & \infty \\
19 & 9 & \infty & 15 & 0
\end{bmatrix}
$$

9.28. Do a topological sort of the following DAG by crossing out rows and columns:

$$
\begin{bmatrix}
0 & 0 & 0 & 1 & 0 & 0 & 0 & 0 & 1 \\
1 & 0 & 1 & 0 & 0 & 0 & 0 & 0 & 0 \\
0 & 0 & 0 & 0 & 0 & 0 & 0 & 1 & 0 \\
0 & 0 & 1 & 0 & 0 & 0 & 0 & 0 & 0 \\
1 & 1 & 0 & 1 & 0 & 0 & 0 & 1 & 1 \\
1 & 0 & 1 & 0 & 1 & 0 & 0 & 0 & 0 \\
0 & 0 & 0 & 0 & 0 & 0 & 0 & 0 & 1 \\
0 & 0 & 0 & 0 & 0 & 0 & 1 & 0 & 1 \\
0 & 0 & 0 & 0 & 0 & 0 & 0 & 0 & 0
\end{bmatrix}
$$

9.29. Trace the execution of a depth-first topological sort on the following graph:

$$
\begin{array}{c}
A \\ B \\ C \\ D \\ E \\ F \\ G \\ H
\end{array}
\begin{bmatrix}
0 & 1 & 0 & 0 & 0 & 1 & 0 & 0 \\
0 & 0 & 0 & 0 & 0 & 1 & 0 & 0 \\
1 & 1 & 0 & 1 & 0 & 1 & 1 & 1 \\
1 & 1 & 0 & 0 & 0 & 1 & 1 & 1 \\
1 & 1 & 1 & 1 & 0 & 1 & 1 & 1 \\
0 & 0 & 0 & 0 & 0 & 0 & 0 & 0 \\
1 & 1 & 0 & 0 & 0 & 1 & 0 & 0 \\
1 & 1 & 0 & 0 & 0 & 1 & 1 & 0
\end{bmatrix}
$$

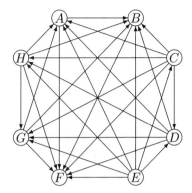

9.30. Write a Pascal procedure for a depth-first topological sort; test it on the graph given in Problem 9.28.

9.31. Trace the execution of a breadth-first topological sort on the graph of Problem 9.29.

9.32. Modify the procedure `Depth_Sort` to perform a depth-first topological sort of a graph represented by an adjacency list.

9.33. In `B_Sort`, there is no `visited` array and hence no protection against visiting a vertex more than once. Why not?

9.34. Modify the procedure `B_Sort` to perform a breadth-first topological sort of a graph represented by an adjacency list.

CHAPTER 10

TEXT COMPRESSION

Data compression seeks to store data in a form that requires fewer bits than the original form did. Text compression is compression applied to data whose original form is characters represented by ASCII codes. The topic of data compression is a good application area to consider for several reasons. First, it is a practical problem in many computer applications. Data stored on a disc or a tape take up space. The capacities of disc storage, even on personal computers, is growing almost daily; the days when a 10-megabyte disc was a *lot* of storage are apparently gone forever. Even so, there is never enough disc space. Magnetic tapes used for backup purposes have enormous capacities, but these days nearly every backup program for tapes includes a data compression capability, in case there is not enough tape. Moreover, transmitting data over a network takes time. Long-haul networks, spanning cities, use telephone lines to transmit data, and the rates these lines can handle are severely limited. Of course, you are billed for the time you use the telephone line. The result is that big files are expensive to transmit; if we can compress these files to perhaps half their original size, the cost saving can be significant.

Second, data compression makes use of much of the theory we have seen. The compression methods we will consider use many of the algorithms we have seen and many of their associated data structures. It is always well to see that the topics included in a course have real, practical applications. We will meet hashing, trees, tries, heaps, and other data structures, and we will always be alert to the complexity of the various algorithms.

Third, many readers have probably used compression utilities like ARC or PKZIP to compress files. (In the UNIX operating system, the utilities `pack` and `unpack` use Huffman coding; `compress` and `uncompress` use LZW.) Any user must occasionally wonder how the magic is done; in this chapter we will find out. We will not cover the field in great detail; data compression is a topic that can, and does, fill books. For more information than I provide here, I recommend Nelson [1992] and especially Bell, Cleary, and Witten [1990].

We can compress a file if it contains more bits than are needed to store the information it contains. We must thus start by considering how to define information in a way that lets us measure it.

10.1 INFORMATION

Data compression methods can be lossy or lossless. A lossless compression method preserves all the information in the original data; a lossy method, as you might expect, loses some of the information. From this you might infer that information is an important issue in data compression, and you would be right.

In 1948, Claude Shannon determined a way of measuring the information a message contains. He built on a more fundamental concept, which he called *entropy*. (Entropy is a term borrowed from thermodynamics. The expression for Shannon's concept took essentially the same form as the expression for thermodynamic entropy, so it seemed a reasonable term to use.[1]) In information theory, entropy is a measure of the uncertainty associated with a set of possible messages. It is a measure of our ignorance before we have received one of the messages. Then the information contained in the message, once we've received it, is the amount of ignorance the message removed. More important for us, entropy will tell us the absolute minimum storage space needed to represent one of the messages.

The entropy associated with a set of messages depends on the probabilities of the individual messages. If there are n possible messages $x_1, x_2, \ldots, x_n$, and if the ith message has a probability p_i, then the entropy of the entire set of messages is

$$H = -\sum_i p_i \log p_i.$$

where the sum is taken over all possible values of x_i. Since probabilities are never more than 1, their logs are never positive; putting the minus sign out in front of the sum makes the result nonnegative. The base of the logarithm determines the unit of measurement. If the log is to the base 2, the measure of H is in *bits*. If we use natural logarithms, to the base e, the unit is the *nat*. We will use bits.

The information content of a single message with a probability p is simply $\log p$. The entropy of a set of possible messages is thus just the average information content, over all the messages, weighted by the probabilities of the individual messages.

To take a concrete example, suppose the probability of precipitation in, let us say, Chicago, is .01 on a certain Summer day. In this case we have two possible outcomes: rain or no rain. The probability of rain is .01, and the probability of no rain is .99. If we are told that it didn't rain, this is no great surprise, and this is reflected by the fact that the information content of a message with probability .99 is lg .99 = .0145 bits. If we are told, instead, that it rained, we will be astonished, and our astonishment is reflected by the information content of lg .01 = 6.644 bits, which is 458 times the information content of the other message. On the other hand, the *uncertainty* associated with this set of possible messages is $-(.01 \lg .01 + .99 \lg .99)$. This is $.01(6.644) + .99(.0145) = .0664 + .0144 = .081$ bits. This low figure reflects the fact that, in the light of a probability of precipitation of only .01, there is not much doubt what will happen, even if we may occasionally be surprised.

---

[1] There's a story that John von Neumann recommended he call it entropy because nobody knew what entropy was; his argument was that this fact "would give Shannon an edge in arguments over information theory." [Horgan, 1992]

One of the properties of the entropy measure is that it is a maximum when all messages are equally likely. This should be intuitively reasonable: If the probability of precipitation is .5, we have no idea beforehand whether it will rain or not and our ignorance is at a maximum. It is not difficult to see that in this case the entropy is $.5(1) + .5(1) = 1$ bit. The maximum information conveyed by a single yes or no answer is thus one bit.

We can see the relation between bits of information and computer bits by considering that a single bit is also equivalent to a yes–no answer: yes corresponds to 1 and no to a 0. Furthermore, if a computer register contains 8 bits, then it can contain 2^8 different bit patterns. If these patterns are all equally likely, then any one value has a probability of 2^{-8}. In that case, the maximum information the register can hold is

$$H = -256 \left(2^{-8} \lg 2^{-8}\right) = \frac{-256}{256} \cdot (-8) = 8 \text{ bits.}$$

The relation of all this to data compression is this: We normally represent a message by a sequence of *codes*. These codes are nearly always strings of bits. The most common code is probably the ASCII code,[2] in which all the letters of the alphabet, upper- and lowercase, all the digits, and a generous selection of punctuation marks and control codes, are represented by strings of seven bits. The ASCII code represents 128 different symbols. If all these symbols were equally likely, the information contained in any of these codes would be

$$H = -128 \left(2^{-7} \lg 2^{-7}\right) = \frac{-128}{128} \cdot (-7) = 7 \text{ bits.}$$

But they are not equally likely. For example, in 177,382 characters of English text, I found 16,709 occurrences of e, 12,132 occurrences of t, and 10,683 occurrences of h. The most frequent character of all was the blank, which occurred 29,933 times. On the other hand, there was only one Q, only one Z, and X never showed up at all. So we conclude that the probabilities of the different characters vary widely, in which case the entropy associated with this character set should be a good deal less than 7 bits. The same program that found these letter counts estimated their probabilites by dividing the count for each letter by the total count; then it used these estimates to compute the entropy. The entropy was 4.5 bits. This means that if the ASCII set is used to represent ordinary English text, it is wasting approximately 2.5 bits per character. These are *redundant* bits, and the heart of all data compression is the removal of redundancy.

We cannot fault the designers of the ASCII code for this redundancy. They had no choice but to use 7 bits per character. The ASCII code is essentially the same as the ISO code, which is an international standard. The letter frequencies in different languages are not the same. For example, the probability of o is about .058 in my

---

[2] We customarily use the word *code* in two senses. A code can be a bit string that represents a particular character or sequence of characters, or it can be the rule that defines the mapping of the letters of an alphabet to specific codes. It will be clear from context which meaning is intended.

body of English text; in German the probability is roughly .035 and in Portuguese it is .115 [Gaines, 1939]. It thus makes no sense to tailor the codes to the letter frequencies of any one language. In addition, ASCII codes are often used to represent numerical data. In the absence of firm, reliable frequency data, the safest course is to assume all characters equally likely and hence to encode all of them with the same number of bits.

But the overriding consideration is that codes of uniform length are easiest to handle. There is no doubt where one code ends and the next begins. Furthermore, in computers, where memory is now generally organized in 8-bit bytes, it is simplest to store every character in a byte. The waste of yet another bit is a small price to pay for avoiding the overhead of pulling a long bit stream to pieces to isolate the individual characters.

In the case of data compression, however, the rules are different. We are not interested in convenience as much as we are in saving space. In that case, we can use statistical methods to ferret out the redundancy and remove it. This frequently results in codes of nonuniform length. The trouble we must take in writing and reading these nonuniform codes is a small price to pay if they sufficiently reduce the storage space or transmission time.

In considering letter frequencies, we can estimate them in isolation or we can consider pairs of letters (*digraphs*) or even triplets (*trigraphs*). The difference can be significant. The probability of *u* in my body of text was .00061, but when the preceding letter is a *q*, the probability of *u* jumped to 1.0. If we could rely on this to happen every time, we could just encode *qu* as *q* when compressing the data and decode *q* as *qu* when decompressing. Unfortunately, we can't rely on it to happen every time, because our text may contain words like *Iraq*. But in general, the conditional probability of a character *y* given that we have just seen a letter *x* can be used to remove more entropy, and the most powerful compression methods make use of this fact in one way or another.

10.2 SHANNON-FANO COMPRESSION

The oldest compression method is probably the one discovered independently by Shannon [1948] and Fano [1949]. It was superseded shortly by Huffman's [1952] method, but since it is still occasionally used and mentioned in the literature, we will consider it briefly here.

The Shannon-Fano code is a variable-length code. It uses bit strings of varying length, assigning the shortest codes to the most commonly occurring characters and the longest codes to the rarest characters. Thus in English the two most commonly occurring characters are the blank and *e*; these get the shortest possible codes. The idea is that the number of bits we save on the most frequently occurring characters more than makes up for the excess bits in rarely occurring characters. Ideally, the length of the code assigned to any character should be proportional to its entropy—that is, to the log of its probability.

This code is effective only if the various characters cover a wide range of frequencies of occurrence, and it helps if these frequencies are nearly the same over a wide range of possible input text files. We hope that the texts will meet this second condition because we would like to be able to use one code for all our input texts; otherwise, we would have to analyze each file for its letter frequencies and store the table of frequencies, or some equivalent information, along with each compressed file. (This is frequently done.)

If the codes are of varying length, then we need a way to determine where one code ends and the next one begins. We can do this without wasting space on delimiters if we impose the rule that no code may be a prefix of any other code. For example, if a particular code is 00, then any longer code must begin with 01, 10, or 11. If this requirement is met, then the decoding algorithm can read bits from the input stream until it has found a legal code. At that point, it emits the corresponding character and starts reading bits again. A code that meets this requirement is said to have the *unique-prefix* property. We will see that both the Shannon-Fano and the Huffman code have this property.

The Shannon-Fano algorithm uses the probabilities of the characters to grow a coding tree. This is a binary tree whose root represents the entire alphabet. The interior nodes represent subsets of the alphabet, the leaves of the tree will be the individual letters, and the form of the tree will give us the desired code.

To construct the tree, we do the following:

1. List the probabilities in descending order.

2. Make the root of the tree, corresponding to the entire alphabet.

3. Look for a place to divide the list into two contiguous sublists so that the summed probabilities of the characters in one sublist are as nearly as possible equal to the summed probabilities of the characters in the other sublist.

4. Make one sublist the left subtree of the root and the other sublist the right subtree. Label the root of the left subtree with a 0 and that of the right subtree with a 1.

5. Recursively apply Steps 3 and 4 to the two subtrees until each sublist contains only one character.

6. Obtain the code for each character from the labels encountered in going from the root of the tree to the leaf containing the character.

Most encoding schemes are impractical to describe if we consider the full ASCII character set, or even if we consider only the full alphabet, *a, b, ..., z*. So all our examples will use some limited alphabet; the generalization to a full character set is always straightforward. To illustrate the operation of the Shannon-Fano algorithm, suppose we have an alphabet consisting only of the letters *a, b, c, d, e, f, g*, and suppose their probabilities are as follows:

e	.39	f	.07
a	.20	g	.06
d	.13	b	.04
c	.11		

The entropy of this alphabet is 2.425 bits.

We have listed the letters in order of decreasing probability. To construct the tree, we look for a place to divide the list into two parts so that the summed probabilities of the characters in one part are nearly equal to the summed probabilities of the characters in the other part.

The letters in the set $\{e, a\}$ have a combined probability of .59, and the letters in the set $\{d, c, f, g, b\}$ have a combined probability of .41. Hence, we split the list between a and d. The sublist $\{e, a\}$ is the left child of the root, and the sublist $\{d, c, f, g, b\}$ is the right child. We label these new nodes with 0 and 1. At this point, the tree looks like this:

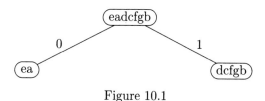

Figure 10.1

(In programming this, we would put the labels 1 and 0 in the children themselves, but the picture is clearer if we place them on the edges leading to the children.)

Now we apply this splitting process recursively to each new node in the tree. This recursion will continue until a node contains only one character. In $\{d, c, f, g, b\}$ the letters d and c have a combined probability of .24 and the letters $\{f, g, b\}$ have a combined probability of .17. Again, these are nearly equal, so we split this sublist between c and f. This split gives us two more nodes $\{d, c\}$ and $\{f, g, b\}$, which are the children of the node $\{d, c, f, g, b\}$:

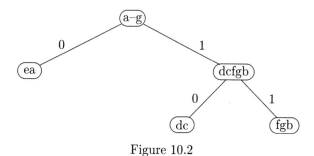

Figure 10.2

The nearest thing to an even split of $\{f, g, b\}$ puts $\{f\}$ in one node and $\{g, b\}$ in the other. Now in the set $\{e, a\}$, there are only two letters. We must split this set, and there is only one way to do so; hence, their probabilities are immaterial and we split them into one node for e and one for a; these become leaves of the tree. We split the nodes for $\{d, c\}$ and $\{g, b\}$ the same way. So we end up with the following tree:

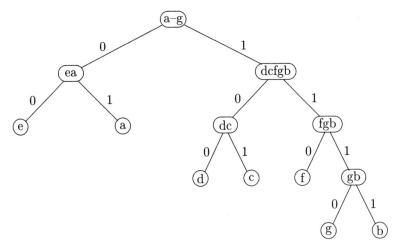

Figure 10.3

The code for each letter is given by the labels on the path to the leaf holding the letter. Tracing out the paths to the leaves of the tree gives us the following code:

a	01
b	1111
c	101
d	100
e	00
f	110
g	1110

The average code length can be computed by summing the individual code lengths weighted by their probabilities:

$$L = \sum_{i=1}^{N} \ell_i p_i, \tag{10.1}$$

where N is the number of characters in the alphabet, 7 in our example, and ℓ_i and p_i are the code length and frequency for the ith character. For this example, if we tabulate the letters, their frequencies, and the lengths of their codes, we can compute the average code length. From this table, we get an average code length of 2.51 bits, which compares favorably with the entropy of the alphabet.

Char	p_i	Code	ℓ_i	$\ell_i p_i$
a	0.20	01	2	0.40
b	0.04	1111	4	0.16
c	0.11	101	3	0.33
d	0.13	100	3	0.39
e	0.39	00	2	0.78
f	0.07	110	3	0.21
g	0.06	1110	4	0.24

10.3 HUFFMAN CODING

The Shannon-Fano code is still encountered, but it is largely of historical interest as the first attempt to generate an optimal code from the probabilities of the characters. The resulting code is always nearly optimal but not always optimal. The best coding of single characters, subject to the requirement that every character be represented by an integer number of bits, is the Huffman code.

The Shannon-Fano code works by splitting the ensemble of characters in the alphabet; the Huffman code works by merging individual characters. Both methods end up with a tree; Shannon-Fano grows the tree top down, whereas Huffman grows the tree bottom up. Since the Huffman code is widely used, we will consider how it is programmed in some detail.

Huffman's algorithm, like the Shannon-Fano algorithm, starts with a list of letter frequencies. It constructs the code by doing the following:

1. Search the list for the two lowest-frequency entries.

2. Create a new entry whose frequency is the sum of the frequencies of those two entries and whose contents are the union of their contents.

3. In a new column, remove the two lowest-frequency entries from the list and replace them with the new entry. (Notice that this always makes the list shorter, since we are removing two entries and adding only one.)

4. Repeat Steps 1–3 until there are only two entries in the list.

5. Mark one of the last pair of entries with a code 0 and the other with a code 1.

6. Move one column to the left, and copy the codes just created. For the merged entries, copy the old code and append a 0 to one of the entries and a 1 to the other.

7. Repeat Step 6 until all columns have been coded.

8. The codes in column 1 are the desired Huffman code.

We will demonstrate this algorithm with the same alphabet we used for the Shannon-Fano algorithm:

e	.39
a	.20
d	.13
c	.11
f	.07
g	.06
b	.04

The easiest way to trace the steps of the algorithm is to show them horizontally, working across the page. The two lowest-frequency characters are b and g. If we consolidate these, we get Fig. 10.4 (a):

```
e  .39        e    .39
a  .20        a    .20
d  .13        d    .13
c  .11        c    .11
f  .07    ┌► bg  .10
g  .06 ┐  │  f    .07
b  .04 ┘
```

Figure 10.4 (*a*)

(For clarity, we will keep the entries in each column sorted by frequency; the merged entry *bg* is thus placed above that for *f*.)

Now the two lowest-frequency items are *f* and the new entry *bg*. Consolidating these, we get Fig. 10.4 (*b*):

```
e  .39        e    .39        e      .39
a  .20        a    .20        a      .20
d  .13        d    .13    ┌► bfg   .17
c  .11        c    .11    │  d      .13
f  .07    ┌► bg  .10 ┐  │  c      .11
g  .06 ┐  │  f    .07 ┘
b  .04 ┘
```

Figure 10.4 (*b*)

Now the two lowest-frequency entries are *c* and *d*. Here the new entry consolidates *c* with *d* and has a frequency equal to the sum of their frequencies:

```
e  .39        e    .39        e      .39        e      .39
a  .20        a    .20        a      .20    ┌► cd    .24
d  .13        d    .13    ┌► bfg   .17        a      .20
c  .11        c    .11    │  d      .13 ┐  │  bfg   .17
f  .07    ┌► bg  .10 ┐  │  c      .11 ┘
g  .06 ┐  │  f    .07 ┘
b  .04 ┘
```

Figure 10.4 (*c*)

We continue this process until we are down to two groups. In this example, we end up with the tableau shown in Fig. 10.4 (*d*).

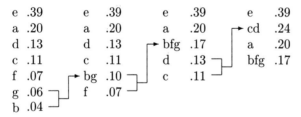

Figure 10.4 (*d*)

This completes the first part of the process. To generate the codes, we mark the entries in the last column with 0 and 1. Then, working left column by column, we copy the codes from the old column to the new *except* for the merged items. For these, we copy the old code but append a 0 to the code for one of the merged items and a 1 to the other. For example, as we work back from the last column to the second-last, we get these codes:

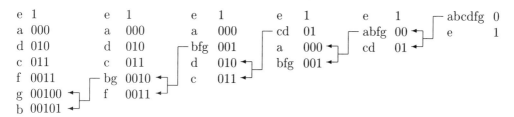

The 0 and 1 distinguish between the two groups that were merged. Continuing in this way, we end up with the codes shown in the first column of Fig. 10.5.

e	1		e	1		e	1		e	1		e	1		abcdfg	0
a	000		a	000		a	000		cd	01		abfg	00		e	1
d	010		d	010		bfg	001		a	000		cd	01			
c	011		c	011		d	010		bfg	001					
f	0011		bg	0010		c	011								
g	00100		f	0011											
b	00101														

Figure 10.5

We can also represent the tableau of Fig. 10.5 as a tree.

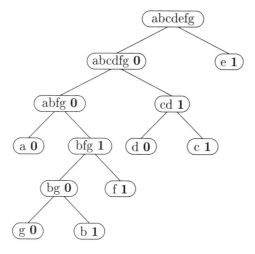

Figure 10.6

The root of the tree represents the entire character set; its two children are the last column of our tableau, marked with 0 and 1. After that, the children of each vertex are the subsets that were merged, and each vertex is marked with the bit that was appended. Each character to be encoded is a leaf of the tree; the code for the character is obtained from the labels in the nodes we encounter as we go from the root to the leaf (although in the program we will find it easier to go from the leaves back up to the root). The code for a is thus 000, since the vertices leading from the root down to the a leaf contain the labels '0', '0', '0'. Similarly, the code for b is 00101, because the path from the root to the b leaf passes through the vertices labelled '0', '0', '1', '0', '1'. We will find this tree useful when it comes to programming compression and decompression.

If we tabulate the letters, their frequencies and codes, and the lengths of their codes, as we did for the Shannon-Fano code, we get

Char	p_i	Code	ℓ_i	$\ell_i p_i$
a	0.20	000	3	0.60
b	0.04	00101	5	0.20
c	0.11	011	3	0.33
d	0.13	010	3	0.39
e	0.39	1	1	0.39
f	0.07	0011	4	0.28
g	0.06	00100	5	0.30

Adding the last column gives us an average code length of 2.49 bits. You will notice that this is closer to the actual entropy of 2.425 bits than the result we got from the Shannon-Fano algorithm. Huffman coding almost always has a slight edge over Shannon-Fano coding. When the full ASCII set of 128 characters is encoded by this method, using frequencies taken from English text, the minimum code length is 4 bits, the maximum is 24 bits, and the weighted average is 4.629 bits. Using Huffman coding to compress a draft of this chapter resulted in a compressed file two-thirds the size of the original.

Notice that the Huffman code for a particular set of letter frequencies is not unique, since at any vertex on the tree we could label the left child '1' and the right child '0' instead of following the convention given above. Any such labelling yields a usable code that is just as efficient as the one we found.

To prove that the Huffman code is the optimal code (subject to the constraint that every character must be represented by an integer number of bits), recall that the construction of the code takes place in two stages: First we consolidate subsets of the characters as we work rightward column by column. Then we construct the codewords by starting at the right and retracing the paths, working to the left a column at a time. The proof likewise starts at the right and works to the left column by column.

We can relate each column to a partial (or *reduced*) code in which each codeword stands for a subset of the character set. In the last column, we have a 1-bit code in which the 0 and 1 represent two subsets of characters. (If we think of this in terms of the coding tree, the last column corresponds to just the root of the tree and its two children.) At this point, the average length is 1 bit times the probability of one subset plus 1 bit times the probability of the other subset; but this is just 1 bit. So at the end we have a 1-bit code, and since the codewords have to have an integer number of bits, this code is optimal.

The proof then works inductively back to the left. We want to prove that if the code in the last column is optimal, then the code in the second-last column will be optimal, too; and if that is optimal, then so is the one in the third-last column, and so on back to the first column. The entries in the first column correspond to the leaves of the tree.

The inductive step thus consists of proving that if the code you get from any column n is optimal, then the expanded code you get by working leftward to column $n-1$ is also optimal. And the proof goes this way: Suppose there were a better code for column $n-1$. In that case, you could work back to the right to column n to get a better code than the one you had. But that's impossible, because the code you had for column n was already optimal.

The details are as follows: Let the code for column n be C_n, and let the code for column $n-1$ be C_{n-1}. Let the average length of the codewords in C_n be L_n. We obtain C_{n-1} by copying all the codes from C_n except for the two subsets we consolidated when we worked rightward to column n. Call these two subsets S_0 and S_1, and call the subset we get when we consolidate them S. That is, $S = S_0 \cup S_1$. For these two subsets we append a 1 and a 0 to the code we had for S. If the probabilities of S_0 and S_1 are p_{S_0} and p_{S_1}, respectively, we may write

$$L_{n-1} = L_n + p_{S_0} + p_{S_1}, \tag{10.2}$$

where p_{S_0} and p_{S_1} are the smallest probabilities in column $n-1$. This follows from Eq. (10.1).

Now to show that if C_n is optimal, so is the expanded code C_{n-1}, assume the contrary and see what happens. Suppose C_{n-1} weren't optimal. Then there would be some other code $\widetilde{C}_{n-1}$ whose average length would be $\widetilde{L}_{n-1}$, and we would have

$$\widetilde{L}_{n-1} < L_{n-1}. \tag{10.3}$$

But then when we consolidated S_0 and S_1 in the process of going to the next column, we would have gotten a new code $\widetilde{C}_n$ in which the code for S would be those for S_0 and S_1 with the last bit dropped. But in that case we could write

$$\widetilde{L}_{n-1} = \widetilde{L}_n + p_{S_0} + p_{S_1}. \tag{10.4}$$

But if we combine Eqs. (10.2)–(10.4), we get the result,

$$\widetilde{L}_n < L_n,$$

which contradicts our assumption. We thus conclude that if C_n is optimal, so is C_{n-1}. Applying this inductive step repeatedly, we see that the code for column 1, which corresponds to the leaves of the tree (and the paths to those leaves), is indeed the best we can do if we are restricted to an integer number of bits per character.

We have thus proved that the Huffman code is optimal. We have also seen a Shannon-Fano code for our sample character set that is not as compact as the Huffman code was; from this counterexample, we see that the Shannon-Fano algorithm does not always yield an optimal code.

In programming this algorithm, we will take the tree as our guide; each vertex on the tree will be a record containing the appended bit and the corresponding frequency. We can outline the program as follows:

1. Let $i =$ length of list.

2. While $i > 1$:

    a. select the two lowest-frequency entries;

    b. remove them from the list;

    c. merge them into a new entry;

    d. insert the new entry in the list;

    e. $i \leftarrow i - 1$.

The merging process consists of creating a new entry whose frequency is the sum of the frequencies of the entries that were removed and making those entries the children of the new entry.

Initially, we have only the list of characters and their frequencies. These correspond to the leaves of the tree, and at the start we do not know how these leaves will relate to the rest of the tree. So we must begin with a forest, each one containing only the leaf for one of the characters in the alphabet. Then when we merge two elements, we remove them from the forest and construct a new tree whose subtrees are rooted in the two elements to be merged. When the process is finished, the forest will consist only of a single tree, which is our desired Huffman tree. We will represent the initial forest by an array of pointers to tree nodes. Thus, at the start we have the data structures shown in Fig. 10.7.

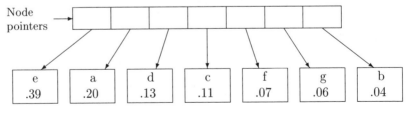

Figure 10.7

Then when we consolidate the two lowest-frequency entries, create a new node to hold these consolidated entries, and make the original nodes the children of the new node, we have in effect replaced two of the original trees in the forest by a new, more elaborate tree; this can be seen in Fig. 10.8:

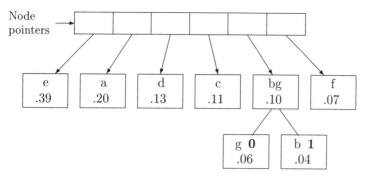

Figure 10.8

Similarly, when we merge *bg* and *f*, we obtain the structure shown in Fig. 10.9.

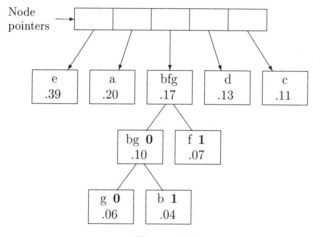

Figure 10.9

The execution time will be dominated by the time required to find the two lowest-frequency entries. In the previous examples, I showed the nodes sorted by frequency for clarity, but in order to minimize the time required for finding these entries, we will organize the array of pointers so that we can use them, and the nodes to which they point, as a priority queue. Since we are interested in finding the lowest-frequency entries, we will make this a heap of losers, with the minimum value at the top of the heap.

But if we use a priority queue, the list entries will lead a double life. They start out as entries in a priority queue and again end up as nodes in a binary tree. We will design the tree structure into the nodes and form them into a heap using our array of node pointers.

The node structure is

```
type
    cstring = string[24];          { Code and character strings    }
    nptr = ^node;
```

```
node = record                      { Data node:                        }
              value: integer;      {    ASCII code for symbol          }
              chars: cstring;      {    Characters (for debugging)     }
              freq: real;          {    Frequency                      }
              code: cstring;       {    Code                           }
              father: nptr;        {    Paternal pointer               }
          end;
```

The array of pointers is

```
    codeptrs = array [1..max] of nptr;
var
    A: codeptrs;
```

where max is the number of characters in the set—typically 128 or 256. Notice that the nodes have pointers to their fathers but not to their children. This is an additional refinement; it lets us work backwards from the leaves of the tree to the root in constructing the code.

The tree-building routine is structured very nearly the same as Heapsort. It uses the SiftUp and SiftDown procedures we saw in Chapter 6; in the present application the comparisons in these procedures are on A[·]^.freq, the frequencies associated with the entries. As usual with a priority queue, it finds the smallest element by swapping from location 1 in the array:

```
procedure MAKE_TREE (var A: codeptrs);
    var                     { First part of Huffman algorithm:     }
        i: integer;         {    Forms Huffman tree                }


    {  ====  SiftUp, SiftDown, & Merge go here  ====  }

begin  { Make_Tree }
for i := max div 2 downto 2 do
    siftup (i);                     { Heapify                }
i := max;
while i > 1 do
    begin
    swap (1, i);                    { Find smallest          }
    siftdown (i - 1);               { Reheapify              }
    swap (1, i - 1);                { Find second smallest   }
    siftdown (i - 2);               { Reheapify              }
                            { The two smallest are now in    }
    merge (i);              { A[i]^ and A[i-1]^. Merge them. }
    i := i - 1;
    siftup (i);                     { Reheapify              }
    end;
end;  { Make_Tree }
```

The differences are that it swaps twice (because it needs the *two* lowest-frequency entries), reheapifying after each swap, and that the two lowest-frequency items are consolidated by the procedure `Merge`. We need the call to `SiftUp` at the end to put the new consolidated entry in its proper place in the heap.

`Merge` creates a new node, makes its frequency the sum of the two given nodes, makes the new node the parent of the given nodes, and puts it at the end of the list:

```
procedure MERGE (i: integer);    { Consolidate two lowest-       }
   var                           {    frequency nodes A[i]^ &    }
      p: nptr;                   {    A[i - 1]^                  }
   begin
   new (p);                      { Get a father node        }
   with p^ do                    { Fill it in               }
      begin
      father := nil;             { Sum frequencies &        }
                                 {    concatenate chars      }
      freq := A[i]^.freq + A[i - 1]^.freq;
      ch := A[i]^.ch + A[i - 1]^.ch;
      code := '';                { No code yet              }
      end;
   A[i]^.father := p;            { Indicate paternity       }
   A[i - 1]^.father := p;
   A[i]^.code := '0';            { Assign codes             }
   A[i - 1]^.code := '1';
   A[i - 1] := p;                { Now insert father        }
                                 {  in place of A[i - 1] }
   end;  { Merge }
```

To find the codes from the tree, we work upwards from the leaves, as described before. This implies that we must have some way of finding the leaves, but since the original pointers in the `A` array have been lost in the course of the tree-constructing process, we need some other way of accessing these nodes. The solution is simple: provide a reference array `ref` of type `codeptrs` and copy the initial contents of `A` into it. We can now change the contents of `A` as required, and at the end we can still use `ref` to access the leaves of the tree. In the following procedure the codes are represented as character strings for convenience.

```
procedure FIND_CODES (var ref: codeptrs);
                 { Second part of Huffman algorithm:     }
   var           {    Read codes from tree               }
      i,
      hc: cstring;       { Holds code    }
      p: nptr;           { Climbs tree   }
   begin
   for i := 1 to max do
      begin
      hc := '';
      p := ref[i];                 { Point to leaf            }
```

```
    while p <> nil do
        begin
        hc := p^.code + hc;     { Copy codes              }
        p := p^.father;         {   & move up tree        }
        end;
    ref[i]^.code := hc;         { Put result into leaf  }
    end;
end;  { Find_Codes }
```

The main loop in `Find_Codes` repeats N times, where $N = \mathtt{max}$, and on each pass the tree-climbing process requires $O(\lg N)$ steps; hence, the cost of constructing the codes is also $O(N \lg N)$.

Encoding a file requires simply looking up the bit pattern for each character in turn and concatenating the bits into an output file. In a byte-oriented language like Pascal, handling individual bits requires some care but is not an insuperable problem.

To restore a compressed file, we construct a tree similar to the one from which we obtained the codes. This time the nodes must have pointers to their children, because we are going to start at the root for each new character. Our data structure now looks like this:

```
type
    nptr = ^node;
    node = record              { Node for decoding tree}
                value: integer;    { Decoded datum if leaf }
                left,              { Pointers to left      }
                right:  nptr;      {   & right sons        }
            end;
```

This tree, in fact, works like a trie. Indeed, it is grown from the codes in the same way that a trie is grown from its strings. When the trie is used for decoding, each bit in the compressed data tells you whether to select the left son or the right son. When you reach a leaf, you know you have reached the end of that particular code and that the character is the entry contained in the `value` field of the leaf.

Huffman coding can be made adaptive, so that it tracks the frequencies of the characters in the input file as they change and ends up matched to the file. We do this by starting with a more-or-less plausible set of frequencies and building the tree from that. But as each new input input character appears, we update the tree to reflect the change in its statistics. The Huffman tree has properties that make this an inexpensive operation, so the tree can be modified continually as compression is going on without slowing the program significantly. The decompression program, knowing the rules, updates its codebook in exactly the same way, so changes at one end are tracked at the other. For further material regarding adaptive compression, see Nelson [1992] and Bell, Cleary, and Witten [1990].

In its nonadaptive form, Huffman coding is fairly resistant to errors. If a bit gets switched as the result of noise or an error in transmitting or writing the file, the decoding algorithm will output some garbage, but the unique prefix property normally helps it to resynchronize again and get back on track after a few characters. Here is what happens when this paragraph is compressed with Huffman coding and then expanded again after one bit has been set incorrectly:

> In its nonadaptive form, Huffman coding is fairly resistant to errors. If a bit gets switched as the result of noise or an error in transmitting or writing the file, the decoding algorithm will output some garbage, but the unique prefix property normally helps it to resynchronize again and get back on track after a few charactersh toa cQchmo^Uhappens when this paragraph is compressed with Huffman coding and then expanded again after one bit has been set incorrectly:

One bit was changed from a 1 to a 0; as a result of this simulated error, the decompression process got lost in the words, `characters.␣␣Here␣is␣what␣` and then resynchronized successfully and reproduced the rest of the text without error. (One of the replacement characters was a nonprinting code, which I have had to represent with ^U.) Such an error is regrettable but not catastrophic. (I might add that it took several tries to get an error this bad; other times only one or two characters were lost.)

10.4 ARITHMETIC COMPRESSION

Suppose we had an alphabet of only ten characters, *a, b, . . . , j*. Suppose, further, that we assigned these letters the codes $0, 1, . . . , 9$. Then a message like *beachhead* has the codes $1, 4, 0, 2, 7, 7, 4, 0, 3$. In that case, what is to keep us from representing the whole word as the number 140,277,403? We have now wrapped up the entire word in a single number. We can accommodate that number in a 32-bit integer. (2^{32} is 4,294,967,296, so we have plenty of room for a number that big.) But this means we have encoded a 9-byte word in a 4-byte integer; this is a compression ratio of 2.25 to 1.

This, in greatly oversimplified form, is the rationale behind arithmetic compression. It outperforms Huffman coding, because it is not subject to the Huffman constraint that every character must be represented by an integer number of bits. Every new character makes a contribution to the output, but that contribution is not necessarily exactly one or more bits. On the other hand, arithmetic compression is slow, it is not robust in the presence of transmission errors, it is complicated to implement, and the improvement over Huffman is normally not great. We will see much more powerful methods later in this chapter. Hence, we will regard it as an interesting curiosity and will discuss it only in outline without providing a detailed implementation. Code (in C) for arithmetic compression may be found in Nelson [1992] and in Bell *et al.* [1990].

As so frequently happens, the basic idea requires a lot of refinements to make it work. First, for simplicity, I have used an integer for this first example, but in fact since there may be more text following that initial word, and since we want the numerical code to reflect the order in which the text appears, we use a fraction instead: Integers grow to the left, whereas fractions grow to the right. Thus *beachhead* would be represented as 0.140277403. Additional words would extend this fraction to the right, and in fact every message will be represented by a number between 0 and 1.

Second, in working with a full set of 128 characters, we will divide the scale from 0 to 1 into 128 parts instead of 10, and we will apply this 128-part division recursively to all the subdivisions of the scale. Thus, we encode the first character of a message—let us suppose it is A, with an ASCII code of (decimal) 65—by going $65/128$ of the way up from 0 to 1. So our resultant number will be somewhere in an interval beginning at $65/128$ and ending at $66/128$. If the next character is s, with an ASCII code of 115, then the resultant number will be $115/128$ of the way up that interval. The resulting fraction will then be $65/128 + 115/128 \left(66/128 - 65/128\right)$. If you work this out, it comes to .51843154296875. We continue this way until we reach the end of the message. It's as if we were using a radix-128 number system instead of a radix-10 system.

That enables us to accommodate 128 characters instead of just ten. The next question is how to represent arbitrarily long fractions with the limited precision available to us. As we keep adding characters, the fraction becomes longer and longer, and it is natural to wonder how we will accommodate it in the computer without resorting to multiple-precision arithmetic. But as the fraction grows, something else happens as well: Its high bits gradually stabilize and never change. We can see this even if we stay in the decimal domain. Suppose the message is "Ask me no questions." When we add the k, we are adding an increment of $107/128^3$; this increases our fraction to .51488256454467773.... But the leading four digits have not changed, and the next character (the space) will increase the fraction by $32/128^4$, which is only .00000012. So at this point we could remove and ship out the leading .5148, normalize what remains by multiplying it by 10,000 (so we have .8256454467773), and work with that. This incremental approach also means that we do not have to wait until the end of the message to start emitting codes.

Finally, in order to achieve optimum compression, we will allot space within the interval from 0 to 1 in proportion to each letter's frequency of occurrence. That is, we started out with the notion of dividing the interval equally into ten parts with one part for each letter:

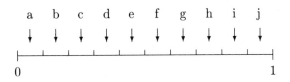

Figure 10.10

But arithmetic compression, like Huffman coding, works by taking into account the unequal frequencies of the various characters. To do this, we will allocate bigger fractions of the range to the more frequent characters and smaller fractions to the less frequent ones. Specifically, let the frequency of the ith character be $f(i)$, where the $\{f(i)\}$ are scaled to make $\sum_i f(i) = 1$. Then the size of the interval allocated for the ith character will be just $f(i)$. For example, suppose the characters from a

to j have the following frequencies:

i	$f(i)$	$c(i)$
a	0.17	0.17
b	0.03	0.20
c	0.06	0.26
d	0.09	0.35
e	0.27	0.62
f	0.05	0.67
g	0.04	0.71
h	0.12	0.83
i	0.15	0.98
j	0.02	1.00

The last column gives the cumulative frequencies, obtained by summing the frequencies in the second column. We can use these cumulative frequencies to show the way the range from 0 to 1 is divided among the characters:

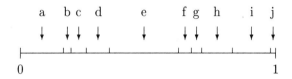

Figure 10.11

The generalization to the full 128-character ASCII set is straightforward.

We can represent the computations on each new character as follows. Let x_i be the ith character to be encoded; let its frequency be $f(x_i)$ and let its cumulative frequency be $c(x_i)$. Let r_i be the range of the fraction after coding the ith character, with a bottom value b_i and a top value t_i. Then the following recurrences apply:

$$
\begin{aligned}
t_i &= b_{i-1} + r_{i-1}c(x_i) \\
r_i &= f(x_i)r_{i-1} \\
b_i &= t_i - r_i
\end{aligned}
\tag{10.5}
$$

with initial conditions $b_0 = 0$ and $r_0 = t_0 = 1$. Arithmetic compression carries out these recurrences repeatedly on each new input character x_i. Then after a complete message of n input characters has been processed, the output code can be any number q for which $b_n \leq q < t_n$.

Because we are continually removing leading digits (or bits) from the fractions representing our range, we are continually making room for more precision at the trailing end. This means that we can carry out the computations of Eq. (10.5) without having to resort to arithmetic of such precision as to be prohibitively expensive; 32 bits are normally enough. It also means that we do not have to wait until we have computed the fraction for the entire message before we start putting out bits.

That summarizes the basic idea behind arithmetic compression; everything beyond this is implementation, which I said we would not consider. I will observe only that we have illustrated everything so far with decimal fractions, and this might naturally lead to the impression that we would compress using floating-point arithmetic. But floating-point arithmetic is slow, and different computers may use different, and incompatible, representations of floating-point numbers. Hence we use fixed-point arithmetic, obtaining fractions by imagining that the binary point is at the left end of the binary representation of the number instead of the right. We represent the range r and its bottom and top values b and t using these fixed-point values. Every time the high bits of b and t agree, that bit is shipped out and the representations of b and t shifted one bit to the left. Most of the complexity of the algorithm arises from making sure the range is updated correctly (modifying Eq. (10.5) to allow for the removal of matching high-order bits) and avoiding potential loss of precision when b and t get too close.

Using an implementation in Pascal, arithmetic coding compressed a draft of this chapter to about 64 percent of its original size; this is just slightly better than Huffman coding. The entropy of that file was computed as 5.11 bits, and the table used by the compressor was constructed from the file. We would then expect the compressed file to use approximately 5.11 bits per character; you will notice that 5.11 bits is approximately 64 percent of 8 bits.

10.5   CODEBOOKS AND LEMPEL-ZIV COMPRESSION

An attractive alternative to Huffman and arithmetic coding, and one which is suitable for a large variety of file types, uses a codebook or dictionary. The basic idea of a codebook is to provide a short numerical code which stands for a long character string. The codebook is a list of character strings—for example, words—with a number assigned to each string. In compression with the codebook, we substitute the string's number for the string; in decompressing, we substitute the string for the number. Thus, we could imagine a 16-word codebook as follows:

Code	Meaning	Code	Meaning
0	big	8	history
1	class	9	homework
2	computer	10	mathematics
3	data	11	more
4	department	12	science
5	discrete	13	technology
6	English	14	universe
7	French	15	world

Then we can code the phrase "big computer science class" as 0, 2, 12, 1. We store these four numerical codes, and to reconstruct the original data we simply look them up in the codebook. We have coded 23 characters as four 4-bit numbers. Codebooks on this model were once used commercially to minimize the cost of overseas communication by cable.

The problem is that such a codebook would have to be immense if it were to be generally applicable, while if it were tailored to a particular file it would have to be stored along with the file itself.

The Lempel-Ziv algorithms solve this problem with a suboptimal codebook that is generated from the text itself, but which can also be *regenerated concurrently as the text is being expanded*, so that it doesn't have to be stored along with the compressed file. The codebook is *implicit* in the compressed file. This is a remarkable accomplishment. The fact that the codebook is derived from the source text means that it is matched to that text; it is like having a dictionary that is custom-made for the text being compressed.

Lempel and Ziv developed two algorithms that do this. One uses the source text itself as the codebook; this is the earlier algorithm and is commonly known as LZ77, since it first appeared in their 1977 paper [Ziv, 1977]. The other forms a separate codebook from bits and pieces of the source text; this is known as LZ78, since it first appeared in 1978 [Ziv, 1978].

10.5.1   LZ77

The simplest codebook to use is that part of the source text that has already been compressed. This guarantees that the compression and decompression codebooks will match. It also makes it likely that the codebook will be well matched to the source, since if you start talking (or writing) about something, you will probably continue talking about it for some time, so the latest word you use has a high probability of appearing in the codebook.

This is the approach used in LZ77. The codebook is taken from the most recent n characters of the source text, n usually being some convenient power of 2 like 1,024 or 2,048. A new string of characters is encoded by searching in this codebook for a match. If a match is found, then the output is a pair of numbers giving the location of the match and the number of characters that were matched. If no match is found, then a single input character is passed to the output with a code indicating that it is not a codebook reference. On every step, the characters that were coded are appended to the end of the codebook and an equal number of characters are deleted from the start of the codebook. This means that the codebook acts as an n-character window that gradually slides through the text.

For example, suppose we are encoding this chapter. Suppose further that the codebook contains 256 characters and that we have reached the beginning of the last sentence in the previous paragraph. At this point, the codebook contains

     `acter␣is␣passed␣to␣...␣start␣of␣the␣codebook.␣␣`

(The ␣ is a blank.)

As it starts in on the next sentence, the compressor will look for a match to "This means ..." and, since there is no capital T in the codebook, the search fails, and the compressor outputs the T. The codebook is now shifted so that it contains

     `cter␣is␣passed␣to␣...␣start␣of␣the␣codebook.␣␣T`

The compressor now looks for a match to "his means ...," and again it fails. (There are several *h*'s, but single-character matches do no good; we can more easily transmit the character itself. In fact, the substring that is matched must be long enough that it is cheaper to output the location and length of the match than to output the substring itself.) The uncompressed *h* is passed to the output, the codebook is shifted to contain

> `ter␣is␣passed␣to␣...␣start␣of␣the␣codebook.␣␣Th`

The program now searches for "is means that ..." and the first three characters are matched by the first three characters of `is␣passed`. The location of the match (4) and its length (3) are sent to the output. The codebook window is now shifted three positions over, since three characters have been encoded, so that it now contains

> `␣is␣passed␣to␣...␣start␣of␣the␣codebook.␣␣This␣.`

...and so on.

Decompression works similarly. The first few characters will normally be uncompressed; they will go directly to the output and into the codebook. The codebook will grow during decompression the same way it grew during compression, and when substrings coded by location and length appear, the parts of the codebook that these numbers reference will be in place. Since no searching is necessary during decompression, it generally runs faster than compression does.

We must do a number of things to make this algorithm effective. First, the codebook must be longer than 256 characters, so that we will have a generous supply of previous text to draw upon; 2,048 characters is a typical size. Second, we must decide how to deal with the fact that, at the start of the process, the codebook is empty. The simplest solution to that problem is simply to let the codebook grow from a length of 0 to its final length as the first *n* characters of the source text are processed. This means that these first *n* characters will not be compressed as well as the rest of the file, but this is usually acceptable. Some implementations preload the codebook with some selection of strings, which, it is hoped, will be useful in compressing the data.

Finally, the cost of the process is dominated by the cost of searching the codebook, since a search must be made for every output code. If this is not done quickly, the process will take unacceptably long. Compressing the beginning of this chapter, using a 2,048-character codebook, shrank a file of 24,662 bytes to 13,914 bytes, 56 percent of its original size. But a sequential search of the codebook, even using Sunday's Quicksearch, was not fast enough: The compression required roughly 4 minutes on a 25-MHz PC. Life would be simpler if we could sort the characters of the codebook into alphabetical order, but that would destroy the patterns on which we want to draw for compression. What we need is a list of subscripts into the codebook that will access it in alphabetical order. We need to impose a structure on these subscripts that will give us quick access to any substring we may be looking for and that will be simple to update as the window slides through the source text. Nelson [1992] recommends using a binary search tree. If the codebook is *n* characters long, then the tree has *n* nodes and, if it is reasonably well balanced, the time to access any substring in the codebook is $\lg n$. The cost of inserting a new node, when the window moves, is similarly cheap, and the cost of deletion is not excessive.

10.5.2 LZ78

There have been many variants of LZ78. The one by Welch [1984] is one of the best known and most widely used; it is commonly called LZW. This is the variant we will describe here.

To form the codebook, we start out with a bare-bones codebook consisting of single characters. Then in compressing, we proceed as follows, starting at the beginning of the text:

1. Find the longest substring that is represented in the codebook.
2. Output its code.
3. Append the very next character from the file and create a new codebook entry for the resulting string.
4. Advance past the end of the substring just encoded and go to Step 1.

And we do this until you have compressed the entire text.

For example, suppose we have an artificial alphabet consisting only of "a", "b", and "c", and suppose the message is "ababcbaba." The codebook initially looks like this:

$$
\begin{array}{ll}
1 & a \\
2 & b \\
3 & c
\end{array}
$$

We start by considering the beginning of the message:

> ababcbaba
> ⇑

Here the longest string that is represented in the codebook is just the initial "a". So we output the code 1 (for "a") and add "ab" to the codebook:

1	a		
2	b	*Output:*	
3	c	1	
4	ab		

Now, picking up where we left off—

> ababcbaba
>   ⇑

the longest string represented in the codebook is "b". So we output the code 2 and add "ba" to the codebook:

1	a		
2	b		
3	c	*Output:*	
4	ab	1, 2	
5	ba		

Now we are here:

ababcbaba

⇑

Notice that we are now in a position to use one of the newer codes: The longest string is now "ab"; so we output code 4 and add "abc" to the book:

1	a		
2	b		
3	c	*Output:*	
4	ab	1, 2, 4	
5	ba		
6	abc		

Having taken care of "ab", we move two characters down the string and resume at "c":

ababcbaba

⇑

... and so on. Viewed this way, the algorithm seems simple-minded, not to say pointless. The codebook keeps getting filled with bits and pieces of text that may or may not be useful later on. It's hard to believe that any good could come of such foolishness. But in fact, this method produces very good compression of text. Why?

First, note that since the strings in the codebook are taken right from the text itself, the codebook is matched to the text. There will be useless entries containing things that appear only once in the text, but there will be many entries containing commonly appearing substrings like "the," "it", "ith", "st", and the like. Furthermore, if the source text contains some unusual word—for example, *zonk*— once, the chances are that the word will appear again, and when it does, part of it will be in the code book the next time. It is in this sense that the codebook is matched to the text. Second, each code emitted to the output file represents the longest substring that can be represented by a codebook entry; hence, there is a tendency for the algorithm to get as much mileage out of any output code as possible. The LZW algorithm compressed a draft of this chapter to 53 percent of its original length. (If you've been noting these figures as they have appeared, you will notice that this is the best compression to date.)

Now, how does the process reconstruct the codebook at the other end? The expansion rule is harder to explain than the compression rule.

(Startup:)

Read a code;

Look it up in the codebook;

Output the codebook entry and save it (call this **save**);

(Loop:)

Read a new code;

Look it up in the codebook;

Output the codebook entry (call this **new**);

Create a new codebook entry consisting of **save** plus the first character of **new**;

Copy **new** into **save**.

and that loop continues until we're done.

In our example, we have the codes, 1, 2, 4, 3, ... and initially our codebook is the bare-bones one with which the compressor started:

$$
\begin{array}{cc}
1 & a \\
2 & b \\
3 & c
\end{array}
$$

For the preliminaries, we read 1, look it up, output "a", and **save** = "a". Then, in the loop, we read 2, look it up, output "b", and **new** = "b". The output so far is "ab". We then create a new codebook entry consisting of **save** plus the first character of **new**; this is "ab":

$$
\begin{array}{cc}
1 & a \\
2 & b \\
3 & c \\
4 & ab
\end{array}
$$

When we copy **new** into **save**, the latter becomes "b".

Now we read 4, look it up, output "ab", and **new** = "ab". The output so far is "abab". The next codebook entry is **save** plus the first character of **new**; this is "ba":

$$
\begin{array}{cc}
1 & a \\
2 & b \\
3 & c \\
4 & ab \\
5 & ba
\end{array}
$$

When we copy **new** into **save**, the latter becomes "ab".

Now we read code 3, look it up, output "c", and **new** = "c". The output has now grown to "ababc". Our next codebook entry is "abc":

$$
\begin{array}{cc}
1 & a \\
2 & b \\
3 & c \\
4 & ab \\
5 & ba \\
6 & abc
\end{array}
$$

and **save** becomes "c" ... and so on.

This peculiar way of proceeding makes the codebook grow upon expansion in a way that parallels the way it grew during compression, and it also guarantees that each forthcoming code will normally be found in the codebook. The growth lags one step behind the compressing program, however, and this means that an undefined code could occur if the compression program used it immediately after it had added it to the codebook. This circumstance arises from a pathological case; I'll take that up shortly.

The basic procedure, as described here, runs slowly and eats up a lot of memory. It runs slowly because of the time required to search the codebook during compression; it uses up memory because of the length of the strings that are stored in the codebook. The first few entries are short, but as the algorithm proceeds, the strings to be coded get longer and longer.

The execution-time problem is solved by hashing. The entry to be stored or found is converted into a subscript by some convenient hash function and entered into the codebook accordingly. This reduces the search time to $O(1)$ if we use chaining.

To avoid excessive storage space for the codebook entries, note that every new entry is built on some previously defined entry. In that case, we could substitute the code for the previous entry and just add the fresh character at the end:

$$
\begin{array}{cl}
1 & (-1, a) \\
2 & (-1, b) \\
3 & (-1, c) \\
4 & (1, b) \\
5 & (2, a) \\
6 & (4, c)
\end{array}
$$

Where $(-1, \cdot)$ means a one-letter entry. You can reconstruct the meaning of code 6 by the steps, $6 \Rightarrow 4c \Rightarrow 1bc \Rightarrow abc$. This is a tedious operation, but tedious operations are what computers are for. We thus define codebook entries as

```
type
   codeptr = ^coderec;
   coderec = record
                code,                { Code for this entry       }
                prefix: integer;     { Code on which we build     }
                extension: char;     { New character              }
                next: codeptr
             end;
```

The **next** pointer is used to chain the records together in the hash table.

With these improvements, the compression algorithm proceeds along the following lines:

```
procedure COMPRESS;
   var
      testentry: coderec;      { Record to be found    }
      loc: integer;            { Code returned by Find }

   begin
```

```
with testentry do
   begin
   read (inf, extension);
   repeat
      prefix := -1;
      repeat
            { Invariant: extension holds current input   }
            {    character; prefix holds code for longest }
            {    substring found in codebook so far.      }
         loc := find(testentry);
         if loc >= 0 then            { Haven't reached end  }
            begin                    {    of substring yet  }
            prefix := loc;           { Chain & keep trying  }
            if not eof(inf) then
               read (inf, extension) { Read next char}
            else
               extension := chr(26)        { Fake eof mark }
            end;
      until (loc < 0);
                                 { Prefix now holds code     }
                                 {    for longest substring  }
         putout (prefix);            { Write it to output  }
         add_code(testentry, last_code) { Add code to book   }
      until prefix = 26;
   end; { with }
end;   { Compress }
```

Find uses hashed storage to find the code for the string represented by `testentry`; if there is no codebook entry for this string, Find returns −1. PutOut writes the code, which is contained in `prefix`, to the output file as a packed 12-bit binary number. The call to Add_Code creates a new codebook entry for `testentry`, increments a global counter `last_code`, assigns that new value to the entry's `code` field, and adds the entry to the hash table.

In the course of compressing a file, all goes well until the codebook fills up. It should be clear from our example that this happens fairly quickly. At that point no new combinations can be entered and the compression degrades rapidly. One surprisingly simple cure for this is simply to flush the entire codebook (except for the bare-bones part) and start building it from scratch. This operation can be postponed by using a larger codebook, but this requires using a longer codeword as well. Note that since the decompression program will build the codebook in step with the compressor, its codebook fills up at the same moment, and so it will know the proper time to flush and start anew.

The codeword length affects the performance of LZW in a number of ways. Presumably, the shorter the output codeword, the fewer bits the compressed file will contain. But every time you add a bit to the length of the code, you double the size of the codebook, which is good, because, as we have seen, the codebook fills up quickly. Most implementations use a 12-bit code, which permits a 4,096-entry codebook. Variants of LZW occasionally start with a short codeword and switch to a longer word as the codebook begins to fill up. If the initial codeword is, say, 9 bits long, then a short file, which may not be long enough to fill a 512-word codebook, can be compressed without using unnecessarily long code words. Since the decompression program's codebook fills up the same way the compression program's codebook does, it is not difficult to recognize the point at which the latter switched to a longer codeword.

The expansion program constructs its own copy of the codebook, again building on a 0 to 255 nucleus. Here we do not need to use hashing, and we declare only

```
entry = record
          prefix: integer;     { Code assigned to prefix     }
          extension: char;     { Character appended to prefix }
        end;
```

We implement expansion as follows:

```
procedure EXPAND;          { Decompresses file compressed      }
                           {    by LZW algorithm               }
   var
      newentry: entry;   { New codebook entry    }
      max_code,          { Highest code so far   }
      old_code,          { Last code             }
      new_code:integer;  { Current code          }
      cc: char;          { Extension character   }
      work: string[32];  { Decoded string        }
   begin
   clear_codebook (max_code);
   unpack (old_code);                  { Unpack & decode first code   }
   decode (old_code, work);
   write (outf, work);
   while not eof(inf) do
      begin
      unpack (new_code);                   { Unpack              }
      if new_code <= max_code then         { If defined,         }
         decode (new_code, work)           {    decode           }
      else                                 { Undefined:          }
         work := work + cc;                {    special case     }
      write (outf, work);                  { Write result        }
      cc := work[1];                       { Save first character }
      newentry.prefix := old_code;         { Construct new       }
      newentry.extension := cc;            {    codebook entry   }
      max_code := max_code + 1;
      if max_code >= max then              { Room in codebook?   }
         begin                             {  --no: clear        }
            clear_codebook (max_code);     {     & start over    }
```

```
        max_code := max_code + 1;
      end;
    codebook[max_code] := newentry;   { Add entry to book   }
    old_code := new_code;
  end;  { while }
end;  { Expand }
```

`Clear_Codebook` creates the bare-bones codebook and returns the number of codes entered so far, normally 128 or 256. `Unpack` reads a single code from the input file. We will discuss the problem of an undefined entry presently.

In the simplified version given previously, we created a codebook entry from `save` plus the first character of `new`. But that was before we learned about building entries on codes used for earlier entries. What we really need is not `save` but the *code* for `save`. But that is `old_code`; and of course the first character of `new` is `cc`. That is why `newentry` is made up from `old_code` and `cc`; it is also why we have `old_code := new_code` at the end of the loop instead of "`save := new`."

It is `Decode`'s job to go through the codebook expanding all those prefix codes until it hits a −1, and to assemble the characters in the variable `save` (or `new`). The logic is simple:

```
procedure DECODE (new_code: integer; var work: cstring);
  begin
  work := '';
  while new_code >= 0 do
    begin
    work := codebook[new_code].extension + work;
    new_code := codebook[new_code].prefix;
    end;
  end;  { Decode }
```

I mentioned the possibility of an undefined code. This can happen if you are compressing a message like this one:

acbcbcbca

(clearly a contrived example), where the initial codebook is 1 = a; 2 = b; 3 = c. The compression goes as follows:

Input	Output	New codes	
a	1	4 = ac	(code 1 + c)
c	3	5 = cb	(code 3 + b)
b	2	6 = bc	(code 2 + c)
cb	5	7 = cbc	(code 5 + c)
cbc	7	8 = cbca	(code 7 + a)
a	1		

The decompression goes like this:

Input	Output	New codes
1	a	
3	c	4 = ac
2	b	5 = cb
5	cb	6 = bc
7	... ?	

Here code 7 appears in the input before a code 7 is added to the codebook. But note that this can only happen if the compression program uses code 7 immediately after it has been created. But that means that the substring that created code 7 appeared immediately after code 7 was defined. Now the group that created code 7 was "cb" plus the next character, "c". But that means that the substring that used code 7 began with a "c", the character that was added to the end of the group for the code. In fact, the group for code 7 must be the most recently encoded group, plus its first character. If you consider the possibilities, you will see that a code that is used immediately after it was created must always represent a group that begins and ends with the same character. The ending character of the group is the start of the next substring; but if that substring uses the code, then it must start the way the code started—*i.e.*, with the same character.

This gives us the key to handling the undefined code. It must represent the group just decoded, followed by the first letter of that group. Hence, when we decode, we do this:

Input	Output	New codes
1	a	
3	c	4 = ac
2	b	5 = cb
5	cb	6 = bc
7	cbc	(This is *cb* followed by its first character)
		7 = cbc
1	a	8 = cbca

This explains the "Undefined: special case" code in **Expand**, shown above. The working string **work** still holds the previously decoded string, and it is necessary only to tack its initial character (contained in **cc**) onto the end.

10.6   OTHER COMPRESSION TECHNIQUES

There are other compression methods besides the ones described here, and there are other kinds of data that can be compressed besides text.

Run-length compression replaces strings of repeated symbols by a single symbol and a repetition count. Long strings of repeated characters other than blanks are rare in text, so this is not a very powerful approach for text compression, although it can be effective in image compression. Finite-state models are the basis of a compression method of potentially great power; these are described in detail in Bell *et al.* [1990].

Lossy compression techniques sacrifice some information in the process of compression, and it is impossible to recover the original data perfectly when compressed by a lossy technique. These methods are hopeless for text compression, where the reconstructed text must match the original character for character, but they can be very effective when compressing speech or images. In compressing speech, for example, one popular method derives a model of the mechanism by which the speech sounds are produced (a model, in fact, of the acoustics of human speech organs) and uses this model to predict what the next digitized speech sample will be. If the prediction is good, then the error will be small and we will require fewer bits to transmit the model and the error than to transmit the original signal. It's like using a player-piano roll instead of a phonograph record: The record stores the sounds of the original performance, whereas the player-piano roll stores the *method* by which the sounds were produced. Within the limits of the technology, the record will reproduce the original sound exactly, whereas the player-piano roll yields a convincing imitation of the original performance.

10.7 SUMMARY

How do we select a compression method? One important consideration is patent protection; for example, LZW is patented, and to use it you must be licensed by the patent holder. Among methods for which this is not a consideration, one simple way to choose a method is to try all the available techniques, see which one will yield the greatest compression, and select that method. Lempel-Ziv coding outperforms Huffman on many files, but not on all; you must not get the idea that it has somehow rendered Huffman's algorithm obsolete. The amount of compression achieved by Huffman and arithmetic coding can be estimated by computing the entropy of the data, but in the case of Lempel-Ziv coding, the compression must actually be carried out before its performance is known. A compression utility like ARC includes among its options no compression at all, in case the data to be compressed are such that all the available techniques result in an output file that is bigger than the input file.

10.8 PROBLEMS

10.1. Show that if there are n possible messages, all equally likely, their entropy is simply $\log n$.

10.2. When $p = 0$, the expression for entropy gives us the undefined form $0 \cdot (-\infty)$. Prove that $\lim_{p \to 0} p \ln p = 0$.

10.3. Compute the entropy for the following set of characters and frequencies:

a	0.32	e	0.09
b	0.24	f	0.04
c	0.15	g	0.03
d	0.12	h	0.01

10.4. Compute the entropy for the following character set:

e	0.33	i	0.07
t	0.27	n	0.05
a	0.13	s	0.04
o	0.11		

10.5. (a) Construct a Shannon-Fano code for the alphabet of Problem 10.2. Draw the encoding tree.

(b) Compute the weighted average code length and compare it with the entropy found in Problem 10.2.

(c) Encode the following string: *beachhead*

10.6. (a) Construct a Huffman code for the alphabet of Problem 10.3. Draw the encoding tree.

(b) Compute the weighted average code length and compare it with the entropy found in Problem 10.3.

(c) Encode the following string: *annotations.*

10.7. Given the following Huffman code, construct the decoding trie and decode the message, 01010010100001001000011001010011.

C	011	R	01001
E	1	S	000
F	0101	U	01000
O	001		

10.8. In the procedure `Find_Codes`, we wrote `hc := p^.code + hc` instead of the usual string-growing operation, `hc := hc + p^.code`. Why?

10.9. In expanding the Huffman code, the trie nodes had pointers to their children instead of their fathers. Why?

10.10. In all these programs, we evaded the issue of sending individual bits to the output in packed form. Write a procedure that will pack bits into a working byte and write the byte out to a file when it is full; write another procedure that will extract individual bits from a working byte and replenish it when it is empty.

10.11. Suppose the letters $a, \ldots, f$ have equal probabilities. Use arithmetic compression to encode the words *cad, feed,* and *deaf.* (Do this by pencil and paper and use floating-point arithmetic.)

10.12. Suppose the letters $a, \ldots, f$ have the following probabilites:

a	0.176
b	0.060
c	0.118
d	0.235
e	0.235
f	0.176

Construct a table of cumulative frequencies and use arithmetic compression to encode the words *cad* and *feed.*

10.13. Why don't we use hashed storage in decompressing a file compressed by
LZW?

10.14. (a) Assume that a file to be compressed by LZW is made from the
alphabet "a"... "f". Starting with an initial codebook,

a = 1   c = 3   e = 5
b = 2   d = 4   f = 6

Trace the compression and codebook growth and list the sequence of output codes
as the following string is compressed: *fababababaabaaabaaac.*
   (b) Using the result of part (a), trace the reconstruction of the original string
from the codes generated during compression.

10.15. An LZW decompression program has the input 3124579. Assume that
the bare-bones codebook with which it starts contains the entries

1   a
2   b
3   c
4   d

Trace the expansion of the message and the growth of the codebook. Show the
output.

CHAPTER 11

DYNAMIC PROGRAMMING

In discussing greedy algorithms, we saw that such an algorithm grabs the alternative that currently looks most attractive without any forethought or consideration of whether this choice will, in the long run, turn out to be the right one. But the greedy approach will not always work; sometimes it may turn out that there are a number of attractive possibilities, but that we won't know which one to choose until we have gone further through the process.

In that case, the sensible thing to do may well be to note the attractive possibilities and follow them up through subsequent stages until we find out which is the best. With luck, some of these initial possibilities will turn out to be unsatisfactory in some later step, at which point they can be eliminated. This approach will work only if one of those possibilities is guaranteed to be the correct one with which to start, so we don't have to go back to the beginning and consider some other possibility.

This approach is used in optimization problems: finding a solution that yields the greatest return (maximization) or that has the lowest cost (minimization). These problems are usually made more complicated by the presence of constraints. The constraints are usually what distinguish reasonable solutions from unreasonable ones, but they also make the solution harder to find. To take a silly-looking example:

> Problem 1: Minimize your taxes.
>
> Solution 1: Don't pay them.
>
> Problem 2: Minimize your taxes *legally*.
>
> Solution 2: ... ??? ...

This example is actually not as silly as it looks. Problem 1 is an *unconstrained minimization problem*, and its solution is simple, but unreasonable; solutions to unconstrained optimization problems frequently are. Problem 2 has a constraint built in: You mustn't break the law; and the difficulty of this *constrained minimization problem* is one of the things that keep accountants in business.

There is a class of constrained optimization problems that can be solved relatively easily by breaking down the solution into a set of steps or stages. (Unfortunately, this class doesn't include tax minimization.) In solving these problems

(1) there is only a finite set of choices; (2) each stage builds on the results of the previous stages; (3) we use the optimization requirement and the constraints to limit the number of choices we must consider in any stage. Many problems in this class can be attacked by the technique known as *dynamic programming* (DP). (The term is a catchy one, but it does not really explain how the process works. Because of property (2), it could better be called stepwise optimization, but that name isn't catchy at all, so we will follow the rest of the world and call it DP.)

In the typical DP application, there is usually a sequence of some sort to be found—in graph problems, for example, some kind of path comprising a sequence of edges. There is a cost associated with each step of the sequence, and these costs are additive. The combinatorics are such as to make an exhaustive search for the optimum prohibitive. We build the sequence one step at a time. At each step, there are a number of alternatives. On each step we look at the results from the previous step in combination with the current alternatives. For each alternative, we ask, if we chose this alternative, how would we get here most cheaply? The alternative will normally have a number of eligible predecessors; so for each predecessor, we compute the total cost:

$$\text{Cost of step } k \;=\; \text{(cost of predecessor)}$$
$$+ \text{(cost of getting from predecessor to step } k) \quad (11.1)$$

The cost will thus depend on which predecessor is under consideration. For each current alternative we note the cost for all possible predecessors and select the predecessor giving the minimum cost. These minimum costs and chosen predecessors usually go into arrays so they are readily accessible the next stage, since the results of this stage will be the predecessors of the next.

DP is typically used on problems with the following characteristics:

1. The problem can be divided into separate steps.

2. The cost mounts up steadily as we go through the steps.

3. The cost at any step depends only on the cost of the steps so far and the cost of the current step.

4. The *Principle of Optimality* applies to the problem:

> If the total solution is optimal, then that portion of the solution up through step k is also optimal.

The last characteristic means that as we work our way from Step $k - 1$ to Step k, we can use an optimal result from Step $k - 1$ without having to go back to the beginning and rethink everything. It is the reason why Eq. (11.1) works. This also brings us back to my original warning: We have to be sure that one of those attractive possibilities is guaranteed to be the right one.

It should be clear that DP isn't really an algorithm; it is a method of proceeding, like divide-and-conquer, that can be used to obtain efficient algorithms. In this chapter, I am going show how we can apply this method to particular problems.

11.1   DIJKSTRA'S ALGORITHM (AGAIN)

Dijkstra's algorithm for finding the cheapest path between two vertices has been characterized as a greedy algorithm—indeed, I introduced it as such—but it can also be viewed as a DP algorithm. Since we are familiar with it already, it is thus probably as good an introduction to DP as we are likely to find.

Let us consider it again from a DP point of view. As we set out from the starting node, we normally have a number of possibilities. In the graph in Fig. 11.1, if we want the shortest path from A to H, we can start by going to B, D, or F.

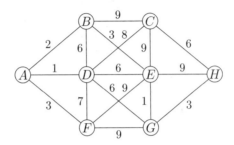

Figure 11.1

It could be argued that the greedy choice would be to go to D, because that edge costs only 1 against 2 for B and 3 for F. As a matter of fact, the correct choice eventually turns out to be B, but in any case, one of these will be the the first edge of the winning path. At the start, we don't know which one it will be, so we save the current costs in the dist array. We maintain the dist array so that it contains the cost of the cheapest known path from the starting node to every possible predecessor, and the preds array contains information from which those cheapest paths can be reconstructed.

As the process continues, we build on the results of the previous steps. In particular, the dist array gives us the optimum distance from the starting node to any node we would currently like to consider as a predecessor. Thus in updating the dist array, we compare the cost of the previous best way of reaching every vertex with the cost of reaching it *via* the new vertex. For example, in updating dist[E] after selecting node B, we consider whether it is cheaper to reach E *via* B or *via* D. To evaluate B as a predecessor, we find the cheapest cost of getting to B (which we have in dist[B]) plus the cost of getting from B to E; this is exactly Eq. (11.1). This is typical of the DP approach: we save old information from previous stages in the process so that we can refer to it again later.

Finally, we note that the cheapest-path problem satisfies the optimality principle. Given the cheapest path from node x to node y, the path from x to any interior node on that path is also cheapest. It is easy to see this: Let P be the cheapest path from x to y and let q one of the interior nodes on that path. Suppose there were a cheaper path from x to q than the one we're using. But if there were, we could use it as the beginning of the path from x to y, and this would be a cheaper path than P, since all the costs are additive.

In that case, why did we call Dijkstra's algorithm greedy? One reason is obviously that there is no point in invoking DP before the topic has been introduced. But we can also argue that if you are going to be greedy, you can be greedy about different things; in this case, we are simply being greedy on a more subtle criterion than simply the cost of an edge: our greed is directed toward the total cost of getting to any particular node as determined with the aid of the `dist` array.

11.2 THE KNAPSACK PROBLEM

Suppose we have a knapsack with a certain capacity (measured in the weight it can hold before it begins to tear). Suppose also that we have a large number of objects to pack, but that the knapsack can't hold them all. Each object has a certain value v_i and a certain weight w_i. The *knapsack problem* is this: Of the various subsets of the objects that will fit in the bag, find the one with the greatest value. (This is the popular way of stating the problem. It's an unfortunate way, because it seems to trivialize a real problem: Optimal packing is clearly of interest in loading planes, freighters, trucks, freight cars, and the like.)

This is a classic problem. It comes in two versions. In Version 1, we are permitted to slice up the objects and put pieces of them into the knapsack—as though we were packing bread, or salami. In Version 2, we either put the whole object in or we don't. In Version 1, we decide what fraction a_i of the ith object goes in; in Version 2, $a_i =$ either 0 or 1. Hence Version 2 is frequently called the Zero-One Knapsack (ZOK) Problem.

Version 1 has a simple solution that turns out to be a greedy algorithm. You find the value-to-weight ratio of every object. (For example, diamonds have a high value-to-weight ratio, and raw sewage has a low value-to-weight ratio.) You then pack everything you can, starting with the highest ratio and working down. You put the entire object in every time. Eventually, you'll reach something that won't go in; then you select the fractional amount of that object that just fills the bag to capacity. The cost of doing this is the cost of computing the value-to-weight ratios, which is $O(n)$, and of sorting the objects by ratio, which is $O(n \lg n)$.

The solution to ZOK is much harder. The brute-force way is:

For every subset:
    if it will fit then note its value.
Select the fitting subset with the highest value.

This means considering every subset. That's the power set of the objects; if there are n objects in our collection, then there are 2^n subsets to consider, and so the cost of the brute-force method is $O(2^n)$. If the weights and the capacity of the knapsack are real numbers, there is no known clever way of doing this that reduces that figure significantly.

If we restrict the numbers to integer values, however, there is a DP solution to the problem. That is what we are going to consider here. Each step of the process will correspond to the insertion of an article into the knapsack. Since the values and weights of the objects are both additive, all the initial subsets of the optimal subset will also be optimal for whatever bag will just hold them, so we can apply the principle of optimality to the problem.

We can state the problem formally as follows: Let the ith object have weight w_i and value v_i, let the number of objects be n, and let the capacity of the knapsack be c. Find the numbers $\{a_i\}$ that maximize

$$f_n(c) = \sum_{i=1}^{n} a_i v_i$$

subject to the constraint that

$$\sum_{i=1}^{n} a_i w_i \leq c.$$

where $a_i \in \{0, 1\}$. Here $f_i(j)$ is the total value of objects 1 through i packed into a knapsack of capacity j.

We will proceed as follows: The first step will be to find the optimal packing of the first object into knapsacks of every capacity up to the final weight limit. Since we are considering only integer capacities, this approach is practical. The values $f_1(j), j = 1, 2, \ldots, c$ that result from this step, saved in an array, are the remembered data to which we will refer in the next step.

For each subsequent article i, we do the following: Again consider knapsacks of every capacity up to the weight limit. If the new article will fit in the knapsack, find out how much capacity is left over. Suppose the current knapsack size we are considering is j. Then the remaining capacity is $j - w_i$. To fill this remaining capacity, we resort to the optimality principle: referring to the saved data, find the optimum packing of articles 1 through $i - 1$ for a knapsack of size $j - w_i$. (This is $f_{i-1}(j - w_i)$.) Since w_i and j are integers, we can use this expression as a subscript into the saved data. This is what makes the integer version amenable to a DP solution; if the capacity and the weights were real numbers, we couldn't use them to obtain an exact subscript.

It may be that the combined value of the latest article, plus the value $f_{i-1}(j-w_i)$ will be less than the value we had when we considered the same size knapsack with only $i - 1$ items, $f_{i-1}(j)$. In that case, we ignore the new article. But if the combined value is more, then we choose the new article and fill the knapsack up with the contents associated with $j - w_i$. So this is how we decide whether to include each new article: If it gives us a better deal, we include it and make up the remaining capacity with a smaller optimum packing; otherwise, we omit it and make do with what we had before.

This policy gives us the following recursion:

$$f_i(j) = \max[f_{i-1}(j), \ v_i + f_{i-1}(j - w_i)]. \tag{11.2}$$

The first item in that comparison is what we would have if we omitted the new object i and stayed with the previous packing, and the second item is the value we would get if we chose the new object and filled as much as possible of the remaining capacity with the packing for $(i-1, j - w_i)$. We get our initial conditions as follows:

$f_i(0)$ is the maximum value packed into a knapsack with capacity zero, and $f_0(j)$ is the value of an empty knapsack of capacity j, so clearly

$$f_i(0) = 0, \quad i = 0, 1, \dots, m$$
$$f_0(j) = 0, \quad j = 0, 1, \dots, c. \tag{11.3}$$

The algorithm thus need only fill in the table $f_i(j)$ with an outer loop on i and an inner loop on j.

If the weights are contained in an array `wgt` and the values in an array `val`, then we can code the algorithm as follows. We will declare

```
const
   cap = 12;     { or whatever: capacity of knapsack    }
   nobj = 5;     { or whatever: number of items to pack }
type
   x_array = array[1..nobj] of integer;
   t_array = array[0..nobj, 0..cap] of integer;
var
   wgt,                     { Weights & values          }
   val: x_array;           {    of objects to be packed }
   totval: t_array;        { Array of packed values     }
   i, j: integer;
   weight: integer;        { Total weight packed        }
```

Then the implementation is as follows:

```
procedure KNAPSACK (wgt, val: x_array; var totval: t_array);
   var                     { Solves the integer knapsack problem   }
      i, j, p: integer;
   begin
   for j := 0 to cap do          { Initial conditions     }
      totval[0, j] := 0;
   for i := 0 to nobj do
      totval[i, 0] := 0;
   for i := 1 to nobj do                      { Loop on objects        }
      for j := 1 to cap do                     { Loop on knapsack size }
         begin
         totval[i, j] := totval[i - 1, j]; { Assume we'll          }
                                            {    leave it out       }
         if j - wgt[i] >= 0 then          { Is there room for it? }
            begin
            p := totval[i - 1, j - wgt[i]] + val[i];
            if p > totval[i - 1, j] then     { Does it pay           }
                                             {    to put it in?      }
               totval[i, j] := p             { --yes: put it in }
            end
         end;
   end; { Knapsack }
```

The `totval` array contains the values of f: $\texttt{totval}[i, j] = f_i(j)$. Its dimensions are [0..nobj, 0..cap], in which $\texttt{nobj} = n$, the number of objects, and $\texttt{cap} = c$, the capacity of the knapsack.

When we return from the call to `Knapsack`, we can find which articles to pack from the `totval` array. We start at the lower-right corner of the array—that is, at `totval[nobj, cap]`—and compare the entry with that just above it. If the two entries are the same, then the last object must not have been packed. Otherwise, we list it as packed, find the remaining capacity, and examine the next row up at the column corresponding to the remaining capacity. This leads to the following code:

```
weight := 0;
i := nobj;
j := cap;
write (' Packed ');
while i > 0 do
    begin
    if totval[i, j] <> totval[i - 1, j] then
        begin                           { Must have packed it:  }
        write (i:3);                    {    List it            }
        weight := weight + wgt[i];      {    Note its weight     }
        j := j - wgt[i]                 {    Find capacity left  }
        end;
    i := i - 1                   { Back off to previous item    }
    end;
writeln;
write (' Total weight = ', weight);
writeln ('; Value = ', totval[nobj, cap]);
```

As shown, this code has a time complexity of $O(nc)$, which is a good deal better than $O(2^n)$ for all reasonable values of n and c. It has a space complexity of $O(nc)$ as well, however, because of the need to store the entire `totval` array. We might consider reducing the cost by saving only the current and previous rows of this array, but then we would need another way of noting what saved items correspond to each new entry. It seems simplest to do it as shown.

11.3 OPTIMAL BINARY SEARCH TREES

In considering binary search trees, we discussed avoiding degenerate cases by means of AVL and red-black trees. DP allows us another approach that is based on a different criterion: If we know how often the various records will be accessed, then we should put the most frequently accessed records at or near the root of the tree, and we should make the least frequently accessed ones leaves, subject to the constraint that the order of the keys still results in a binary search tree. This policy will not necessarily reduce the time required for a traversal, but it will minimize the average time required for a successful search. It will avoid degenerate trees except in the rare case where a degenerate shape just happens to offer the best deal. (An example of this appears in the problems.)

The shape of the tree will be determined, not by the order in which the data arrive or by some self-balancing mechanism, but by the values of the keys and their weights. We will grow the tree once for all, *i.e.*, with no allowance for subsequent additions of deletions. (Reoptimizing a tree after insertions or deletions is an expensive undertaking.)

To apply DP to this problem, we need a cost function. Let p_i be the probability that we will search for record i $(i = 1, 2, \ldots, n)$. Then for the most frequently accessed records p_i will be large and for the least frequently accessed ones p_i will be small. Let d_i be the length of the path from the root to the node containing record i. Then the number of comparisons for a successful search will be $d_i + 1$, and the average number of comparisons over the entire tree will be $\sum_{i=1}^{n} p_i(d_i + 1) = \sum_{i=1}^{n} p_i d_i + \sum_{i=1}^{n} p_i$. The sum of the probabilities is independent of d_i (in fact, it is 1); so it is sufficient to minimize the first sum. This first sum is the *weighted internal path length* $\sum_{i=1}^{n} p_i d_i$, and we will take this as the cost function we wish to minimize. (I have introduced this in terms of probabilities. We will find it more convenient to use integer weights, presumably the access counts from which we could estimate the probabilities. It should be clear that either approach will give us the optimum tree, since the probability estimates are proportional to the access counts.)

The DP approach considers all attractive solutions to the first step in the process and then saves these solutions and builds on them in subsequent steps. Here the first step will be to optimize the smallest subtrees, the ones containing only two vertices. The subsequent steps will then optimize larger and larger subtrees, forming them from the subtrees we have already found, until we have the entire tree. We thus grow the tree from the bottom up. It should be clear that the cost function is additive and that the principle of optimality applies, since an optimal tree must have optimal subtrees. (If it didn't, we could get a better tree by substituting optimal subtrees with the same contents.)

Let the records, listed in sorted order, be $(r_1, r_2, \ldots, r_n)$, and let T_{ij} be an optimal subtree containing only the records from r_i through r_j. The root will contain r_k, where $i \leq k \leq j$, as shown in Fig. 11.2.

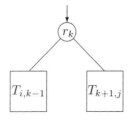

Figure 11.2

If we choose to put r_k in the root, then the binary-search-tree constraint means that the left subtree must contain $r_i, r_{i+1}, \ldots, r_{k-1}$ and the right subtree must contain $r_{k+1}, r_{k+2}, \ldots, r_j$. All the subtrees will thus contain consecutive records.

In order to specify the tree from the bottom up, we will use two nested loops. The outer loop will be on the size of the subtrees to be considered, starting with the smallest. The inner loop will be on i, and in this loop, j will be computed from i and the current size. It helps to see how i and j vary over the course of the outer loop. Let the size of the subtrees currently under consideration be m and let the number of vertices be n. Then, for example, if $n = 8$, we have the following sets of values for (i, j):

m	Ranges (i, j)						
2	(1, 2)	(2, 3)	(3, 4)	(4, 5)	(5, 6)	(6, 7)	(7, 8)
3	(1, 3)	(2, 4)	(3, 5)	(4, 6)	(5, 7)	(6, 8)	
4	(1, 4)	(2, 5)	(3, 6)	(4, 7)	(5, 8)		
5	(1, 5)	(2, 6)	(3, 7)	(4, 8)			
6	(1, 6)	(2, 7)	(3, 8)				
7	(1, 7)	(2, 8)					
8	(1, 8)						

In each pass through the loop on m, $j = i + m - 1$. When $m = 2$, we find the seven optimal subtrees consisting of only two consecutive nodes. When $m = 3$, we find the six optimal subtrees consisting of three consecutive nodes, using the results we just obtained for $m = 2$, and so on.

To find the optimal subtree T_{ij}, we consider each vertex from i to j as a possible root and see which choice gives the smallest weighted internal path length—that is, the smallest cost. We will remember the winning vertex and the resultant cost, which we will call $cost_{ij}$. We will save these costs in an array, because as we work up to larger subtrees, we will refer to these numbers in computing the costs of the larger subtrees. Saving and reusing intermediate results this way is the hallmark of DP.

We can obtain $cost_{ij}$ as follows: The cost of a tree consisting of a single vertex r_k with no children is just p_{r_k}, that is, how often we expect r_k to be referenced. Since this single node can be written as T_{kk}, we will put the probability p_{r_k} into $cost_{kk}$ at the start.

For any other tree with root r_k and subtrees $T_{i,k-1}$ and $T_{k+1,j}$, the cost will be made up of three components, as we can see from Fig. 11.2. These components are the cost of the root, which is $cost_{kk}$, a corrected cost for $T_{i,k-1}$, and a corrected cost for $T_{k+1,i}$. We need the corrections to allow for the fact that when $T_{i,k-1}$ is made a subtree of r_k, all its nodes are one level down from where they were in the tree itself. Thus, the correction for $T_{i,k-1}$ is the sum of $cost_{ss}$ as s runs from i to $k - 1$, and similarly for $T_{k+1,i}$. So

$$cost_{ij} = cost_{kk} + cost_{i,k-1} + \sum_{s=i}^{k-1} cost_{ss} + cost_{k+1,j} + \sum_{s=k+1}^{j} cost_{ss}. \qquad (11.4)$$

But notice that the corrections, together with $cost_{kk}$, comprise the sum of all the probabilities from i to j, and that sum, which I'll call w_{ij} (the *weight* of the subtree), is independent of whichever node k we are currently considering. This has two consequences that simplify life for us: First, in finding the minimum over k, we can ignore the corrections and just find

$$best\_deal_{ij} = \min_{i \le k \le j} (cost_{i,k-1} + cost_{k+1,j}). \qquad (11.5)$$

Second, we can reduce Eq. (11.4) for the optimal cost by substituting the weight of the subtree, as follows:

$$cost_{ij} = best\_deal_{ij} + w_{ij}. \qquad (11.6)$$

The algorithm uses Eqs. (11.5) and (11.6) to fill in the *cost* array in a pair of nested loops on m and i.

At this point, we are ready to consider the implementation. In the following code, I have chosen to use `size` for m and `n` for the number of nodes; `n1` is `n + 1`. The input parameter is the array of probabilities; the output parameters are the the choices for every possible T_{ij} and the final cost. We will see the definitions of `p_array` and `r_matrix` presently.

```
procedure OPT_TREE (var probs: p_array; var rootchoice: r_matrix;
                    var totalcost: real);
                            { Constructs optimal BST        }
    var
       cost: c_matrix;
       i, j,              { Current range                   }
       k,                 { Current candidate for root      }
       size               { Current subtree size            }
       kmin: integer;     { Root giving minimum cost        }
       best_deal,         { Minimum cost                    }
       temp,
       weight: real;      { Weight of this subtree          }

    begin
    for i := 0 to n1 do         { Preliminaries:            }
       for j := 0 to n1 do      { Clear all of cost array   }
          cost[i, j] := 0;
    for i := 1 to n do          { Put key subscripts on main }
       begin                    {    diagonal of rootchoice  }
       rootchoice[i, i] := i;
       cost[i, i] := probs[i]   {    & probabilities on main }
       end;                     {    diagonal of costs       }

    for size := 2 to n do       { Loop on subtree size       }
       for i := 1 to n + 1 - size do      { Loop on starting node }
          begin
          j := i + size - 1;                { Determine ending node }
          best_deal := HUGE;
          kmin := 0;
```

```
      for k := i to j do     { Loop on possible roots       }
         begin
         temp := cost[i, k - 1] + cost[k + 1, j];
         if temp < best_deal then    { Find minimum cost      }
            begin
            best_deal := temp;
            kmin := k
            end;
         end;
      rootchoice[i, j] := kmin;
      weight := 0;
      for k := i to j do                { Find weight          }
         weight := weight + cost[k, k];
      cost[i, j] := best_deal           { Get total cost       }
            + weight;
      end;  { for size; for i }
   totalcost := cost[1, n]
   end;  { Opt_Tree }
```

As usual, HUGE is a constant defined in advance as some very large number guaranteed to be greater than any of the costs being considered. The array types are declared as follows:

```
type
   c_matrix = array [0..n1, 0..n1] of real;
   r_matrix = array [1..n, 1..n] of integer;
   p_array = array [1..n] of real;
```

The costs go in the c_matrix array cost; the probabilities (from the parameter probs) go on the main diagonal of cost, and all the other entries are initially zero. The r_matrix array rootchoice holds the roots chosen by the loop on k; rootchoice[i, j] will hold the best root found for T_{ij}. This array is returned as a parameter so that it can be used in growing the tree. Since the optimum root for T_{kk} cannot be anything but k, we put the root subscripts into the main diagonal of rootchoice.

The DP process is carried out in the loop on size. For each of the possible roots in any subtree T_{ij}, it finds the cost and selects the root giving the minimum cost following Eq. (11.5). This root and its actual cost (found from Eq. (11.6)) go into the [i, j] entries of rootchoice and cost, respectively.

For example, suppose we have the following nine keys and their weights:

Key:	1	3	5	7	8	12	14	18	23
Weight:	14	4	14	15	8	2	13	17	1

(Remember that any weights that reflect the access probabilities will do; here we have used integer values, as I said we would.) With this combination of keys and weights, the program produces these `cost` and `rootchoice` arrays:

$$
cost = \begin{bmatrix}
0 & 0 & 0 & 0 & 0 & 0 & 0 & 0 & 0 & 0 & 0 \\
 & 14 & 22 & 54 & 84 & 108 & 116 & 159 & 210 & 214 & 0 \\
 & & 4 & 22 & 52 & 71 & 77 & 113 & 164 & 168 & 0 \\
 & & & 14 & 43 & 59 & 65 & 101 & 151 & 154 & 0 \\
 & & & & 15 & 31 & 37 & 70 & 109 & 112 & 0 \\
 & & & & & 8 & 12 & 35 & 69 & 72 & 0 \\
 & & & & & & 2 & 17 & 49 & 51 & 0 \\
 & & 0 & & & & & 13 & 43 & 45 & 0 \\
 & & & & & & & & 17 & 19 & 0 \\
 & & & & & & & & & 1 & 0 \\
 & & & & & & & & & & 0
\end{bmatrix}
$$

$$
rootchoice = \begin{bmatrix}
1 & 1 & 1 & 3 & 3 & 3 & 4 & 4 & 4 \\
 & 2 & 3 & 3 & 4 & 4 & 4 & 4 & 4 \\
 & & 3 & 4 & 4 & 4 & 4 & 7 & 7 \\
 & & & 4 & 4 & 4 & 5 & 7 & 7 \\
 & & & & 5 & 5 & 7 & 7 & 7 \\
 & & 0 & & & 6 & 7 & 8 & 8 \\
 & & & & & & 7 & 8 & 8 \\
 & & & & & & & 8 & 8 \\
 & & & & & & & & 9
\end{bmatrix}
$$

If you consider the loops in the procedure, you will see that they start using the weights on the main diagonal of `cost` and fill in the diagonal just above it. Then on the next pass through the `size` loop, they use that new diagonal and fill in the diagonal above *it*, and so on. At the end of the procedure, the only remaining item of interest in the `cost` matrix is `cost[1, n]` (in this case `cost[1, 9]`), which gives us the total weighted internal path length of the optimized tree; this is returned as the parameter `totalcost`.

From the three nested loops that constitute the main part of `Opt_Tree`, it should be clear that the cost of the procedure as shown is $O(n^3)$. This is expensive; but since the total number of binary trees with n vertices is the nth Catalan number $\frac{1}{n+1}\binom{2n}{n}$, as shown in Appendix B, it is clear that an exhaustive search is out of the question. We have two possible speedups, however. One minor one stems from the observation that the weight of a subtree can be written as

$$
w_{ij} = \sum_{k=i}^{j} cost_{kk} = w_{i-1,j\dot-1} + cost_{jj} - cost_{i-1,i-1}.
$$

Hence we may rewrite the computation of the weight as follows:

```
if i = 1 then
   begin
   weight := 0;
   for k := i to j do           { Find weight           }
```

```
        weight := weight + cost[k, k];
      end
  else
      weight := weight + cost[j, j] - cost[i - 1, i - 1];
```

A more important speedup arises from the form of the rootchoice array: every element has a value no less than the element to its left and no greater than the element below it. In fact, Knuth [1973] shows that we may write

rootchoice[i, j - 1] $\leq$ rootchoice[i, j] $\leq$ rootchoice[i + 1, j].

Knuth's proof is difficult, but we can make the following plausibility argument: T_{ij} is just $T_{i,j-1}$ with an additional vertex r_j stuck on at the end. Appending r_j may shift the optimum root to the right, but it certainly won't shift it to the left unless its weight is negative. Hence, in looking for rootchoice[i, j], there is no need to try any vertex coming before rootchoice[i, j - 1]. Similarly, T_{ij} is just $T_{i+1,j}$ with an additional vertex r_i at the beginning. If you add r_i, the optimum root may move to the left, but it certainly won't move to the right. Therefore, there is no need to try any vertex past rootchoice[i + 1, j].

Because of this, we can narrow the limits on the loop on k:

```
for k := rootchoice[i, j - 1] to rootchoice[i + 1, j] do
```

Knuth shows that this reduces the execution time of the procedure to $O(n^2)$. On the other hand, there is considerable space complexity as well, because of the need to carry along all those **cost** and **rootchoice** entries, and the sizes of these arrays are both $O(n^2)$.

After we return from the procedure, we use the **rootchoice** array to control the shape of the tree, which we are now at last ready to grow. We can grow it recursively, as follows: rootchoice[1, n] gives the best choice for the root of the entire tree, in this case, record 4. Then the left subtree must contain records 1 through 3. To grow that left subtree we look at rootchoice[1, 3], which tells us that the best choice for this subtree's root is record 3. We can interrogate this array similarly for all the other subtrees. This leads to the following procedure for growing the tree:

```
    procedure GROW_TREE (i, j: integer);      { Grows optimal BST    }
                                              {    from rootchoice   }
        var                                   {    array             }
            p: treeptr;
            k: integer;
        begin
        if j >= i then                  { This is an upper      }
            begin                       {    triangular matrix  }
            k := rootchoice[i, j];
            new (p);                    { Make a node           }
            with p^ do
                begin
```

```
            data := key[k];          { Stuff it with goodies }
            left := nil;
            right := nil;
            end;
         insert (root, p);           { Put it in the tree     }
                           { Then do left & right subtrees }
         grow_tree (i, rootchoice[i, j] - 1);
         grow_tree (rootchoice[i, j] + 1, j);
         end
      end;  { Grow_Tree }
```

Insert is the regular recursive insertion procedure we saw back in Chapter 5. In the main program, we set `root = nil` and then call `Grow_Tree[1, 9]` (or, in the general case, `Grow_Tree[1, n]`). For the keys and weights given in our example, the resultant tree looks like Fig. 11.3. The upper number in each node is the value of the key and the lower number is its weight.

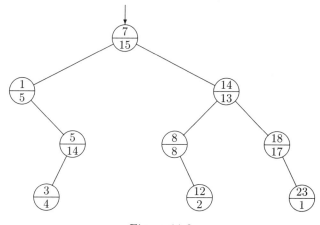

Figure 11.3

11.4 PARAGRAPH FORMATTING

Computer typesetting attempts to equal or exceed the performance of human type-setters. Among many other things, it lines up the left and right margins of paragraphs, so that they are even; printers call this *justification*. Computers and human compositors alike justify text by inserting extra space between words until the line fits snugly in the allotted width.

Ideally there should be as little extra space as possible. It sometimes happens, however, that if you allow a little more looseness in a particular line, you can set some other line much more tightly later on. Compositors normally justify one line at a time, however, and if they could make a better deal by going back and shifting the last word of some line down to the next line, they rarely do so. In trade books or textbooks, it isn't worth the trouble. This is particularly true of mechanical typesetting (that is, using Linotype or Monotype equipment); these machines are intended to maximize productivity, and going back to fiddle with previous lines defeats their purpose. But taking trouble is one of the things for which computers are made, and so a fair amount of research has been devoted to finding the optimum points at which to break lines so that the paragraph is as well formatted as possible.

For example, in the TEX system in which this book is set, there is a penalty associated with any line that is shorter than the maximum permitted width. (The penalty is proportional to the cube of the shortfall.) Hyphenating long words makes the lines come out more nearly uniform in length, but excessive hyphenation is considered bad style, so there is an additional penalty for hyphenating a word. This makes hyphenation a last resort, used only when it alleviates a particularly bad problem. (Since it is particularly bad style to hyphenate two consecutive lines, there is a special penalty applied in this case so that this is done only out of sheer desperation.) TEX determines the line breaks for an entire paragraph, using a DP algorithm that breaks the lines in such a way as to minimize the sum of all the penalties.

The TEX algorithm is described in detail in a fascinating paper by Knuth and Plass [1981]. The elaborate system of spacing and penalties described there is too complicated for our purposes, however. I will take as our example a greatly simplified method for breaking lines in typewritten text so as to have as smooth a right margin as possible. Typewritten characters have a uniform spacing (the technical term for this is *monospaced*), and the spaces are normally a single space between words and two spaces between sentences. We will use the following paragraph as our example:

```
    A line that hangs out on the right past its neighbors is known as a
"buck tooth."  Buck teeth do not show up often, but when there is one,
there is frequently a place earlier in the paragraph where a more
intelligent line break would result in a more nearly even right margin and
avoid the buck tooth.  But a line breaking algorithm that considers only
the current line will miss such a point.  This is a concern even if the
text is right justified, as is usual in printed text, because in that case
the typesetter will expand a short line by enlarging the space between
words, and in extreme cases these wide spaces will look odd and may
distract the reader.
```

The line width in this example is 74 characters, a width that fits conveniently on a textbook page. The text as shown was formatted by a conventional line-breaking algorithm of the kind that looks only at the current line.

It should be clear immediately that we do not have to consider every word as a possible line break, because some choices are ridiculous. (We would not want only one word per line, for example.) To bring the problem under control, we will first find out where the line breaks will come if every line is given its maximum length. We do this by going 74 characters out on the first line. (If we run off the end, we concatenate the proper amount of space and then the start of line 2.) If the first line is indented six characters, then doing this takes us just past the end of the word a. This is the absolute maximum length for this line; we back off one character to the end of the word. This is column 73, one short of the maximum, so we associate a penalty of $1^3 = 1$ with this choice.

We then start the next line with "buck and carry it out to its maximum length; this puts us in the middle of the word there. We back off to the end of the preceding word one, and end this line at column 69. This is five columns short of 74, so we give this line break a penalty of $5^3 = 125$. We continue this until we have reached the end of the paragraph.

It may turn out, however, that we get a more evenly spaced paragraph by ending some lines early. To keep the size of the problem within bounds, we will consider only three possibilities per line: breaking after the word we have selected for each line, or breaking after one of the two preceding words. For each line, we determine how long the line would be for each of these three possibilities, taking into account what happens if the *preceding* line ended with each of its three possible line-break words. For each of these lines, we find the penalty by cubing the shortfall.

For example, we have considered breaking the first line after a. The other two possible breaks will be after as and after known. We considered breaking the second line after one,; the other two possible breaks are after there and after is.

We then must find the penalties associated with all combinations of line breaks in these two lines. So, for example, we consider the following possible second lines, depending on where line 1 ended:

```
as a "buck tooth."  Buck teeth do not show up often, but when there is one,
a "buck tooth."  Buck teeth do not show up often, but when there is one,
"buck tooth."  Buck teeth do not show up often, but when there is one,
```

where the $\vee$ symbols indicate the break points. We compute the penalties for all these combinations:

Line 1 ending	Line 2 ending		
	there	is	one,
known	8^3	5^3	0
as	11^3	8^3	3^3
a	13^3	10^3	5^3

$\left.\begin{array}{c} \\ \\ \end{array}\right\}$ Line 2 penalties

We form a similar table for every pair of consecutive lines, considering all possible combinations. Some combinations will not be possible, however. For example, the possible breaks for line 3 are after where, a, and more, and those for line 4 are after right, margin, and and. But if we break line 3 after where, then the only break in line 4 that doesn't exceed the allowable line length is the one after right. This process of computing penalties for all combinations is laborious, but we will let the computer do it for us.

We must now use these penalties to find the combination of line breaks that minimizes their sum. At the moment, the problem may look hopelessly complicated. But note that we can represent our choices and their consequences by a weighted digraph, in which the vertices are our various line-ending choices and the weights of the edges are the penalties associated with the various combinations. Where a combination results in a line of more than the maximum length, the corresponding edge is omitted. The digraph for our example is shown in Fig. 11.4. (The penalties for the last line are zero, because it is all right for this line to end early.)

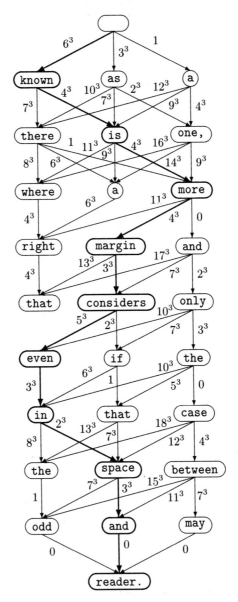

Figure 11.4

But with this figure, the whole problem falls apart in our hands. This is a big, messy graph, but it is just a graph, and we are back to a problem we know how to solve: We can use Dijkstra's algorithm to find the cheapest path through this digraph, and the vertices along that path will give us the optimal line breaks. These are large, sparse graphs, so we will want to use adjacency lists to represent them in memory. Beyond that, the problem offers nothing new.

The most troublesome part of the entire process is writing the program to analyze the source text and determine the possible line breaks and their demerits. Knuth and Plass recommend using two arrays, one for the lengths of the words and another for the spaces between the words; I have found this the simplest approach. For our simplified version of the problem, it is sufficient to determine the line breaks for the longest possible lines (these are the rightmost vertices in each row of Fig. 11.4) and then back off one and two words from these points, as described previously.

Using this process on our example, we get the path shown by the heavy lines in Fig. 11.4. Placing the line breaks as indicated by that path gives us the following result:

```
       A line that hangs out on the right past its neighbors is known
as a "buck tooth."  Buck teeth do not show up often, but when there is
one, there is frequently a place earlier in the paragraph where a more
intelligent line break would result in a more nearly even right margin
and avoid the buck tooth.   But a line breaking algorithm that considers
only the current line will miss such a point.  This is a concern even
if the text is right justified, as is usual in printed text, because in
that case the typesetter will expand a short line by enlarging the space
between words, and in extreme cases these wide spaces will look odd and
may distract the reader.
```

You will notice that we have now come full circle; we started by considering the shortest-path problem from a DP point of view, and we have ended by reducing the line-breaking problem to a shortest-path problem. Many DP problems can be transformed into shortest-path problems, in fact, and this is frequently the logical starting point in seeking a DP solution to a problem.

11.5 SUMMARY

DP algorithms have been used to allocate scarce resources, to manage inventories intelligently, in guidance systems, and in decoding processes. A lot of applications reduce to some kind of minimum-path or optimum-path problem, as paragraph formatting and time warping did for us.

As we saw from our second look at Dijkstra's algorithm, DP is a distant relative —a *very* distant relative—of the greedy algorithms. It grabs the most attractive possibility, but it grabs it in a particularly intelligent way, and it keeps records of what it did so it can grab with equal intelligence in the next stage of the process.

There is no cookbook rule for writing a greedy algorithm. We study the problem, we try something, it works, and after congratulating ourselves on our success we realize we have devised a greedy algorithm. We may have had an inkling, if we are experienced, and lucky, that a greedy approach would pay off. Much the same is true of DP: that is, there is no cookbook rule for designing such an algorithm. There are some clues that a DP approach may pay off, however. There are usually a number of attractive possibilities; it is not clear which one will pay off, and until the process is done, we won't know which will be the winner. The combinatorics usually rule out an exhaustive search. Something like Eq. (11.1) can be found for the process. And above all, the optimality principle holds.

11.6 PROBLEMS

11.1. Argue that because of the principle of optimality, the set of cheapest paths from the starting vertex to all other vertices will normally be a tree. When may it not be?

11.2. Trace the execution of `Knapsack` with the following data: $c = 12$, $n = 5$, $w_i = (3, 6, 1, 7, 8)$, $v_i = (4, 5, 2, 6, 5)$.

11.3. As we described the knapsack problem, either we put each object in or we didn't. Suppose we have an indefinite number of objects in each weight-value category and that we will pack as many objects from each category as possible. (This means that each $a_i \in \{0, 1, 2, \ldots\}$.) Modify the knapsack program to handle this case.

11.4. Construct an optimal binary search tree using the following keys and weights.

Key:	2	4	5	8	10	12	17	29
Weight:	12	5	17	6	9	13	7	10

11.5. Construct an optimal binary search tree using the following keys and weights.

Key:	1	2	3	4	5	6	7	8	9
Weight:	256	128	64	32	16	8	4	2	1

Explain your results. How can this tree be called optimal?

11.6. (Chained array multiplication.) Let $A_1, A_2, \ldots, A_n$ be a set of arrays that are to be multiplied. For conformability, they must have orders $(d_0, d_1), (d_1, d_2), \ldots, (d_{n-1}, d_n)$. It should be clear that the total number of scalar multiplications required to find the product $A_1 A_2 \cdots A_n$ will depend on the order in which they are multiplied: for example, it may be cheaper to find $A_1(A_2 A_3)$ than to find $(A_1 A_2) A_3$. The optimum parenthesization can be found by DP using the fact that

$$cost_{ij} = \min_k(cost_{ik} + cost_{kj} + a_{i-1} a_k a_j).$$

where $cost_{ij}$ is the minimum cost of finding the product $A_i \cdots A_j$.

The procedure for computing this optimum parenthesization is parallel to that for computing the optimum binary search tree. Write a program that will compute the minimum cost and display the corresponding parenthesization.

11.7. Take the first two sentences of the "buck tooth" sample paragraph and find the possible line endings if the paragraph is set to be 67 characters wide. (In this case, we have a maximum of five lines to worry about.) Compute the penalties associated with all resulting combinations of line breaks. (When a particular combination of breaks results in a line that is too long, indicate a negative penalty. A program constructing a graph from these numbers would not include edges with negative penalties.)

11.8. (Major project.) Write a program that will scan a paragraph of monospaced text and construct an output file describing a weighted digraph like the one in Section 11.4.

CHAPTER 12

RANDOM NUMBERS

A computer is an inherently deterministic device; unless there is something wrong with the hardware, everything in a program is predictable. The only exceptions to this arise when execution depends on the timing of some unpredictable external event, like an input/output operation. But sometimes we need random numbers. It may be necessary to select records from a file at random, possibly because the customer wants a random sample; or it may be necessary for some kinds of simulation or for data encryption. Some signal processing programs must be able to generate a noisy signal, and noise is commonly simulated by generating random numbers. Random numbers are used in computer games, in which the next event must be unpredictable, or where the fall of the dice or the selection of a card must be random. Random data are also frequently used in debugging a computer program. If we wish to test a sorting routine, it's handy to give the routine lots of lists of random numbers to sort.

But random numbers are inherently impossible on a deterministic system like a computer. Random numbers are unpredictable, whereas everything a deterministic system like a computer does is (in principle, at least) predictable. What to do? The solution is to find a way to make the computer generate a sequence of numbers that *look* random. These are technically called "pseudorandom numbers," but we will mostly overlook the pseudo aspect here and call them random numbers.

I should mention that it is possible to get truly random numbers from physical systems. After all, if you provided the computer with a peripheral device that tossed a coin, you could reasonably expect a random series of heads and tails. More realistically, for cryptographic purposes, a little bit of radioactive material is used; every time the material gives off a particle, this is noted and the times between particles can be used to provide a sequence of random numbers. But this is an expensive device to make and use, and the use of radioactive substances is unpopular in our culture. Hence, we will consider only ways of producing pseudorandom numbers by means of computer arithmetic.

John von Neumann, the great computer pioneer, once said, "Anyone who considers arithmetical methods of producing random digits is, of course, in a state of sin." Since von Neumann himself devised a random number generator—which wasn't very good—he obviously didn't intend to be taken seriously; but if you *do* take him seriously, then in this chapter we're going to be in a state of sin.

We will discuss "arithmetical methods" of generating random numbers on a computer and will then consider some of the more common applications of random numbers.

12.1 PSEUDORANDOM NUMBERS

There has been a great deal of thought about what "truly random" numbers are like. If we are to generate pseudorandom numbers on a computer, we need to have some way of evaluating the result—that is, of deciding how random they are. Most people think of random numbers as being somehow unpredictable and as lacking any kind of pattern. This is mostly true, but truly random numbers can behave in disconcerting ways. After all, it is possible to get 20 heads in a row when tossing a fair coin. Twenty heads in a row seems very unlikely; its probability is 2^{-20} which is about 9.5×10^{-7}, but in a sequence of roughly a million tosses, it's as likely to happen as not. It may seem silly to imagine tossing a coin that many times, but computer programs that require random numbers may require them in vast numbers, and we don't want some pattern like 20 heads to come up along the way. So it may be better to say that we want our computer-

Intuitive notions of randomness can be misleading. The following example may help to illustrate this. Many people, shown Fig. 12.1 (a),

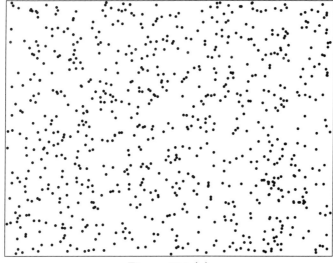

Figure 12.1 (a)

will find it "less random" than Fig. 12.1 (b).

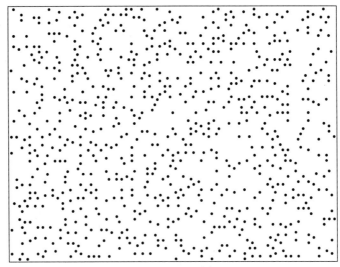

Figure 12.1 (*b*)

But the first diagram consists of 800 random points plotted in a 128-by-96-point box, whereas the second consists of the same number of random points plotted under the restriction that no two points may be closer to each other (horizontally, vertically, or on a diagonal) than a certain minimum distance. This restriction makes the points *less* random. Random numbers tend to cluster (which is why 20 heads in a row isn't such a crazy notion), and the bunching that may make Fig. 12.1 (*a*) seem less random is actually a mark of randomness.[1]

Clearly, we need some more definite way of defining what looking random means. We can say, roughly, that a sequence of numbers looks random if (1) the probability of a number x coming out is just the same as the probability of some other number y coming out. More precisely, if the random numbers are supposed to fall in some range (p, q), then all numbers in this range are equally likely. (We say that the probability density is *uniform*.) Next, (2) the numbers are independent: if the first number that comes out is 2, this should have no effect on what the next number is going to be. Finally, (3) the numbers should not run in cycles: a sequence 0, 7, 12, 3, 6, 0, 7, 12, 3, 6, 0, 7, 12, 3, 6, ... is not random. There are more exacting tests for randomness, but these will do for a start.

In practice, we can get uniformity fairly easily. (After all, 0, 1, 2, 3, 4, 5, 6, 7, ... is uniform.) But condition (2) is never satisfied; the best we can say of a practical random-number generator is that if 2 comes out, it is not immediately obvious what number is going to come out next, unless we happen to know the inner workings of the generator. Worse yet, if 2 is followed by (say) 31,679, then if 2 ever shows up again, it will be followed by 31,679 again, as we will see. The most we can hope for is that consecutive pairs of numbers will be *uncorrelated*. (Two variables x and y are uncorrelated if their correlation $\langle x_i y_i \rangle = (1/N) \sum_{i=1}^{N} x_i y_i = 0$.

---

[1]Fig. 12.1 (*a*) and (*b*) are adapted, with permission, from similar figures in Gould [1991].

In very crude terms, y_i will be greater than x_i as often as it is less than x_i as you run over all the i's.)

Finally, if the sequence goes on long enough, it is bound to run in cycles. This happens because practical random number generators use integer arithmetic and, as we will see, one of these integers is eventually going to repeat. Once that happens, in fact, the whole cycle will repeat. We will call the length of the cycle the *period* of the generator, and we want the period to be a long as possible. If the period is equal to some large number like `maxint`, we will be satisfied with that.

Just to show that random-number generation can be tricky, let's look at von Neumann's method. He proposed taking some starting number, squaring it, and selecting a chunk of digits from the middle of the square as the new random number. For example, if the number is 4 digits long, the square will be 7 or 8 digits long and we will pick the middle 4 digits. The next random number is generated by repeating the process, using the number you just got. This looks very promising: when you square a number, you do a scrambling operation on the digits; surely the middle digits will be scrambled the most. For example, if you start with the number 1,234, you get

$$1234^2 = 01522756 \rightarrow 5227 \qquad \text{(Middle four digits are 5227.)}$$
$$5227^2 = 27321529 \rightarrow 3215$$
$$3215^2 = 10336225 \rightarrow 3362$$
$$3362^2 = 11303044 \rightarrow 3030$$

This looks reasonably promising (although three numbers in a row beginning with 3 may not be so great); but after 50 repetitions of this process, you get

$$4003^2 = 16024009 \rightarrow 0240$$
$$0240^2 = 00057600 \rightarrow 0576$$
$$0576^2 = 00331776 \rightarrow 3317$$
$$3317^2 = 11002489 \rightarrow 0024$$
$$0024^2 = 00000576 \rightarrow 0005$$
$$0005^2 = 00000025 \rightarrow 0000$$
$$0000^2 = 00000000 \rightarrow 0000$$

and from here on you just get zeroes. From this it should be clear that you must be very careful in choosing a starting value. With a starting value of 1490, the sequence enters the following cycle after 15 repetitions: (2100, 4100, 8100, 6100, 2100, 4100, 8100, ...), and this cycle is very common. There are a few middle-square generators with extremely long periods, but they require bigger numbers than most computers can handle using integer arithmetic, and floating-point arithmetic is unacceptably slow. Probably nobody uses von Neumann's method any more.

Short periods are a persistent problem in random-number generation. Knuth [1981] describes a random-number generator he once devised that used a large number of different methods and selected the method *at random* for each new number. In spite of this ingenious approach, the generator quickly entered a cycle. Part of the problem is that the generator may not fall into the cycle until very many numbers have been produced; hence, if you merely look at the output and search for cycles, the cycle may not show up until a point after which you have lost patience and given up.

The best published pieces on random-number generation include Knuth [1981], Press *et al.* [1986], and Park and Miller [1988]. Knuth is tough reading but thorough; Park and Miller, and Press, are easier but restricted to only one method. Knuth's book describes a number of alternative methods but devotes most of the space to the method described by the others. We will discuss only that method.

12.1.1   Lehmer's Method

The method of choice is known as the *Linear Congruential Method*, also called Lehmer's [1951] method. This uses three integer constants (sometimes only two):

    a, the multiplier,
    m, the modulus,
    c, the increment.

(The increment, c, isn't really necessary, which is why I said sometimes only two. Lehmer used $c = 0$. When $c \neq 0$, the method is also called the *mixed* congruential method, and when $c = 0$, the *multiplicative* congruential method.) The rule for generating new numbers is this:

$$x_{n+1} = (ax_n + c) \bmod m. \tag{12.1}$$

Here $\{x_n\}$ are the random numbers, which are nonnegative integers; the equation says you get a new random number (x_{n+1}) from the old one (x_n) by the operation shown on the right-hand side. The "mod" is the regular Pascal `mod` operation: the remainder after dividing by m.

It's called the linear congruential method because you can rewrite Eq. (12.1) as a linear congruence. If the right-hand side is the remainder after dividing $(ax_n + c)$ by m, then it must be that

$$ax_n + c = qm + x_{n+1} \quad (q \ some \ integer)$$

or

$$x_{n+1} - (ax_n + c) = -qm,$$

and therefore, by the definition of congruence,

$$x_{n+1} \equiv ax_n + c \pmod{m}, \tag{12.2}$$

which is a linear congruence. About all the increment c buys you is the ability to generate 0 as a random number; clearly, if $c = 0$ and $x_n = 0$, then all subsequent "random" numbers will also be 0. Failure to generate 0 is seldom crucial, and in most of what follows, I will assume that $c = 0$.

If we leave c in, we can program this as follows:

```
procedure RAND (var x: integer);    { Random number generator:  }
   const                            {    first version           }
      m = 32;   { Or some other }
      a = 25;   {    suitable   }
      c = 7;    {    values     }
   begin
   x := (x*a + c) mod m;
   end;  { Rand }
```

Every time we call the generator, it does the computation of Eq. (12.1) for us on the previous random number and gives us a new one. To start the generator going, we must have some initial value x_0, commonly called the "seed" of the generator. (Von Neumann's method required a seed, too.) If this seed is always the same, then we will get the same sequence of random numbers every time we run our program. This can be a good thing: If we discover a bug in a program while testing it with random numbers, we will probably want to rerun it with the same set of numbers in the process of debugging it; sometimes also we want to rerun a simulation with exactly the same random numbers we used before. For getting different sequences, some programming languages have a special procedure called something like **randomize**; this changes the seed of the generator. (One popular method is to ask the operating system for the date and time; the seed is generated from the answer, and this guarantees that we'll practically never get the same seed twice.)

In our example, the random number is returned in the parameter **x**. Notice that the user must save the latest number for reuse on the next call. In programming languages that provide a built-in random-number generator, the generator is usually written as a parameterless function, and the problem of saving the old random number for reuse on the next call is handled by the function and hidden from the user.

Selecting the constants. There is no proof that this method gives a good sequence of random numbers; indeed, if the magic numbers a, m, and c are chosen badly, it is a miserable generator. There are a lot of miserable Lehmer generators around, which is one reason why we are going to consider the construction of Lehmer generators in some detail: you can't necessarily trust your language implementation to have a good one. (For some horror stories, see Park and Miller [1988].) But if these constants are chosen well, the multiplication and **mod** operations have the effect of bouncing the sequence $\{x_n\}$ around in the range from 0 to $m-1$ in a way that looks random and that fools most statistical tests for randomness.

The period of this generator is at most m. We are using integer arithmetic, after all, and the mod m operation will give us integers in the range from 0 through $(m-1)$. There are exactly m numbers in this range; by the pigeon-hole principle, if we select $m+1$ numbers from this range, there is bound to be a repetition, and once a number repeats, it will begin a new cycle. So the longest possible period is

m, and we will want as large a value of m as we can get. (Generators whose period is m are called *full-period* generators.)

If we choose the wrong a, the period may turn out to be less than m. But there is more to it than that, because $a = c = 1$ will produce a sequence with a period of m which is (as Knuth points out) anything but random. Knuth gives a set of necessary conditions for a mixed congruential generator to be have a period of length m:

c must be relatively prime to m;

$(a - 1)$ must be divisible by every prime factor of m;

If m is a multiple of 4, $(a - 1)$ must also be a multiple of 4.

Beyond this, a lot of work has been done by trial and error, especially for generators for which $c = 0$. (Such a generator can have a period of at most $(m - 1)$, because the value 0 will be missing from the random sequence.) Park and Miller provide a good discussion of choosing a and m and list a few values that have been found to give good results. They recommend $m = 2^{31} - 1 = 2,147,483,647$ and $a = 16,807$, with $c = 0$, although there is some evidence that $a = 48,271$ may be a better choice. We will use 16,807 in what follows; Park and Miller regard this as the "minimal acceptable standard."

Implementation.   There are several things we must do to implement this in a practical programming language. First, since the multiplier and the intermediate results are so big, we will have to use a large data type to hold our results. The Turbo Pascal `longint` type is just big enough to hold m, but after the multiplication the result may overflow, resulting in a number that appears to be negative. It is better to avoid this than to try to correct it; the corrections frequently introduce new bugs. Second, we would like to save the seed in the function itself between calls. Standard Pascal doesn't provide a way of handling this, but Turbo Pascal's typed constant does. This is an unsatisfactory makeshift, because we're stuck with the seed we choose. It is better to provide the user with a way of setting the seed to any desired value. This requires a programming language that permits static storage of a local variable and alternative entry points to a procedure. FORTRAN and C support these; they can also be handled in a Turbo Pascal `unit`.

To avoid overflow, we can write the generator in assembly language. But this is troublesome; we then have the problem of linking the resulting generator to the high-level language that is to use it, and the program is not portable from one machine to another.

For a portable generator that avoids overflow, we must make sure that all intermediate results lie within the range that can be accommodated by the language's integer data type. This usually means breaking up the computation into stages that produce suitably bounded values that can then be combined to get the final result. Because of this, we can no longer get by with just one multiplication and one division. The process is more laborious, but the results are guaranteed to be right.

The technique we consider here is due to Schrage [1979]; the exposition is based loosely on Park and Miller. We start with two numbers $p = m$ div a and $q = m$ mod a, in which a is our multiplier, as before. If we choose a suitable m and a, we can guarantee that $q < p$. Note that these numbers can be precomputed and entered in the program as constants. Then we do the following:

```
d := x div p;
e := x mod p;
f := a*e - q*d;
if f > 0 then
    x := f
else
    x := f + m;
```

The value of x coming into this procedure is x_n; the value that results is x_{n+1}.

Proving that this works involves simple algebra but involved reasoning. Recall, first, that in languages that do not provide a mod function, we can fake it by doing an integer division by m, multiplying the result by m again, and then subtracting this product from the original number. Therefore, we can write our computation as

$$\begin{aligned} x_{n+1} &= ax_n \bmod m \\ &= ax_n - m(ax_n \text{ div } m). \end{aligned} \tag{12.3}$$

Here we are using "div" to represent integer division. Next, let $p = m$ div a and let $q = m$ mod a, so that $m = ap + q$. Then we may write

$$x_{n+1} = a(x_n \bmod p) - q(x_n \text{ div } p) + m[(x_n \text{ div } p) - (ax_n \text{ div } m)]. \tag{12.4}$$

You will notice that the first two terms correspond the quantity we named f in the code above. To see why equation is equivalent to Eq. (12.3), consider those first two terms:

$$\begin{aligned} a(x_n \bmod p) - q(x_n \text{ div } p) &= ax_n - ap(x_n \text{ div } p) - q(x_n \text{ div } p) \\ &= ax_n - (ap + q)(x_n \text{ div } p) \\ &= ax_n - m(x_n \text{ div } p). \end{aligned}$$

The first line comes from the same kind of reasoning that gave us Eq. (12.3); the rest comes from elementary algebra and the fact that $m = ap + q$. Substituting this result in Eq. (12.4), we have

$$x_{n+1} = ax_n - m(x_n \text{ div } p) + m(x_n \text{ div } p) - m(ax_n \text{ div } m).$$

The two middle terms cancel, and we're back to Eq. (12.3) again.

The point of Eq. (12.4) is this: We can rewrite it more compactly as

$$x_{n+1} = f(x_n) + mg(x_n), \tag{12.5}$$

where $f(x_n) = a(x_n \bmod p) - q(x_n \text{ div } p)$
and $g(x_n) = (x_n \text{ div } p) - (ax_n \text{ div } m)$.

The significance of this is that neither f nor g will overflow; in addition, we will find that the values of f and g are such that we can skip computing g.

It should be clear that f lies in the range from $-(m-1)$ to $m-1$. Since all the terms in f are nonnegative, the most positive value it can have is determined by the first term and the most negative value is determined by the second. But the first term is $a(x_n \bmod p) = a[x_n \bmod (m \text{ div } a)] < a(m \text{ div } a) \le m$, so $f \le m-1$. The second term is $q(x_n \text{ div } p) \le qx_n/p < x_n$, because we made $q < p$. Since x_n itself $\le m-1$, it follows that $f > -(m-1)$.

Moreover, g is either 0 or 1. This follows because $x_n \text{ div } p = x_n \text{ div } (m \text{ div } a) = \lceil ax_n/m \rceil$ and $ax_n \text{ div } m = \lfloor ax_n/m \rfloor$; but the floor and ceiling of a number can differ by at most 1.

But the fact the g is either 0 or 1 means that in Eq. (12.5) we either do or do not add m to f. Since the result has to lie between 1 and $m-1$, clearly we add m if f is negative and not otherwise. That gives us the code we had above; the complete function may be written as follows:

```
procedure RAND(var x: longint); { Random number generator:     }
   const                         {    uses Schrage's method      }
       a = 16807;
       m = 2147483647;
       q = 127773;        { This is m div a }
       r = 2836;          { This is m mod a }
   var
       d, e, f: longint;
   begin
   e := x div q;
   d := x mod q;
   f := a*d - r*e;
   if f > 0 then
       x := f
   else
       x := f + m;
   end;  { Rand }
```

The lattice problem. Lehmer pseudorandom numbers are extremely good but not perfect. Consider the sequence with $m = 32$, $c = 7$, and $a = 25$: This is a full-period generator yielding the following numbers:

7, 22, 13, 12, 19, 2, 25, 24, 31, 14, 5, 4, 11, 26, 17, 16, 23, 6, 29, 28, 3, 18, 9, 8, 15, 30, 21, 20, 27, 10, 1, 0, 7, ...

a sequence that certainly *looks* random, since it contains all the numbers from 0 through 31, and it bounces wildly around the interval $(0, 31)$. But suppose we plot pairs of consecutive numbers in order as they come out of the generator—that is, suppose we plot x_{n+1} against x_n, as in Fig. 12.2.

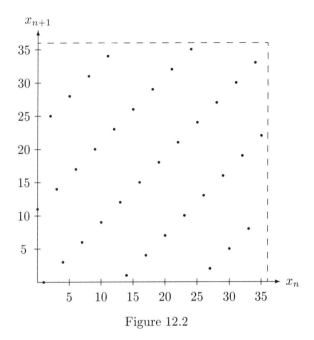

Figure 12.2

The dashed box represents the range of these combinations of consecutive values. These points form a regular lattice that isn't random looking at all. The points are generated in a random order, but they do not fill the box in a random manner; they lie along a set of five straight lines. This problem occurs generally with Lehmer generators. If you pick sequences of three consecutive random numbers, the points they define will lie in a set of planes, and in general if you pick sets of k consecutive Lehmer numbers, they will define points lying on a set of $(k - 1)$-dimensional hyperplanes in a k-dimensional hyperspace. (This may be hard or impossible to visualize, but the problem can be a very real one, nevertheless.) There will be at most $m^{1/k}$ of these hyperplanes. If your application relies on their filling a space of this sort in a random manner, this method is going to get you in trouble. The general feeling is that these hyperplanes should not be too far apart; Fishman and Moore [1982] have proposed that the multiplier a be chosen so that the distance between planes be no more than 25 percent more than the minimum possible, but this may be too restrictive.

This pattern of consecutive subsequences can be broken up by the following method, due to Bays and Durham [1976] and quoted in Knuth [1981]: Using Lehmer's method, we set up an initial table of something like 100 random numbers. (The length of the table has to be shorter than the period of the generator; since practical generators have a period of thousands of numbers, as we have seen, this is assured.) On each call, we scale the seed to fit within the size of this table and use the scaled seed to select a number from the table. This is the number we will return as the value of the function. *Then* we use Lehmer's algorithm to generate a new random number and put it in the table to replace the entry selected by the seed.

12.1.2   Floating-Point Random Numbers

Most built-in random-number generators return a real value in the range from 0 to 1. So far, we have learned only how to find random integers in the range from 0 to $m - 1$ or from 1 to $m - 1$. Generating random numbers with floating-point arithmetic is not attractive, because floating-point computations are nearly always slower than integer arithmetic. Integer random numbers can be converted to reals in the range, $(0 \ldots 1)$, however, simply by dividing by m. (This has to be a floating-point division, of course.) The result will be random numbers running from 0 (or $1/m$) to $1 - 1/m$. The granularity of these numbers is $1/m$, but if m is truly large, then the results will *seem* to be continuous on $(0, 1)$. A practical floating-point random-number generator would thus look like this:

```
function RAND: real;              { Floating-point random number  }
   const                          {    generator                  }
      a = 16807;
      m = 2147483647;
      q = 127773;
      r = 2836;
      seed: longint = 1;     { Hidden in Turbo typed constant }
   var
      d, e, f: longint;
   begin
   e := seed div q;
   d := seed mod q;
   f := a*d - r*e;
   if f > 0 then
      seed := f
   else
      seed := f + m;
   rand := seed/m;                { Convert to floating point      }
   end;   { Rand }
```

12.2   APPLICATIONS

Now that we have seen what is inside the typical random-number function, we will ignore the works entirely and will consider how to use real random numbers between 0 and 1 (but always less than 1) as returned either by a built-in random-number generator or by one you've written yourself. We will assume that it is a parameterless function named **Random** and that it maintains its own seed, so that to set y to some random value, we need only write

```
y := random;
```

12.2.1   Random Numbers Within a Specified Range

If we get numbers from 0 to 1 and need numbers from a to b, then it should be clear that this statement will do the job:

$$y := a + (b - a)*\text{random}; \tag{12.6}$$

If `Random` returned 0, then y would be a; if it returned 1, then y would be $a+b-a = b$; and if it returns some fraction k, then y will be $100 \cdot k$ % of the way from a to b.

If we require integers in the range from i to j (i and j integers), then we can write

$$y := i + \text{trunc}((j + 1 - i)*\text{random}); \tag{12.7}$$

This follows from Eq. (12.6). `Random` gives us numbers from 0 to slightly less than 1. When we get 0, clearly y will be i; when we get slightly less than 1, then the product will be slightly less than $j + 1 - i$. Since i and j are integers, the `Trunc` function will reduce this to $j - i$, so in that case y will be $i + j - i = j$.

In particular, to get a random integer between 1 and some integer p, we write

$$y := 1 + \text{trunc}(p*\text{random});$$

12.2.2   Random Events

We will see a couple of cases later in which we want some event to occur with a specified probability. We can take advantage of the fact that the real numbers generated by `Random` are uniformly distributed on $(0, 1)$. Clearly, if p is some number in this range, then `Random` $< p$ with probability p. Hence, all we need to do is write

```
if random < p then
   { event }
```

12.2.3   Normal Random Numbers

When we use random numbers in simulation, we frequently need to simulate a random variable with a normal (Gaussian) probability density. This is the familiar bell-shaped probability curve, given by

$$p(x) = \frac{1}{\sigma\sqrt{2\pi}} e^{-(x/2\sigma)^2} \tag{12.10}$$

(The constant σ is the *standard deviation*; it is a measure of how wide the bell-shaped curve is. Roughly two-thirds of the area under the curve lie between $x = -\sigma$ and $x = \sigma$.) Enormous numbers of naturally occurring random quantities have probability densities of this form. In such applications, we have the problem of transforming the uniformly distributed random numbers provided by `Random` into this form. There is a trick for doing this. We use our `Random` function to get two random numbers s and t for which $-1 < s, t < 1$, making sure that $s^2 + t^2 < 1$. (If they don't meet this requirement, we must go back for two more random numbers. This happens less than a quarter of the time.) We then compute

$$p = s^2 + t^2$$
$$q = \sqrt{(-2\ln p)/p}$$
$$u = sq$$
$$v = tq$$

The random variables u and v are independent and normally distributed with zero mean and $\sigma = 1$.

There is no way of proving this that doesn't draw on probability theory, and even with probability theory, the proof is difficult. A proof may be found in Papoulis [1984, p. 143].

Every use of this procedure requires two random numbers from **Random**, but it gives you two independent normal variables back. The code is as follows:

```
procedure GAUSS2 (var u, v: real);
                              { Returns two independent  }
     var                      {    zero-mean Gaussian     }
         s, t, p, q: real;    {    random variables with  }
     begin                    {    variance unity in para- }
     repeat                   {    meters u, v.            }
         s := 2.0*random - 1.0;
         t := 2.0*random - 1.0;
         p := sqr(s) + sqr(t);
     until p < 1.0;
     q := sqrt(-2.0*ln(p)/p);
     u := s*q;
     v := t*q;
     end;   { Gauss2 }
```

Computing a square root and a log is expensive, but the strength of this method is that it is *exact* (subject to the precision of the computer's floating-point arithmetic and the quality of the random-number generator); for most nonuniform random variables, one has to resort to approximations.

*Correlated Gaussian random numbers. Some simulations require sets of Gaussian random variables with a specified correlation coefficient. This can easily be managed with the use of **Gauss2**; it will give you two uncorrelated values; all that is necessary is to arrange the correlation. This is done as follows: If the numbers returned by **Gauss2** are u and v and if the desired correlation is r, then

$$x = u$$
$$y = rv + \sqrt{1 - r^2}\, u \qquad (12.11)$$

will be random variables with correlation r. This is relatively easy to verify: the correlation coefficient is given by $\langle xy \rangle / (\sigma_x \sigma_y)$. Since **Gauss2** gives us uncorrelated numbers with zero mean and unity variance,

$$\langle uv \rangle = 0, \qquad \langle u^2 \rangle = \langle u^2 \rangle = 1.$$

Then we have

$$
\begin{aligned}
\sigma_x^2 &= \langle x^2 \rangle = \langle u^2 \rangle = 1. \\
\sigma_y^2 &= \langle y^2 \rangle \\
&= \langle (ru + \sqrt{1 - r^2}\, v)^2 \rangle \\
&= r^2 \langle u^2 \rangle + 2r\sqrt{1 - r^2}\,\langle uv \rangle + (1 - r^2)\langle v^2 \rangle \\
&= 1. \qquad\qquad \text{(since } \langle uv \rangle = 0) \\
\langle xy \rangle &= \langle u(ru + \sqrt{1 - r^2}\, v) \rangle \\
&= r\langle u^2 \rangle + r\sqrt{1 - r^2}\,\langle uv \rangle \\
&= r.
\end{aligned}
$$

Putting these results together, we find that the correlation coefficient is just r, as promised.

If the random variables are to have some specified means, standard deviations, and correlation coefficients, the operations to obtain these should done in the following order:

1. Obtain the Gaussian variables from `Gauss2`.
2. Find x, y from Eq. (12.11).
3. Scale x and y to have the desired standard deviations.
4. Shift x and y to have the desired means.

If the operations are done in this order, each new operation will leave the results obtained by the previous ones undisturbed.

12.2.4   Generating a Random Permutation

Sometimes it's necessary to "un-sort" an array—that is, to take an array that is in some sort of order and randomize it. For example, if you join a professional society like ACM, you will occasionally receive ballots for electing officers in the society. The names of the candidates are generally presented in random order, just in case someone might claim that there's an advantage to being first on the list. Another application where scrambling is necessary is in data encryption, where the data elements are usually jumbled in a pseudorandom order in addition to being further encrypted by other methods.

The easiest way to do this is to swap the array contents at random. Suppose our list is

```
list: array [1..n] of {something};
```

We use `Random` to generate random subscripts and use these to select the element to be swapped. The code is

```
for i := n downto 2 do
  begin
  j := 1 + trunc(i*random);
  swap (list[i], list[j])
  end;
```

This works just the way permutations are sometimes described in discrete math. For the nth element, there are n possible choices, and the subscript j selects a random element between 1 and n. For the $(n-1)$st element, there are $n-1$ choices remaining, and this time j is a random number between 1 and $n-1$, and so on.

An alternative way to do this is to generate a *permutation vector*. This is useful if you have several lists that are to be scrambled in exactly the same way, or if you want to save the original list in its original order. If the list has n items in it, the permutation vector **p** is an array of integers containing the numbers from 1 to n in scrambled order. Then you get your randomized list (called scramble here) by saying

```
for i := 1 to n do
  scramble[i] := list[p[i]];
```

The permutation vector is generated by scrambling the numbers from 1 to n in exactly the same way as shown above:

```
for i := 1 to n do
  p[i] := i;          { P now contains integers      }
                      {    in natural order          }
for i := n downto 2 do
  begin               { Scramble them }
  j := 1 + trunc(i*random);
  swap (p[i], p[j])
  end;
```

12.2.5   Selecting Random Elements from a List

Sometimes it is necessary to go through a list or a file and select a record at random. This may be done in the course of some sort of spot checking, or because a client wants a random sample for some reason or other. If we know the size of the list in advance, then we can use Eq. (12.2.1) to decide which element we want. If the list is an array with bounds [1..p], then we can write simply

```
i := 1 + trunc(p*random);      { Subscript between 1 and p }
y := list[i];
```

If the list is a linear linked list, then we must traverse the list and count nodes as we go until we reach the ith node, but otherwise, the principle is the same.

If we wish to select m records at random from a file of N records, the picture is more complicated. We will consider, first, the case where the total number of records is known. We are looking for a subset of m things drawn from a pool of N

things. It is well known that there are $\binom{N}{m} = N!/[m!(N-m)!]$ such subsets. In deriving this formula, we usually argue that there are N possible choices for the first element in the subset, $N-1$ choices for the second, and so forth. But here the problem is turned inside-out: when we read a particular record, we must decide then and there whether to include it, and we must make this decision in such a way that all of those $\binom{N}{m}$ subsets are still equally likely.

We reason as follows: When we have just read the first record and are wondering whether we should include it, we have a choice of $\binom{N}{m}$ subsets, since we haven't yet put anything in the subset. Now of those $\binom{N}{m}$ subsets, $\binom{N-1}{m-1}$ of them will include the first record and the rest won't. Since all subsets must be equally likely, the probability that this record will go in is the number of favorable outcomes divided by the total number of possibilities:

$$\text{Prob}\{x_1 \text{ in subset}\} = \frac{\binom{N-1}{m-1}}{\binom{N}{m}}.$$

This is

$$\text{Prob}\{x_1 \text{ in subset}\} = \frac{(N-1)!}{(m-1)!(N-m)!} \cdot \frac{m!(N-m)!}{N!} = \frac{m}{N}.$$

So the first record goes in with probability m/N.

If the first record wasn't chosen, then the probability of choosing the second record is the same.

If the first record was chosen, then we have $m-1$ elements to go out of a pool of $N-1$ available records, so that there are now $\binom{N-1}{m-1}$ possibilities left. Of these possibilities, the second record will be in $\binom{N-2}{m-2}$ of them. So the probability will be

$$\text{Prob}\{x_2 \text{ in subset}\} = \frac{\binom{N-2}{m-2}}{\binom{N-1}{m-1}} = \frac{m-1}{N-1}.$$

Now suppose we jump ahead to a point where j records have been chosen and k records have been considered. Then there are $m-j$ records to go and the number of remaining available records is $N-k$. The total number of possibilities is now down to $\binom{N-k}{m-j}$, and the next record will be in $\binom{N-k-1}{m-j-1}$ of them. So the probability of selecting the next record must be, again,

$$\text{Prob}\{x_{k+1} \text{ in subset}\} = \frac{\binom{N-k-1}{m-j-1}}{\binom{N-k}{m-j}} = \frac{m-j}{N-k}. \tag{12.12}$$

Notice that this fraction is just the number of output records to go divided by the number of input records still available.

To implement this in code, it is probably easiest if we call $N - k$ by the variable name `avail` and $m - j$ by the name `to_go`. Then the probability of selecting the next record is just `to_go/avail`. Initially, $avail = N$ and $to\_go = m$. Every time we have read and considered a record, `avail` is decreased by 1 whether we have selected it or not (because the number of available records is decreased in either case). Every time we select a record, we decrement `to_go`. So if we assume we are reading records from a file `inf` and writing the chosen ones to a file `outf`, then our procedure looks like this:

```
procedure SAMPLE1 (m, n: integer);        { Selects random subset }
                                          {    from file of known  }
    var                                   {    size                }
        avail, to_go: integer;
        inrecord: rectype;
    begin
    avail := n;
    to_go := m;
    while not eof(inf) and (to_go > 0) do
        begin
        read (inf, inrecord);
        if random < to_go/avail then
            begin
            write (outf, inrecord);
            to_go := to_go - 1
            end;
        avail := avail - 1
        end
    end;  { Sample1 }
```

What assurance have we that we will not run through the file and, at the end, discover that we stalled too long and cannot make up the required number of selections? At the point when that possibility is imminent, `to_go` will be equal to `avail` and our threshold will be 1. At that point every record will be chosen, because `Random` will always return a value < 1. Hence, if `Random` makes us stall too long (a very unlikely possibility), the remaining records will all be crammed in to make up the number. Indeed, we could add an assertion after the end of the `if`: `{ to_go <= avail }`. If the size of the file is N, then the cost of this method is $O(N)$.

Selecting from a file of unknown size. If we don't know how big the list is going to turn out to be, then the problem becomes more interesting. This situation can arise, for example, if we need a random sample from a database of unknown size, or if the records from the database must meet a set of certain criteria before they can be even considered for sampling. In such a case, we normally won't be able to anticipate how many records will qualify. Furthermore, it is desirable for practical purposes to be able to make our decision on each record as it arrives; hence, we want an algorithm that can be carried out *on-line*.

Again, we will consider selecting a single record first. We do it this way: We will copy the first record from the file into our selected item. But then as we continue reading records, we count the records as we read them and replace the selected item at random. Specifically, if we have just read the nth record, we replace the selected item with probability $1/n$. So our procedure looks like this:

```
procedure SAMPLE2 (var select: rectype);
                            { Selects single sample from   }
        var                 {    file of unknown size       }
            inrecord: rectype;
        begin
        read (inf, inrecord);       { Read the first record }
        select := inrecord;         { Select it              }
        n := 1;                     { One record read so far}
        while not eof(inf) do
            begin
            read (inf, inrecord);   { New record             }
            n := n + 1;             { Update count           }
            if random < 1/n then    { Decide whether         }
                select := inrecord; {    to replace          }
            end
        end;  { Sample2 }
```

To show why this works, suppose, first, there is only one record in the file. Then we will read the first record and select it; that's all we can do. Next, suppose the file contains two records. We read and select the first record. When we read the second record, $n = 2$. If Random $< 1/2$, we will replace the selected record with the new one. Since the random numbers are uniformly distributed between 0 and 1, this means that half the time we'll end up with the first record and half the time with the second record.

Next, suppose we have read k records and that this method has worked so far. Then of the k records we've read so far, each one has had a $1/k$ chance of being selected. Now we read the $(k+1)$st record. We select it with probability $1/(k+1)$. This means that the current selection will be unchanged $k/(k+1)$ of the time and replaced $1/(k+1)$ of the time. Then each of the first k records now has a probability of $(1/k) \cdot [k/(k+1)] = 1/(k+1)$ of being selected, and the $(k+1)$st record also has a probability of $1/(k+1)$ of being selected. When the entire file of N records has been read, every record has a $1/N$ chance of being selected.

If we are selecting a random subset of m records from a file of unknown length, we proceed as follows:

1. Read the first m records from the file and put them into the subset. Count how many you have read. (Call this count k; at this point $k = m$ if the file did not end.)

2. While the file is not exhausted:

   a. Read a record in and increment k.

b. With probability m/k, pick an element at random from the subset and replace it with the current record.

We can program this as follows. Here we are reading from `inf` as before; we assume that the file has at least m records, and the selected records are held in `subset`, an `array [1..m]` of the appropriate record type.

```
procedure SAMPLE3 (m, n: integer; var subset: recarray);
                        { Selects random subset from file  }
    var                 {    of unknown size               }
        i, k: integer;
        inrecord: rectype;
    begin
    for k := 1 to m do        { Initialize the subset         }
        read (inf, subset[k]);
    k := m;
    while not eof(inf) do
        begin
        read (inf, inrecord);
        k := k + 1;
        if random < m/k then   { Decide whether to substitute  }
            begin
            i := 1 + trunc(m*random);   { Pick random record   }
            subset[i] := inrecord       {    & substitute       }
            end
        end   { while }
    end;   { Sample3 }
```

If the random-number generator is a good one, this algorithm will select a subset at random. When selecting a sample of size m from a file of N records, the probability of any given record ending up in the subset must be

$$\text{Prob}\{j\text{th record in subset}\} = \frac{m}{N}, \qquad 1 \leq j \leq N,\ m \leq N.$$

We can prove that this holds for our algorithm by induction on N.

It's trivially true for $N = m$: When m records have been read, they are all in the subset. So $\text{Prob}\{j\text{th record in subset}\} = 1 = m/N$. Next, suppose it is true for $N = k$ and show it is true for $N' = k + 1$. We've read k records, and the inductive hypothesis says that each one has a chance m/k of being included. Now read the $(k + 1)$st. This new record gets in with probability $m/(k + 1) = m/N'$, so it's all right. An existing record is replaced with probability

$$\frac{1}{m} \cdot \frac{m}{k + 1} = \frac{1}{k + 1}.$$

Therefore, the probability that any of the first k records is in the subset is

$$\text{Prob}\{j\text{th record in subset}\} = \text{Prob}\{\text{in set so far}\} \cdot \text{Prob}\{\text{not replaced}\},$$

$(1 \leq j \leq k)$. By the inductive hypothesis, this is

$$\text{Prob}\{j\text{th record in subset}\} = \frac{m}{k}\left(1 - \frac{1}{k+1}\right)$$

$$= \frac{m}{k} \cdot \frac{k}{k+1}$$

$$= \frac{m}{k+1} = \frac{m}{N'}.$$

So those are all right, too.

Notice that in the special case in which $m = 1$, this algorithm reduces to the method for a single sample.

*Fast random sampling. When we are selecting a single sample, the average number of substitutions from a file of N records will be the sum of the probabilities, $\sum_{i=1}^{N} 1/i$. This is the Nth harmonic number, $H_N \approx \ln n$. If we have a file of 50,000 records (and in large databases this is not at all unusual), we will make about 11 substitutions. This means that 49,989 of these random numbers have, in effect, been useless. Similar arguments can be made in the case of selecting a random subset of m records.

Vitter [1984] has devised fast methods for random sampling. These methods are based on the idea of *predicting* what the next record to be chosen will be. If you know that the next record to be chosen will be record j, then you can quickly skip over all intervening records and just wait for record j to show up. In order to provide a general idea of the approach, I will describe a simple method for selecting a single sample that uses prediction. Imagine that we had a list, drawn up in advance, telling us just when we should make a substitution. Call this list $\{S_i\}$. Then we wait for the S_1th record to appear, and when it does, we make the replacement; then we wait for the S_2th, and so on. The following method for computing the S_i values on-line is due to Glaser [1992].

To do this, we must find a way to generate the sequence $\{S_i\}$ from the uniformly distributed random numbers we get from Random. The general method for converting uniform random variates to obtain a specified probability distribution is given in Papoulis [1984], freely paraphrased here:

Find $P(n)$, the probability of event n.

Find the distribution $C(n) = \sum_{i=1}^{n} P(i)$.

If the uniform random variate is r, solve $C(n) = r$ for n. The solution n will have the required distribution.

If $S_i = k$, the probability that the next replacement record will be the nth is

$$\text{Prob}\{S_{i+1} = n \mid S_i = k\} = \frac{k}{n(n-1)}. \tag{12.13}$$

Proof: Writing $\text{Prob}\{S_{i+1} = n \mid S_i = k\}$ as $P(n|k)$ for brevity, we observe that $P(n|k)$ is the probability that it *was* the nth record and that it *wasn't* any of the intervening ones. So we have

$$P(n|k) = \text{Prob}\{S_{i+1} \neq k+1 \wedge S_{i+1} \neq k+2 \wedge \cdots$$
$$\wedge S_{i+1} \neq n-1 \wedge S_{i+1} = n\}.$$

Since $\text{Prob}\{S_i = k\} = 1/k$, $\text{Prob}\{S_i \neq k\} = (k-1)/k$. Furthermore, these are all independent events. Hence,

$$P(n|k) = \frac{k}{k+1} \cdot \frac{k+1}{k+2} \cdot \frac{k+2}{k+3} \cdot \ldots \cdot \frac{n-3}{n-2} \cdot \frac{n-2}{n-1} \cdot \frac{1}{n}.$$

The intermediate numerators and denominators cancel, and the result follows. This completes the first step of Papoulis's method.

For the second step, we must now find the distribution

$$C(n|k) = \sum_{i=k+1}^{n} P(i|k) = \sum_{i=k+1}^{n} \frac{k}{i(i-1)}, \qquad (12.14)$$

set it equal to r, and solve for n. It is well known that

$$\sum_{i=1}^{n} \frac{1}{i(i+1)} = \frac{n}{n+1}. \qquad (12.15)$$

(This is shown in Appendix A.) If we rewrite $C(n|k)$ as

$$C(n|k) = k \sum_{i=k}^{n-1} \frac{1}{i(i+1)},$$

then

$$\begin{aligned}
C(n|k) &= k \left[\sum_{i=1}^{n-1} \frac{1}{i(i+1)} - \sum_{i=1}^{k-1} \frac{1}{i(i+1)} \right] \\
&= k \left[\frac{n-1}{n} - \frac{k-1}{k} \right] \\
&= \frac{k(n-1) - n(k-1)}{n} \\
&= \frac{n-k}{n} \\
&= 1 - \frac{k}{n}. \qquad (12.16)
\end{aligned}$$

We now require that

$$C(n|k) = r. \qquad (12.17)$$

Solving for n gives us

$$1 - \frac{k}{n} = r,$$

$$n = \frac{k}{1-r}. \qquad (12.18)$$

Since we had $S_i = k$, $S_{i+1} = n$, this gives our result:

$$S_{i+1} = \left\lceil \frac{S_i}{1-r} \right\rceil . \tag{12.19}$$

in which the ceiling operator is needed to assure an integer result.

This leads to the following procedure:

```
procedure SAMPLE4 (var select: rectype);
                            { Fast random selection of a    }
                            {    record from file of unknown }
                            {    size (Glaser's method)      }
    var
        i,                { Record count          }
        s: integer;       { Selected record number}
        inrecord: rectype;
    begin
    i := 0;
    s := 1;
    while not eof(inf) do
        begin
        i := i + 1;
        read (inf, inrecord);
        if i = s then                { If this is to be selected,  }
            begin
            select := inrecord;          { Select it            }
            s := trunc(s/(1 - random)) + 1 { Find next record    }
            end                          {    to select          }
        end
    end;  { Sample4 }
```

This requires $H_n \approx \ln n$ random numbers instead of n of them. The difference can be significant; one sampling program using Sample2 was found to spend a third of its time just generating random numbers.

12.2.6   Random Numbers Without Repetitions

Many applications require a random sample of m numbers in a range from 1 to N without duplicates. For example, we have seen some sorting algorithms that assume that the unsorted data contain no repeated keys. In testing procedures based on these methods, it's handy to use random keys. (A full test suite needs more than that, but that's a good starting point.) How do we generate random keys with no repetitions?

This code obviously won't work:

```
for i := 1 to m do
    x[i].key = 1 + trunc(N*random);
```

Here m is the size of the array and N is the desired range of the keys (1 to 100 or 1 to 1,000 or whatever); obviously $N \geq m$. The problem is that there is no protection against repeated keys. A good random-number generator makes random-looking numbers with a long period, but there's no guarantee that `trunc(N*random)` won't give you the same key twice within m iterations.

The usual tack is to get a random number and see whether it is already in the list. If it isn't, we use it; otherwise, we get a new random number and try again:

```
for i := 1 to m do
   begin
   repeat
      p := 1 + trunc(N*random);      { Pick a number      }
      ok := true;
      j := 1;
      while (j < i) and ok do   { Already there?      }
         if x[j].key = p then
            ok := false          { --yes: pick another  }
         else
            j := j + 1;
   until ok;
   x[i].key := p
   end;
```

The search has to be sequential because the keys are in random order; the cost of the search is $O(m)$. If we use a **set** data type, and if N is small enough that the set can accommodate all possible values in the range, then we can put each new key in the set and use the set-membership test to find duplicates:

```
s := [];                  { Set initially empty    }
for i := 1 to m do
   begin
   repeat
      p := 1 + trunc(N*random)       { Find a number      }
   until not (p in s);               { that isn't in set }
   x[i].key := p;
   s := s + [p];                     { Include p in s     }
   end;
```

This is shorter, but it is still wasteful to keep generating random numbers until we have gotten a fresh one. The cost of the main loop is at least m, and more if we get a duplicate key. The probability of a duplicate key is i/N. If we let $i/N = a$, then we can find the expected length of the inner loop easily: The probability that its length is k is the probability that we got $k - 1$ duplicate keys and then a fresh one; this probability is $a^{k-1}(1 - a)$. The expected length is thus

$$E\{k\} \;\; = \;\; \sum_{k=1}^{\infty} k[a^{k-1}(1 - a)]$$

$$= \left(\frac{1}{a} - 1\right) \sum_k ka^k$$

$$= \frac{1-a}{a} \frac{a}{(1-a)^2}$$

$$= \frac{N}{N-i}. \tag{12.20}$$

The cost of the main loop is the sum of $E\{k\}$ as i runs from 1 to m; this is

$$N \sum_{i=1}^{m} \frac{1}{N-i} = N \sum_{j=N-m}^{N-1} \frac{1}{j}$$

$$= N(H_{N-1} - H_{N-m})$$

$$\approx N \ln \frac{N-1}{N-m}. \tag{12.21}$$

This has an N-lg-Nish look to it, which is usually good news, but in fact we can do better than this.

Bentley [1988] shows a clever way, due to R. Floyd, for avoiding the inner loop altogether by adding a new, different random number each time whether there is a duplicate or not: First, we find a set of $m-1$ random numbers in the range from 1 to $N-1$. (We do this with a recursive call.) Then we pick a number T between 1 and N. If T isn't in the set, we use it; otherwise, we put N in. It is easiest if we nest the recursive part inside a nonrecursive shell, so that the set and the array subscript will be external to all activations of Floyd's procedure:

```
procedure MAKE_DATA1 (var x: sortarray; m, n: integer);
                            { Fills x with random keys from }
                            {   1 to n without repetitions  }
                            {    (Floyd's method)           }
   var
      j,                  { Array subscript       }
      t: integer;         { New random number     }
      s: set of byte;

   procedure FLOYD (m, n: integer);     { Recursive part          }
      begin
      if m = 0 then
         begin
         s := [];
         j := 0
         end
      else
         begin
         floyd (m - 1, n - 1);                { Make the smaller set }
         j := j + 1;
         t := 1 + trunc(n*random);            { Add new number       }
```

```
        if t in s then
            begin                              { If duplicate,        }
                x[j].key := n;                 {    select n          }
                s := s + [n]
            end
        else
            begin
                x[j].key := t;                 {    else select t     }
                s := s + [t]
            end
    end
end;  { Floyd }


begin   { Make_Data1 }
floyd (m, n)
end;   { Make_Data1 }
```

(Sortarray is an array [1..m] of some suitable record type.) The algorithm will be correct if N goes in with probability m/N on each recursion. There are two ways that N can get into the set: Either T was a duplicate or T was N. The probability that it was a duplicate is $(m-1)/N$ and the probability that it was N is $1/N$; these are disjoint events and their probability sums to m/N. The cost of Floyd's method depends on the depth of the recursions. If the cost of testing for set membership is $O(1)$ (which it may or may not be, depending on the way the set is represented), then the cost of each recursion is $O(1)$ and the depth is clearly m; hence, subject to this assumption, Floyd's time complexity is $O(m)$.

If the language we are using does not include the set data type, then we must either implement our own sets or find some other way of avoiding duplicates. We can modify the sampling procedures of Section 12.2.5 to do the latter; here is a method based on Sample3:

```
procedure MAKE_DATA2 (var x: sortarray; m, n: integer);
                                        { Fills x with random keys from }
                                        {    1 to n without repetitions  }
    var                                 {    (based on Sample3)          }
        i, j,
        avail, to_go: integer;
begin
avail := n;
to_go := m;
j := 0;
for i := 1 to n do
    begin
    if random < to_go/avail then
        begin
        j := j + 1;                     { Select this number     }
        x[j].key := i;
```

```
            to_go := to_go - 1
            end;
        avail := avail - 1
        end;
    end;  { Make_Data2 }
```

The price we pay to avoid searching for a duplicate is a cost of $O(N)$ instead of $O(m)$. This is not as good as Floyd's method, but it is better than the brute-force method with which we began.

Neither `Make_Data1` nor `Make_Data2` can be relied on to produce the keys in random order. Indeed, `Make_Data2` generates the numbers in sorted order. The nonrandomness of Floyd's method is more subtle, but it should be clear that whenever N is selected, it goes in at the end of the array and that the N's that go in this way appear in increasing order; so there is a subset of the array, spaced at irregular intervals, that is already sorted. We can deal with either of these problems by jumbling the array after we have gotten it, using the scrambling procedure described previously; scrambling costs only $O(m)$.

12.3   SUMMARY

Random numbers are used in computer games to avoid presenting the player with the same circumstances repeatedly; they are used in simulations to imitate the randomness of real life; they are used to test programs and procedures with a wide variety of data; and they are used to encrypt data and messages. In all these cases, we require numbers that at least look random.

Many random-number generators in programming languages and in mathematical subroutine packages are suspect. (The subroutine **randu** in the old IBM System/360 Scientific Subroutine Package [1968] was notorious.) If the quality of your random numbers is crucial in your application, you should refer to Knuth [1981], study the statistical tests for randomness, and apply them to the random-number generator available on your system; otherwise, you would do well to use the generator described at the end of Section 12.1.1. "A poor workman blames his tools," Dr Franklin tells us, but a good programmer can blame a dubious random-number generator with a clear conscience.

12.4   PROBLEMS

12.1. Run the random-number generator, Eq. (12.1) (on paper) with $a = c = 1$ and $m = 8$. Verify that the random-number sequence has a period of 8 and that it is "anything but random."

12.2. Run the random-number generator Eq. (12.1) (again on paper) with $a = 20$, $c = 15$, and $m = 19$, and verify that the period is 19. Consider how "random" the numbers look: is there a pattern to the sequence?

12.3. Test Knuth's criteria for a full-period generator by using the following sets of values. Use a seed of 1.

(a) $m = 18$, $a = 7$, $c = 3$. (Violates third requirement.)

(b) $m = 18$, $a = 12$, $c = 5$. (Violates second requirement.)

(c) $m = 18$, $a = 7$, $c = 1$.

12.4. Find the first six random numbers generated by Eq. (12.1) with $a = 16{,}807$, $c = 0$, and $m = 2{,}147{,}483{,}647$. Use a seed, $x_0 = 1$.

12.5. Suppose we had two random number generators, `random1`, with a period of x, and `random2`, with a period of y. Consider a generator that combines the outputs of these generators as follows:

```
z := (random1 + random2) mod p;
```

(a) If x, y, and p are coprime (i.e., have no factor in common other than 1), what would you expect the period of z to be? (b) If x and y have a common factor k, what would you expect the period of z to be?

12.6. Code and try out Bays and Durham's method for avoiding the lattice problem.

12.7. In Eq. (12.2.1), shouldn't that be `round` instead of `trunc`? Examine the consequences of using

```
y := 1 + round((p - 1)*random);
```

12.8. In describing the algorithm for generating normal random numbers, we said that $s^2 + t^2$ will exceed 1 less than $1/4$ of the time. Prove this assertion.

12.9. Write a function that takes mean, variance, and correlation coefficient as parameters, calls `Gauss2`, and returns a pair of floating-point random numbers with the specified mean, variance, and correlation.

12.10. The code for randomizing an array in Section 12.2.4 runs from the end of the array back to the beginning. Can it be modified to start at the beginning and run to the end?

12.11. In discussing random numbers without repetitions in Section 12.2.6, we said, rather rashly, that there was no guarantee that our first attempt might not give us the same key twice over m iterations. But if the generator is a full-period generator, doesn't that *guarantee* no repetitions if m is less than the period? Explain.

12.12. We saw an adaptation of `Sample3` for generating random numbers in a specified range with no duplicates. But `Sample1` also selects records at random from a file of known size. What happens if you adapt `Sample1` to generate numbers for testing a sorting procedure?

12.13. The *chi-squared* statistic is a popular test for randomness. We define

$$\chi^2 = \frac{\sum_{i=0}^{r-1}(n_i - N/r)^2}{N/r}.$$

in which n_i is the number of times the generator returned the value i, N is the number of random numbers generated, and the range of the numbers is from 0 to r. If $N \gg r$, then we decide that the numbers are random if, on a number of repeated tests, $|\chi^2 - r| < 1.35\sqrt{r}$ about half the time. (This is because $|\chi^2 - r|$ will lie in this range with probability 0.5.)

(a) Program the chi-squared test. (b) Use the real random-number generator with Eq. (12.7) to generate random integers in the range from 0 to 20 and apply the chi-squared test to the results. Make sure you use a big enough N (3,000 is a good value). (c) If your version of Pascal includes a built-in random-number generator, try the same test on the numbers provided by that generator.

APPENDIX A

MATHEMATICAL BACKGROUND

There is very little in the body of this book that is not normally covered in a course in discrete mathematics. It is useful to summarize the more important topics here, however, in case any of them have been omitted from discrete math, and to add one or two new things that we need occasionally.

A.1 SUMMATIONS

We find the cost of an algorithm by counting things and adding them up. The conventional notation for adding a series of items $a_1, \ldots, a_n$ is as follows:

$$a_1 + a_2 + \cdots + a_n = \sum_{i=i}^{n} a_i. \qquad (A.1)$$

The expression after the big sigma is a typical element of the sum; we call this the *summand*. In this case the summand is a subscripted variable, but it can be any expression as well. The numbers below and above the sigma are the *limits*, the beginning and final values of i. When a sum is displayed on a line by itself, we write the limits below and above the sigma, as above; but when the sum appears in a line of text, we save space by writing the limits next to the sum: for example, $\sum_{i=1}^{n} a_i$.

There is nothing magical about the use of i; we could use any variable that isn't spoken for elsewhere in the typical element or the limits. Hence,

$$\sum_{i=1}^{n} a_i = \sum_{j=1}^{n} a_j = \sum_{k=1}^{n} a_k.$$

Next, suppose we only want to add up a_4 through a_7. We can do that by adjusting the limits:

$$\sum_{i=4}^{7} a_i.$$

406

If we want to keep adding a's *forever*, we can write,

$$\sum_{i=1}^{\infty} a_i.$$

That "∞" means "...to infinity." Of course, such a sum might be infinitely big—might "blow up"—but some such sums, in fact, *don't* blow up, and in that case, the sum has a definite meaning.

We can even sum from infinity in both directions, if the result has a meaning. That is, we're allowed to write

$$\sum_{i=-\infty}^{\infty} a_i,$$

and if the result doesn't blow up, we can work with this. We are specifying a sum over all possible i's here, and in that case it is sometimes simpler to leave off the limits and just write

$$\sum_{i} a_i.$$

We also omit the limits if they don't matter or if it's obvious from the context what they are.

We are also allowed to use an *expression* in the subscript of the typical term—for example,

$$\sum_{n=1}^{3} a_{2n+1}.$$

In this case, the expression is evaluated for each value of n:

$$\sum_{n=1}^{3} a_{2n+1} = a_{(2\cdot1+1)} + a_{(2\cdot2+1)} + a_{(2\cdot3+1)} = a_3 + a_5 + a_7.$$

(In order to get used to summations like this one, it helps to write them out the long way a few times.)

We can sum all sorts of things besides a_i. For example, mathematics deals a lot with things called *power series*, sums of the form,

$$a_5 x^5 + a_4 x^4 + a_3 x^3 + a_2 x^2 + a_1 x + a_0. \tag{A.2}$$

(These are the polynomials we talk about in Chapter 1.) This is also troublesome to write; but notice that the typical term of the sum is just $a_i x^i$. In that case, we can wrap up the whole works by writing

$$\sum_{i=0}^{5} a_i x^i. \tag{A.3}$$

A.1.1   Operations on Sums

There are a few things that make life easier when working with sums. First, we know from elementary algebra that we can rewrite $cx + cy$ as $c(x + y)$. We can factor out the c, since it is common to both terms. Then clearly we can factor the c out of

$$ca_1 + ca_2 + ca_3 + ca_4 + ca_5 + ca_6 + ca_7 + ca_8 + ca_9$$

so it must be that

$$\sum_{i=m}^{n} ca_i = c \sum_{i=m}^{n} a_i. \qquad (A.4)$$

This is called the *distributive law*.

A second law arises from the fact that we can add numbers in any order that's convenient. Thus,

$$(a_1 + b_1) + (a_2 + b_2) + (a_3 + b_3) + (a_4 + b_4)$$

is the same as

$$(a_1 + a_2 + a_3 + a_4) + (b_1 + b_2 + b_3 + b_4),$$

so we can break a single sum into two sums if it's convenient to do so:

$$\sum_{i=m}^{n} (a_i + b_i) = \sum_{i=m}^{n} a_i + \sum_{i=m}^{n} b_i. \qquad (A.5)$$

This is the *associative law*.

A third thing we can do is to subtract sums. We may know what $\sum_{i=1}^{a} x_i$ is but not what $\sum_{i=a}^{b} x_i$ is; but by the associative law we can write,

$$\sum_{i=a}^{b} x_i = \sum_{i=1}^{b} x_i - \sum_{i=1}^{a-1} x_i, \qquad (A.6)$$

and that will give us our result.

A fourth operation that is frequently useful is *removing the last term*. We do this, for example, if we want to express the sum in terms of something simpler. Suppose we have a sum,

$$\sum_{i=1}^{n+1} x_i = x_1 + x_2 + x_3 + \cdots + x_n + x_{n+1}.$$

When we remove the last term, we reduce the upper limit of the sum by 1 and write that last term separately:

$$\sum_{i=1}^{n+1} x_i = \sum_{i=1}^{n} x_i + x_{n+1}. \qquad (A.7)$$

The new sum covers everything up through x_n, and the missing term x_{n+1} is written separately. This operation is frequently useful in verifying sums by induction. It should be clear that we can remove the first term similarly. We will see an application of this shortly.

A.1.2   Some Special Sums

A few sums come up repeatedly in computer science. Many of these can be rewritten in a way that gets rid of the summation sign. (We say that the expression is *in closed form.*) We will look at seven of these sums.

1. $S_1 = \sum_{i=1}^{n} i$. The trick is to note that if we sum these numbers *in reverse order*, we get the same result:

$$S_1 = \sum_{i=1}^{n} i = \sum_{i=1}^{n} (n + 1 - i)$$

By the associative law, this is

$$2S_1 = \sum_{i=1}^{n} (n + 1 - i + i).$$

In every term of this sum, the i and the $-i$ cancel, so the result is just

$$2S_1 = \sum_{i=1}^{n} n + 1 = (n + 1) \sum_{i=1}^{n} 1 = n(n + 1)$$

by the distributive law. Hence,

$$\sum_{i=1}^{n} i = \frac{n(n + 1)}{2}. \tag{A.8}$$

2. $S_2 = \sum_{i=1}^{n} i^2$. We saw that S_1 gave us an expression containing n^2; we guess that S_2 will be an expression containing n^3. To be completely general, assume that

$$S_2(n) = an^3 + bn^2 + cn + d.$$

It is easy enough to evaluate S_2 by hand for $n = 0, 1, 2,$ and 3. Substituting these in our assumed formula, we get

$$
\begin{aligned}
0 + 0 + 0 + d &= 0 \\
a + b + c + d &= 1 \\
8a + 4b + 2c + d &= 5 \\
27a + 9b + 3c + d &= 14
\end{aligned}
$$

It is obvious that $d = 0$. This leaves us with three equations in three unknowns; solving them yields $a = 1/3$, $b = 1/2$, $c = 1/6$. Hence,

$$\sum_{i=1}^{n} i^2 = \frac{n(n + 1/2)(n + 1)}{3}. \tag{A.9}$$

We have a result that we know is right for $n = 0, 1, 2,$ and 3; we can verify that it is right for all n by induction.

3. $S_3 = \sum_{i=0}^{\infty} x^i$. Evaluating this also requires a trick. The first thing we notice is that if $x > 1$ or $x < -1$, this sum will blow up. So we assume that x lies between -1 and 1. Then the trick is to multiply S_3 by x and subtract:

$$
\begin{array}{rcccccccccc}
S_3 & = & 1 & + & x & + & x^2 & + & x^3 & + & x^4 & + & \cdots \\
x S_3 & = & & & x & + & x^2 & + & x^3 & + & x^4 & + & \cdots \\
\hline
S_3 - x S_3 & = & 1 & & & & & & & & & &
\end{array}
$$

Since both sums are infinite, we never run out of terms, and all the terms cancel except the 1. So we conclude,

$$S_3(1 - x) = 1, \quad \text{or}$$

$$\sum_{i=0}^{\infty} x^i = \frac{1}{1-x}, \quad |x| < 1. \tag{A.10}$$

$\big($If you don't believe we can get away with this, try dividing 1 by $(1-x)$ using long division.$\big)$ Remember that this works only for $-1 < x < 1$.

4. We can also find the *finite* sum, $S_4 = \sum_{i=0}^{n-1} x^i$. Consider the somewhat bigger sum,

$$\sum_{i=0}^{n} x^i.$$

Here is where removing the last term will lead us to a solution. Doing so, we get $\sum_{x=0}^{n-1} x^i + x^n$, which is our original sum S_4 plus x^n. If we remove the *first* term instead, we get $x^0 + \sum_{x=1}^{n} x^i$. But these two must be equal:

$$1 + \sum_{x=1}^{n} x^i = \sum_{x=0}^{n-1} x^i + x^n = S_4 + x^n. \tag{A.11}$$

(Remember that $x^0 = 1$.) Next, note that we can pull an x out of the left-hand side:

$$1 + \sum_{x=1}^{n} x^i = 1 + \sum_{x=0}^{n-1} x^{i+1} = 1 + x \sum_{x=0}^{n-1} x^i = 1 + x S_4.$$

So we have

$$1 + x S_4 = S_4 + x^n.$$

If $x \neq 1$, then solving for S_4 gives us our result:

$$\sum_{i=0}^{n-1} x^i = \frac{1 - x^n}{1 - x}, \quad x \neq 1. \tag{A.12}$$

(A modified version of this formula is used for computing mortgage payments.) An immediate application of this sum is finding $\sum_{i=0}^{n-1} 2^i$; by Eq. (A.12), this is $2^n - 1$.

5. $S_5 = \sum_{i=0}^{n} i2^i$. Again, we start by considering a bigger sum $\sum_{i=0}^{n+1} i2^i$. This can be written two ways:

$$\sum_{i=0}^{n+1} i2^i = S_5 + (n+1)2^{n+1}$$

and

$$\sum_{i=0}^{n+1} i2^i = \sum_{i=0}^{n} (i+1)2^{i+1}.$$

(We can leave the lower limit at 0 on the right-hand side since the term for $i = -1$ is 0.) We equate these two expressions for the bigger sum and apply the distributive law:

$$S_5 + (n+1)2^{n+1} = \sum_{i=0}^{n} i2^{i+1} + \sum_{i=0}^{n} 2^{i+1}.$$

The first sum on the right-hand side is $2S_5$, and the second sum is $2^{n+2} - 2$ from our formula for S_4. Hence, we have

$$S_5 + (n+1)2^{n+1} = 2S_5 + 2^{n+1} - 2.$$

Now we need only solve for S_5: $S_5 = (n+1)2^{n+1} - 2 \cdot 2^{n+1} + 2$. Therefore,

$$\sum_{i=0}^{n} i2^i = (n-1)2^{n+1} + 2. \tag{A.13}$$

6. $S_6 = \sum_{i=1}^{\infty} i2^{-i}$. We can use a similar trick for this sum:

$$\sum_{i=1}^{\infty} i2^{-i} = \sum_{i=0}^{\infty} (i+1)2^{-(i+1)}$$

$$= \sum_{i=0}^{\infty} i2^{-(i+1)} + \sum_{i=0}^{\infty} 2^{-(i+1)}$$

The first sum is just $\frac{1}{2}S_6$, and the second sum is 1. Hence, we have

$$S_6 = \frac{1}{2}S_6 + 1,$$

or

$$\sum_{i=1}^{\infty} i2^{-i} = 2. \tag{A.14}$$

7. $S_7 = \sum_{k=1}^{n} 1/[k(k+1)]$. At first glance, this looks forbidding: how do you sum a bunch of reciprocals of products? Putting everything over a common denominator looks hopeless. Fortunately, we don't have to do

that; we can resort to yet another trick: *rewriting the summand*. Note that

$$\frac{1}{k(k+1)} = \frac{1}{k} - \frac{1}{k+1}.$$

In that case, we can write this sum as

$$
\begin{aligned}
S_7 &= \sum_{k=1}^{n}\left(\frac{1}{k} - \frac{1}{k+1}\right) \\
&= \left(\frac{1}{1} - \frac{1}{2}\right) + \left(\frac{1}{2} - \frac{1}{3}\right) + \left(\frac{1}{3} - \frac{1}{4}\right) + \cdots + \left(\frac{1}{n-1} - \frac{1}{n}\right).
\end{aligned}
$$

All terms but the first and last cancel, and we are left with $1 - 1/n$, or

$$\sum_{k=1}^{n}\frac{1}{k(k+1)} = \frac{n-1}{n}. \tag{A.15}$$

A.2 HARMONIC NUMBERS

A sum that comes up particularly often in the analysis of algorithms is this one:

$$H_n = \sum_{i=1}^{n}\frac{1}{i}. \tag{A.16}$$

There is no closed-form solution to this sum; we just have to live with it. The numbers H_n are called *harmonic numbers*. We can get a feel for their size from the following table:

n	H_n
1	1
2	1.5
3	1.8333
4	2.0833
5	2.2833
10	2.9290
20	3.5977

The numbers grow more and more slowly, but they never stop growing. In books of tables (*e.g.*, Tuma [1970]), you will find what looks like a closed-form expression:

$$\sum_{i=1}^{n}\frac{1}{i} = \psi(n) + \gamma, \tag{A.17}$$

but that merely postpones the inevitable, because $\psi(n)$ is the *digamma function*, which can't be expressed in closed form, either.

We can derive an approximation to H_n as follows: Suppose we approximate $1/n$ by a continuous curve, as in Fig. A.1.

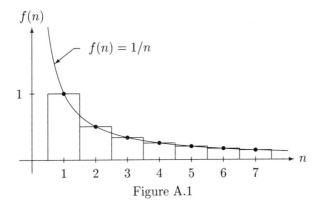

Figure A.1

Then the exact value of H_n is the sum of the areas inside the rectangular boxes (since each box is of width 1 and height $1/i$), and the area under the curve from $1/2$ to $n + 1/2$ should be a reasonably good approximation. The curve is too high at the left edge of each box and too low at the right edge, and we may hope that these errors will approximately cancel. The area under the curve is

$$
\begin{aligned}
A &= \int_{1/2}^{n+1/2} \frac{1}{u}\, du \\
&= \ln u \Big|_{1/2}^{n+1/2} \\
&= \ln(n + 1/2) - \ln 1/2
\end{aligned}
$$

This is roughly $\ln n$, and we will always use this as an approximation to H_n. A closer approximation is

$$
H_n = \ln n + \gamma + \frac{1}{2n} + O(n^{-2}), \tag{A.18}
$$

in which $\gamma = 0.5772156649\cdots$ is called Euler's ("Oiler's") constant.

If we need a sum of reciprocals in which the lower limit is greater than 1, we can resort to subtracting sums. Specifically,

$$
\sum_{i=a+1}^{b} \frac{1}{i} = \sum_{i=1}^{b} \frac{1}{i} - \sum_{i=1}^{a} \frac{1}{i} = H_b - H_a. \tag{A.19}
$$

From our approximation, this is roughly $\ln b - \ln a$ or $\ln(b/a)$.

A.3 FACTORIALS AND STIRLING'S APPROXIMATION

The factorial of a number, written $n!$, is defined as follows:

$$
n! = 1 \cdot 2 \cdot 3 \cdot \cdots \cdot n, \tag{A.20}
$$

with the special value, $0! = 1$. We can also define factorials recursively,

$$n! = \begin{cases} 1, & n = 0, \\ n(n-1)! & \text{otherwise.} \end{cases} \qquad (A.21)$$

Factorials come up most frequently in combinatorics and particularly in the binomial coefficients, which we will discuss in the next section.

Factorials get bigger faster than any other common function. It is believed that there are something like 10^{70} particles in the universe; this is less than $54! \approx 2.308 \times 10^{71}$. When someone says that the combinatorics make a problem too expensive to solve, this is shorthand for the fact that the cost involves factorials and that the factorials result in enormous values like 2.308×10^{71}.

Factorials are discrete samples of a continuous function called the gamma function. In particular, for integer n, $n! = \Gamma(n+1)$. (This is one justification for defining $0!$ as 1 since $\Gamma(1) = 1$.) The gamma function is defined over all real numbers except for 0 and all negative integers, where it goes infinite. (The digamma function, which we mentioned in connection with harmonic numbers, is the derivative of the log of the gamma function.)

For our purposes, probably the most important thing about factorials is Stirling's approximation, which allows us to estimate large factorials without going through the labor of multiplying them out. We can get a rough idea of how this approximation must look by reasoning as follows: Since we can multiply numbers by adding logs, it must be true that

$$\ln n! = \ln 1 + \ln 2 + \cdots + \ln n.$$

We can approximate this sum by an integral, the way we did with the harmonic numbers. If we pass a curve through the points and integrate the curve from 1 to n, we get

$$\begin{aligned} \ln n! &\approx \int_1^n \ln u \, du \\ &= u \ln u - u \Big|_1^n \\ &= n \ln n - n + 1. \end{aligned}$$

You will notice the $n \ln n$ term; this is the basis of our observation that the best sorting method that uses key comparisons is $O(n \lg n)$. Taking exponentials, we get

$$n! \approx e \left(\frac{n}{e} \right)^n.$$

which is pretty close. Stirling's approximation, arrived at by much subtler means than we have used, is

$$n! \approx \sqrt{2\pi n} \left(\frac{n}{e} \right)^n \left[1 + \frac{1}{12n} + \frac{1}{288n^2} + O\left(\frac{1}{n^3} \right) \right]. \qquad (A.22)$$

A.4 BINOMIAL COEFFICIENTS

We learn in discrete math that there is a general formula for the number of subsets of k elements that can be selected from a set of n elements:

$$\text{Number of subsets of } k \text{ objects in a set of } n \text{ objects} = \frac{n!}{k!(n-k)!}$$

This is sometimes written $C(n, k)$; some authors also write ${}_nC_k$. Probably the most common abbreviation is

$$\frac{n!}{k!(n-k)!} = \binom{n}{k}.$$

This is read as either "n upon k" or as "n choose k."

The numbers $\binom{n}{k}$ are called the *binomial coefficients*. This section provides additional information about these useful numbers.

A.4.1 Properties

The binomial coefficients have all sorts of useful properties; here are some of the more important ones.

Symmetry:

$$\binom{n}{k} = \binom{n}{n-k}. \tag{A.23}$$

This can be proved in two ways. First, the number on the left is the number of ways we can select subsets of size k and the number on the right is how many ways we can select subsets of size $n - k$. But selecting a subset of size $n - k$ is like *excluding* a subset of size k. It should be clear that we can exclude subsets in the same number of ways as we can select them; hence, the two numbers must be equal. Second, from the definition,

$$\binom{n}{k} = \frac{n!}{k!(n-k)!},$$

it should also be clear that interchanging n and $n - k$ leaves the number unchanged.

Recurrence: This is also called the addition property.

$$\binom{n}{k} = \binom{n-1}{k} + \binom{n-1}{k-1} \tag{A.24}$$

You can show this by algebra, but probably the easiest way to see this is to remember that $\binom{n}{k}$ is the number of ways you can choose a subset of k objects from a pool of n objects.

When you choose the subset, you can either (a) pick the very first one or (b) *not* pick the very first one. Choice (a) will lead to the second term, choice (b) will give you the first, and since these are two completely different ways of getting what you want, the two terms add up.

If you've picked the very first one, you now have a set of $(n-1)$ objects left, from which you must still select $(k-1)$ objects. This can be done in $\binom{n-1}{k-1}$ ways; that gives you the second term.

If you aren't going to pick the very first one, then you have only $(n-1)$ other objects from which you must still select k objects. That can be done in $\binom{n-1}{k}$ ways, and that gives you the first term.

The addition property is what gives us Pascal's triangle:

n \ k	0	1	2	3	4	5	6	7
0	1							
1	1	1						
2	1	2	1					
3	1	3	3	1				
4	1	4	6	4	1			
5	1	5	10	10	5	1		
6	1	**6**	**15**	20	15	6	1	
7	1	7	**21**	35	35	21	7	1

The addition property tells you how to construct each new row; each entry $\binom{n}{k}$ is the sum of the one to the north $\binom{n-1}{k}$ and the one to the northwest $\binom{n-1}{k-1}$. For example, 21 (written in **boldface** above) is the sum of 15 and 6.

Special values:

$$\binom{n}{k} = \begin{cases} 1, & k = 0 \\ 1, & k = n \\ n, & k = 1 \\ 0, & k < 0 \text{ or } k > n \end{cases}$$

The subset of zero elements is the empty set, and there's only one empty set; that proves the first line. The second line follows from symmetry (or you can argue that you can select the whole set only one way). The third line follows from the definition. To show the last line, we argue that it's *impossible* to choose fewer than 0 elements or more than n. From this last line it follows that the blank entries in Pascal's triangle are zeroes.

A.4.2   The Binomial Theorem

$$(a + b)^n = \sum_k \binom{n}{k} a^k b^{n-k}. \tag{A.25}$$

We don't need any limits on the sum; you can think of k as running from $-\infty$ to ∞. This is because the binomial coefficients are 0 for $k < 0$ and for $k > n$, so terms outside this range just don't appear. (We assume that $\lim_{k \to \infty} \binom{n}{k} a^k b^{n-k} = 0$.)

Proof (by induction on n):

It should be clear that the Binomial theorem works for $(a+b)^1$. Then suppose it's true for $(a+b)^n$. I will show that it's also true for the $(a+b)^{n+1}$.

We have

$$(a+b)^n = \sum_k \binom{n}{k} a^k b^{n-k}$$

and we must show

$$(a+b)^{n+1} = \sum_k \binom{n+1}{k} a^k b^{n+1-k}.$$

In decomposing the right-hand side to make use of the inductive hypothesis, note that if we multiply $(a+b)^n$ by $(a+b)$ to get the $(n+1)^{\text{st}}$ power, we have

$$(a+b)^{n+1} = (a+b)(a+b)^n = (a+b)\sum_k \binom{n}{k} a^k b^{n-k}.$$

This last form can be broken up by the distributive law:

$$(a+b)\sum_k \binom{n}{k} a^k b^{n-k} = a\sum_k \binom{n}{k} a^k b^{n-k} + b\sum_k \binom{n}{k} a^k b^{n-k}.$$

The first sum on the right is

$$a\sum_k \binom{n}{k} a^k b^{n-k} = \sum_k \binom{n}{k} a^{k+1} b^{n-k}.$$

I will turn this into something more manageable by changing $k+1$ to k (and k to $k-1$); then we have

$$\text{First sum} = \sum_k \binom{n}{k-1} a^k b^{n-(k-1)}$$

$$= \sum_k \binom{n}{k-1} a^k b^{n-k+1}.$$

The second sum is

$$b\sum_k \binom{n}{k} a^k b^{n-k} = \sum_k \binom{n}{k} a^k b^{n-k+1}.$$

Now we put these two sums together:

$$(a+b)^{n+1} = \text{first sum} + \text{second sum}$$

$$= \sum_k \binom{n}{k-1} a^k b^{n-k+1} + \sum_k \binom{n}{k} a^k b^{n-k+1}.$$

But now both sums contain that factor $a^k b^{n-k+1}$. So we can pull it out and combine the two sums this way:

$$(a + b)^{n+1} = \sum_k \left[\binom{n}{k-1} + \binom{n}{k} \right] a^k b^{n-k+1}.$$

But we know what $\binom{n}{k-1} + \binom{n}{k}$ is: it's $\binom{n+1}{k}$, by the addition property. So we have the result,

$$(a + b)^{n+1} = \sum_k \binom{n+1}{k} a^k b^{n+1-k},$$

which is the result we need.

A.4.3   Operations

Working with binomial coefficients is easier if we know some tricks. Here are a few of the more important ones.

Summing on lower number:

$$\sum_k \binom{n}{k} = 2^n. \tag{A.26}$$

This follows from the binomial theorem with $a = b = 1$. You can also argue that the sum is the number of all subsets of any size; but that's the power set, and we know that the cardinality of the power set is 2^n.

Summing on upper number:

$$\sum_{n=0}^{p} \binom{n}{k} = \binom{p+1}{k+1}, \qquad k, p \geq 0. \tag{A.27}$$

Proof (by induction on p):
Base: It's true for $p = 0$:

$$\text{LHS} = \binom{0}{k} = 0; \qquad \text{RHS} = \binom{1}{k+1} = 0.$$

Induction: Suppose it's true for $p = q - 1$:

$$\sum_{n=0}^{q-1} \binom{n}{k} = \binom{q}{k+1}.$$

We must show it's true for $p = q$:

$$\sum_{n=0}^{q} \binom{n}{k} = \binom{q+1}{k+1}.$$

We break up the sum on the left-hand side by pulling out the last term. This gives us

$$\text{LHS} = \sum_{n=0}^{q-1} \binom{n}{k} + \binom{q}{k}$$

$$= \binom{q}{k+1} + \binom{q}{k}.$$

We get the second line from the inductive hypothesis. But by the addition property,

$$\binom{q}{k+1} + \binom{q}{k} = \binom{q+1}{k+1},$$

which is the desired result.

Pulling out n/k:

$$\binom{n}{k} = \frac{n}{k}\binom{n-1}{k-1}. \tag{A.28}$$

Proof: Starting with the right-hand side,

$$\frac{n}{k}\binom{n-1}{k-1} = \frac{n}{k} \cdot \frac{(n-1)!}{(k-1)![n-1-(k-1)]!}$$

$$= \frac{n(n-1)!}{k(k-1)!(n-k)!}$$

$$= \frac{n!}{k!(n-k)!}$$

$$= \binom{n}{k}.$$

We can also write this as

$$\binom{n+1}{k+1} = \frac{n+1}{k+1}\binom{n}{k}.$$

Notice that this gives us a way to go diagonally down Pascal's triangle. If we know that $\binom{6}{2} = 15$, then this property gives us the result, $\binom{7}{3} = \frac{7}{3}\binom{6}{2} = \frac{7 \cdot 15}{3} = 35$.

*The Expression, $\binom{-1/2}{n}$. In finding the number of possible binary trees, in Appendix B, we come across the following strange-looking binomial coefficient:

$$\binom{-1/2}{n}.$$

With some ingenuity, we can convert this to a more manageable form. By definition,

$$\binom{-1/2}{n} = \frac{(-1/2)(-3/2)(-5/2)\cdots}{n!}.$$

We can get rid of the minus signs and the fractions by pulling $-\frac{1}{2}$ out of every factor in the numerator. This gives us

$$\binom{-\frac{1}{2}}{n} = \left(\frac{-1}{2}\right)^n \frac{1 \cdot 3 \cdot 5 \cdot 7 \cdot \; \cdots \; \cdot (2n-1)}{1 \cdot 2 \cdot 3 \cdot 4 \cdot \; \cdots \; \cdot n}.$$

Now we multiply numerator and denominator by $2^n n!$ to get

$$\binom{-\frac{1}{2}}{n} = \left(\frac{-1}{2}\right)^n \frac{1 \cdot 3 \cdot 5 \cdot 7 \cdot \; \cdots \; \cdot (2n-1)}{1 \cdot 2 \cdot 3 \cdot 4 \cdot \; \cdots \; \cdot n} \frac{2 \cdot 4 \cdot 6 \cdot 8 \cdot \; \cdots \; \cdot 2n}{2^n(1 \cdot 2 \cdot 3 \cdot 4 \cdot \; \cdots \; \cdot n)}.$$

Combining the two fractions gives us $(2n)!$ in the numerator and $2^n n! n!$ in the denominator. Moving the 2^n out to the fraction in front gives us

$$\binom{-\frac{1}{2}}{n} = \left(\frac{-1}{4}\right)^n \frac{(2n)!}{n!n!}, \qquad \text{or}$$

$$\binom{-\frac{1}{2}}{n} = \left(\frac{-1}{4}\right)^n \binom{2n}{n}.$$

A.5 PROBLEMS

A.1. Evaluate the following sums:

(a) $\sum_{i=1}^{8} 1$

(b) $\sum_{k=0}^{5}(k^2 + 1)$

(c) $\sum_{j=1}^{4} 2^k$

(d) $\sum_{n=1}^{7}(n+1)/n$

A.2. Prove that

$$S_2 = \sum_{i=1}^{n} i^2 = (2n^3 + 3n^2 + n)/6$$

works for all n. (Do it by induction on n.)

A.3. We know that

$$\sum_{i=0}^{n-1} x^i = \frac{1 - x^n}{1 - x}$$

provided $|x| \neq 1$. What is the value of this sum if $x = 1$? What is its value if $x = -1$?

A.4. Show that

$$\sum_{i=1}^{n} H_i = (n+1)H_n - n.$$

Hints: (a) $H_1 = 1$; (b) $H_{n+1} = H_n + 1/(n+1)$.

A.5. Find $(a+b)^5$.

A.6. Find $(a+2b)^3$.

A.7. (a) Find $(a+b)^4$. (b) Evaluate the result you got in part (a) term by term using $a = 2$ and $b = 3$. Check your result by finding 5^4.

A.8. Find $(a+a^{-1})^3$.

A.9. How much is $\binom{7}{0} + \binom{7}{1} + \binom{7}{2} + \binom{7}{3} + \binom{7}{4} + \binom{7}{5} + \binom{7}{6} + \binom{7}{7}$?

A.10. How much is $\binom{0}{4} + \binom{1}{4} + \binom{2}{4} + \binom{3}{4} + \binom{4}{4} + \binom{5}{4} + \binom{6}{4}$?

A.11. If $\binom{31}{6} = 736{,}281$, how much is $\binom{32}{7}$?

APPENDIX B

THEOREMS ABOUT TREES

B.1 THE PATH LENGTH THEOREM

In a full binary tree, the internal path length I and the external path length E are related by

$$E = I + 2n, \qquad (B.1)$$

where n is the number of interior vertices in the tree.

Proof (by induction on the number of interior vertices in the tree): For the base step, consider the empty tree. Clearly, $I = 0$ and likewise $E = 0$. Since $n = 0$, the base step holds.

For the induction, assume the theorem is true for a tree with k interior vertices. We will write this as

$$E_k = I_k + 2k. \qquad (B.2)$$

We must show that

$$E_{k+1} = I_{k+1} + 2(k+1). \qquad (B.3)$$

Add an interior vertex by changing any leaf x to a vertex with two children:

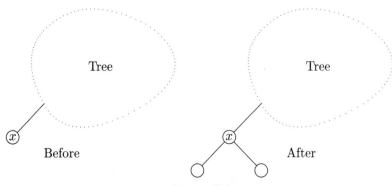

Before   After

Figure B.1

Let the length of the path from the root to x be p. Then the fact that x is now an interior vertex increases the internal path length by p:

$$I_{k+1} = I_k + p. \tag{B.4}$$

In the case of the external path length, it is reduced by p since x is no longer a leaf, but it is also increased by $2(p+1)$ because of the two new leaves, each of which is at a distance of $p+1$ from the root. Hence, the net change in the external path length is $p+2$:

$$E_{k+1} = E_k + p + 2. \tag{B.5}$$

When we put these together with the inductive hypothesis, the p's cancel and we get

$$E_{k+1} = I_{k+1} + 2k + 2, \tag{B.6}$$

which completes the proof.

B.2 HOW MANY BINARY TREES ARE THERE?

There are huge numbers of possible binary trees. For our purposes here we will say that two binary trees are the same if they have the same shape, regardless of the contents of their vertices. In that case, we can find a way of counting them, following the development in Knuth [1969]. It is based on the technique of making bigger trees from existing ones; this approach leads to a recursion relation, which, when solved, gives us the number of binary trees with any given number of vertices. The recursion relation is tricky to solve, but it is an important one that comes up in several other enumeration problems. I will solve it by applying it to two other enumeration problems and using the solutions we get for those to count binary trees.

Binary Trees. It is clear that there is only one empty tree; this gives us our starting point. There is also only one binary tree with one vertex. In order to construct bigger trees, we observe that we can get a tree with n vertices by making a root, giving it a left subtree with, say, k vertices, and giving it a right subtree with $n-1-k$ vertices:

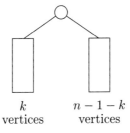

The subtrees provide $n-1$ vertices, and the nth is the new root.

How many different ways can we do this? Let b_n be the number of trees with n vertices. Then for any particular k there are b_k possible left subtrees and b_{n-1-k}

possible right subtrees. By the multiplication rule we learn in combinatorics, this means that for any particular k there are $b_k b_{n-1-k}$ possibilities. But k could be anything from 0 to $n-1$, and the sets of possibilities for different k's are disjoint; hence, by the addition rule, the total number of possibilities is

$$b_n = \sum_{k=0}^{n-1} b_k b_{n-1-k}, \qquad n > 0, \qquad (B.7)$$

with initial conditions $b_0 = 1$, $b_1 = 1$.

This is a particularly nasty recurrence relation. You can solve it by brute force using generating functions, but the math is far from obvious and doesn't yield any new insight. Another way to tackle such a problem is to find some other problem that is easier to solve and has the same solution. That's what we will do here.

Parentheses.   I will show that the number of properly nested strings of n open parentheses and n close parentheses—call it p_n—is the same as b_n; then I will find p_n, and that will give us b_n.

We will use P_n to represent the set of all legally nested strings of n open parentheses and n close parentheses. Then $p_n = |P_n|$—that is, the cardinality of P_n. A recursive method for arriving at P_n as follows: Clearly

$$
\begin{aligned}
P_0 &= \{\epsilon\} \qquad \text{(the empty string)} \\
P_1 &= \{\,(\,)\,\}.
\end{aligned}
$$

So $p_0 = p_1 = 1$. We can get P_n by taking a new pair of parentheses, nesting one legal string inside the new pair, and concatenating another legal string after it, making sure that the sizes of these two strings add up to p_{n-1} (because the new pair brings the count up to p_n). So we may write

$$
\begin{aligned}
P_n &= (P_0)P_{n-1} \cup (P_1)P_{n-2} \cup (P_2)P_{n-3} \cup \ldots \cup (P_{n-1})P_0 \\
&= \bigcup_{k=0}^{n-1} (P_k)P_{n-1-k},
\end{aligned}
$$

with the understanding that $(P_i)P_j$ means the set of all strings made from some element of P_i and some element of P_j.

There are $|P_k| = p_k$ ways to put something inside the new parentheses and $|P_{n-1-k}| = p_{n-1-k}$ ways to concatenate something onto the end. Hence, by the multiplication and addition rules, we get the recursion

$$p_n = \sum_{k=1}^{n-1} p_k p_{n-1-k}, \qquad n > 0, \qquad (B.8)$$

with initial conditions $p_0 = 1$, $p_1 = 1$. This has exactly the same form as Eq. (B.7); if we can solve this problem we can solve the binary-tree problem.

It should be clear that if we drop the requirement that the parentheses be well formed, there are

$$Q_n = \binom{2n}{n}$$

strings of n opens and n closes altogether. (You have a set of $2n$ positions to fill, and you must choose a subset of n positions to be occupied by open parentheses; you can do this in $\binom{2n}{n}$ ways.)

If you form such a string at random, the odds are that it will be illegal. Specifically, for every such string that is properly nested, there are n improperly nested ones. This is awkward to prove, however, so to prove it, we will resort to our third instance of this recursion.

Stack operations. We will define a legal sequence of stack operations as a sequence of **pushes** and **pops** with the property that if the stack is initially empty, the operations will never try to pop an empty stack and will leave the stack empty at the end.

It should be clear that we can get these sequences from our legally nested parentheses by replacing each open parenthesis with **push** and each close parenthesis with **pop**. (Then the stack height at any point corresponds to the current level of nesting in the parentheses.) So if the number of such sequences with n **pushes** and n **pops** is s_n, then we have the same recurrence:

$$s_n = \sum_{k=1}^{n-1} s_k s_{n-1-k}, \qquad n > 0, \tag{B.9}$$

with initial conditions $s_0 = 1$, $s_1 = 1$. We also have the property that the total number of such sequences, legal or illegal, is $\binom{2n}{n}$.

To account for the illegal operations, we resort to the following strategem, based on Graham *et al.* [1989]: imagine a legal sequence S_n with an extra **push** added at the beginning. If we start with an empty stack, then at the end of this sequence the stack height will be 1, because of the extra **push**, and during the sequence the stack height will never be less than 1. We will call this a legal *modified* sequence. If we were to repeat this legal modified sequence, the stack height would end up being 2, another repetition would make it 3, and so on.

The reason this modified sequence helps is this: We can get other modified sequences from cyclical permutations of the one with which we start. That is, we can rotate the sequence, shifting it to the left and putting the operations that fall off the left end back onto the right end. For example, suppose we represent **push** with $+1$ and **pop** with -1. Then one of the legal sequences $\{S_3\}$ is

$$(+1, +1, +1, -1, -1, -1).$$

The modified sequence is then

$$(+1, +1, +1, +1, -1, -1, -1).$$

In this case $n = 3$; for any legal sequence S_n the modified sequence has a length of $2n + 1$. The cyclical permutations are

$$(+1, +1, +1, +1, -1, -1, -1) \quad \text{(the original)}$$
$$(+1, +1, +1, -1, -1, -1, +1) \quad \text{(shifted left once)}$$
$$(+1, +1, -1, -1, -1, +1, +1) \quad \text{(shifted left again)}$$
$$(+1, -1, -1, -1, +1, +1, +1) \quad (\dots \text{etc.})$$
$$(-1, -1, -1, +1, +1, +1, +1)$$
$$(-1, -1, +1, +1, +1, +1, -1)$$
$$(-1, +1, +1, +1, +1, -1, -1)$$

(There are $2n + 1$ such permutations; another shift and we are back where we started.)

Of these permutations, only one will be legal in the sense that the stack height will never be less than 1 at any point in the sequence. To see this, plot the stack height h against the steps $\{i\}$ in the modified sequence, as in Fig. B.2.

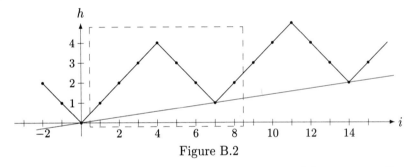

Figure B.2

The repetitions show the possible cyclical permutations of the sequence; for example, the dotted box corresponds to the first of the permutations we listed above. The slanted line shows the trend of stack height as this sequence is repeated over and over again: it increases by 1 every time i is increased by 7. The only place this line touches the plot of stack height is at the beginning of the original sequence. If you tried to draw the line through the beginning of any other permutation, some part of the stack height would fall below the line. We conclude that only one of these permutations is legal, and that means that for every legal modified sequence there are $2n$ illegal ones, these being the other permutations.

There are $\binom{2n+1}{n}$ sets of $n + 1$ pushes and n pops. But since only $1/(2n + 1)$ of these are legal, we conclude that there are

$$\frac{1}{2n+1}\binom{2n+1}{n} = \frac{1}{n+1}\binom{2n}{n}$$

legal modified sequences. But for every legal modified sequence there is exactly one legal *un*modified sequence. So we conclude that there are

$$\frac{1}{n+1}\binom{2n}{n}$$

legal sequences of n pushes and n pops. Because the recursion for stack operations is exactly the same as those for parentheses and for trees, we conclude that there are $\frac{1}{n+1}\binom{2n}{n}$ sets of $2n$ legally nested parentheses and $\frac{1}{n+1}\binom{2n}{n}$ binary trees with n vertices.

These numbers are known as *Catalan numbers* (for E. C. Catalan, who discovered them). We may write the nth Catalan number as

$$C_n = \frac{1}{n+1}\binom{2n}{n} \approx \frac{4^n}{\sqrt{\pi}\, n^{3/2}}.$$

(The approximation can be obtained from Stirling's approximation for factorials.) The Catalan numbers quickly become enormous. The following table gives the first few values:

n	C_n	n	C_n
0	1	6	132
1	1	7	429
2	2	8	1,430
3	5	9	4,862
4	14	10	16,796
5	42	11	58,786

*The Hard Way. We have derived this result by an extremely roundabout process. In order to show why I have chosen this route, here is a more conventional derivation using generating functions. (This section is for the mathematically bold only; others can skip to Section B.3.)

Let us make a table of the first few values of b_n:

$$
\begin{aligned}
b_0 &= 1 \\
b_1 &= 1 = b_0 \\
b_2 &= b_0 b_1 + b_1 b_0 \\
b_3 &= b_0 b_2 + b_1 b_1 + b_2 b_0 \\
b_4 &= b_0 b_3 + b_1 b_2 + b_2 b_1 + b_3 b_0 \\
&\quad \dots \text{ etc.}
\end{aligned}
$$

The trick to solving this is to make use of a generating function. Let

$$B(z) = b_0 + b_1 z + b_2 z^2 + b_3 z^3 + \cdots \tag{B.10}$$

In this generating function, the coefficient of z^n gives us the number of trees with n vertices. In that case, for any particular step in the recurrence we must have

$$b_n z^n = \left(\sum_k b_k b_{n-1-k} \right) z^n. \tag{B.11}$$

So we can include the powers of z in our table:

$$
\begin{aligned}
b_0 &= 1 \\
b_1 z &= (b_0)z \\
b_2 z^2 &= (b_0 b_1 + b_1 b_0)z^2 \\
b_3 z^3 &= (b_0 b_2 + b_1 b_1 + b_2 b_0)z^3 \\
b_4 z^4 &= (b_0 b_3 + b_1 b_2 + b_2 b_1 + b_3 b_0)z^4 \\
&\quad \dots \text{ etc.}
\end{aligned}
$$

If equals are added to equals, the results are equal. If we add up these equations, we get

$$ B(z) = 1 + z[B(z)]^2. $$

The right-hand side is not at all obvious, but if you work out the first few terms of $[B(z)]^2$, you will see that they match the entries in our table. This is a quadratic in $B(z)$. We can solve it like any other quadratic; the result is

$$ B(z) = \frac{1}{2z}(1 - \sqrt{1 - 4z}). \qquad (B.12) $$

But we need to write this as a power series in z, so we can display a formula for the coefficient of z^n. Since that coefficient is b_n, we will then have our answer. We expand the square root by the Binomial theorem:

$$ \sqrt{1 - 4z} = \sum_n \binom{1/2}{n}(-4z)^n. $$

Substituting this in Eq. (B.12) gives us

$$ B(z) = \frac{1}{2z}\left[1 - \sum_n \binom{1/2}{n}(-4z)^n\right]. $$

We can clean this up with the aid of the identity,

$$ \binom{1/2}{n} = \left(\frac{-1}{4}\right)^n \binom{2n}{n}, $$

which we proved in Appendix A. Thus, after a few more steps,

$$ B(z) = \sum_n \frac{1}{n+1}\binom{2n}{n} z^n. $$

The coefficient of z^n then gives us b_n, which is

$$ b_n = \frac{1}{n+1}\binom{2n}{n}. \qquad (B.13) $$

B.3 DEGENERATE AND ALMOST-DEGENERATE TREES

A degenerate tree is one in which every interior vertex has only one nonempty subtree. We will say that an almost-degenerate tree is one in which most interior vertices have only one nonempty subtree but some have two, one of which is of height 1. In particular, an AD_k tree is one in which exactly k interior vertices have such subtrees. (Then a degenerate tree is AD_0.) Thus the trees I have in mind look like (a) or (b) below, but not (c). Trees like (a) and (b) are the kind that most seriously mess up the nice $\lg n$ properties of binary search trees.

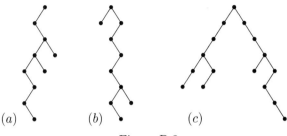

Figure B.3

We observe, first, that the number of degenerate trees with n vertices is 2^{n-1}. This can be proved by induction on n. For the base step, it is clear that there can be only one degenerate tree with one vertex, and $2^0 = 1$. For the inductive step, it is enough to note that, every time you add a new vertex to the tree, the number of possibilities doubles, since the new vertex can be either a left kid or a right kid.

I will refer to an almost-degenerate tree of n vertices in which exactly k interior vertices have two kids as $AD_k(n)$. It should be clear that no tree with fewer than three vertices can be AD_1 and that there is only one $AD_1(3)$ tree: $\diagdown\!\!\diagup$. For $n > 3$, we can grow AD_1 trees with n vertices in four distinct ways:

1. Make a root and make its left subtree an AD_1 tree with $n - 1$ vertices.
2. Make a root and make its right subtree an AD_1 tree with $n - 1$ vertices.
3. Make a root, give it a right kid, and make its left subtree a degenerate (AD_0) tree with $n - 2$ vertices.
4. Make a root, give it a left kid, and make its right subtree an AD_0 tree with $n - 2$ vertices.

These possibilities are shown in Fig. B.4:

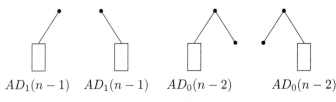

$AD_1(n-1)$ $\qquad$ $AD_1(n-1)$ $\qquad$ $AD_0(n-2)$ $\qquad$ $AD_0(n-2)$

Figure B.4

Let $A_1(n)$ be the number of AD_1 trees with n vertices. Then, from the figure we have

$$A_1(n) = 2A_1(n-1) + 2A_0(n-2), \qquad n > 3.$$

We know that $A_0(n) = 2^{n-1}$. So we have the recurrence relation

$$A_1(n) = 2A_1(n-1) + 2^{n-2}, \qquad n > 3,$$

with the initial condition, $A(3) = 1$.

We can use the same argument to determine how many AD_k trees there are. Let $A_k(n)$ be the number of AD_k trees with n vertices. Then we have the picture,

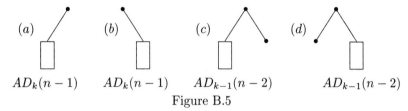

$$(a) \quad AD_k(n-1) \qquad (b) \quad AD_k(n-1) \qquad (c) \quad AD_{k-1}(n-2) \qquad (d) \quad AD_{k-1}(n-2)$$

Figure B.5

From this it should be clear that $A_k(n) = 2[A_k(n-1) + A_{k-1}(n-2)]$, for sufficiently large n.

As for how much is sufficiently large, we can also show that the smallest AD_k trees have $2k + 1$ vertices and that there are 2^{k-1} such trees. This can be verified for $k = 1$ by inspection. We then proceed by induction: Given the smallest AD_k tree, you can get the smallest AD_{k+1} tree by the construction of Fig. B.5 (c) or (d); this adds two vertices and doubles the number of possibilities, and the result follows.

To summarize our findings, we can write

$$A_k(n) = \begin{cases} 2^{n-1}, & k = 0, \\ 0, & n \leq 2k, \; k > 0, \\ 2^{k-1}, & n = 2k + 1, \; k > 0, \\ 2[A_k(n-1) + A_{k-1}(n-2)], & n > 2k + 1, \; k > 0. \end{cases} \qquad (B.14)$$

Solving these recurrences takes a great deal of labor and a certain amount of cunning. For $k = 1, 2, 3, 4$, the solutions are

$$\begin{aligned} A_1(n) &= (2n - 5)2^{n-3}, & n \geq 3, \\ A_2(n) &= (n^2 - 8n + 16)2^{n-4}, & n \geq 5, \\ A_3(n) &= \tfrac{1}{6}(2n^3 - 33n^2 + 181n - 330)2^{n-5}, & n \geq 7, \\ A_4(n) &= \tfrac{1}{12}(n^4 - 28n^3 + 293n^2 - 1358n + 2352)2^{n-6}, & n \geq 9. \end{aligned}$$

It should be clear that $A_k(n)$ is $O(n^k 2^{n-k-2})$, $n > 2k + 1$, $k > 0$.

It is easy to write a program that uses the recurrence of Eq. (B.14) to construct a table of $A_k(n)$ out to any reasonable values of k and n. Furthermore, we can then sum the table entries over k to find the total number of AD trees for any n. The results of such a program are as follows:

n	$\sum_k A_k(n)$	n	$\sum_k A_k(n)$
1	1	14	3.23×10^5
2	2	15	8.82×10^5
3	5	16	2.41×10^6
4	14	17	6.58×10^6
5	38	18	1.80×10^7
6	104	19	4.91×10^7
7	284	20	1.34×10^8
8	776	21	3.67×10^8
9	2,120	22	1.00×10^9
10	5,792	23	2.74×10^9
11	15,824	24	7.48×10^9
12	43,232	25	2.04×10^{10}
13	1.18×10^5	26	5.58×10^{10}

These are impressive numbers, but the numbers for b_n given above and in Section 5.8 are larger still: For 26 vertices, $b_{26} = 1.84 \times 10^{13}$; hence, the number of *AD* trees is only 0.03 percent of the total.

APPENDIX C

FINITE-STATE AUTOMATA

Finite-state automata (FSA's, also called finite-state machines) are the simplest of several models of computation. They are also used for carrying out certain special tasks; they occur in the text when we discuss the Knuth-Morris-Pratt algorithm for pattern matching in strings.

FSA's are sometimes taken up as an application of graph theory in discrete mathematics. This appendix is intended to provide a brief summary in case you haven't heard of them.

We will start with an example. Consider a vending machine with a slot for coins, one or more buttons for selecting what you want to buy, and a coin return. We will assume it is selling candy bars. The days when you could buy anything from a vending machine for 25 cents are long gone, but for simplicity we will assume a candy bar costs a quarter. When we walk up to the machine, it is sitting there waiting for something to happen; we designate this state of the machine as State A. We will normally start by inserting coins into the slot. As it receives each coin, it goes into a new state to reflect how much money it now has. The states thus serve as a simple kind of memory.

We can represent this machine by the directed graph shown in Fig. C.1.

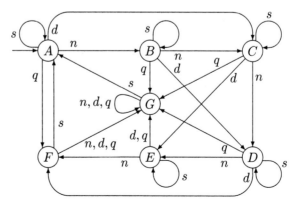

Figure C.1

State A, the starting state, is identified by the arrow coming in out of nowhere. If the first coin we insert is a nickel, then the vending machine changes from State A to State B; this is the significance of the arrow between these states marked n. If we then insert a dime, the machine goes from State B to State D, as indicated by the arrow marked d. Other transitions are made similarly. The states clearly correspond to different amounts of money received; for example, any combination of coins totalling 20 cents will put the machine into State E. If we try to cheat by pressing the select button while the machine is in State D, it ignores us; that is the significance of the self-loop on State D. When the machine has received the full 25 cents, it is in State F; now pressing the select button makes it deliver the candy bar and return to State A. State G represents an overpayment; we assume the excess goes into a special area for return, along with the candy bar, when we press the select button.

FSA's are used for many purposes. They may be implemented in hardware or software, or they may be used to model processes. The control logic of a digital computer is a FSA.[1] Our own concern is with FSA's that recognize strings of characters; these are the basis of the Knuth-Morris-Pratt pattern searching algorithm described in Chapter 3.

We are now ready for a formal definition of a FSA considered as a recognizer. A FSA M consists of

> An input alphabet Σ;
>
> A finite set of states Q;
>
> An initial or starting state $q_0 \in Q$;
>
> A set of accepting states $F \subseteq Q$;
>
> A set of state-transition rules $f\colon Q \times \Sigma \to Q$.

The states can be identified by letter or by number. Σ specifies the set of inputs that M will find meaningful. M starts in the state q_0; as inputs from Σ arrive, M makes state transitions that depend on the current state and the current input. If M is in an accepting state after the last input character has been read, we say that it *accepts* the input string; otherwise, it does not. (In most applications, if M passes through an accepting state in the course of reading the input string, this normally makes no difference. All that counts is the state it's in at the end of the string. The Knuth-Morris-Pratt machine is an exception to this: it is so designed that any time it enters an accepting state, it has recognized the pattern it is supposed to be searching for.)

The state transition rules can be described by a digraph like the one in Fig. C.1 or by a state table. The state table for the vending machine example is as follows:

---

[1] Actually, the entire computer is a FSA, but there are other models that embody its strengths and weaknesses more effectively.

This State	Input n	d	q	s	
A	B	C	F	A	
B	C	D	G	B	
C	D	E	G	C	
D	E	F	G	D	Next state
E	F	G	G	A	
F	G	G	G	A	
G	G	G	G	A	

We can define acceptance as follows. Let the state table be represented by a digraph. Then a character string w is accepted by M if and only if there is a path from the starting state to any accepting state whose edges spell out w.

For example, consider M_1, shown in Fig. C.2. Its state table is as follows:

This State	Input a	b	c
1	2	3	4
2	4	3	2
3	4	3	2
4	1	4	3

In this machine, $Q = \{1, 2, 3, 4\}$, $F = \{2, 4\}$, and $\Sigma = \{a, b, c\}$. The starting state is listed first by convention and accepting states are underlined. In the state diagram, the starting state is indicated by an arrow and the accepting states are drawn as double circles.

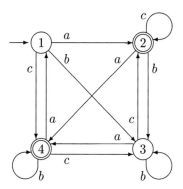

Figure C.2

To see how this machine responds to different inputs, consider what happens if it is presented with the string $abcabc$. The transitions are as follows:

$$\rightarrow \textcircled{1} \xrightarrow{a} \textcircled{2} \xrightarrow{b} \textcircled{3} \xrightarrow{c} \textcircled{2} \xrightarrow{a} \textcircled{4} \xrightarrow{b} \textcircled{4} \xrightarrow{c} \textcircled{3}$$

You can envision time as running from left to right on this diagram. The starting state is shown at the left, and the arrows indicate the transitions resulting from the various input characters. In this case, M_1 ends up in State 3; this isn't an accepting state, so the string is not accepted.

Here is the result when we apply the string *cbacba*:

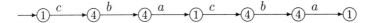

This time M_1 ends in State 1; that is not an accepting state, so this string is not accepted either. If we give it the string *aabbcc*, we get the following history:

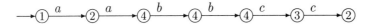

Since State 2 is an accepting state, M_1 accepts this string.

Here is another FSA. M_2, shown in Fig. C.3, is a machine constructed by the Knuth-Morris-Pratt (KMP) algorithm for recognizing the pattern **murmurs**:

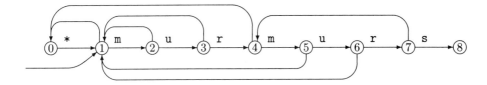

Figure C.3

The KMP automata are slightly different from the others we have seen. The starting state is State 1, not State 0. State 0 is a dummy state. The transition marked $*$ is taken on any character at all. The unmarked transitions occur on any non-matching character, and they take place *without moving on to the next character*. For example, in State 4, M_2 expects an m; if it gets one, it goes to State 5; if it gets anything else at all, it returns to State 0, where it will look at this character again.

The transition of particular interest is the error transition out of State 7. If the next character is not s, it goes back to State 4 instead of State 1, in case the second **mur** is the prefix of the desired word. We can see why it does this if we run M_2 over the string **murmurmurs**:

$$\textcircled{1} \xrightarrow{m} \textcircled{2} \xrightarrow{u} \textcircled{3} \xrightarrow{r} \textcircled{4} \xrightarrow{m} \textcircled{5} \xrightarrow{u} \textcircled{6} \xrightarrow{r} \textcircled{7} \xrightarrow{m*} \textcircled{4} \xrightarrow{(m)} \textcircled{5} \xrightarrow{u} \textcircled{6} \xrightarrow{r} \textcircled{7} \xrightarrow{s} \textcircled{8}$$

The third m (marked by the star) is an error: M_2 expected an s here. When it goes back to State 4, it continues to look at the m, on the chance that this may turn out to be the fourth character of **murmurs** (as in fact it does). This is the reason for the repeated m in parentheses: that's that same character. It then correctly advances through States 5–8 and recognizes the pattern.

APPENDIX D

REFERENCES

Adel'son-Vel'skiĭ, G. M., and E. M. Landis, *Doklady Akademiia Nauk SSSR*, vol. 146, pp. 263–266, 1962. Translation in *Soviet Math.*, vol. 3, pp. 1259–1263.

Aho, A. V., J. E. Hopcroft, and J. D. Ullman, *The Design and Analysis of Computer Algorithms.* Reading, Mass.: Addison-Wesley, 1974.

Baeza-Yates, R., and G. H. Gonnet, "A new approach to text searching," *Comm. Assoc. Comp. Mach.*, vol. 35, no. 10, pp. 74–82, October 1992.

Bayer, R., and E. McCreight, "Organization and maintenance of large ordered indexes," *Acta Informatica*, vol. 1, no. 3, pp. 173–189, 1972.

Bays, C., and Durham, S. D. *Assoc. Comp. Mach. Trans. on Mathematical Software*, vol. 2, pp. 59-64, 1976.

Bell, T. C., J. G. Cleary, and I. H. Witten, *Text Compression.* Englewood Cliffs, N. J.: Prentice-Hall, 1990.

Bentley, J., *Programming Pearls.* Reading, Mass.: Addison-Wesley, 1986.

———— *More Programming Pearls: Confessions of a Coder.* Reading, Mass.: Addison-Wesley, 1988.

Boyer, R. S., and J. S. Moore, "A fast string searching algorithm," *Comm. Assoc. Comp. Mach.*, vol. 20, no. 10, pp. 762–772, October 1977.

Bright, H. S., and R. L. Enison, "Quasi-random number sequences from a long-period TLP generator," *Assoc. Comp. Mach. Computing Surveys*, vol. 11, no. 4, pp. 357–370, December 1979.

Dijkstra, E. W., "A note on two problems in connexion with graphs," *Numerische Mathematik*, vol. 1, pp. 269–171, 1959.

Even, S., *Graph Algorithms.* Rockville, Md.: Computer Science Press, 1979.

Fagin, R. *et al.*, "Extendible hashing—a fast access method for dynamic files," *Assoc. Comp. Mach. Trans. on Database Systems*, vol. 4, no. 3, pp. 315–344, September 1979.

Fano, R. M., "The transmission of information," Tech. Report 65, Research Laboratory of Electronics, MIT, 1949.

Fishman, G. S., and Moore, L. R., "An exhaustive analysis of multiplicative congruential random number generators with modulus $2^{31} - 1$," *SIAM Jour. Sci. Stat. Comput.*, vol. 7, no. 1, pp. 24–45, 1986.

Floyd, R. W., "Algorithm 97 (SHORTEST PATH)," *Comm. Assoc. Comp. Mach.*, vol. 5, no. 6, p. 345, June 1962.

Fredkin, E., "Trie memory," *Comm. Assoc. Comp. Mach.*, vol. 3, no. 9, pp. 490–499, September 1960.

Gaines, H. F., *Elementary Cryptanalysis*. American Photographic Publishing Co., 1939. Reprinted New York: Dover, 1956.

Glaser, D., Personal communication.

Gould, S. J., *Bully for Brontosaurus*. New York: W. W. Norton, 1991.

Graham, R. L., D. E. Knuth, and O. Patashnik, *Concrete Mathematics*. Reading, Mass.: Addison-Wesley, 1989.

Guibas, L. J., and R. Sedgewick, "A dichromatic framework for balanced trees," *Proc. Annual IEEE Symp. on Foundations of Computer Science*, pp. 8–21, 1978

Hamming, R. W., *Numerical Methods for Scientists and Engineers*. New York: McGraw-Hill, 1962.

Hoare, C. A. R., "Quicksort," *Computer Journal*, vol. 5, no. 1, pp. 10–15, 1962.

Horgan, J., "Claude E. Shannon," *IEEE Spectrum*, vol. 29, no. 4, p. 72, April 1992.

Huffman, D. A., "A Method for the construction of minimum-redundancy codes," *Proceedings of the IRE*, vol. 40, pp. 1098–1101, 1952.

IBM Corporation, *System/360 Scientific Subroutine Package (360A-CM-03X) Version III: Programmer's Manual*. White Plains, New York: IBM Corporation, 1968.

Kernighan, B. W., and P. J. Plauger, *The Elements of Programming Style*, second edition. New York: McGraw-Hill, 1987.

Knott, G. D., "Expandable open addressing hash table storage and retrieval," *Proc. ACM SIGFIDET Workshop on Data Description, Access, and Control*, 1971, pp. 186–206.

Knuth, D. E., *Fundamental Algorithms*, vol. 1 of *The Art of Computer Programming*. Reading, Mass.: Addison-Wesley, 1968.

———— *Literate Programming*. Palo Alto: Center for the Study of Language and Information, Leland Stanford Junior University, 1992.

———— *Seminumerical Algorithms*, vol. 2 of *The Art of Computer Programming*. Reading, Mass.: Addison-Wesley, 1981.

———— *Sorting and Searching*, vol. 3 of *The Art of Computer Programming*. Reading, Mass.: Addison-Wesley, 1973.

Knuth, D. E., J. H. Morris, and V. R. Pratt, "Fast pattern matching in strings." *SIAM Jour. Comput*, vol. 6, no. 2, pp. 323–350, June 1977.

Knuth, D. E., and M. F. Plass, "Breaking paragraphs into lines," *Software—Practice and Experience*, vol. 11, no. 11, pp. 1119–1234, 1981.

Kruse, R. L., *Data Structures and Program Design*, second edition. Englewood Cliffs, N. J.: Prentice-Hall, 1984.

Kruskal, J. B., "On the shortest spanning subtree of a graph and the travelling salesman problem," *Proc. Amer. Math. Soc.*, vol. 7, pp. 48–50, 1956.

Larson, P., "Dynamic hashing," *BIT*, vol. 18, pp. 184–201, 1978

Lehmer, D. H., "Mathematical methods in large-scale computing units," *Annu. Comput. Lab. Harvard Univ.* vol. 26 (1952), pp. 141–146.

Litwin, W., "Virtual hashing: a dynamically changing hashing procedure," *Proc. Very Large Data Bases Conf.*, Berlin, 1978, pp. 517–523.

Miller, G. A., "The magical number seven, plus or minus two: some limits on our capacity for processing information," *Psychological Review*, vol. 63, no. 2, pp. 81–97, March 1956.

Minsky, M., *Computation: Finite and Infinite Machines*. Englewood Cliffs, N. J.: Prentice-Hall, 1967.

Morrison, D. R., "PATRICIA—Practical Algorithm To Retrieve Information Coded in Alphanumeric," *Jour. Assoc. Comp. Mach.*, vol. 15, no. 4, pp. 514–534, October 1968.

Nelson, M., *The Data Compression Book*. San Mateo, Calif.: M & T Books, 1992.

Papoulis, A., *Probability, Random Variables, and Stochastic Processes*. New York: McGraw-Hill, 1984.

Park, S. K., and Miller, K. W., "Random number generators: good ones are hard to find," *Comm. Assoc. Comp. Mach.*, vol. 31, no. 10, pp. 1192–1201, October 1988.

Press, W. H. *et al.*, *Numerical Recipes*. Cambridge: Cambridge Univ. Press, 1968. Chapter 7: "Random Numbers."

Prim, R. C., "Sortest connection networks and some generalizations," *Bell System Tech. Jour.*, vol. 36, pp. 1389–1401, 1957.

Reingold, E. M., and W. J. Hansen, *Data Structures in Pascal*, Boston: Little, Brown, 1986.

Schrage, L. "A more portable FORTRAN random number generator," *Assoc. Comp. Mach. Trans. on Mathematical Software*, vol. 5, no. 2, pp. 132-138, June 1977.

Sedgewick, R., "Implementing Quicksort programs," *Comm. Assoc. Comp. Mach.*, vol. 21, no. 10, pp. 847–857, October 1978.

———— *Algorithms*. Reading, Mass.: Addison-Wesley, 1988.

Shannon, C. E., "The mathematical theory of communication," *Bell System Technical Journal*, vol. 27, pp. 379–423, 623–656, July and October, 1948. Reprinted in Shannon and Weaver [1949].

Shannon, C. E., and W. Weaver, *The Mathematical Theory of Communication.* Urbana, Ill.: Univ. of Illinois Press, 1949.

Sunday, D. M., "A very fast substring search algorithm." *Comm. Assoc. Comp. Mach.*, vol. 33, no. 8, pp. 132–142, August 1990.

Tarjan, R. E., "Updating a balanced search tree in $O(1)$ rotations," *Information Processing Letters*, vol. 16, no. 5, pp. 253–257, June 1983.

Tausworthe, R. C., "Random numbers generated by linear recurrence modulo 2," *Math. of Computation*, vol. 19, p. 201–209, 1965.

Tuma, J. J., *Engineering Mathematics Handbook*, third edition. New York: McGraw-Hill, 1970.

Vitter, J. S., "Faster methods for random sampling," *Comm. Assoc. Comp. Mach.*, vol. 27, no. 7, pp. 703–718, July 1984.

Warshall, S., "A theorem on Boolean matrices," *Jour. Assoc. Comp. Mach.*, vol. 9, no. 1, pp. 11–12, January 1962.

Welch, T. A., "A technique for high-performance data compression," *IEEE Computer*, vol. 17, no. 6, pp. 8–19, June 1984.

Ziv, J., and A. Lempel, "A universal algorithm for sequential data compression," *IEEE Trans. on Information Theory*, vol. 23, no. 3, pp. 337–343, May 1977.

———— "Compression of individual sequences via variable-rate coding," *IEEE Trans. on Information Theory*, vol. 24, no. 5, pp. 530–536, September 1978.

INDEX